Advances in
Parapsychological
Research

2 Extrasensory Perception

Advances in Parapsychological Research

Volume 1   **Psychokinesis**
Edited by Stanley Krippner

Volume 2   **Extrasensory Perception**
Edited by Stanley Krippner

A Continuation Order Plan is available for this series. A continuation order will bring
delivery of each new volume immediately upon publication. Volumes are billed only upon
actual shipment. For further information please contact the publisher.

Advances in Parapsychological Research

2 Extrasensory Perception

EDITED BY

Stanley Krippner
Humanistic Psychology Institute
San Francisco, California

MANAGING EDITOR

Mary Lou Carlson

ASSOCIATE EDITORS

Montague Ullman and Robert O. Becker

PLENUM PRESS · NEW YORK AND LONDON

133.88

Ad 95

Library of Congress Cataloging in Publication Data

Main entry under title:

Advances in parapsychological research.

   Volume 2: managing editor, Mary Lou Carlson.
   Includes bibliographies and indexes.
   CONTENTS: v. 1. Psychokinesis. v. 2. Extrasensory perception
   1. Psychokinesis—Addresses, essays, lectures. 2. Psychical research—Addresses, essays, lectures. I. Kripper, Stanley. [DNLM: 1. Parapsychology. BF1031 A244]
BF1371.A35   133.8'8   77-9518
ISBN 0-306-40082-0(v.2)

75869

©1978 Plenum Press, New York
A Division of Plenum Publishing Corporation
227 West 17th Street, New York, N.Y. 10011

Printed in the United States of America

To J. B. Rhine and Louisa E. Rhine,
who helped bring science into parapsychology,
and parapsychology into science

Contributors

Stanley Krippner, Humanistic Psychology Institute, San Francisco, California

Robert L. Morris, University of California, Santa Barbara, California

John Palmer, John F. Kennedy University, Orinda, California

K. Ramakrishna Rao, Institute for Parapsychology, Durham, North Carolina and Department of Psychology, Andhra University, Visakhapatnam, India

Montague Ullman, American Society for Psychical Research, New York, New York

Contents

Introduction   1
  Montague Ullman

1. A Survey of Methods and Issues in ESP Research   7
  Robert L. Morris

2. Extrasensory Perception: Research Findings   59
  John Palmer

3. Theories of Psi   245
  K. Ramakrishna Rao

Name Index   297

Subject Index   303

Introduction

Montague Ullman

The second volume of this series includes essays on methods and issues in ESP research (Morris), research findings in ESP (Palmer), and theories of psi (Rao). It thus complements the areas covered in Volume 1, the two volumes taken together providing the reader with a sound grounding in the progress and achievements of parapsychological research from its inception to the present day. What is immediately striking is the rapid increase in the amount and variety of experimental reports appearing in the last decade and the increasing number of centers in which research is being carried out. Work in parapsychology is moving toward a broader disciplinary base, the use of more imaginative technology, greater academic support, and more activity on an international scale. These are promising signs of a rapprochement between parapsychological research and the mainstream of science.

Robert O. Becker, in his preface to Volume 1, holds out the hope that parapsychology will lead the way to a new view of the biological organism, one going beyond mechanism to "a new vision of the human being and his place in the universe" (Becker, 1977). Heavy as this responsibility may be, a careful reading of the present volume should persuade the reader that a new view is very much in order. Such a view will have to do what the old order seems to find so difficult, namely, accommodate to the mounting evidence that psi effects have a reality of their own regardless of their present state of incomprehensibility.

It is obvious that if parapsychology is to complete its rites of passage into the mainstream of science, it will have to come to terms with the issue of replicability, the need for a theory that will contain both parapsychological and nonparapsychological data, and ultimately, the issue of the application of such data to our everyday life. Taken together, all three essays tell us how far we have come in each of these areas. The future seems hopeful, not because we have any foreseeable solution to any of these problems, but because research ingenuity and powerful technology are now being mobilized, involving many more scientifically trained workers in many more disciplines than ever before. If we project in a fanciful way it may well be that the Americans, in their love affair with technology, will come up with the research findings; the English, with their predilection for philosophical and theoretical inquiry, will bring these findings under a theoretical umbrella; and the Russians, oriented to the materiality of human existence, will lead the way to the applications of psi.

The first essay focuses on the research strategies that have been employed in the pursuit of those anomalies commonly referred to as ESP. The second presents a comprehensive review and evaluation of the entire range of experimental work carried on by means of these various strategies. The third considers the various theoretical strategies that have been devised to make sense out of these findings. These essays are evaluative as well as descriptive. The research literature has been accumulating for over half a century. Morris and Palmer have done an exceptionally fine job of organizing an enormous range of disparate data in ways that convey to the reader the main trends, the problems encountered, the steps taken to overcome them, and the results obtained.

Rao's task was quite different. Many imaginative thinkers have struggled with theoretical formulations that will fit the observational data and move us further along the path of replicability and predictability. These have ranged from general philosophical challenges, such as Jung's synchronicity principle that takes issue with the exclusivity of causal relations, to mathematically based formulations derived from quantum physics, such as Walker's particular application of the notion of a hidden variable. Rao has brought order into this theoretical mélange. His critical judgment sharpens our appreciation of the value, as well as the limitations, of each theoretical contribution.

Where does this survey of methods, results, and theories leave the reader? My guess would be with some clarity as to where we have been and some uncertainty as to where we are going. Let me focus on some of the philosophical and theoretical issues involved since, explicitly or implicitly, they form the underpinnings of any research effort.

In a current work in progress (G. Murphy and M. Leeds, in prep.) Gardner Murphy assesses the various monistic and dualistic approaches to the mind–body problem in historical perspective. Their failure to accommodate the data of psi research is not surprising, he notes, considering the fact that these systems came into being before these data had to be taken seriously. The issue is not monism or dualism in the usual sense of the terms, turning on the question of whether there are two basically different kinds of substance in nature. Taking the existence of psi phenomena into account, the question is more properly asked: Are there two different ways of ordering experience — one conditioned to the spatial and temporal ordering of events and one seemingly independent of such ordering? We now require a philosophy for a more complex reality, one that embraces the essential meaning of parapsychological data, namely, that whereas most mental events seem to have intrinsic correlation with physical events, there are some that seem to follow a lawfulness of their own that we do not yet comprehend.

The call for a broadening of our scientific base comes from many quarters other than the progress now being made in parapsychological research. Hess (1967) challenges the concept of causality; Weiskopf (1977) emphasizes the need for recognizing other modes of dealing with human experience; Stent (1975) suggests the need for new a priori categories with which to understand the transcendental features of the self; and Boss (1962) calls attention to the limitations mechanism and positivism have imposed on medicine and psychology. All are harbingers of the effort to outline the dimensions of the challenge confronting the scientific endeavor.

In some instances the plea is for a better blend of the two cultures (Weiskopf, Stent). How much of a help is this in the struggle to understand how psi fits into the nature of things? Parapsychology appears to pose the problem of the extruded middle. It does not seem to fit comfortably into either camp. It continues to elude the net that scientific strategies set for it and it falls short of identifiable connections with man's creative urgings, at least as these urgings are individually expressed. Nevertheless, it may prove interesting to add to the scientific concern with discovery and control the artist's concern with creativity.

The aspect of that experience that may be relevant is the struggle to give form to feeling in a way that evokes a response of aesthetic satisfaction in others. Experiences of this kind seem essential to a sense of ourselves in our closeness to each other as common members of a single species. Spontaneous psi events also seem to have the effect of closing the space between the people involved. To draw a limited analogy, perhaps there is an aspect to these events that can be only partially grasped by the objectifying goals of science but that can be directly experienced given certain emotional constellations in an interpersonal field. There appears to be no way of sparking across this gap at the present time but there are interesting conjectures that appear to be moving toward that closure. Some of this arises out of the structuralist inquiry into the existence of "deep structures" that shape our relatedness to the world. For the parapsychologist the possibility exists that such structures may have evolved phylogenetically in order to limit the role that psi could play in the life of discrete organisms.

Also pertinent to this inquiry is the current interest in a more sophisticated pursuit of phenomena that occur during altered states of consciousness. Associated with this is the recognition of the need for new linguistic and conceptual tools with which to examine such phenomena.

There have been beginning attempts at viewing psi events in terms of the emotional field. We know that belief systems among people generally help or hinder the emergence of psi events. We also know from psychoanalytic studies of psi induction (Ehrenwald, 1957) that there is a tendency to generate more psi effects as interest in and involvement with their occurrence affects a small group. What has not been sufficiently investigated is the nature of the creative elements that enter into these effects as the component parts weave themselves into dynamic patterns. Clinical studies have provided us with insight into the kind of interpersonal situation that favors the appearance of psi in the special and limited field of the therapeutic relationship. To transpose this into the experimental arena would entail significant changes in experimental design. It would involve a shift away from the agent–target–subject arrangement that has characterized so much of psi research, and toward a concern with generating field relationships in which psi events come into being as the outcome of the dynamics of the field. Such an approach would embody the intuitive resources of the clinical approach with the objectifying goals of the experimental approach.

These speculations may strike the reader as somewhat at odds with the rigorous pursuit of experimental strategies and the concern with quantifiable and replicable results so meticulously considered in the pages to follow. But the subject matter of parapsychology occupies an extraordinary position in the realm of experience and, by its very nature, will compel us to the furthermost reaches of our speculative imagination either to accommodate psi effects within our present world view or to transform that view in such a way that these effects no longer seem anomalous.

References

Becker, R. O. Preface. In S. Krippner (Ed.), *Advances in parapsychological research*. Vol. 1: Psychokinesis. New York: Plenum Press, 1977.

Boss, M. The conception of man in natural science and daseinanalysis. *Comprehensive Psychiatry*, 1962, *3*, 193–214.

Ehrenwald, J. The telepathy hypothesis and doctrinal compliance in psychotherapy. *American Journal of Psychotherapy*, 1957, *11*, 359–379.

Hess, W. R. Causality consciousness and cerebral organization. *Science*, 1967, *158*, 1279–1283.

Stent, G. S. Limits to the scientific understanding of man. *Science*, 1975, *187*, 1052–1057.

Weiskopf, V. F. The frontiers and limits of science. *American Scientist*, 1977, *65*, 405–411.

A Survey of Methods and Issues in ESP Research

1

Robert L. Morris

1. The Basic Logic

1.1. The Traditional Forms of ESP, as Illustrated by Spontaneous Cases

Interest in psychic phenomena in general, now often referred to as psi, was based originally on a wealth of anecdotal material. We will first define some basic terms and then go on to use anecdotes to illustrate some of the main forms of psi.

Psi includes all interactions between organisms and their environment which are apparently not mediated by the organisms' sensory or motor functions. If an organism exerts apparent influence on the environment without the use of known means, such as motor functions, we have a case of psychokinesis, or PK, the subject of the first volume in this series. The present volume describes what is known about extrasensory perception, or ESP: an organism's apparent access to external information without the use of the known senses or known means of rational inference. There are four traditional subcategories of ESP: telepathy, clairvoyance, precognition, and retrocognition.

Robert L. Morris • University of California, Santa Barbara, California.

1.1.1. Telepathy

Telepathy (literally, "distant feeling") is apparent direct mind-to-mind communication. One organism appears to have access to the thoughts or experiences of another remote organism.

In a typical anecdote, a young man in Argentina has not communicated with his family in North America for over six months. One day he decides to call them. He picks up the receiver, but before he can dial, he hears an operator's voice speaking his name. She announces that she has a call for him from his parents.

In another example, a family leaves its pet dog behind at a boarding kennel and goes on a trip. The dog's behavior is normal until one morning at 10:00, when it becomes very agitated, howls, and runs around the cage in circles. An hour later the dog returns to normal. The keepers describe the dog's behavior to its owners when they return. The owners are amazed and tell the keepers that at 10:00 that particular morning they were suddenly trapped on the roof of their car in a flash flood and were later rescued.

These examples suggest that one organism was somehow aware of the experiences, intentions, etc., of another and took some appropriate action.

1.1.2. Clairvoyance

Clairvoyance (literally, "clear viewing") means apparent awareness of remote physical, rather than mental, events. The organism appears to have access to remote events in the environment of which other organisms are unaware.

For example, an archaeologist gets a sudden impression that if he digs in a certain somewhat unlikely location he will locate the ruins of an early religious meeting place. He digs and discovers such a ruin.

In another example, a woman goes to a psychic and claims to have lost a valuable jewel. The psychic suggests that she look in the top drawer of her dresser, under some letters. The woman goes home and locates the jewel in the place described by the psychic.

The examples suggest that an individual was somehow aware of a remote physical circumstance unknown to others.

1.1.3. Precognition

Precognition (literally, "before-knowing") means that an individual seems to have access to information that has not yet been determined, e.g., appears able to "see into the future" through some direct means rather than through some process of rational inference.

For example, during the course of an evening, a woman becomes very ill at ease about the safety of her car in the driveway. Finally she feels compelled to move her car into the garage. Early next morning lightning strikes a tree that crashes into the driveway where her car had been parked.

In another example, a young man has a vivid dream about meeting his new roommate when he moves into the school dormitory. A week later he moves in and finds his new roommate has the same first name and general physical appearance as was the case in his dream.

In each case an individual had an impression that seemed to indicate an awareness of a specific future event.

1.1.4. Retrocognition

Retrocognition (literally, "backward knowing") is an individual's apparent access to information about events that took place in the past, without knowledge of available records in the present or rational inference. Such a category of ESP exists as a logical possibility; however, in order to establish the validity of any retrocognitive experience one must have access to information that exists at present. Such records may well themselves have served as the target, or source of information, thus allowing the other forms of ESP to take place. Retrocognition is generally considered not to be a separately researchable category of ESP; research tools for its investigation have not been developed, and it will not be considered further in the present chapter.

1.1.5. Summary

The above anecdotes were selected for their illustrative value only. As will be seen below, they do not serve as a demonstration of the existence of ESP. All involve examples of a strong coincidence between an event or events in an organism's environment and some aspects of the organism's behavior (e.g., a reported experience, a set of body movements) which indicate the organism at some level was aware of the event in the environment. If the anecdote is to be construed as psychic, all known means of communication should be ruled out. Such anecdotes can involve highly specific imagery of one sort or another, as in dreams, as well as unspecific feelings, as in the case of the woman who simply felt uneasy about her car being parked outside. They can involve completely spontaneous, unplanned events, or deliberate attempts "to use ESP." They can be once-in-a-lifetime occurrences or frequent happenings. In truth, since it is we humans who interpret and label any specific anecdote as "psychic," the variety and form of purported psychic events are limited only by the limits to human creativity.

1.2. General Strategies for Investigating ESP

1.2.1. Spontaneous Case Collections

Since our interest in ESP has its origins in personal observations of anomalous experiences, it is logical to attempt to study ESP by collecting well-documented spontaneous experiences suggesting ESP. Such cases can then be compiled and analyzed for overall evidence of ESP as well as for trends suggestive of underlying processes.

1.2.1a. Spontaneous Cases as Evidence for ESP. Researchers attempting to use spontaneous cases as evidence for various forms of ESP must collect enough data from the individual cases involved to be able to make a persuasive case that whatever happened could not be due to nonpsychic factors. Cases either may be actively solicited via public announcements and advertisements or may be gradually acquired from people who volunteer anecdotes in correspondence or in person to individuals and organizations publicly identified with parapsychology.

Such cases must then be screened by diligent interviewing, gathering of corroborating documents, and personal inspection of the places and materials involved. If someone claims to have had a psychic impression of some remote event, it is necessary for that impression to have been registered sometime in advance of the "psychic" having learned the truth of his or her impression; such a registration must be located and documented. The environmental event that matched the psychic impression must likewise be documented. Additional descriptive data bearing on the possibility of any causal connection between the two must also be documented. Any statements by witnesses should be taken separately, to avoid mutual tracing by witnesses. Even such independent taking of witnesses' statements, ideally by separate interviewers, cannot rule out the possibility of witnesses having met earlier to develop a consistent story. Stevenson (1971) argues that spontaneous cases can be adequately documented to constitute excellent evidence for the existence of various forms of psi, although he acknowledges that no method may be capable of providing a perfect proof of the existence of psi.

1.2.1b. Spontaneous Cases as Sources of Hypotheses. L. E. Rhine (e.g., Rhine, 1977) argues that since spontaneous cases can never be completely documented after the fact, they should be used rather as sources of ideas about the nature of psi functioning which can then be assessed in controlled studies. In her analyses of case collections, Rhine attempted very little documentation, screening them primarily on the basis of face validity, plus limited follow-up correspondence. This allowed her a wider variety of cases from which to draw. In her published research, she attempted fairly simple content analyses of such factors as the state of awareness of the percipient, emotional importance of the target, and level of accuracy of the psychic impression. Such a breakdown of written cases can be extended to very fine units of meaning; relationships among categories can be studied, and hypotheses generated for further research.

1.2.1c. Methodological Problems with Spontaneous Case Investigations. Such surveys have had relatively little impact upon modern researchers, beyond suggesting useful hypotheses. Their value is limited by several factors.

First, participants' descriptions of what took place may be inaccurate, due to faulty initial perceptions or interpretations, poor memory, selective memory, exaggeration, elaboration, and intentional fabrication. Corroborative testimony can reduce these problems but still leaves open the possibility of shared inaccuracies or that one persuasive person may have influenced the perceptions and/or memories of others.

Second, one can never totally reconstruct the initial circumstances or their determinants, to rule out hidden factors unknown to the participants which may have produced the apparent psychic event. As a result, assessing the likelihood that any given coincidence of event with impression occurred simply by chance is generally impossible. Coincidences do occur by chance, but to specify how likely chance coincidences are to occur in a given circumstance, we must know all of the factors involved.

Third, there are "sampling errors" in the reporting of cases to investigators. Only certain kinds of people under certain circumstances will take steps to report their cases to an investigator and allow them to become public. Many are shy, have embarrassing elements in their cases, or fear being regarded as unusual. Many may exaggerate or report only those cases that fit their own theories or those theories held by the investigator. Also, the nature and abundance of cases received may be influenced by the media. For instance, if an article appears in a Sunday supplement on ESP and dreams, the researchers mentioned will likely receive several dream anecdotes in the mail shortly afterwards. Thus any statistic reflecting the proportion of cases that fall within a particular category (such as dreams) will be biased and inaccurate (see Rhine, 1977, for a more thorough discussion of this point). Stevenson (1971) has advocated the use of systematic sampling procedures such as those used by pollsters, as well as sampling from captive groups, as strategies to reduce these problems.

Fourth, researchers may themselves differ in the ways they select and process their data. Cases may be judged as valid or not, in accordance with the investigator's prejudices, and may be classified in accordance with the concepts, definitions, and underlying assumptions of the investigator. Before too long we hope we will have enough information to strive for an international terminology and criteria to reduce such problems.

1.2.2. Field Investigations

To overcome some of the above difficulties, many researchers focus their attention upon recurring spontaneous or intentional psi occurrences in real-life situations. For ESP, this generally means work with a selected individual or group that frequently reports being able to do psychic readings of people, foretell the future, etc. The investigator works in a naturalistic setting, yet hopes to be physically present during the psychic occurrences to allow more detailed observation and, where possible, to study the effect of specific manipulations of the conditions.

Field studies are generally initiated when an investigator learns about a specific person (the psychic) or group that seems to be able to produce evidence of ESP fairly consistently and in the presence of strangers. The initial stage generally involves collecting background data on the people involved, including whether they have a reputation for fraud, plus good descriptions of specimen events suggesting psychic functioning. Each event can be treated functionally as though it were a spontaneous case, as described in the section above.

If the investigation seems at this stage to be worth pursuing, in terms of the credibility of the witnesses and psychic(s) and strength of the psychic anecdotes, the investigators may become more directly involved. Sometimes an incognito personal appearance and observation is helpful as a next step. One can join the group or sit in the audience, for example. To embark upon a specific study, it is generally necessary to discuss the investigation in detail with the psychics involved. If a manager suddenly appears, demanding loose conditions, payment in advance of a large fee, or control over publication of results, then there is a strong likelihood that the psychic is too commercial and would be inclined to cheat and/or exploit the investigator. A great deal of common sense and interpersonal skill is needed in setting up the conditions for the investigation. The experimenter must guard effectively against fraud and exploitation but must also not take such a hard line at the start that it turns off the psychic for personal reasons or leads the psychic to devalue the worth of the investigation. There are no fixed rules here, but in general it seems very appropriate for the investigator to clarify at the start what the purposes and procedures of the investigation will be so that its value is apparent and no surprises will occur later to disturb the psychological conditions. The exact nature of the conditions often must be a compromise between what the psychic claims to do and is used to doing and what the investigator would ideally like to have happen. Somewhat more relaxed conditions at the start may be tolerated to help the psychic adjust, as long as it is understood by all parties that claims for ESP success will not be made if conditions, in the investigator's opinion, are inadequate. If the psychic refuses to eventually work under controlled conditions, the investigator may decide to proceed anyway, to obtain descriptive data that may be of use in other studies, with the understanding that the investigation and its results will not be put forth as evidence for the psychic's psi ability.

How does the investigator set up controlled conditions? This depends upon the claims of the psychic and the psychic's desired working conditions. The investigator must know in detail what phenomena are to be expected. For ESP, this generally means the psychic has agreed to respond to a remote piece of information (the target) of some sort, such as a personal description of an absent person, location of a lost object, or knowledge of an important future event. The investigator must therefore know about the psychic's immediate past doings before a session, the layout of the psychic's house or place of business and its contents, the nature of the intended target, its environment, how it was selected, and other details. During the time the psychic is attempting to get impressions of the target, the investigator should continue to collect as much descriptive data as possible about what is happening. Care must be taken to collect data unobtrusively and with sensitivity for the feelings of all concerned. Complex physical monitoring systems, frequent interruptions, endless questionnaires, and the like can easily wear out their welcome. Specifics of how to handle target selection and other such details will be covered later in the chapter.

Ideally the investigator should be present on many occasions, so as to build up a body of systematic observations that can be analyzed for patterns, correlations, etc. These may suggest hypotheses about the processes underlying the phenomena which can perhaps be put to a further test in the field by deliberately manipulating some of the conditions, such as the emotional salience of the target, which have been found to correlate with success.

Although field investigations have the advantage of collecting data under natural conditions, the conditions in which we are ultimately most interested, there are still disadvantages. The investigator or investigative team should be highly trained observers, skilled in physics; experimental, personality and humanistic psychology; and techniques of detecting fraud. In the field, one's capacity to describe all the relevant aspects is still somewhat limited—one cannot X-ray all the furniture in the building to check for hidden gimmicks or monitor all entrances for unwanted visitors, for example, without being an extraordinary nuisance. This is especially important when the unexpected happens. Science records many occasions when more was learned from the unanticipated than from an intended experiment, but it was often found after the fact that vital information was missing that the scientist did not know in advance would be needed. In the field, investigators are also largely reliant upon human testimony based on human observation. Automatic recording equipment can be used where feasible, but it can be psychologically and physically inconsistent and can also be subject to deception, since it observes only what it is given to observe. Also, an investigator in the field is basically a combination of intruder and guest, and must make the necessary social adjustments to keep the situation as natural as possible.

1.2.3. Controlled Laboratory Investigations

The most detailed and sophisticated investigation procedures are those that involve controlled, precise experimentation in a laboratory setting. The environment is designed and constructed to meet the needs of the researcher. Its characteristics can be manipulated at will and can be described quite accurately and thoroughly in any research report. The ESP targets can be specific events or objects in the environment defined and selected by the researcher to answer specific questions about psi functioning. The target can be screened from the percipient (the subject) in a variety of ways. Measurements of various sorts—physical, biological, and psychological—can be taken conveniently. A wide variety of conditions can be manipulated or held constant. Alternative, nonpsychic explanations including fraud can be more thoroughly controlled and ruled out, and success and failure can be measured much more precisely, allowing more effective comparisons of psi functioning under different conditions. This in turn enables more effective research aimed at understanding the processes involved. The capacity to describe one's procedures and results in greater detail increases the ability of one investigator to repeat the procedures of another as thoroughly as possible.

Although these are powerful advantages, controlled laboratory studies do have their drawbacks, as Stevenson (1971) and others have pointed out. The laboratory environment is artificial, can be quite sterile in appearance and mood, and can be either boring, trivial, or frightening if not handled properly. Many people disdain laboratory research and refuse to participate, thus restricting the generality of laboratory findings. Being on someone else's territory and being asked to perform psychically at a specific time by responding to a remote target whose emotional relevance exists only because it is part of an agreed-to experiment is psychologically quite different from being able to respond spontaneously, and often incidentally, to whatever seems relevant at the time. The psychology of psi should be quite different for our three main modes of ESP testing, and many findings from one mode will doubtless not generalize to the others. In fact, one last reason for focusing on controlled laboratory research is that it is doubtless the toughest situation of all; if psi is controlled and understood in the laboratory, whatever techniques we have found to work should be most effective in producing controlled successful ESP under a variety of natural conditions.

1.3. Introduction to the Basic Elements of Controlled ESP Research

For present purposes, ESP studies (as well as most spontaneous cases) may be described by a model of apparent communication, for which no channel (or physical means) can yet be identified. All controlled ESP studies involve a percipient or subject (an organism whose ESP skills are being tested) and a target or event in the environment to which the subject is expected to respond. The target is separated from the subject by barriers to known relevant means of communication from target to subject, either direct means (sensory) or indirect means (rational inference). The target's content is varied in some way and the subject's behavior (including verbal behavior) is monitored to see if it consistently reflects the nature of the target. If the subject's behavior is significantly related to the target's content to a greater degree than one would expect by chance, then some form of communication apparently took place. If the lines of known communication from target to subject have been truly blocked and yet some information seems to get through, there apparently is at least one new form of communication taking place.

2. The Basic Elements of an ESP Communication System

2.1. The Subject

2.1.1. The Gifted Subject

Many researchers prefer to work with especially gifted subjects. There are several advantages. Such subjects are likely to have more confidence in their own abilities and better control over them, perhaps because they have been experimenting on their own and with others for some time. They may therefore have worked through any emotional problems they might have with personally displaying ESP, may have acquired a more thorough understanding of their own psychic functioning, and may be able to contribute their own insights about research with them to the parapsychological literature (e.g., Garrett, 1939; Harribance, 1976; Swann, 1975; Tanous, 1976). Additionally, since gifted subjects are more likely to produce strong and sustained results, they are well suited for certain kinds of research: research in which it is necessary to establish quickly that the procedure is conducive to ESP and is not amenable to alternative interpretations; research in which an unusually difficult procedure is being tested, simply to see if it can be made to work, which calls for confidence from the percipient; and research that, for whatever reason, will call for a sustained strong psi performance.

It could be argued that most process-oriented research is best done with gifted subjects, except for research deliberately aimed at investigating the nature of psi functioning in people in general, or studies of learning in beginners. However, there are several specific disadvantages to working with gifted individuals. A person publicly known as a gifted psychic may be at least in part a deliberate fraud or someone heavily dependent upon the sensory cues generally presented in the public arena. These possibilities must be guarded against in the research procedures as well as in procedures used in selecting the gifted individuals with whom to work. Gifted individuals are more likely to be considered frauds than the non-gifted (e.g., Randi, 1975). Also, gifted individuals may have a hard time adjusting to controlled conditions and may find them threatening if not introduced to them gradually and with a sensitive explanation of why they are necessary. A well-known individual may have a reputation to protect, which may create pressure to do well and may lead to tension over whether or not to publicize negative results. Also, the generality of results from gifted individuals can be called into question. Such a person may have developed ESP in a very particular way, within the context of a highly specific belief system; any results obtained may be quite incorrect for individuals who did not develop within that tradition.

To bring a gifted person from the field situation into a controlled setting generally involves a thorough review of the goals of the overall project, the procedures to be used, and the costs and gains to all concerned. The explainer must decide how much to emphasize that the procedures involve extensive safeguards against fraud. Some take offense that they might be accused and leave; others are grateful that care is being taken to safeguard them against reasonable charges of fraud after the fact.

Deception in any aspect of the study should be either eliminated or cleared with the psychic in advance within a general context, with the reason for deception made clear. The same can easily be done if facts occasionally are going to be withheld from the psychic. If these details are ignored, interpersonal tension and loss of confidence can easily result. If informing the psychic in even general terms will destroy the value of the experiment, then perhaps another way to approach the question should be found. In general, the needs and goals of the psychic need to be taken into account as much as possible, as long as the soundness of the procedures used is not jeopardized.

If the goal of a project is simply to see whether or not such and such a psychic feat can be accomplished by *anyone*, then a single confident individual can often provide the answer. If any generality to one's data is desired, including general repeatability by other researchers, then a pool of gifted individuals should be used. A large, diverse pool will produce more general results than a small one. If several psychics are used, their social interactions become important. If they know of each other and do interact, this can be a valuable source of information as experiences are shared, notes compared, etc. It can also make the results of each interdependent; e.g., if person A finds she does better on visual imagery than auditory imagery, person B may expect to do better on visual imagery also. Also, a sense of competition may develop that can easily get out of hand. Unless competitiveness is specifically desired, it is up to the researcher to maintain a general research environment that values and reinforces cooperation. Often competitiveness can be reduced by the process of initial subject selection.

2.1.2. Other Selected Subjects

Many researchers investigate ESP in specific subject populations such as the blind, hyperactive children, meditators, native Americans, and other categories. Such people must be solicited for research in ways that consider their special needs as well as the experimental goals of the researchers. If a special group is to be compared for ESP with the population as a whole, then a "nonspecial" control group must be tested for ESP under the same circumstances as the special groups, without allowing the special group to regard itself as special or to be regarded by experimenters as special. Otherwise subject or experimenter expectations could lead to the special group artifactually scoring higher (or lower) than the control groups. Keeping the two groups the same within all respects is difficult at best and is rarely even attempted in parapsychological research. The control group is necessary in the first place to enable the researchers to know that whatever results they found with the special groups were not solely due to the experimental conditions, experimenters' expectations, or similar factors. For instance, research on the blind or on youngsters seems in general to produce fairly strong results. Yet this may be due simply to the tendency of researchers to treat such people with special care and understanding.

2.1.3. The Unselected Subject

Many researchers do studies with "unselected" subjects, meaning subjects not deliberately selected for some outstanding characteristic such as deafness or psi ability. Such subjects are not truly unselected, of course; they are generally volunteers who are taking a course related to parapsychology, visitors to a parapsychology research unit, or respondents to a public announcement asking for volunteers for an ESP test. No study in parapsychology or any other branch of the behavioral sciences has ever used a truly random or representative sample of human beings. The handicapped, institutionalized, and undereducated segments of society are rarely well represented.

An important part of any research is the technique used for recruiting subjects, yet it is rarely described in any detail in procedural writings. Subjects solicited from classes may be heavily influenced in their approach to the study by the public attitudes of the instructor and the content of the course. The exact wording of a public notice or an article in the media can bias strongly who volunteers and who doesn't. Nonvolunteer subjects such as members of a large class suddenly called upon to take an ESP test may be actively hostile to the notion of ESP and may contribute unnecessary noise to the data (see the sheep–goat effect, p. 153). Some researchers have drawn primarily from friends, acquaintances, and research staff for their subjects, thus greatly reducing the generality of the results but also in all likelihood reducing the initial anxiety experienced by subjects.

Procedures for soliciting subjects should take into consideration the goals and needs of the researcher. Captive audiences of one sort or another will give more diversity in general and may be better for purely exploratory, correlational questions, such as the relationship between attitude toward ESP and initial scoring on a guessing ESP test. Volunteers are more likely to be interested in ESP, to be more open to experimentation, and to place a real value upon their performance. Unfortunately, no real research on the personality dynamics of volunteers versus nonvolunteers for ESP experiments has been done, but it is likely that volunteers may be somewhat special with regard to other characteristics such as openness to personal disclosure and social extroversion. Volunteers can be solicited through announcements on bulletin boards and in classes, by advertisements in newspapers, by word of mouth, or through mention of the proposed research in the media, among other ways. Unsolicited volunteers are generally visitors and people who have learned indirectly of the study.

The initial attitudes of volunteers vary considerably but may be affected by the wording of any preliminary solicitation announcement. Some researchers prefer simply to announce that ESP volunteers are needed; others describe the study in detail; others solicit general volunteers and then describe the particulars of a given study over the phone. The more information a subject has in advance, the more opportunity to avoid a study that has no appeal; the subject also has more opportunity to build specific motivation. Advance knowledge of the specifics of a study can often lead to too much introspection and hypothesis construction, however. The overall apparent warmth of the announcement may also affect people; a cold brief announcement in type calling for "experimental subjects" may attract fewer people than a pleasantly colored poster soliciting "participants in studies of psychic communication." A garish poster with a picture of light beams zigzagging between two foreheads may have great appeal to some but may turn others off completely.

Once initially selected, a large group of subjects may then be put through a screening process of some sort, to select especially talented subjects. Tart (1976) used a two-stage ESP-test screening procedure to increase the likelihood that participants in his learning studies would be able at the start to manifest ESP under experimentally controlled procedures. Subjects who did poorly on the screening tests were not invited to participate in the extensive follow-up study. Subjects can also be screened for any other characteristic, through the use of behavioral measures, questionnaires, and other methods.

2.1.4. Animals

Some researchers prefer to work with animals, either to investigate specifically the role of psi in different biological systems or because in certain respects it is easier to keep conditions constant and under control in animal studies. The species selected generally depends upon the question being asked and the equipment and housing facilities available. Several general factors should be borne in mind, however. The species chosen should be one that might reasonably be expected to show evidence of ESP, such as one frequently mentioned in spontaneous cases (e.g., cats, dogs, and horses), or one for which ESP would be useful, such as a species involved in violent prey–predator relationships. The species should also be one whose behavior and physiology is well understood and is relatively easy to motivate within an experimental context, e.g., through rewards and/or punishments. If a telepathy procedure is to be used, then a species having strong social bonds or at least a well-defined social structure should be used. Finally, a species should fit the practical requirements of controlled research such as reasonable size, ease of handling, and freedom from disease.

A final point with regard to animals is that they are never, strictly speaking, volunteer subjects and have no direct control over what happens to them. The general thought prevailing in the parapsychological research community is that the researcher should exercise humane considerations in the design and conduct of animal studies. Although some research questions may be impossible to investigate without recourse to punishment, surgery, etc., alternatives to these procedures should be sought whenever possible (see Morris, 1970, 1971).

2.1.5. The Researcher as Subject

A few researchers have used themselves as subjects, either exclusively or as part of a general group of subjects. Being one's own subject is often an excellent way to detect and deal with the problems of an experimental procedure in its developmental stages, since it allows one to view the experimental situation from the subject's perspective. If there is only one researcher, this is of course not feasible. The researcher's data would be hard to compare with data from others, especially if a specific experimental hypothesis known to the researcher is being tested. Thus the researcher's own data should not be, and rarely are, included in the official data. If, however, the only question being asked is whether or not *anyone* can accomplish a certain ESP task, then perhaps the researcher's data may be useful due to his or her high motivation, as long as someone else is actually conducting the study and adequate experimental safeguards have been taken.

The researcher as subject occurs in another context as well. As the researcher(s) involved in a given study go about the business of making decisions, behaving toward the subjects, and observing physical events, they may inadvertently be using ESP to gather the information they need to make favorable decisions or may be using PK to influence physical events to take place in a favorable way. Although this possibility may seem farfetched, it is at present taken quite seriously by parapsychologists and will be considered later in more detail.

2.2. The Target

What kinds of information have been used as targets? Essentially almost no limits have been placed on target material, except that it be some information that can be meaningfully linked to the behavior of subjects.

2.2.1. General Characteristics of Targets

Targets can be characteristics of objects (e.g., what's in the box), events (e.g., what's happening in the box), or representations of either (e.g., what's the content of the picture in the box). The target can be set up in any of a variety of ways. It can be microscopic (e.g., Pratt and Woodruff, 1939) or an entire landscape (e.g., Targ and Puthoff, 1974). It can be information existing in the present or information that has not yet been determined at the time the subject attempts to respond to it, as in studies of precognition.

In many experiments the target is known to another individual, the agent, who is also concealed from the subject. Agents may be active: concentrating on the target and trying to communicate it to the subject (who is also known as the receiver or percipient in this case). Agents may also be passive: aware of the target but not actively oriented toward communicating with the subject. When the experimental design includes both an agent and a target object or event, it is impossible to determine conclusively whether the source for any information transfer is the agent's mental processes (telepathy) or the target itself (clairvoyance). In such cases, the term *GESP* (general ESP) is used to describe the information transfer.

It is possible that active agents function at times as PK subjects. If one human being tries to influence another person's behavior, we usually label that influence telepathy or GESP, with the agent part of the target and the receiver the subject (e.g., Rhine 1945; Rhine and Pratt, 1957). If a human being tries to influence the behavior of a mammal, insect, protozoan, plant, virus, enzyme, organic soup, inorganic chemical reaction, electromechanical event, or rolling die, we at some point in this series start to view the agent as PK subject and stop viewing the receiver as subject.

Passive agents, on the other hand, are rarely regarded as subjects; in some designs (e.g., Kreitler and Kreitler, 1972), the agent and receiver are not even aware of each other's existence. I prefer to use the terms *active and passive information sources* and *receivers* rather than *targets* and *subjects* but will continue the more traditional subject–target usage throughout the chapter. Perhaps, as we shall reconsider later, the most appropriate view will be to regard all participants in psi studies as having the potential to contribute psychically to the outcome of these studies. For a further consideration of active versus passive agency, see Schmeidler (1961).

Targets can be distorted or totally unfamiliar to the subject, so that a cognitively complex translation is necessary to render the target meaningful to the subject. Rao (1963), for instance, asked subjects to match cards containing standard English words with their equivalents in a language and alphabet unknown to the subjects: Telugu or Hindi. Targets can be hidden aspects of the environment of which the subject is totally unaware but which are nevertheless functionally important for the subject, who does not even know that he or she is in an ESP study, (e.g., Stanford and Stio, 1976).

Subjects can often respond to more than just the specific target intended by the experimenter. Any record kept of the identity of the target—e.g., a separate listing of the order of the suits in a stacked deck of cards—may also serve as the target for the subject's ESP. Given the possibility of precognition, this also pertains to records made after the subject's responses, in the course of tallying results.

For the above reasons, most researchers feel that it is probably impossible to conduct a pure telepathy study, so as to rule out clairvoyance or precognition as alternative descriptions of what happened. Any attempt to study "mind-to-mind" communication must sooner or later rely upon an objective record of what the agent has been assigned to think about or image, which record could then have served as the target for clairvoyance or precognition by the subject. An attempt to avoid this problem was proposed by McMahan (1946). The agent would compose a private code, translating digits into known visual symbols (e.g., one equals circle, two equals star, etc.). A list of random numbers could be given to the agent, to serve as fixed instructions as to what symbol to think about at any given time that the receiver was concentrating. The subject would write down the symbol that came to mind during each concentration period. Then the agent could compare the subject's record of symbol guesses with the original list of random numbers to tally the subject's accuracy, bearing in mind the code needed to do so. To guard against mistakes or motivated errors by the agent, however, an independent checker would be needed, one to whom the agent had somehow indirectly (e.g., through reference to shared past events) communicated the code. Unfortunately, the behaviors used to communicate the code as well as the actions and record keeping involved in eventually tallying the scores could also have served as targets for clairvoyance or precognition. The subject could have used such cues rather than true mind-to-mind communication. Since the presence of even an active agent is not enough to rule out alternative forms of psi, many researchers prefer to use the term *GESP* for procedures in which an agent of any sort is involved, thus avoiding an arbitrary decision as to whether or not the agent's thoughts constitute part of the target.

The environment around the target may also conceivably serve as part of the target. Stanford and Pratt (1970), for instance, found evidence that the inner of two envelopes used to conceal colored cards led the subject to respond consistently in the same way each time a particular envelope was used, even though the subject could not see the envelope and was consciously attempting only to guess which side of a card inside the envelope was facing upward. West and Fisk (1953) found evidence that subjects responded differently to target materials prepared by the two different experimenters. Targets prepared by Fisk tended to be guessed correctly; those by West tended to be guessed incorrectly. Osis and Carlson (1972) found evidence that the moods of distant experimenters preparing target materials were significantly related to subjects' success at responding to the remote targets. Carpenter (1971) found that erotic pictures placed next to the target card in a concealing envelope affected subjects' accuracy in guessing the identity of the card, even though the subjects were quite unaware that any erotic pictures were being used.

The upshot of all this confusion is that, since the target in an ESP study can be literally almost anything, most studies give the subject more things to respond to than just the simple target envisioned by the re-searcher. This should be borne in mind by the researcher in the course of designing the study. Depending on the research question being asked, one may wish to restrict the redundancy of the target information (e.g., have no independent record of its existence and no agent) or one may wish to have many potential sources of information about the target available. Of course, all sources of information about the target must be concealed from the subject. Also, the researcher may wish to vary the target environment and handling so as to compare targets with emotionally salient histories and environments with those whose environments have been more pedestrian.

2.2.2. Restricted-Choice Targets

Many spontaneous ESP cases involve someone who is a consistently accurate guesser or chooser. When faced with a decision about which of several alternatives to select (e.g., which exit door is unlocked), this person chooses the correct one more frequently than others do. Researchers have attempted to study whether such people are using ESP, rather than simply good logic or subtle sensory cues, by presenting subjects with a set of alternative choices and asking them to choose the correct one. The earliest work of this sort (e.g., Richet, 1884) involved guessing the suit of each card in a series of concealed playing cards. If the subject guessed at only one card and got it right, one could conclude nothing since this should happen about 25% of the time by chance. Thus subjects must be asked to guess the identities of several cards, to see whether they are successful consistently enough to exclude mere coincidence. This necessitated the development of a set of specific procedures involving groups of target cards to be guessed in a specific order.

2.2.2a. Basic Card-Guessing Techniques. In the "broken technique" (also known as the BT or "basic technique") a stack of cards is randomly arranged (see below) and concealed from the subject. A handler removes the cards one by one and places them aside. The subject's job is to guess the identity of each card either before or after it has been transferred from the top of the deck. The cards can be either face up in view of the handler-agent (GESP) or face down (clairvoyance). The subject must know when each change of cards takes place. This can be done in three ways. The experimenter can signal the subject verbally, mechanically, or electronically in some way. This procedure is inappropriate if the cards are not adequately concealed from the experimenter, since he or she may inadvertently signal in a slightly different way for some targets than others, e.g., by signaling more quickly or for a shorter duration on certain suits. Alternatively, the subject can decide on each trial when he or she is ready for the next target to be selected and can signal the experimenter verbally, mechanically, or electronically. This procedure has the advantage of allowing the subject to set the pace of the trials. A third procedure is to have both experimenter and subject paced by a third party who signals both at the same time. A variant of this is to use synchronized chronometers and begin new trials every X seconds, an interval agreed upon in advance.

A simpler version of the above procedure, useful only in clairvoyance testing, is to conceal an entire deck of randomized cards and ask the subject to guess "down through" the deck, card by card, until all of the cards have been responded to. This procedure, called the "down through technique" (DT), is very flexible, in that the cards can be placed anywhere appropriate and need not be monitored card by card as the subject makes responses. The subject, therefore, is given more control over the pacing of the experiment.

Some card-guessing procedures ask the subject to identify each card in a deck of target cards by placing it in front of one of several "key cards," one for each possible type of card. The simplest matching procedure is called "open matching" and is exemplified by the "Four Aces Test." One takes a standard deck of cards, removes the four aces, and places each ace face up in a row (the key cards). The remaining cards are then randomized and are given to the subject. This person then guesses the suit of the remaining "target cards" by placing them one by one in front of the ace of whichever suit one guesses the target to be. Once completed, the target cards are turned over and scored for hits.

Blind matching (BM) is similar, except that key cards are randomly arranged face down, so that their identity is not known by those present. The subject's task is still to place each target card in front of the appropriate key card. The subject presumably must now identify both key card and target card to be correct, a task that should be much more difficult than open matching. However, as Foster (1940) has pointed out, a comparison of results with the two methods shows less of a discrepancy in success than one would expect. This led Foster to hypothesize that ESP seems to work in some sort of direct fashion, so that the apparent cognitive complexity of the task does not matter. The blind matching technique is well adapted to explore this line of reasoning, since the key cards can be set up to be only cognitively related to the target cards, and the complexity of the cognitive relationship can be varied. Carpenter (1965), for instance, employed key cards with numerical equations written on them and target cards with the numerical solutions. The subject's job was cognitively complex: to put the target card where it belongs, e.g., in front of the key card that it solves mathematically. In similar fashion Rao (1963) used target cards in one language and key cards of the same words in not only another language but another alphabet.

A rarely used matching procedure, known mainly through its use in the Pratt-Woodruff study (1939), is the screened touch matching (STM) procedure. Key cards are hung, face up or face down, on pegs placed in a row on a vertical board suspended a few inches off the ground. Blank indicator cards are placed beneath the vertical board, just under each key card, so that someone shielded by the board from the key cards can nevertheless see the indicator cards and tell where each key card is located. In the usual procedure, the subject sits on the key card side of the board and the experimenter sits on the other side of the board, so that he or she cannot see the key cards. The experimenter holds the deck of randomized target cards, and the subject guesses the suit of each card by tapping the indicator card under the key of his or her choice. The experimenter can see the subject's response and places the top target card behind the indicator card tapped by the subject. After the subject has completed making guesses, the board containing the key cards is turned over and the results are scored. This procedure is considered tighter than the other forms of matching, since the subject never handles or even sees the actual target cards.

The above procedures are the main strategies for arranging a target deck of cards. Such a deck need not be playing cards and their suits; researchers have also used cards with numbers written on them or cards of different colors, as well as other kinds of symbols. In his early work at Duke, Rhine (1935/1973) became aware that subjects' personal preferences or habits could influence their guessing behavior, so that they might call more spades than clubs just because spades rank higher in many card games, or might call numbers in numerical sequence (e.g., seven after six) simply through habits picked up in learning how to count. Since such biased guesses would constitute a source of unwanted noise detracting from the subjects' ESP success, Rhine asked a colleague in perceptual psychology at Duke, Dr. Karl Zener, to suggest a set of symbols likely to be emotionally neutral to the average subject. Zener suggested a set of symbols, which, with minor modifications, became the well-known circle, cross, three wavy lines, square, and star of the standard ESP cards (occasionally still referred to as Zener cards). A standard deck of ESP cards contained 5 cards of each symbol, 25 in all.

Such cards have often been used in the procedures mentioned above. Each guess is labeled a "call" or "trial." A set of consecutive calls, such as 25 calls down through a deck, is a "run," and a set of runs at a single sitting is a "session."

2.2.2b. Other Kinds of Restricted-Choice Targets. In addition to cards or analogous surfaces such as pieces of paper with symbols on them, several other choice-related targets have been used. Several researchers have used mere lists of symbols as targets; the subject's job is to guess in order each symbol in a concealed list of randomized symbols. Some studies (e.g., Bleksley, 1963) have used randomly set times on clock faces as targets. Such targets allow the results to be scored for near misses as well as direct hits, although there is the disadvantage of a likelihood of guessing biases—calling preferred times, etc.

Many targets deal with location. Some researchers (e.g., Freeman, 1964) have asked subjects to circle which of five symbols or pictures in a row is in the "correct" position, e.g., positions one through five, moving from left to right. Stanford (e.g., 1967) presented subjects with a grid marked off in the circular shape of a radar screen and asked them to guess which sectors had targets in them. Child and Singer (1976) presented subjects with a complex paper maze having over a hundred numbered "doorways" leading from one compartment to another. Subjects were asked to find their way out of the maze by going from compartment to compartment until the outer edge of the maze was reached. The subject would make a choice as to which doorway to use to leave the starting compartment. The experimenter would then consult a concealed complex code to learn whether an odd or even digit had been randomly assigned to the number of that chosen doorway. If odd, the door was "open" and the subject could advance to the next compartment. If even, the door was "closed" and the subject would have to select another doorway. Once in another compartment, the process would be repeated until the subject had either left the maze or was hopelessly sealed in. For this procedure as well as those of Stanford and Freeman, the subjects are responding by making correct or incorrect locational choices. The correctness of these choices may be represented by an actual duplicate of the material seen by the subject, with the target location marked off, or simply by a coded set of numbers used to determine the correctness of the response. As discussed earlier, the true target may be very difficult to specify.

Other kinds of locational targets may involve guessing where, from several possibilities, a missing object is. This procedure has even been adopted for animals—food is hidden in a maze and the animal is allowed to run the maze, to see if it goes toward the food. Osis and Foster (1953) ran cats in a two-choice maze and used fans to blow away the food odors. In some studies (e.g., Duval and Montredon, 1968) animals were allowed to roam in a confined area. If they were in the correct place when a target location was selected, they would avoid shock.

A final form of target involves guessing the outcome of an automated random number generator attached to a display and recording system. Such random number generators and their workings will be described in more detail in section 2.4.2. Such devices basically produce random electrical events that lead to the activation of one of several alternative electrical circuits. Each circuit has its own specific consequence, e.g., will allow its own light to be lit when a button is pushed. In its most typical version, as developed mainly by Schmidt (1969, 1970), the subject is confronted by a row of differently colored lights, each with a button below it. He or she is told that each time one of the buttons is pressed, one of the lights will turn on. The subject's job is to anticipate which circuit has been activated (or will be activated, if the test is for precognition) and to press the corresponding button. Such equipment can be made extremely flexible, so that the subject can press a pass button if nothing is coming through and a new target is desired (e.g., Puthoff and Targ, 1974), or a confidence button if one has just made a call, feels especially good about it, and wishes it to be scored separately. The choices and targets can be automatically tallied and recorded. The display to the subject can be greatly varied: For GESP studies, an agent in another room sees the target light on another console (e.g., Tart, 1976); for pure clairvoyance studies, feedback to the subject can be withheld so that the light never comes on, although the machine still tallies hits and misses, etc. Thus the range of target material, at least for the last procedure, must include minute electromechanical events.

To summarize, in restricted-choice studies, we are basically studying the possible role of psi in decision making, as an organism selects from among a finite number of alternatives. Subjects for most of these procedures clearly get a hit or a miss. There is no ambiguity of the sort that plagues some of the other procedures, as we shall see below.

2.2.3. Free-Response Targets

As the name implies, free-response targets are targets drawn from a wide sample of target material rather than from a limited number of alternatives already known to the subject. The subject is thus free to respond in whatever way seems appropriate.

2.2.3a. Pictorial Material. Most of the free-response studies have emphasized pictures of complex objects and events, ranging from simple line drawings (e.g., Sinclair, 1962) on through to picture postcards (Braud and Braud, 1973), famous art prints (e.g., Ullman, Krippner, and Feldstein, 1966) and sets of Viewmaster slides (e.g., Honorton and Harper, 1974). The target picture can be a concealed picture not known to anyone present or it can be a picture concentrated upon by an active agent. If the agent is attempting to aid the information transfer by drawing the picture, then the agent's drawing may also be serving as target. When extremely complex target pictures are used, many researchers use only one or two for an entire session, since there is enough information available to allow assessment of whether or not anything was transmitted.

Free-response material in principle has always been popular as target material, since it more easily captures the interest of the subject, leads to qualitatively rich responses, and is more appropriate for investigating ESP during enhanced imagery states. Its drawback, as we shall see below, is that it is far more complex to assess information transfer mathematically in free-response procedures. Pictures, both drawings and photographs, have the advantage of being both interesting and varied (if well selected), can be tailored in content to the specific needs of a particular study, and yet can be very conveniently and easily catalogued by content, selected by some randomizing process, and concealed from the subject.

Free-response pictures have been selected for many specific criteria; most researchers prefer pictures that are in color, are perceptually and thematically distinct, are emotionally salient, and are unambiguous in interpretation. Such pictures have more appeal for subjects, are easier for agents to attend to, and facilitate any judging procedure in which a judge is comparing the subject's responses with several pictures, one of which was the target (see below for a description of data analyses).

Unfortunately, many researchers have given too little care to the development of an effective, well-coded pool of target pictures. An exception is a pool of 1,024 slides developed at Maimonides Medical Center in Brooklyn (Honorton, 1975). These slides were designed to be codable for gross content. A survey by Hall and Van de Castle (1966) of dream content yielded several categories of frequently encountered dream material of which ten were selected: color, activity, human being, human body part, mythological (fictional) character, food, animal, artifact/implement, architectural object, and nature scene. The Maimonides team reasoned that such categories are likely to be those found in internally generated imagery in general. They therefore composed a set of 1,024 pictures and collages, converted to slides, representing all possible combinations of the presence and absence of the ten content categories—ranging from a picture with all categories absent to a picture with all present. Thus, in the target pool as a whole, each category is represented in exactly half of the slides and no two slides have the same distribution of content categories present. Each slide can thus be represented by ten binary digits, representing the presence or absence of each content category. The slides vary greatly in visual complexity and thematic cohesiveness; their main value, in addition to being amenable to more precise quantification (see below), is that they represent a great variety of images that are often dreamlike in their frequent juxtaposition of unrelated themes.

2.2.3b. Real Events and Locations. Basically any object or event of interest can be concealed from the subject and used as a target, if handled properly. One example of this is the "remote viewing" procedure (e.g., Targ and Puthoff, 1974). In its basic form, the target is a specific geographical location. A target pool is composed of note cards giving detailed instructions on how to reach a specific location. An agent receives one of these cards, selected randomly by a third party, and drives to the target site, arriving at a prearranged time. He or she may then have further specific instructions, written on the card, such as "sit on the large rock by the pond and splash your hand in the water." The subject is asked at the same time to "view" the agent at the target location, to describe it, and to report on anything that the agent may be doing. Variants on this procedure include asking the subject to describe where the agent will be at some specified time in the near future, or asking the subject simply to describe the location defined by a set of geographical coordinates. The target in each case is a large physical location; subjects are asked to describe the location without any specific limits to how much territory to take in, although such limits could easily be built into the subject's instructions. Also, subjects could easily be asked to focus to varying degrees on the actual experience of the agent. In many locations, for instance, agents may be able to see mountains close by without actually being in the mountains. A subject who responds with images of the mountains is doing well if the target is defined in terms of what the agent sees, but is doing poorly if the target is defined in terms of where the agent is. The latter procedure is most often used with remote viewing research, since part of its value and appeal is that it makes use of long-standing physical objects as its target rather than transient events (including experience) and has the potential for use in locating lost objects and people.

   2.2.3c. People. One of the most frequent claims of persons with supposed ESP abilities is that they can "read" people—that is, tell about a person's past, present, and future—having had only minimal contact with the person. We thus have the concept of the "target person," whose personal characteristics become the target for the subject. The subject is oriented toward a specific target person at the onset of a session by being told something quite neutral about the person, e.g., that the target person is seated at a desk in a room known to the subject. The subject may be given a "token object," something that belongs to the target person, to further orient the subject toward that one specific individual. Roll, Morris, Damgaard, Klein, and Roll (1973) took Polaroid pictures of the target person and gave them, undeveloped, to the experimenter working with the subject. The subject, Lalsingh Harribance, was allowed to place his hand on top of the still-unopened picture in its development casing. His reading of the person was then tape-recorded and the picture casement was not opened until later.

   Characteristics of the target person that are fair game for a reader include: physical appearance; physical and mental health; actuarial data; socioeconomic and educational background; family details including spouse, children, pets; emotional ties; goals and ambitions; childhood details, including traumatic events, childhood emotional ties; interests and hobbies; details about other relatives and acquaintances, living and nonliving; and future events in the person's life.

   Lore maintains that some people consistently make better target persons than others, but the topic has not been adequately researched. Those people may simply lead more varied lives, thus increasing the likelihood that correct statements will be made by the subject sooner or later. Harribance (personal communication, 1972) once suggested that the best target persons were people who had had varied, interesting lives, with emotional ups and downs, and who were genuinely interested in participating in a reading.

In summary, free-response ESP targets are ones to which the subject can respond freely, so that any imagery or impressions that come to mind may be directly or indirectly related to the target, even if the subject knows it is only a postcard or that it is a male human over 20 years of age.

2.2.4. Emotional Events Having a Specific Onset and Termination

Some targets do not fit so neatly into the restricted-choice versus free-response dichotomy. Chief among these are the targets designed specifically to have brief emotional impact upon the subject. Many anecdotes involve people who suddenly became uneasy or felt ill, without any accompanying thoughts or images, only to learn later that a tragedy had befallen someone close to them at the time.

Generating emotionally powerful targets under controlled laboratory circumstances is very difficult, and despite the abundance of anecdotal data on emotional targets, very little research has been done. Those who have investigated the area have largely confined themselves to mildly noxious stimuli applied to an agent, or concealed symbols or words of emotional importance to the subject.

Some researchers have used periodic short duration stimuli. Rice (1966) fired blank cartridges behind the agent or asked the agent to place one foot briefly in ice water. Tart (1963) periodically shocked the agent (Tart himself) through electrodes strapped to his legs. Targ and Puthoff (1974) periodically pulsed a strobe in the agent's eyes. Others asked the agent to think about something of emotional interest to the subject. Dean (1962; Dean and Nash, 1967) gave the agent a stack of 20 note cards, 5 containing names of emotional importance to the subject as of the day of the test, 5 containing comparable names important to the agent, 5 containing names randomly taken from the phone book, and 5 blank. The deck was arranged in random order and placed face down in front of the agent. During the experimental session the agent would turn the cards over at preselected times and concentrate on the name for 20 seconds. The subject, some distance away, was monitored for emotion-related activity throughout the session. The aim of these and related procedures was basically to see whether the subject showed increased emotional activity at the same time the agent was having an induced emotional experience or was experiencing something of emotional interest to the subject. Thus the presence or absence of the emotional stimuli and its qualitative nature, as well as its exact time of onset and duration, all served as aspects of the target.

2.3. Modes of Response

An important distinction should be drawn between the target in an ESP experiment and the goal of an ESP experiment. The goal of an ESP experiment is not just to see whether the subject can "tune in" to a remote target; rather, the goal is to see whether the subject responds consistently in ways that can be meaningfully related to the target by researchers. If the latter does not occur, the former cannot be inferred. The subject's job in each study is to make a correct response, in whatever manner the research team has defined a correct response. The job of the research team in this respect, of course, is to define a correct response intelligently. The issues involved are best considered according to the general style of the study involved.

2.3.1. Restricted-Choice Responses

In most respects these responses are the most straightforward. The organism is placed in a situation in which it has a limited number of alternative behaviors at its disposal, one for each possible target alternative. Most studies are carried out with humans who are aware that they are in an ESP test and have had the relationship between their behavioral options and the target alternatives thoroughly explained to them. A few studies have involved humans unaware that they were participating in an ESP test, and/or unaware of the contingencies between their behavioral alternatives and a target of relevance to them. Finally, some studies have used nonverbal species such as cats or mice as subjects, who presumably are not aware that they are in an ESP test and must have "natural," strongly motivating target material to prompt an appropriate response from them.

2.3.1a. Responses by Humans Aware of the Existence of Their Targets. From the outset it should be noted that the experimenter's role in explaining the nature of the study is very important. Generally the new subject is shown a sample of each of the target alternatives and is shown how to register a response in each case.

For the basic technique for card guessing, the subject may be asked simply to wait for the signal to begin each trial, then to call out the name of whatever he or she feels to be the card suit or standard ESP symbol for the top card. A coexperimenter nearby then records each call on a standard record sheet. Any such recorder should not be aware of the target's identity, to avoid simple scoring errors. Tape-recording the subject's calls is one way of avoiding this problem, as long as it does not intrude upon the subject. Subjects can also be asked to record their own calls on a record sheet. The Duke Laboratory even developed its own record sheets, designed specifically for recording standard ESP card runs of 25 trials each. The sheets contained ten pairs of columns of 25 blank squares each; pairs were numbered from one to ten. The first pair in each column was marked "call" and the second was marked "card." Across the top was a list of the five standard ESP card symbols, plus shorthand symbolic abbreviations of each symbol. The subject (or experimenter) would then write each guess in the appropriate square of the call column, until 25 had been completed. A carbon underneath would ensure that there were duplicate records of the subject's calls. Later on, depending on the exact procedure used, the target order could be entered in the card column, once the call column had been folded back out of sight (once again, to reduce scoring errors). Thus hits could be scored whenever the symbol in the call column matched the symbol in the card column.

The above procedures for recording calls would also work with the down through technique. The main difference between the two techniques is that in the basic technique there must be coordination of response with the card-handler's actions, whereas in the down through technique the subject alone sets the pace. This is important, because subjects have reported making their responses in two different ways: by letting some sort of impression drift into awareness, consciously deciding what the target is and then making the response; or by making a purely motor response, e.g., calling a symbol or writing it without this response reflecting a conscious decision. The latter procedure, perhaps a minor form of motor automatism, can only be made effectively when the subject sets his or her own pace, and is often made extremely rapidly. If one is making a conscious decision, which only then produces a response, a variety of different internal strategies can be deployed. The subject generally has a set of the target symbols in view as a reminder of the alternatives; many let their eyes wander across the symbols until one stands out in some way, or move a hand over each symbol until it feels unusual in some way. Most subjects rely on imagery, generally visual but often auditory; this imagery is generally direct but is sometimes symbolic (e.g., seeing water for wavy lines or a shovel for spades). Some rely upon intellectual impressions or call the first symbol that comes to mind.

Timing may occasionally present a problem to the subject in terms of distinguishing one response from another. For instance, some subjects report that they will get firm impressions of three or four symbols at a time. Is this a part of their attempts to sort out impressions of their particular target of the moment, or is it perhaps a set of responses, in a burst, not only to the target card of the moment but to the next three target cards as well? When responding down through, subjects often just go ahead and write down all four as consecutive responses. When being paced, as by the basic technique, the subject is presented with more of a problem. Also, during such a paced procedure, the subject may start getting an impression just before the signal to respond is given and must then decide whether it "counts" or not. If the target order is already fixed and in existence, of course, there is no real reason not to go ahead and respond. If it is yet to be determined, i.e., if the target order is being randomly generated trial by trial, then the subject may be mixing clairvoyance with precognition or PK, at which he or she may for some reason not be as adept.

In any procedure in which subjects make a run of consecutive restricted-choice calls, they may show systematic biases in their calling patterns. There are three main kinds: (1) symbol preference, a tendency to call one symbol more often than the others; (2) position biases, a tendency to call certain symbols more often at different positions in the run, e.g., to call stars early and wavy lines toward the end; and (3) sequential interdependence, the tendency to have one's calls on a given trial dependent in part upon what calls one made just before. An example of the latter is the tendency to avoid doubles, or two consecutive calls of the same symbol. This bias shows up very consistently and makes an excellent classroom demonstration, not only for consecutive calls by one individual but also for consecutive calls made by different people, one at a time, going around the classroom. Basically, we all seem to assume that to call the same symbol as the immediately preceding one is somehow not random, is a biased choice, and so we avoid it. Essentially, such calling patterns constitute a source of noise in that, if we make a choice for some "logical" reason, that reason may well override any "psychic" impression competing for our attention.

There are few effective strategies for discouraging such biases, other than to give subjects a brief description of some of the more common biases plus encouragement to be aware of them (but not to become too self-conscious about avoiding them, lest an opposing bias be developed). If a subject is new to a specific set of target symbols, it may help to make sure that examples of each symbol are visually available; otherwise someone may temporarily forget a particular symbol for a while, then overcall it later to compensate. A related procedure is to use an "open deck" rather than a "closed deck" in preparing the target order. A closed deck is a deck of target cards as sold by the manufacturer, with the same number of cards for each symbol. If a subject knows that there will be exactly 13 cards of each suit or 5 cards of each of the standard ESP symbols, he or she will tend to keep track of how many have been called before, so as to call each symbol the same number of times. This produces biased calling, especially toward the end of the run. To avoid this an open deck is generally used, one in which each card is determined independently of the others so that some symbols may occur more often than others.

For the matching procedures, the subject's response is a motor rather than a verbal act—the target card is placed "where it belongs" or, in screened touch matching, a pointer is tapped on the "correct" indicator card so the experimenter can register the response by placing the card correctly. As with the above card-calling procedures, subjects can collect an impression first, then make a conscious, deliberate motor response; or they can simply turn off cognitive and imaging activity and do the equivalent of a motor automatism, letting their hands place the cards rapidly and on the basis of spontaneous impulse. In matching procedures the subject is much freer to be self-paced, with the minor restriction that in screened touch matching the experimenter may fall behind and lose track if the subject points too rapidly.

Calling biases can also emerge in matching procedures. If a subject is faced with five key cards in a row, he or she may tend to avoid placing cards on the end positions, especially the left end if one is placing with the right hand and vice versa. Conversely, if the subject knows or suspects that the deck is closed, he or she may deliberately place exactly the same number of cards in each pile. Also, a subject may consistently avoid placing two cards in a row on the same pile, may consistently place a card to the immediate left of the previously placed card, etc. Unfortunately, one of the disadvantages of the matching studies is that, unless the whole procedure is videotaped or some other record is kept of each response as it is made, no assessment of sequential patterns can really be made.

Once the placement of cards has taken place, their placement must be permanently recorded. Although it is little used today, the Duke Laboratory developed a standard record sheet for use with the standard ESP symbols, with five boxes across the top for the key card symbols to be written and, below each key card box, a column of boxes for the target card symbols to be written. As with the other recording procedures, it is necessary that the target cards be recorded by someone not aware of the key card identities and the key cards recorded by someone not aware of the target card identities, to reduce the possibility of motivated scoring errors.

It should be noted that matching can be used as a response even when key cards are not actually in use. In much of the work with Stepanek, for instance, Ryzl (e.g., 1962) had Stepanek guess whether the green or white side of a colored card was face up by sorting a stack of sealed opaque envelopes containing the cards into two piles, the green to his left (for instance) and the white to his right. Ideally, whenever the responses are recorded, this should be done by someone not aware of the designation for each pile. Such a general sorting procedure can be used under a variety of circumstances.

A somewhat more complex version of the matching procedure is what has come to be known as the "psychic shuffle" (e.g., Rhine, Smith, and Woodruff, 1938). Basically, the subject is given a concealed record sheet upon which are written 25 symbols (for example), randomly arranged. The subject is then given a deck of 25 cards to be shuffled until the subject feels there is a strong match between the order of the shuffled deck and the target order. Once the subject stops shuffling and sets the deck aside, someone not aware of the concealed symbol order then records the order of the shuffled deck. It can then be compared with the concealed order, position by position, to see to what extent the two orders match. It is as though the concealed order were functioning as a complex key card and the subject's cards were the target cards, to be set aside whenever a significant match occurred.

Note that as stated, the subject could be using psi at more than one time in the course of a run. As the subject shuffles, he or she could be using ESP and/or PK to generate an order that matches the concealed order. Once a single shuffle is completed, however, the subject must then pause and decide whether or not to shuffle again before tallying. This decision also may involve ESP but it does not necessarily have to for the subject to do well, if in fact the subject is shuffling effectively. Minor modifications can render the procedure even more complex. For example, in one study I supervised, (Morris, 1973), the subject was asked to write out 50 standard ESP symbols in a row. An experimenter seated on the other side of a screen then took a fresh deck of cards and gave it a series of dovetail shuffles, stopping only when told to do so by the subject. The subject could have been using precognition in writing down the original order of symbols, or clairvoyance in telling the experimenter when to stop shuffling. We attempted to resolve this question by examining the behavior patterns of the subject on both occasions, to see if patterns associated with either tended to correlate with success. We found that patterns present in the initial writing out of symbols did not correlate with overall success, whereas one specific pattern associated with telling the shuffler when to stop did correlate. It is therefore likely that whatever psi was taking place occurred during the subject's response to the experimenter's shuffling activity. Such a line of reasoning has its imperfections and is far from a proof, but it does illustrate the kinds of procedures that may become useful in teasing out where psi is taking place in some of the more complex restricted-choice designs.

The entire psychic shuffle procedure is rarely used, in part because it is potentially so fraught with complexities. It came into being for the reason that in the early card-guessing precognition research, the subject would guess down through a deck of cards whose order was yet to be determined. Once the subject's responses were recorded, the experimenter would shuffle the deck of cards several times to determine the final target order. Critics of precognition argued that perhaps since the experimenter wanted the procedure to succeed, he or she may have used psi in the course of the shuffle to affect the final order favorably. Thus an empirical test was developed for what seemed at the time to be a rather farfetched notion. For a further discussion of this complex issue, see Rhine (1941; Rhine and Pratt, 1957).

Various other choice behaviors have been used, tailored to the nature of the target and the needs of the researchers. If the target is something familiar, such as the position of the hands on a clock face, the subject may be asked to draw a clock with the hands correctly placed, or he or she may be presented with a real clock with movable hands and asked to move the hands into the correct position. If the target involves guessing a location, the subject may be asked to respond to a drawing of the overall target environment and asked to shade in the correct area or to put an X over it. In the maze tests described earlier (e.g., Child and Singer, 1976) the subject responded by tracing a path through the maze by pen. In the studies using automated apparatus (e.g., Schmidt, 1969; Tart, 1976) the subjects generally responded by pressing one of several buttons, throwing one of several switches, or similar actions. In most cases with such apparatus the response is automatically recorded; otherwise an experimenter must do the recording, as with certain of the card-guessing procedures.

Also, as mentioned earlier, an important feature of some types of automated apparatus is that the subject can also register a confidence call if one trial somehow felt especially good, and can pass, calling for a new target, if nothing seems to be coming through. Even without such apparatus, many researchers (e.g., Fahler and Osis, 1966; McCallam and Honorton, 1973) have asked subjects to register confidence calls by placing a check beside those responses that felt good, placing those cards above rather than below the key cards, etc. If confidence calls are allowed, the researcher generally gives the subject some sort of guidelines to follow in making the differentiation, such as some sort of special internal feeling, unusually vivid imagery, or even simply an estimated percentage (e.g., marking somewhere between 5 and 10% of the calls as "confident").

2.3.1b. Responses by Humans Unaware of the Existence of Their Targets. Throughout the above procedures, one problem that remains unsolved is that subjects aware they are being tested for ESP may become self-conscious, overly reflective, biased by a plethora of hidden attitudes about being psychic or being considered psychic; may in short become very "unnatural." One strategy recently employed to deal with this problem, especially by Stanford (e.g., Stanford and Thompson, 1974; Stanford and Stio, 1976) and the Kreitlers (e.g., Kreitler and Kreitler, 1972, 1973) is to mask the psychic component of a particular procedure so that the subjects believe themselves to be either in an orthodox psychology study or at least in an ESP study for which the particular procedure in question is designed to measure something other than ESP.

For example, Stanford and Stio (1976) employed a procedure in which subjects were given a word association test. Their response latency to each word (the time it took them to speak a word of their choosing associated meaningfully to whatever word they were just given by the researcher) was timed very precisely. Unknown to the subjects, one of these words had been designated in advance by someone not present as the "target" word. If the subject's response latency to that word was shortest of all, the subject would next be given an enjoyable task to do. If not, the subject would next be given an unenjoyable task. Thus the subjects were responding in a somewhat complex way behaviorally, but their ESP task as defined by the experimenter was to unconsciously choose the target word to respond to most quickly. Since the subject was not motivated by consciously wanting to be correct in a psychic fashion, Stanford relied upon the hidden-reward-related contingency to provide the needed motivation.

The Kreitler studies (1972, 1973) employed a set of procedures in which subjects participated in standard perceptual and clinical psychology tasks, unaware that a remote agent was concentrating on one potential behavior pattern available to the subject. In one procedure, subjects were to tell whether a stationary point of light in a darkened room moved vertically or horizontally; such a light will appear to move, even though it in fact remains stationary. The agent concentrated part of the time on vertical movement, part of the time on horizontal movement. Subjects showed some tendency to respond in accordance with the agent's assigned instructions. In a related study, subjects were shown ambiguous pictures of people interacting and were asked to compose stories about them. A remote agent periodically concentrated upon various basic emotional themes likely to occur in stories about such pictures. The Kreitlers hypothesized that a remote agent might bias the behavior of someone nearby undergoing an experience in which he or she is making choices related to the content of the agent's concentration. The subjects received no reward for responding "correctly" and were unaware of the true nature of the study throughout the session.

Essentially, any choice behavior may potentially be amenable to research procedures of this sort. The main criteria are that there be definable alternatives, each of which the subject is able and reasonably likely to select, and that enough choices be made to allow assessment of whether or not information transfer was above that expected by chance.

2.3.1c. Animal Choice Responses. Choice behavior in animals has been studied mainly by placing the animal in standard laboratory situations in which it can select from among alternative behaviors, one of which leads to a reward or punishment for the animal.

Osis and Foster (1953) and Bestall (1962) used simple variants of the T-maze, in which the animal is placed in a start box, then allowed to travel down an alley to the T-intersection, at which point it has its choice of going either to the left arm or to the right. One arm has been designated as correct—either there is a concealed but real reward awaiting the animal, as in the Osis study, or there is a contingent award awaiting the animal shortly after the animal has completed the maze and been removed from it, as in the Bestall study. A concrete definition of choice must be made; e.g., the animal has chosen one particular arm if in fact all of it but the tail has entered the arm. Such mazes can be easily adapted to most species, even those that live in water.

Another frequently used animal choice apparatus is the "Skinner Box," or variants thereof, a box with one or more levers for the animal to press in order to receive a reward. Generally the animal is trained to expect a reward, such as mechanically regulated access to a food pellet or water, each time it presses any of the levers. Once this has been adequately learned, the apparatus can be arranged so that, on any given occasion, only one lever will produce a reward when pressed. The animal's task is to press the correct lever, correctness determined by a random electromechanical event, and get the reward. The animal's target is, apparently, an electromechanical event and contingency presumably considerably beyond its understanding. If the animal succeeds, as it has upon occasion (e.g., Parker, 1974; Schouten, 1972; Terry and Harris, 1975), then it would seem as though either (1) Foster's (1940) notion of "diametric" or direct ESP regardless of target complexity, as previously discussed for blind matching, is in operation; (2) a human researcher is somehow serving as an unconscious psychic intermediary by using ESP to learn the identity of the target and PK (or GESP) to affect the animal's behavior; or (3) somehow the animal is using the contingent future sequences of events as target, to enable selection of the desired future sequence. All three seem rather complex; (1) and (3) make assumptions beyond the intended scope of this chapter. Despite their implicit theoretical problems, such procedures have been used with animals, with enough success that their further usage seems warranted.

Additional use of such automated devices connected to electromechanical target selectors has been made by several researchers (e.g., Duval and Montredon, 1968; Levin, 1975; Terry, 1976; Eysenck, 1975) with standard shock-avoidance procedures. A small animal is placed in a compartment divided in two by a low partition over which the animal can easily jump. The floor of the compartment is a shock grid, such that the animal can receive shock on either side of the barrier. An electromechanical random number generator periodically selects one side or the other as the "shock" side; the animal's position is detected and compared with the target selection electronically. If the animal is on the "shock" side, the animal gets shocked; if the animal is on the other side, it does not. The hypothesis in these studies has been that the animal can by ESP (either clairvoyance or precognition, depending on when the target is selected) detect which side of the barrier to be on in order to avoid shock. An alternative in such studies, as mentioned earlier, is that either the animal or (more likely) the human researcher is affecting the random number generator to generate target selections that favor the animal's recorded position.

Essentially, the above procedures represent minor modifications of standard highly artificial, well-controlled laboratory testing apparatus and procedures. Many more exist in the animal research literature, for many species, and could easily be explored by an imaginative researcher. One interesting procedure for nonlaboratory testing is well worth noting and derives from the work with "clever" animals in the early 1900s (e.g., Pfungst, 1911/1965). Many horses, dogs, and pigs were trained to respond to simple numerical questions by pawing, barking, etc., the correct number of times. In the mid-1950s George Wood (Wood and Cadoret, 1958) taught his dog, Chris, to paw once when he held up a circle, twice for a cross, and so on for the five ESP card symbols. Then he presented Chris with a stack of ESP cards, each in an opaque envelope, their identities unknown to Wood. He held up each envelope, gave Chris the signal to respond, and recorded the number of paws Chris made. Later this number was compared with a record of the target order. Although Chris did quite well when just tested by Wood, his scores became significantly negative when Cadoret, the professional investigator, arrived to observe. One suggestion made later (Pratt, personal communication, 1969) was that Wood may have used his own ESP to discern the target identity and then cued Chris unconsciously by subtle muscle movements when to stop pawing. At any rate, the general strategy of training an intelligent species to respond in different ways to specific symbols or objects, then concealing the objects for ESP tests and recording the animal's responses, is one that deserves further usage.

2.3.2. Free Responses

In free-response studies, the subject is not being asked to produce a short-duration, highly specific choice-related behavior pattern. Rather, the subject is being asked for a more complex, detailed response to complex, detailed targets. Thus the main responses of interest are those that reflect cognitive impressions and detailed imagery. The general sequence of events in most free-response ESP studies is as follows: The subject is given a general introduction to the experimental environment as a whole, is introduced in general to the target material, interacts with the agent, if any, and has the specific procedure explained. Following this, the subject may undergo some specific imagery enhancement procedure. Then the subject generates impressions, including imagery. These impressions are recorded and edited, if necessary. Then a blind judge, often the subject, compares this impression record with each target in a pool of targets, from which the actual target was originally selected by some random process. If the judge consistently rates the impression transcript as more like the actual target than the other targets in the general target pool, then some information seems to be getting through.

2.3.2a. Setting the Stage for Impressions. When the subject is being prepared for the session, he or she is generally given some idea of the nature of the targets involved. Often a general verbal description is given: e.g., "a physical location within a half hour's drive," "a famous art print selected for emotional salience." One must be careful not to give too specific an example, lest one bias the expectations of the subject and affect the content of the later impressions.

Since the subject is being asked to generate complex impressions and imagery, various imagery-enhancement procedures are now being used. Most of them essentially aid the subject in redirecting attention away from competing external information toward internally generated information. Hypnosis has often been used as a tool, and an excellent review of this research is available (Honorton and Krippner, 1969). Subjects familiar with meditation procedures or other mind-clearing exercises may be asked to use them.

Several techniques for reducing sensory input have recently been used. Braud and Braud (e.g., 1973) have recently popularized the use of progressive relaxation at the start of free-response sessions. The subject is asked, with variations, to focus attention at the tips of the toes, then alternately tense and relax the muscles of the body, working gradually up from feet to legs, trunk, hands, arms, neck, and face. Some researchers prefer to deliver these instructions by tape, to hold this aspect constant from session to session. Others prefer to deliver these instructions personally, to allow adjustments for individual differences in circumstances from session to session.

Honorton, Drucker, and Hermon (1973) employed a device called a witch's cradle to block out sensory input. The subject is strapped gently but firmly into an aluminum support frame that is suspended off the ground and free to rotate. He or she is blindfolded, is played white noise over earphones, and is spun around, thus producing feelings of sensory isolation and disorientation.

Honorton and Harper (1974) introduced the "ganzfeld" procedure, in which subjects have a halved Ping-Pong ball placed over each eye and sealed around the edges. The subject relaxes in an easy chair or bed and a diffuse white or red light source is placed about two feet in front of the subject's eyes. This produces the visual experience of seeing a uniformly colored visual field, a circumstance that many find especially conducive to enhanced visual imagery. The subject may hear white noise or pleasant music or the sound of waves through earphones at the same time.

Charlesworth (1975) played subject and agent a synchronized, taped "guided imagery" trip, in which they were asked to picture themselves drifting along a stream in a boat, then getting out, traveling through a pleasant meadow, and having an interesting adventure once the other side was reached. The agent's tape continued to describe a randomly selected specific adventure; the subject's tape, identical up to this point, continued on only with the suggestion to experience a further adventure, followed by pleasant but neutral background sounds.

Many related procedures for inducing alterations of imagery exist, most of which have never been seriously tried in ESP research. The above examples illustrate the basic ideas. One additional point of method: When a state induction procedure is used, it is very useful to take some measure of the subject's reported change of state. Some subjects are basically little affected by these procedures, in which case the data from those subjects may not be comparable with data from the others.

In some cases, naturally occurring enhanced imagery states can be utilized. At Maimonides (e.g., Ullman and Krippner, 1970), dreams have been used in a long and successful research project. Subject and agent spend some time together during the evening. Then the subject is physiologically monitored and allowed to fall asleep in a sound-attenuated room, while the agent retires to another room where a target art print is concealed in an envelope. When the subject's EEG and eye movements indicate the onset of a dream, the agent is signaled to open the envelope and concentrate on the picture. After a fixed period of time or the termination of the eye movements, the subject is gently awakened by the experimenter and asked to describe the just-completed dream. Similar procedures for hypnagogic and hypnopompic imagery could easily be put to use.

2.3.2b. *Generating and Reporting Imagery.* Although some enhanced imagery states such as dreams are under no apparent conscious control, for the most part subjects have some control over their impressions and the retention of those impressions. The subject may on the one hand be flooded with impressions and must decide to which to pay the most attention. Should everything be reported, or just the strongest impressions? Should all impressions be reported in their crudest, raw sensation form, or should they be interpreted and labeled (e.g., "I see a gray band surrounded by green" vs. "I see a road through hills")? Should mundane, familiar impressions and impressions related to the subject's recent past experiences be regarded as strongly as unusual, unfamiliar, and unexpected impressions? How can one tell the difference between one's own fantasies, telling oneself a story, and a true psychic impression? Should impressions that follow too logically from the immediately preceding impressions be discarded? Should one attempt on the spot to interpret one's impressions or should they just be passively recorded? If an impression lingers, should this lingering be reported? Should visual imagery be emphasized over the other senses? These questions are essentially not answerable at present, and strong differences from subject to subject and even within the same subject from session to session undoubtedly occur. Most researchers would probably agree that active censorship should be avoided.

On the other hand, one may experience a dearth of impressions and be faced with a bit of stress, the "obligation" to have impressions. If one tries too hard, one may just be drawing from one's surface cognitive content; e.g., it may be cold in the room, thus one gets a snowy image. In general, the best advice seems to be to relax and let impressions come as they may. At present there is no real evidence that imagery abundance is correlated with success—the person with few images may simply be filtering out noise below the level of conscious experience, rather than having to rely upon conscious filtering as would the abundant imager.

An important variable may be the length of the imagery period. The longer the period, the more diverse and abundant the imagery is likely to be. Conversely, a short imagery period may not provide enough time to clear out the noise produced by recent experiences, or may be stressful for the poor imager who needs time to develop and recognize impressions.

Another set of important variables are those relating to the actual reporting of the impressions. They can be reported either as they happen ("on-line") or at the end of the impression period. If reported on-line, the very act of reporting may interfere with a subject's internal state and may lead to too much introspection and interpretation at the time. If reported only after the fact, on the other hand, much may be lost and the subject may be tempted to pause after each impression to be sure it is committed to memory, thus also interfering with his or her internal state.

One's impressions can be reported in the presence or absence of an experimenter. If an experimenter is present, the subject may feel especially relaxed or inhibited, depending upon the relationship already established and the experimenter's general demeanor. The experimenter's role generally is that of passive recorder. However, the experimenter can interact with a subject during the on-line reporting of impressions by asking questions, calling for clarification, reminding the subject of the specific task, and so on. As such, the experimenter can be doubly effective or ineffective as a facilitator of the subject's attempts to report impressions.

2.3.2c. Recording Impressions. There are several ways a subject's impressions can be recorded, on-line or later. The subject can voice the impressions, which are then tape-recorded and/or written down by the experimenter. If the latter, they should be read back to the subject immediately afterward, for double-checking and embellishment. Subjects reporting on-line often do not have time to describe an impression in full detail; they may prefer to say a key word or two, which, when read back to them, will allow a fuller description to be given immediately afterwards. Subjects can also write down a lengthy description of their experiences themselves; if so, they should read it to a researcher afterward, so that no handwriting problems develop. Also, subjects can draw any impressions, keying the drawings to the verbal report, and can use gestures or other body movements to convey information to the researcher.

Such a recording of impressions can become rather complex, and it does not truly constitute the final data of the study. The report must be reduced and/or judged in some way so as to allow an evaluation of how much information transfer took place.

2.3.2d. Judging the Impression Transcript. The impression record must somehow be compared with the actual target, to evaluate the extent of correspondence between the two. There are two general strategies for doing this. The first strategy is to use a target that has been numerically coded in some way whereby the subject's imagery can also be coded. The best example of this is the Maimonides slide pool described earlier. Each of the 1,024 slides in that pool can be described by ten binary digits: a 1 means the slide has a specific content category and a 0 means the slide does not, and there are ten content categories in all. A slide numbered 1100000000 has only the first two categories (color and activity) and none of the other. The subject's imagery can be coded in a similar manner. If the only impressions generated were "swirling yellows and oranges, pulsing in and out, then nothing but a mass of dark green," this imagery would be coded for the presence of each of the ten categories by someone reading it afterward as 1100000000, exactly as was the target. This would be numerically a direct hit and its likelihood of occurring could be assessed by the laws of chance. The standard procedure in the Maimonides studies (e.g., Honorton, 1975) is to have the subjects code their own imagery immediately after the impression period, although this could be done by someone else later on who read a typed version of the transcript or heard it on tape, and who had no knowledge of the actual target. It is important to note that these studies use a random selection process so that each of the targets is equally likely to be selected. Not all of the content categories are equally likely to occur in the imagery of a given subject, and the number of categories occurring in a subject's imagery is of course affected by the length of the impression period. Thus, although the subject's responses are likely to be biased, as is always the case to an extent, the target selection process is quite random and thus allows the analysis of the results by standard statistical tools. It should be noted, by the way, that if the above procedure is the only one being used to evaluate the results, it could be argued that the actual content of the target slide is not the true target at all. What determines success and failure in the eyes of the researcher (and probably, therefore, in the eyes of the subject) is the numerical coding of the target. The subject's job is really to generate imagery that will be coded so as to match the code of the target. The target's code, in other words, may in some real sense be the true target.

A second strategy for evaluating free-response results is to use judges who subjectively evaluate the extent of correspondence between the subject's impressions and the target itself. If a judge simply looked at the two, this would provide a biased assessment of the true correspondence— someone favorable toward ESP might read in many correspondences, whereas someone unfavorable might deliberately overlook the obvious. Thus the judge must evaluate the correspondence under circumstances in which the judge is "blind" as to which target is the actual target. The judge is presented with one or more impression transcripts and a pool of possible targets but is not told which target belongs to which transcript and is asked to compare each transcript with each target. The judge may be asked simply to assign a number between 1 and 100 to each possible transcript–target combination (or an analogous procedure) or may be asked to consider each transcript separately and rank each of the possible targets as to which is most like the transcript, next most, etc., on down to least. If a rating is done, the ratings assigned to correct transcript–target combinations are compared statistically to the ratings assigned to incorrect combinations. If information transfer is taking place, the correct ratings should be consistently higher than the incorrect ratings. Likewise, if rankings are used, the rankings given correct combinations should be consistently higher than those given incorrect rankings.

The blind judges may be the subjects themselves. For instance, a recently developed procedure (Morris, Robblee, Neville, and Bailey, 1977) goes as follows. An agent two rooms away from a receiver has an envelope in front of him or her containing two Maimonides slides. One of these was selected randomly by an outside experimenter; the other slide is its exact opposite in category content (e.g., 1100000000 and 0011111111). A random number generator lights up one of two lights, telling the agent which picture to remove and send. The agent then projects it on the wall and draws it. The subject delivers imagery for about four minutes and then is shown a duplicate set of the two possible target slides. The subject then judges which of the two is most like his or her imagery and registers this vote automatically by pressing one of two buttons. The central processing unit records the subject's choice, compares it with the target it told the agent to send, records a hit or a miss, and signals back to the subject which target was actually sent. The target pool, in this case, is the two slides selected from the larger pool, and all parties concerned know that each member of the pool is equally likely to be selected as target.

In addition to the subject, outside blind judges may be used. Such judges can make their judgments on a trial-by-trial basis, using the single transcript and target pool used in each trial. Or, such judges may be given a set of transcripts plus each of the actual targets used for these transcripts. This latter procedure guarantees that each member of the judging pool was actually used as a target on one occasion, thus in some respects providing better control over the possibility that the targets selected from the initial target pool were inadvertently more of interest to the subject purely by accident. However, it also means that special care must be taken in the presentation of the target transcripts to the judge. Two specific examples should make this clear. Suppose the study involves attempts to do psychic readings on subjects and one subject is done per day. Even though the subjects are selected randomly, there is the strong likelihood that a target person run on a sunny day may dress differently and be in a different mood from a target person run on a wet, cold day. Likewise the subject may see the target person as dressed in bright colors and wearing shorts on the first day and dressed warmly and with a raincoat on the second day. This would artifically create correspondence between transcript and target person as a result of weather. To control for this, Roll et al. (1973), in their work with Harribance did two things. First, they had an outside experimenter edit their transcripts to remove any references to clothes or other aspects of appearance that could be related to weather. The target persons were then given ten transcripts to read and were asked to rank the transcripts as to which were most like themselves. Once these rankings were obtained, the researchers checked to see whether target persons run on days having similar weather tended to rate each other's transcripts higher than those from target persons run on days having different weather. There was no such tendency, indicating that the transcript editing had apparently been adequate to take care of any bias intruded by weather conditions. For a further discussion of such problems in the transcripts of psychic readings, see Roll *et al.* (1973).

A similar example occurs in the remote viewing research of Targ and Puthoff (e.g., Hyman, 1977). In one series, a single subject attempted to describe the target person's geographical location on nine separate days. As part of the procedure, the subject was taken to the target location immediately after each session to inspect it. This meant that two forms of bias might occur in the transcripts from later sessions. First of all, if the subject learned that the target location for the first trial was a marina, he or she would know to avoid talking about marinas in later transcripts, so as not to tempt the judges into ranking one of those later transcripts as most like the marina, the earlier target. Secondly, it is possible that the subject might inadvertently refer to the earlier session, commenting on the nature of the earlier session's impressions and their relations to the actual target. All such references should be edited out, of course.

We have here a problem in free-response methodology. If the target pool and judging pool are separate for each trial, we do not have to worry about the fact that a subject's responses in successive sessions are likely to be interdependent, especially if feedback for success is given. On the other hand, if the target pool and judging pool are composed exclusively of actually used targets, we have finer control over the possibility of an accidental (or even PK-induced) selection of those targets in the target pools that best fit the subject's predisposition.

One may wonder why all of the above is included in a section on responses rather than on analysis techniques. The answer is that the judges' decisions are really the final responses upon which assessment of success is based, and there is no reason to expect the judges not to be using ESP themselves in performing this task. When researchers ask the subjects to judge, for instance, they are giving them an extra opportunity to show ESP. On some occasions the judging task may be straightforward—the subject imaged a tree; one target was a tree, the other an indoor scene. On other occasions the job may be more ambiguous and thus amenable to ESP—the subject imaged a tree; one target was an overhead view of a thick forest, the other a picture of a treelike sea anemone. Which should the judge rate highest? It becomes very analogous to restricted-choice ESP procedures.

One solution is to use both subjects and outsiders as blind judges and to use more than one outside judge, taking an average of their ratings as the measure of information transfer. Another is to have judges give only ratings and to compare success rates on those trials in which the ratings are greatly different, indicating the judge had no difficulty deciding, with those in which the ratings are very similar.

There has also been debate on whether to use subjects' ratings or only outsiders' ratings. The subject is the only one who really is fully aware of the impressions obtained of the target; on the other hand, the act of judging may make him or her self-conscious and too introspective, especially if more than one trial is being run per session. The outside judge may also actually have an advantage in working only with the transcript of the impressions, in that the transcript undoubtedly represents a filtering of sorts since only the major impressions of the subject would be likely to be reflected there.

Because of the above complexities, many regard free-response work as less tidy methodologically than restricted-choice research, even though it is clearly richer qualitatively.

2.3.3. Somatic Responses

As mentioned earlier, a third form of ESP study involves the use of measures of emotionally related bodily responses, to see whether changes in bodily activity correspond with changes in the emotional salience of a remote target. The general procedure involves monitoring a subject's bodily responses for an extended period of time. During that time a set of events takes place, at randomly assigned intervals. Some of these events are emotionally activating, others are neutral or quieting. If the subject's bodily responses are more active during the former than the latter, this indicates that some form of information transfer took place.

Several methods have been used to monitor bodily activity. To describe the exact methods involved and the current debates in the methodology of each measure would be a chapter in itself; for this information the reader should go to the original sources. Some examples of measures used include:

1. Characteristics of the subject's brain electrical activity pattern, including alpha abundance (e.g., Duane and Behrendt, 1965), as well as general characteristics (e.g., Tart, 1963; Targ and Puthoff, 1974; Kelly and Lenz, 1976). Generally the occipital EEG output was recorded and processed to give an overall picture of changes in EEG characteristics

throughout the EEG spectrum from that site, considered the best for recording alpha abundance. In some cases subjects had been preselected for having a monochromatic EEG spectrum.

Additional EEG-related measures include the averaged cortical evoked potential, in response to the sudden onset of a remote stimulus (e.g., Lloyd, 1973; Millar, 1976) and the contingent negative variation (CNV), also known as the expectancy wave (Levin and Kennedy, 1975), in anticipation of an event about to occur to the subject.

2. Galvanic skin response, a general measure of level of arousal, largely determined by the activity of the sweat glands near the surface of the skin (e.g., Rice, 1966; Barron and Mordkoff, 1968).

3. Vasomotor activity, as measured by plethysmograph (e.g., Dean, 1962, 1971; Sanjar, 1969). As a subject becomes more aroused, the amount of blood in the surface tissues may increase (blushing) or decrease (paling).

4. Animal activity level in an "open field" environment (e.g., Morris, 1967; Morris, Harary, Janis, Hartwell, and Roll, 1978; Craig, 1973). Essentially an animal's activity level when placed in a large enclosure can be measured by counting the number of times the animal crosses from one section to the next. Depending on the species and the nature of the target, a change in activity level can be used as an indicator of information transfer.

Other measures of physiology, including respiration rate, heart rate, and muscle activity from various muscle systems, should also be appropriate for such procedures. As more comes to be understood about Kirlian photography (e.g., Krippner and Rubin, 1974, 1977; Pehek, Kyler, and Faust, 1976), it is hoped that this process also can be useful as an indicator of information transfer in ESP experiments.

Such measures must be analyzed and scored either electronically or, if such facilities are not available, by an evaluator and scorer who does not know which activity periods were for the activating stimulus and which for the neutral or quieting stimulus. The first method is expensive, the second time-consuming, and both require technical expertise. Perhaps for these reasons little research has been done in this general ESP response mode, although the results with it have been no less promising than with restricted-choice or free-response procedures.

2.4. Barriers between Subject and Target

All of the above is for naught if in fact the subject and target have not been adequately separated by barriers preventing sensory information from flowing from target to subject. The subject must be prevented from sensing the target's characteristics, or inferring them from other information available. The latter means that subjects should not have access to any of the final determinants of the characteristics of the target, that these determinants should not be predictable events in themselves (should be random), that subjects should not have access to other records of the target identity, and that subjects should not have access to other individuals who know the characteristics of the targets or could infer them, lest such individuals provide cues. All of the above pertains to the time up through the subject's response. The recording of the subject's response should be done either automatically or by people who know nothing of the target, to prevent biased recording errors. Any further processing of the data should be done in such a way that the biases of the individuals involved cannot affect the results—i.e., all judges of free-response material should be blind as to the nature of the target, all judges and scorers of physiological responses should be blind as to when the target periods took place, etc. In general, anybody making decisions about the target should be blind to the subject's responses; anybody making decisions about the subject's responses should be blind as to the nature of the target.

This all sounds complex, and in many respects it is, but recently several advances have allowed adequate studies to be run with a minimum of difficulty. Targets can now be selected through adequate random processes immediately before the subject is signaled to begin responding, thus eliminating the possibility of subjects getting prior access to the target or its determinants. Subjects can be shielded from the targets by being in totally different rooms from the target and agent, often heavily sound-proofed rooms. Subjects' responses can be recorded and scored automatically (except for free-response data, which cannot yet be scored automatically) and the data stored on tape, computer card, or printout, thus eliminating motivated scoring errors.

2.4.1. Physical Barriers

Based on considerations mentioned just above, in any given research design the researcher can easily figure out who should be physically separated from what and whom. Physical separation means that physical information propagation systems capable of carrying information relevant to the study in question are all prevented from operating. The simplest device for physical separation is distance, since distance seems to have little if any (other than psychological) influence upon results. If large distances are used, then it is necessary to have an adequate system for coordinating those experimenters with the target and those experimenters with the subject, bearing in mind that the people with the target should not be able to communicate with the subject once they know anything relevant about the target.

If the target or a representation of it is near the subject, it should be concealed in an opaque container, soundproofed if appropriate. A target that is at all volatile chemically should probably be maintained at a distance, since it would be difficult to shield guaranteeably at short distances. ESP cards should be kept either in a box or in another room, or hidden completely from view in some other way. A concealed picture should be kept in an opaque envelope, ideally wrapped in tinfoil or in some other way guarded against the possibility of being rendered visible by a light shining through the envelope or any of a variety of magician's tricks. If a subject is to judge the target pool, one of which is the actual target, precautions must be taken to ensure that the target picture has not been handled selectively so as to provide cues to the subject. If the agent has been viewing a slide it should not be given to the subject while still warm. Handling of targets should be indirect, to avoid fingerprints, dirt, frayed edges, etc. If the agent wears perfume or has any distinctive odor, then the other members of the target pool should receive equal treatment. The only really adequate solutions are (1) to find a way to treat all members of the target pool the same as the target or (2) to use a duplicate set of targets for the subject to use in judging (e.g., Morris *et al.*, 1977).

2.4.2. Randomization Procedures

Targets must be selected randomly, rather than by any human decision or fixed set of rules, because such rules and decisions are inevitably patterned or biased and thus are either potentially inferrable by the subject or else may inadvertently match a similar pattern or bias in the subject's responses.

In restricted-choice studies, randomization must be used to produce a target order that is without pattern or bias. This generally means that for each trial each possible target has an equal probability of occurring and that there be no sequential patterning of targets. An exception to this is that one might wish to increase the probability of occurrence of one symbol over the others to study response biases, for instance, and this could be done by simply adjusting the probability of success for that symbol when analyzing the data. Totally random processes in nature are fairly rare and there is even debate (e.g., Wilson, 1965) that they exist at all. For present purposes, the target order must be random enough that any significant correspondence with subject's guesses could not be interpreted as simply two coinciding biases or patterns and that, if given feedback, the subject cannot derive information that would be useful in inferring the remaining targets. An extreme example of the latter, of course, is the use of a closed deck with feedback. If the subject gets feedback after each trial, e.g., is told the correct target, then the last card is known for certain and the next-to-last card has been at worst narrowed to only two possibilities and perhaps to only one.

The earliest techniques for randomizing cards simply involved shuffling them. Rhine and Pratt (e.g., 1957, p. 141) advised a minimum of four dovetail shuffles followed by a knife cut (to avoid sticky cards, etc.). Later, tables of computer-generated random number tables were published, the best known of which is the Rand Table of a Million Random Digits (Rand Corporation, 1955). This table became widely used, especially for determining precognition targets. As was mentioned earlier, precognition targets must be selected so as to be as free as possible from researcher psi influences, lest the researcher psychically produce a target order that significantly matches the subject's guesses. Not only was card shuffling rejected due to the possibility of the "psychic shuffle"; simply opening the table of random numbers and pointing to a starting place with eyes closed was also ruled out, since psi could enter in there also. To solve this problem, Rhine's group (Rhine and Pratt, 1957) devised a complex procedure that ensured that for the experimenter to use psi, he or she would have to combine ESP and PK and be a mathematical genius to boot. The experimenter started by throwing a ten-sided die (actually 12-sided with two opposite sides rounded) 12 times, thus generating four three-digit numbers. The first number was multiplied by the second, that product by the third, that product in turn by the fourth, and that overall product by itself backward. The last ten digits of that overall product are isolated and their square root extracted to six places. This six-digit figure, with minor conversions of the first and fifth digits, then served to determine a fixed entry point in the standard Rand table. The digits in this table ranged from 0 to 9 and could be easily converted to the standard five ESP symbols (e.g., 1 and 6 = circle, 2 and 7 = cross, etc.) or, with an appropriate conversion code, to any other set of symbols, in such a way as to generate a quite adequately random target order. I have challenged (Morris, 1968) the notion that such a procedure ruled out experimenter "superpsi" and have obtained some preliminary evidence to the contrary, badly in need of replication. For present purposes, most researchers consider Rhine's method adequate.

A significant breakthrough in randomizing procedures came at the turn of the decade when Helmut Schmidt developed an inexpensive and portable electromechanical random number generator that could be interfaced with a variety of automated data acquisition, storage, and retrieval devices. For an excellent description of such devices and their logic, see Schmidt (1974). Additional devices have been constructed and adapted for a variety of purposes by many researchers (e.g., Tart, 1976; Targ, Cole, and Puthoff, 1974; Millar, 1973; Placer, Morris, and Phillips, 1977). Basically, each device has at its core some natural source of events that occur very rapidly and at random time intervals, e.g., sources of radioactivity such as Strontium 90, or Ziner diodes, which maintain a constantly fluctuating electrical field. These rapidly occurring events are periodically sampled and allowed to interrupt some sort of repeating electromechanical event such as the alternation of a flip-flop circuit or the rotation of an electrical impulse around a ring counter. This interruption stops the electromechanical system at one of X possible choice points, which number can ultimately become rather large, e.g., by cascading flip-flop circuits. Whichever choice point is finally selected then is set to activate one of X possible electrical circuits, lighting a particular light or in some other way reflecting the desired random event. If processed properly, such a random event can serve to select an ESP target either directly, to be automatically recorded and scored within the overall device, or indirectly, as a signal to the agent or researcher as to which of X targets to select (as in the Morris study cited earlier, in which the agent was told which of two target slides to remove from an envelope and send).

Such devices have extraordinary flexibility and, with the advent of microprocessors, should quickly and inexpensively find their way into even the most poorly funded parapsychology research facility. They can be used to determine targets on the spot, thus eliminating many alternative nonpsychic explanations (including many forms of fraud). Unfortunately, there still exists the possibility that the experimenter or subject may exert a PK influence over the equipment, so as to produce the target having most appeal for the subject. This is especially true when a target is being randomly selected from a target pool in a free-response study.

3. Miscellaneous Considerations

The sections covered above provide a picture of the basic building blocks of modern ESP research, as well as a description of many of the underlying methodological complexities.

Unfortunately, a full description of the statistical procedures used in evaluating the amount, if any, of information transfer that takes place in any ESP study is beyond the scope of the present chapter. Most studies involve a comparison of how well the subject actually did with how well one would be expected to do if no information transfer were actually taking place, and/or an assessment of whether more information transfer is taking place under one circumstance than under another. The former tells us something unusual may be going on. The latter, it is hoped, tells us something about the nature of the processes involved. By using the appropriate statistical tool, we can assess the likelihood that any such comparisons reveal meaningful differences. Any result so unusual that it would be likely to occur less than once in 20 times by chance ($p < .05$) is considered statistically suggestive; any result likely to occur less than once in 100 times by chance ($p < .01$) is considered statistically significant. Such statistical tools can tell us not only that significantly positive results are occurring (psi-hitting) but also that, upon occasion, the results may be significantly worse than expected by chance (the functional equivalent of bad luck, called "psi-missing"). For a fuller discussion of the logic and problems of statistical description of ESP data, refer to Rhine, Pratt, Stuart, Smith, and Greenwood (1940/1966) for the early work and Burdick and Kelly (1977) for a splendid up-to-date overview.

There are many other aspects of method to consider, but there comes a point at which they become a matter of research findings and their consequences, and as such belong appropriately in the next chapter. I have tried in this chapter to consider the major methodological issues currently confronting active researchers in the field. The complexities are great and, unfortunately, not all the published research has followed the best procedure or been sensitive to many of the very human issues that often stand very much in the way of research as one would ideally conduct it. With healthy consideration of the full range of issues, however, it now seems all but inevitable that we shall advance to understandings of ourselves not previously conceptualized.

4. References

Barron, F., and Mordkoff, A. M. An attempt to relate creativity to possible extrasensory empathy as measured by physiological arousal in identical twins. *Journal of the American Society for Psychical Research*, 1968, *62*, 73–79.

Bestall, C. M. An experiment in precognition in the laboratory mouse. *Journal of Parapsychology*, 1962, *26*, 269.

Bleksley, A. E. H. An experiment on long-distance ESP during sleep. *Journal of Parapsychology*, 1963, *27*, 1–13.

Braud, W. G., and Braud, L. W. Preliminary explorations of psi-conducive states: Progressive muscular relaxation. *Journal of the American Society for Psychical Research*, 1973, *67*, 26–46.

Burdick, D. S., and Kelly, E. F. Statistical methods in parapsychological research. In B. Wolman (Ed.), *Handbook of parapsychology*. New York: Van Nostrand Reinhold, 1977.

Carpenter, J. C. Unpublished manuscript. 1965.

Carpenter, J. C. The differential effect and hidden target differences consisting of erotic and neutral stimuli. *Journal of the American Society for Psychical Research*, 1971, *65*, 204–214.

Charlesworth, E. A. Psi and the imaginary dream. In J. D. Morris, W. G. Roll, and R. L. Morris (Eds.), *Research in parapsychology 1974*, Metuchen, New Jersey: Scarecrow Press, 1975. Pp. 85–89.

Child, I., and Singer, J. Exploration of the paper maze technique for the experimental study of psi. *Journal of Parapsychology*, 1976, *40*, 269–287.

Craig, J. G. The effect of contingency on precognition in the rat. In W. G. Roll, R. L. Morris, and J. D. Morris (Eds.), *Research in parapsychology 1972*. Metuchen, New Jersey: Scarecrow Press, 1973. Pp. 154–156.

Dean, E. D. The plethysmograph as an indicator of ESP. *Journal of the Society for Psychical Research*, 1962, *41*, 351–353.

Dean, E. D. Long-distance plethysmograph telepathy with agent under water. *Proceedings of the Parapsychological Association No. 6, 1969*, Durham, North Carolina: Parapsychological Association, 1971. Pp. 41–42.

Dean, E. D., and Nash, C. B. Coincident plethysmograph results under controlled conditions. *Journal of the Society for Psychical Research*, 1967, *44*, 1–14.

Duane, D. T., and Behrendt, T. Extrasensory electroencephalographic induction between identical twins. *Science*, 1965, *150*, 367.

Duval, P., and Montredon, E. ESP experiments with mice. *Journal of Parapsychology*, 1968, *32*, 153–166.

Eysenck, H. J. Precognition in rats. *Journal of Parapsychology*, 1975, *39*, 222–227.

Fahler, J., and Osis, K. Checking for awareness of hits in a precognition experiment with hypnotized subjects. *Journal of the American Society for Psychical Research*, 1966, *60*, 340–346.

Foster, A. Is ESP diametric? *Journal of Parapsychology*, 1940, *4*, 325–328.

Freeman, J. A precognition test with a high-school science club. *Journal of Parapsychology*, 1964, *28*, 214–221.

Garrett, E. J. *My life as a search for the meaning of mediumship*. New York: Oquaga, 1939.

Hall, C., and Van de Castle, R. *The content analysis of dreams*. New York: Appleton-Century-Crofts, 1966.

Harribance, L. (as told to H. R. Neff). *This man knows you*. San Antonio: Naylor, 1976.

Honorton, C. Objective determination of information rate in psi tasks with pictorial stimuli. *Journal of the American Society for Psychical Research*, 1975, *69*, 353–359.

Honorton, C., Drucker, S., and Hermon, H. Shifts in subjective state and ESP under conditions of partial sensory deprivation: A preliminary study. *Journal of the American Society for Psychical Research*, 1973, *67*, 191–196.

Honorton, C., and Harper, S. Psi-mediated imagery and ideation in an experimental procedure for regulating perceptual input. *Journal of the American Society for Psychical Research*, 1974, *68*, 156–168.

Honorton, C., and Krippner, S. Hypnosis and ESP. A review of the experimental literature. *Journal of the American Society for Psychical Research*, 1969, *63*, 214–252.

Hyman, R. Psychics and scientists:"Mind-reach" and remote viewing. *The Humanist*, 1977, *37*, 16–20.

Kelly, E. F., and Lenz, J. EEG changes correlated with a remote stroboscopic stimulus: A preliminary study. In J. D. Morris, W. G. Roll, and R. L. Morris (Eds.), *Research in parapsychology 1975*. Metuchen, New Jersey: Scarecrow Press, 1976. Pp. 58–63.

Kreitler, H., and Kreitler, S. Does extrasensory perception affect psychological experiments? *Journal of Parapsychology*, 1972, *36*, 1–45.

Kreitler, H., and Kreitler, S. Subliminal perception and extrasensory perception. *Journal of Parapsychology*, 1973, *37*, 163–188.

Krippner, S., and Rubin, D. (Eds.). *The Kirlian aura*. Garden City, New York: Anchor/ Doubleday, 1974.

Krippner, S., and Rubin, D. Preliminary investigation of Kirlian photography as a technique in detecting psychokinetic effects. *International Journal of Paraphysics*, 1977, *11*, 69–73.

Levin, J. A series of psi experiments with gerbils. *Journal of Parapsychology*, 1975, *39*, 363–365. (Abstract)

Levin, J., and Kennedy, J. The relationship of slow cortical potentials to psi information in man. *Journal of Parapsychology*, 1975, *39*, 25–26.

Lloyd, D. H. Objective events in the brain correlating with psychic phenomena. *New Horizons*, 1973, *1*, 69–75.

McCallam, E., and Honorton, C. Effects of feedback on discrimination between correct and incorrect ESP responses: A further replication and extension. *Journal of the American Society for Psychical Research*, 1973, *67*, 77–85.

McMahan, E. A. An experiment in pure telepathy, *Journal of Parapsychology*, 1946, *10*, 224–242.

Millar, B. An inexpensive portable electronic ESP tester. *Journal of the Society for Psychical Research*, 1973, *47*, 90–95.

Millar, B. An attempted validation of the "Lloyd effect." In J. D. Morris, W. G. Roll, and R. L. Morris (Eds.), *Research in parapsychology 1975*. Metuchen, New Jersey: Scarecrow Press, 1976. Pp. 25–27.

Morris, R. L. Some new techniques in animal psi research. *Journal of Parapsychology*, 1967, *31*, 316–317.

Morris, R. L. Obtaining non-random entry points: A complex psi task. In J. B. Rhine and R. Brier (Eds.), *Parapsychology today*. New York: Citadel Press, 1968.

Morris, R. L. Psi and animal behavior: A survey. *Journal of the American Society for Psychical Research*, 1970, *64*, 242–260.

Morris, R. L. Correspondence. *Journal of the American Society for Psychical Research*, 1971, *65*, 237–241.

Morris, R. L. Complex psi and the concept of precognition. In W. G. Roll, R. L. Morris, and J. D. Morris (Eds.), *Research in parapsychology 1972*. Metuchen, New Jersey: Scarecrow Press, 1973. Pp. 95–97.

Morris, R. L., Robblee, P., Neville, R., and Bailey, K. Free response ESP training with feedback to agent and receiver. *Journal of Parapsychology*, 1977, *41*, 259–260.

Morris, R. L., Harary, S. B., Janis, J., Hartwell, J., and Roll, W. G. Studies of communication during out-of-body experiences. *Journal of the American Society for Psychical Research*, 1978, *72*, 1–24.

Osis, K., and Carlson, M. L. The ESP channel—open or closed? *Journal of the American Society for Psychical Research*, 1972, *66*, 310–320.

Osis, K., and Foster, E. A test of ESP in cats. *Journal of Parapsychology*, 1953, *17*, 168–186.

Parker, A. ESP in gerbils using positive reinforcement. *Journal of Parapsychology*, 1974, *38*, 301–311.

Pehek, J. O., Kyler, H. J., and Faust, D. L. Image modulation in corona discharge photography. *Science*, 1976, *194*, 263–270.

Pfungst, O. [*Clever Hans*] (R. Rosenthal, Ed.) New York: Holt, Rinehart & Winston, 1965. (First American edition, C. L. Rahn, trans., 1911.)

Placer, J., Morris, R. L., and Phillips, D. MCTS: A modular communications testing system. In J. D. Morris, W. G. Roll, and R. L. Morris (Eds.), *Research in parapsychology 1976*. Metuchen, New Jersey: Scarecrow Press, 1977. Pp. 38–40.

Pratt, J. G., and Woodruff, J. L. Size of stimulus symbols in extra-sensory perception. *Journal of Parapsychology*, 1939, *3*, 121–158.

Puthoff, H., and Targ, R. Psychic research and modern physics. In J. White (Ed.), *Psychic exploration: A challenge for science*. New York: Putnam's, 1974.

Rand Corporation. *A million random digits*. Glencoe, Illinois: Free Press, 1955.

Randi, J. *The magic of Uri Geller*. New York: Ballantine Books, 1975.

Rao, K. R. Studies in the preferential effect: II. A language ESP test involving precognition and "intervention." *Journal of Parapsychology*, 1963, *27*, 147–160.

Rhine, J. B. *Extra-sensory perception* (Rev. ed). Boston: Bruce Humphries, 1973. (Originally published, 1935.)

Rhine, J. B. Experiments bearing upon the precognition hypothesis: III. Mechanically selected cards. *Journal of Parapsychology*, 1941, *5*, 1–58.

Rhine, J. B. Telepathy and clairvoyance reconsidered. *Journal of Parapsychology*, 1945, *9*, 176–193.

Rhine, J. B., and Pratt, J. G. *Parapsychology: Frontier science of the mind*. Springfield, Illinois: Thomas, 1957.

Rhine, J. B., Smith, B. M., and Woodruff, J. L. Experiments bearing on the precognition hypothesis: II. The role of ESP in the shuffling of cards. *Journal of Parapsychology*, 1938, *2*, 119–131.

Rhine, J. B. Pratt, J. G., Stuart, C. E., Smith, B. M., and Greenwood, J. A. *Extrasensory perception after sixty years*. Boston: Bruce Humphries, 1966. (Originally published, 1940.)

Rhine, L. E. Research methods with spontaneous cases. In B. Wolman (Ed.), *Handbook of parapsychology*. New York: Van Nostrand Reinhold, 1977.

Rice, G. Emotional closeness, communication of affect, and ESP. *Proceedings of the Parapsychological Association No. 3, 1966*. Durham, North Carolina: Parapsychological Association, 1967. P. 25.

Richet, C. La suggestion mentale et le calcul des probabilités. *Revue Philosophique*, 1884, *18*, 609–674.

Roll, W. G. Morris, R. L., Damgaard, J. A., Klein, J., and Roll, M. Free verbal response experiments with Lalsingh Harribance. *Journal of the American Society for Psychical Research*, 1973, *67*, 197–207.

Ryzl, M. Training the psi faculty by hypnosis. *Journal of the Society for Psychical Research*, 1962, *41*, 234–252.

Sanjar, M. A study of coincident autonomic activity in closely related persons. *Journal of the American Society for Psychical Research*, 1969, *63*, 88–94.

Schmeidler, G. R. Evidence for two kinds of telepathy. *International Journal of Parapsychology*, 1961, *3*, 5–43.

Schmidt, H. Precognition of a quantum process. *Journal of Parapsychology*, 1969, *33*, 99–108.

Schmidt, H. A quantum mechanical random number generator for psi tests. *Journal of Parapsychology*, 1970, *34*, 219–224.

Schmidt, H. Instrumentation in the parapsychology laboratory. In J. Beloff (Ed.), *New directions in parapsychology*. London: Elek, 1974.

Schouten, S. Psi in mice: Positive reinforcement. *Journal of Parapsychology*, 1972, *36*, 261–282.

Sinclair, U. *Mental radio* (2nd rev. ed.). Springfield, Illinois: Thomas, 1962.

Stanford, R. G. Response bias and the correctness of ESP test responses. *Journal of Parapsychology*, 1967, *31*, 280–289.

Stanford, R. G., and Pratt, J. G. Extrasensory elicitation of sensorially acquired response patterns? *Journal of the American Society for Psychical Research*, 1970, *64*, 296–302.

Stanford, R. G., and Stio, A. A study of associative mediation in psi-mediated instrumental response. *Journal of the Amerinan Society for Psychical Research*, 1976, *70*, 55–64.

Stanford, R. G., and Thompson, G. Unconscious psi-mediated instrumental response and its relation to conscious ESP performance. In W. G. Roll, R. L. Morris, and J. D. Morris (Eds.), *Research in parapsychology 1973*. Metuchen, New Jersey: Scarecrow Press, 1974. Pp. 99–103.

Stevenson, I. The substantiality of spontaneous cases. In W. G. Roll, R. L. Morris, and J. D. Morris (Eds.), *Proceedings of the Parapsychological Association, No. 5, 1968*. Durham, North Carolina: Parapsychological Association, 1971. Pp. 91–128.

Swann, I. *To kiss earth goodbye*. New York: Hawthorn Books, 1975.

Tanous, A., with Ardman, H. *Beyond coincidence: One man's experiences with psychic phenomena*. Garden City, New York: Doubleday, 1976.

Targ, R., and Puthoff, H. Information transmission under conditions of sensory shielding. *Nature*, 1974, *251*, 602–607.

Targ, R., Cole, P., and Puthoff, H. *Development of techniques to enhance man/machine communication*. Stanford Research Institute Project 2613 Report, 1974.

Tart, C. T. Physiological correlates of psi cognition. *International Journal of Parapsychology*, 1963, *5*, 375–386.

Tart, C. T. *Learning to use extrasensory perception*. Chicago: University of Chicago Press, 1976.

Terry, J. C. Continuation of the rodent precognition experiments. In J. D. Morris, W. G. Roll, and R. L. Morris (Eds.), *Research in parapsychology 1975*. Metuchen, New Jersey: Scarecrow Press, 1976. Pp. 11–14.

Terry, J. C. and Harris, S. A. Precognition in water-deprived rats. In J. D. Morris, W. G. Roll, and R. L. Morris (Eds.), *Research in parapsychology 1974*. Metuchen, New Jersey: Scarecrow Press, 1975. P. 81.

Ullman, M. and Krippner, S. Dream studies and telepathy. (*Parapsychological Monographs No. 12*). New York: Parapsychology Foundation, 1970.

Ullman, M., Krippner, S., and Feldstein, I. Experimentally induced telepathic dreams: Two studies using EEG-REM monitoring technique. *International Journal of Neuropsychiatry*, 1966, *2*, 420–437.

West, D. J. and Fisk, G. W. A dual ESP experiment with clock cards. *Journal of the Society for Psychical Research*, 1953, *37*, 185–197.

Wilson, R. Generation of random numbers for ESP experiments. *International Journal of Parapsychology*, 1965, *7*, 285–293.

Wood, G. H. and Cadoret, R. J. Tests of clairvoyance in a man-dog relationship. *Journal of Parapsychology*, 1958, *22*, 29–39.

Extrasensory Perception: Research Findings

2

John Palmer

1. Does This Stuff Really Exist?

1.1. The Early Years

Although claims of psychic phenomena have been with us since antiquity, the beginning of organized research into the nature of these phenomena is usually associated with the founding in 1882 of the Society for Psychical Research in London. The S.P.R. was the brainchild of a group of distinguished scholars who were concerned primarily with the question of survival after death, and who believed that scientific research might provide a more satisfactory resolution of this problem than had the current religious dogma (Gauld, 1968). The S.P.R., as well as its sister society established a few years later in America, devoted its energies to two principal lines of ESP research. The first was a thorough investigation of reports of "real-life" psychic experiences (e.g., telepathy, apparitional experiences, hauntings) with the purpose of demonstrating that they could not be adequately explained by "normal" causes (e.g., Gurney, Myers, and Podmore, 1886/1970; Myers, 1903/1975). The second approach involved the investigation of spiritualist mediums who claimed the ability to communicate with the dead. Although some of these mediums proved to be fraudulent, others consistently were able to provide investigators with remarkably detailed information about deceased persons, information that

John Palmer · John F. Kennedy University, Orinda, California.

it is difficult to conceive of their having acquired by normal means. Perhaps the most outstanding of these mediums were Leonore Piper (Hodgson, 1897–1898) and Gladys Leonard (Smith, 1964). Whether the information received by these mediums originated from the "other side" or simply reflected their own ESP is still an unresolved issue in parapsychology, although most parapsychologists today recoil from the spiritualistic interpretation.

The observational approach only gradually gave way to laboratory experimentation. Although a handful of quantitatively analyzed laboratory experiments were reported in the first quarter of the 20th century in both Europe (e.g., Brugmans, 1922) and the United States (e.g., Coover, 1917; Estabrooks, 1927/1961), the dominant status that the experimental method enjoys today is largely attributable to J. B. Rhine. Although Rhine did not originate the card-guessing paradigm in parapsychology, he employed it more extensively and successfully than had previous investigators. In 1934 he published a monograph describing an extensive series of card-guessing tests with eight college students, each of whom achieved highly extrachance scores with a great degree of consistency (Rhine, 1934/1973). Unfortunately, most of this research was conducted under informal conditions that were not always well controlled, and the monograph itself reads more like a popular book than a detailed scientific report. Combined with the dominance of both methodological and metaphysical behaviorism in American psychology at this time, these facts caused the monograph to become the object of severe attacks from more orthodox segments of the scientific community. Although these attacks were not always rational, they did push Rhine to tighten experimental controls, and by 1940 he and his colleagues were able to publish a more scholarly volume, which purported to demonstrate that later card-guessing experiments effectively overcame the legitimate criticisms of other scientists (Rhine, Pratt, Stuart, Smith, and Greenwood, 1940/1966).

1.2. Evidence from Selected Subjects: The Psychic Superstars

Probably the most important and evidential of the early Rhine experiments was the so-called Pearce–Pratt distance series (Rhine et al., 1940/1966; Rhine and Pratt, 1954). Hubert Pearce was a divinity student at Duke and one of the eight star subjects referred to in Rhine's 1934 monograph. For this experiment the BT clairvoyance procedure was selected, with the subject (Pearce) and the experimenter (Pratt) located in different buildings.* Duplicate records were made of both the call and target sequences,

---

*The meanings of abbreviations used to define forced-choice testing procedures such as BT, DT, and STM are discussed in Chapter 1, pp. 24–25.

and the scoring was checked independently by Rhine and Pratt. There were 37 sessions conducted, generally consisting of 2 runs each. Pearce's average score was 7.5 hits per run, where the expected number of hits was 5. The probability of such a scoring rate occurring by chance over this number of runs is less than 10^{-22}.

Of course, no single experiment, regardless of how significant the results or tight the controls, can be accepted without reservation as conclusive verification of any scientific hypothesis, especially one as controversial as the existence of ESP. The case for ESP rests not on any one study but on the cumulative results of literally hundreds of controlled experiments. The bulk of these experiments have used groups of unselected subjects (mostly high school and college students) who claim no outstanding psychic ability. While the pooled scores from such samples frequently provide statistically significant evidence of ESP, the results are rarely dramatic. Although equating the magnitude of an effect with its evidential value is a questionable tactic, it is the smaller number of experiments with "gifted" subjects—who produce highly significant individual scores under controlled laboratory conditions—that usually are considered as providing the strongest evidence in support of the ESP hypothesis. Generally speaking, these are the only studies that have captured what little interest scientists outside the field of parapsychology have shown in ESP research. For a historical perspective on research with outstanding ESP subjects, see Pratt (1975).

Not counting subjects tested at Rhine's laboratory prior to 1940, six subjects stand out as having demonstrated the ability to achieve high scores in forced-choice ESP tests over a protracted period of time. It is the reliability of their performance as much as, if not more than, the magnitude of their scores that causes these subjects to assume prominent positions in the annals of parapsychological research. Two of these subjects, a photographer named Basil Shackleton and a housewife named Gloria Stewart, were tested by the British parapsychologist S. G. Soal, whom we will discuss shortly. The other four I will briefly discuss now, in chronological order.

The first was a college student identified only as C. J., who was tested at the University of Colorado (Martin and Stribic, 1938a, b, 1940). This subject excelled at card-guessing tests of the conventional DT (or UT) type, in which he averaged better than 7 hits per run over 2,000 runs; but he also performed well on other card-guessing tests.

The second outstanding subject is a library information clerk in Czechoslovakia by the name of Pavel Stepanek (Pratt, 1973). Stepanek, who was discovered by the Czech parapsychologist Milan Ryzl, has been tested over a period of more than 10 years. He probably has retained his card-guessing abilities longer than any other subject in the history of parapsychology, although his ability has seemed to decline since 1968. Stepanek has been able to succeed on only one type of test, one which involves guessing which side of a green-and-white card is facing upward inside a cardboard envelope. Although he was able to succeed at guessing the correct color early in his career, his success has always been combined with a strong tendency to base his calls on visual cues from the envelopes. The significance of his later results derived in large part from the continuation of these secondary scoring patterns when the envelopes were concealed in progressively larger containers that shielded the inner containers from Stepanek's view. We will discuss this "focusing effect" in greater detail toward the end of the chapter. Stepanek has succeeded with tests conducted by a number of investigators, including a neutral scientist not previously associated with parapsychology (Blom and Pratt, 1968).

The third subject is a professional psychic from Trinidad named Lalsingh Harribance (Altrocchi, 1971; Child and Kelly, 1973; Damgaard, 1972; Dukhan, 1971; Kanthamani, 1974; Kelly and Lenz, 1976b; Klein, 1972; Morris, 1972, 1973; Morris, Roll, Klein, and Wheeler, 1972; Roll, 1972; Roll and Klein, 1972; Stump, Roll, and Roll, 1970). Harribance has succeeded in a number of different forced-choice tests under well-controlled conditions, but his unique specialty is guessing the sex of persons in concealed photographs. He also succeeded in a free-response experiment where he was asked to give "blind readings" of 20 volunteer subjects. He was particularly accurate in identifying the physical aspects of these persons (Roll, Morris, Damgaard, Klein, and Roll, 1973).

The fourth subject is a former law student named Bill Delmore (Kanthamani and Kelly, 1974a, b; Kelly and Kanthamani, 1972; Kelly, Kanthamani, Child, and Young, 1975). Although he has been tested less extensively than the other subjects described in this section, Delmore also has succeeded on a variety of forced-choice tests. His most outstanding results have involved correctly and completely identifying concealed playing cards.

Although free-response testing methods have been employed at times throughout the history of parapsychology (e.g., Sidgwick, 1924) and are enjoying increasingly widespread use, the published literature fails to reveal any subjects who have achieved outstanding scoring levels with such methods under controlled conditions over a large number of trials. Perhaps the individual most closely approaching this ideal was the wife of novelist Upton Sinclair, who evidenced striking success over several years at duplicating hundreds of line drawings made by her husband or others in a different room (Sinclair, 1962). Unfortunately, the results could not be adequately analyzed statistically and the sender was allowed to arbitrarily select the target picture, a fatal flaw in the design of any ESP experiment. Nevertheless, many of the correspondences were extremely striking.

A number of subjects have produced striking free-response results under better controlled conditions in short series, however. Many of these occurred during dreaming, a topic to be discussed later. Several subjects have achieved impressive results with a technique called "remote viewing," where an experimenter travels to a randomly selected location several miles from the laboratory and the subject is asked to both describe and draw his impressions of the location (Bisaha and Dunne, 1977; Puthoff and Targ, 1976; Targ and Puthoff, 1977). In a very sophisticated experiment, an Argentine psychiatrist obtained highly significant results in duplicating 90 freehand drawings under both GESP and clairvoyance conditions (Musso and Granero, 1973).

The above listing is by no means intended as a complete catalogue of all persons who have demonstrated exceptional ESP talents in either the forced-choice or free-response modes. I have simply selected those who have provided the most striking and consistent evidence of ESP in well-controlled experiments reported in detail in the scientific literature.

No discussion of star ESP subjects would be complete without mentioning the Israeli psychic Uri Geller. In a controversial experiment published in *Nature*, Geller was seated in a visually, acoustically, and electrically shielded room and asked to reproduce freehand drawings that were located in another room. The results were highly significant statistically, and many of the correspondences were quite impressive (Targ and Puthoff, 1974).

The greater-than-average controversy surrounding these results stems from the fact that there is at least a great deal of circumstantial evidence that many of Geller's ostensibly psychic stage and "cocktail party" feats are nothing more than magician's tricks (Randi, 1975). Nonetheless, critics so far have been unable to convincingly explain away Targ's drawing experiment. The editorial reviewers for *Nature* were split concerning whether the paper should be published (Investigating the Paranormal, 1974). There were general criticisms concerning the lack of methodological detail in the report but no indications as to what information the reviewers felt was lacking. The only specific criticism stated in the editorial concerned the less-than-ideal method of assuring unbiased selection of target pictures, a technically valid but trivial argument given the magnitude of the effects. Suggestions by others as to how Geller might have cheated either misrepresented the experimental conditions as outlined in Targ's report (Randi, 1975; noted by Tart, 1976b) and/or delved into such exotic speculations as that Geller had a radio receiver implanted in his tooth (Hanlon, 1974).

The controversy over whether or not Geller has genuine psychic ability has become such a media event that serious scientists interested in coming to terms with the paranormal would be best advised to look elsewhere. However, fraud in ESP experiments (on the part of subject, experimenter, or both) is an important issue that must be confronted, however unpleasant and distracting such a task may be.

1.3. Is It All a Hoax?

1.3.1. The Hume Game

In the first presidential address delivered to the Society for Psychical Research, Henry Sidgwick made the following prophetic statement: "We have done all that we can when the critic has nothing left to allege except that the investigator is in the trick" (Sidgwick, 1882, p. 12). By 1940, it appeared that the skeptics were in just such a position. It took them 15 years after that to fulfill Sidgwick's prophecy.

The logic of their attack can be traced back to David Hume, a member of the British empiricist school of philosophy, which helped to provide the philosophical foundation of American behavioristic psychology. In Hume's book, *An Enquiry Concerning Human Understanding*, originally published in 1748 (Hume 1748/1952), one finds the following quote: "No testimony is sufficient to establish a miracle, unless the testimony be of such a kind that its falsehood would be more miraculous than the fact which it endeavors to establish . . . the knavery and folly of men are such common phenomena, that I should rather believe the most extraordinary events to arise from their concurrence, than admit to so signal a violation of the laws of nature." (p. 491). In other words, it is more reasonable to believe that those who participate in ESP experiments are cheaters than to believe in the "miracle" of ESP.

One could question the relevance of Hume's quotation to parapsychology because if ESP does exist, it is not a miracle (i.e., a temporary suspension of natural law). On the contrary, it itself represents a natural law, albeit one currently not well understood by science. Such technicalities were insufficient, however, to deter a young research scientist named George Price from publishing in *Science* an article proposing that ESP research that could not be explained away on more conventional grounds could be accounted for as deliberate fraud or "mildly abnormal mental conditions" (Price, 1955, p. 360). He thus became the first highly visible player of what I will hereafter call the Hume Game.

Although no one has ever set down an official set of rules for the

Hume Game, my own observations suggest the following salient features. The object is to take any ESP experiment, preferably one that seems on the surface to provide conclusive proof of ESP, and to figure out a way the experiment could have been faked. Considerable stress seems to be laid on the elegance of the solution. The best solutions would seem to be the ones where it is necessary to assume that only the subject is a cheat, while the less ideal solutions are apparently the ones where the principal investigator must be implicated as a culprit. Solutions also seem to be more elegant the fewer persons are assumed to be involved in the conspiracy.

Price (1972) eventually decided that his earlier promotion of the Hume Game had been unfair, but by that time other players had come along to take his place. Probably the best known of these newcomers is the British psychologist C. E. M. Hansel. In 1966, he published a book entitled *ESP: A Scientific Evaluation*, in which he played the Hume Game with several of what were considered to be the most "conclusive" ESP experiments published up to that time. At the beginning of the book he defines his own rules for the game: "An experiment that has any defect such that its result may be due to a cause other than ESP cannot provide conclusive proof of ESP. In parapsychological research, the process being investigated is both hypothetical and a priori extremely unlikely. *Any possible known cause* [italics mine] of the result is far more likely to be responsible for it than the hypothetical process under consideration" (p. 17). In an earlier paper, we find an even more sweeping quote: "Any experiment that has any defect such that the result may be due to *any cause* [italics mine] other than the hypothetical cause being investigated must be rejected" (Hansel, 1960, p. 8). In other words, all a critic has to do to destroy the evidence for ESP (or any other hypothesis he or she doesn't like) is to demonstrate that for each relevant experiment there is some alternate hypothesis that does not invoke ESP or whatever other construct happens not to be fashionable in the current scientific orthodoxy. Since there are no limits to the lengths one can go in applying such "orthodox" hypotheses, the failure to do so would seem to be more a reflection on the dullness of the critic than on the rigor of the experimental design. Perhaps this is why the Hume Game is so popular with certain critics: *It is almost impossible to lose*!

One experiment that Hansel subjected to the Hume Game was the Pearce–Pratt series. It will be recalled that this was the clairvoyance experiment in which subject and experimenter were located in different buildings. Although the results seemed to provide strong support for the ESP hypotheses, Hansel proposed an alternate explanation, which assumed fraud on the part of the subject. In a nutshell, Hansel claimed that

Pearce could have left his building during the session and stationed himself in a room across the hall from Pratt's room. From there he could have stood on a chair, peeked through the transom above the door in Pratt's room, copied the target order as Pratt was recording it after the run, returned to his own room, and recorded his guesses so as to obtain the desired number of hits.

Unfortunately for Hansel, the building in which Pratt was located had since been renovated, and Hansel was unable to obtain the original blueprints. He therefore could not document his assumption that Pearce could have had a direct line of sight onto Pratt's desk. Pratt, however, was more successful in obtaining the blueprints and they discredited Hansel's theory (Stevenson, 1967).

A second experiment that received Hansel's attention was by Pratt and Woodruff (1939). In the more tightly controlled second series of this experiment, 32 unselected subjects were tested using an STM procedure. The overall results, although not dramatic, were highly significant. In this case, Hansel's villain was the experimenter (Woodruff) who controlled the deck of target cards. One of the control features supposedly introduced into this series was that this experimenter should not know the order of the key cards hung in a row by the subject on the opposite side of the screen, so that he could not cheat by occasionally matching a target card to the corresponding key card contrary to the subject's call. However, Hansel discovered that one could determine the location of at least some key cards by noting their order on the preceding run (which was revealed during the scoring of that run). This assumes that the subject did a poor job of rearranging the key cards between runs, thus allowing the experimenter to keep track of them. Hansel also found that for himself it was easiest to keep track of the cards that occupied the end positions on the previous run (E-cards), and he concluded that the misplacement of target cards should be concentrated on these key cards.

Hansel then went a step further and actually demonstrated that in the case of the highest scoring subject in the series, the significance indeed was attributable to an excess of hits on the E-cards. This effect also was found to a lesser but still significant degree in the combined results of the four other subjects whose overall scores were independently significant (Medhurst and Scott, 1974).

Pratt argued that parapsychological interpretations could account for this finding (Pratt and Woodruff, 1961; Pratt, 1974a), and he succeeded in providing evidence for such an explanation in a later paper (Pratt, 1977). He suggested that subjects might score best on the E-cards simply because these cards were most salient to them, as a result of their positions on the previous run. As we will see later (see section 4.1.1.) such salience effects have been found in other ESP data. He reasoned that if the

E-cards were salient to the subject, he would be more likely to re-member to change their locations on the next run than he would if these E-cards were not salient. Pratt in fact found, at least with the highest scoring subject, that there were significantly more hits on the E-cards when their locations had been shifted than when they had not been shifted.

Although parapsychologists so far have had the last word in the controversies surrounding the Pearce–Pratt and Pratt–Woodruff experiments, it would be hazardous to assume that either controversy is over. But it really doesn't matter. As a last resort, all Hansel (or any other player of the Hume Game) has to do is argue that Rhine, Pratt, Pearce, and a few of the subjects in the Pratt–Woodruff experiment fabricated the data. While this argument lacks the elegance of Hansel's earlier solutions, it is preferable to the ESP solution, according to the logic of the Hume Game.

1.3.2. Toward a More Balanced Approach

The excesses of the Hume Game should not blind us to the fact that fraud can occur in any science, and that there are legitimate means of both detecting and demonstrating it. A case where the accusations or insinuations of fraud possess more credibility than in those cases discussed above is the research of the late British mathematician and parapsychologist S. G. Soal. He obtained highly significant evidence of psi over a number of years from two selected subjects, a photographer named Basil Shackleton and a housewife named Gloria Stewart, using adaptations of Rhine's forced-choice GESP techniques (Soal and Bateman, 1954). Soal's research, which seemed to be among the most tightly controlled in parapsychology up to that time, became the object of speculative attacks in the tradition of the Hume Game (Hansel, 1960, 1966; Price, 1955), attacks to which Soal vigorously replied (Soal, 1955, 1960).

However, a new element was added to the controversy when one of Soal's assistants reported that she saw Soal altering figures in the target sequences (Soal and Goldney, 1960), a fact that Hansel, curiously enough, mentioned only briefly in his lengthy attack on Soal's work. More recently Scott and Haskell (1974) found internal evidence in the data which was consistent with the assistant's allegation, while another investigator was unable to find the recorded target sequences in question in any of the sources Soal claims to have used (Medhurst, 1971). Several prominent parapsychologists were invited to defend Soal (who was at the time senile and unable to defend himself and has since died) in a debate published in the *Proceedings of the Society for Psychical Research* (Scott *et al.*, 1974), but none of them was able to refute the heart of the critics' argument, at least in the reviewer's opinion. Nonetheless, the case against Soal cannot, at this point, be considered conclusive.

What sets the criticism of Soal's research apart from, say, that of the Pratt–Woodruff experiment was that fraud was not just assumed to have occurred on an ad hoc basis but was actually alleged by a participant. A similar allegation of fraud by an experimental assistant recently led to the exposé of W. J. Levy and the discrediting of his extensive research on psi in animals (Rhine, 1974).

It is thus undeniable that at least one professional parapsychologist whose work was considered of high scientific quality did not live up to the standards of integrity maintained by the vast majority of other scientists in the field, a human frailty not unknown in the more orthodox sciences. Because of this fact, any suspicion of experimenter fraud *based upon empirical evidence of fraud* should be vigorously pursued. Moreover, experimenters should take all reasonable precautions to eliminate the possibility of cheating by subjects (precautions, incidentally, that I have found most good psychics insist upon). On the other hand, it is both unrealistic and unfair to assume cheating just because the results of a particular experiment are distasteful or do not readily fit into the current paradigm—not because such an assumption will not on occasion be correct but because science cannot function in the climate of paranoia and "witch hunting" (of the secular variety) that such an attitude inevitably produces. *No* branch of scientific inquiry can reach its full potential if those who engage in it know that their honesty or competence will be questioned simply for advancing and defending bold ideas or "disparate" findings. Such persecution has been with us throughout the history of science, but never in modern times has it been so blatantly defended as by those critics of parapsychology who have played the Hume Game. The implications of their attacks are by no means limited to parapsychology.

A more reasonable guideline for evaluating the likelihood of fraud in parapsychology experiments has been presented by Ransom (1971):

> If you have a situation where fraud or ESP are the only explanations for an experimental result, the result is evidence for (not proof of) ESP to the degree that the evidence for an honestly conducted experiment outweighs the evidence for fraud; and it is evidence for (not proof of) fraud to the degree that the evidence for fraud outweighs the evidence for an honestly conducted experiment. (p. 294)

1.4. The "Crucial Experiment"—and Other Myths

A great deal of energy has been wasted over the years by both parapsychologists and their critics in efforts to either proclaim or debunk the "crucial experiment" that once and for all will provide conclusive proof of ESP. By this time we all should know better. There is no such thing as a conclusive experiment in parapsychology or any other science. Beyond the lowest levels of abstraction, the results of any experiment can potentially be interpreted in more than one way, even if one assumes the competence and integrity of the experimenters.

It is likely that many scientists who do not feel that ESP has been convincingly demonstrated would change their minds if a well-controlled (although not "conclusive") ESP experiment could be replicated by any competent investigator in his or her own laboratory. However, parapsychologists must concede that no such "repeatable experiment" exists, a concession, incidentally, that must be echoed by investigators in many areas of orthodox psychology. While lack of replicability is often cited as a reason for outright rejection of the ESP hypothesis (see Ransom, 1971), it is not at all clear that such absolute repeatability should be expected, even assuming the validity of the hypothesis. It is important to recognize that the behavioral sciences, including parapsychology, are probabilistic rather than absolute sciences. This is why statistical methods must be used to evaluate most results in these disciplines. One often overlooked implication of this fact is that valid relationships that are not exceptionally strong are likely not to reach conventional levels of statistical significance in a replication attempt simply as a result of sampling variability.

A second cause of the failure of ESP experiments to replicate by conventional criteria is the fact that it is difficult, if not impossible, to precisely replicate the original methodology in all potentially crucial respects. For example, any independent replication attempt by definition involves a different experimenter, and, as we shall see later, there is evidence that different experimenters conducting the same ESP experiment frequently obtain significantly different results. The ways in which different experimenters interact with their subjects is difficult to control but likely has a profound effect on experimental outcomes in this area. We are only beginning to understand the situational variables that determine the success or failure of ESP experiments.

Even if one concedes all of the above, the fact still remains that the repeatable ESP experiment does not exist. Any scientist who chooses to cite this fact as a reason for concluding that the existence of ESP has not been proven is on firm ground, at least in terms of scientific tradition. But why all the fuss over whether ESP has been "proven"? *Proof* is a term that is appropriate in mathematics and logic but not in empirical science. Sciences that are based on probabilistic models and use probabilistic methods of analysis should restrict themselves to probabilistic conclusions. The proper question is not whether ESP has been proven but what is the subjective probability one can reasonably attach to the validity of the ESP hypothesis?

Unfortunately, such a judgment must be largely subjective, although there are certain objective factors that should enter into it. One factor that in my opinion should *not* enter into it is the so-called a priori improbability of ESP. One often hears the argument that if ESP exists, it would violate other well-established laws of nature. This simply is not true. The ESP hypothesis deals with a set of observations totally outside of those that serve as the data base for evaluating other physical laws or theories. ESP in no way threatens the validity of currently accepted scientific laws with respect to the observations to which those laws were intended to apply. The only threat posed by parapsychology is to the *universality* of those laws, a universality that should never be assumed in the first place. When and if the "existence" of ESP is finally accepted by the majority of orthodox scientists, the preferred explanation of how you are assimilating the information on this page will have to do with patterns of light processed by your physical sense organs and brain, not with ESP.

A factor that *should* enter into the judgment is the massive evidence in support of the ESP hypothesis accumulated over the years by parapsychologists and others. First of all, while "anecdotal" reports of ESP experiences by laymen do not and should not carry the conviction of well-designed experiments, a substantial proportion of the population have reported ESP experiences that they found convincing, both in the United States (Greely, 1975; Palmer and Dennis, 1975) and elsewhere (Haraldsson, Gudmundsdottir, Ragnarsson, Loftsson, and Jonsson, 1977). Furthermore, many such cases have been carefully documented (Gurney *et al.*, 1886/1970; Stevenson, 1970). The detail of correspondence between these experiences and the target events is often greater, and the likelihood that the experiences would have occurred without the target events is often less, than is often supposed by critics.

However, the bulk of the case for ESP rests on the numerous controlled laboratory experiments carried out by trained investigators that have provided statistically significant evidence of ESP in the data. While the quality of these experiments varies, few have flaws I would consider fatal as far as the demonstration of ESP is concerned, and the best ones compare favorably with the best I have seen in the psychological literature from the standpoint of methodological rigor. Secondly, although there is far from perfect repeatability in ESP research, it would be equally erroneous to say that there is no repeatability at all, especially when one considers the results of attempts by experimenters to repeat their own results. Generally speaking, I would say that the level of repeatability is about what one would expect given a genuine but weak phenomenon subject to the vagaries of sampling error and changes of conditions described above. Finally, and perhaps most important of all, the results of many experiments fall into consistent patterns that make psychological sense.

After reading the evidence presented in this chapter, the reader, one hopes, will be in a position to attach his or her own subjective probability to the validity of the ESP hypothesis. (The reader will be in an even better position, of course, if he or she consults the original reports.) In all likelihood, if the reader is open-minded, this probability will be greater than zero but less than one.

Once one has decided upon one's own subjective probability, the important question then becomes whether that probability is high enough to justify assuming the existence of ESP as a working hypothesis on which to base further research. I have little sympathy for the kind of logic that says that since parapsychologists have failed to "prove" the existence of ESP after close to a hundred years of research, further research is a waste of time. Progress is being made in this most difficult field of research, even though the progress is slow. Progress would be much faster if the educational and financial resources available to the other sciences were equally available to parapsychology. Just because parapsychologists lack the "repeatable experiment" now does not mean that such will always be the case. Further research well may bring to light the variables that must be exploited or controlled to produce this ultimate breakthrough. When one considers the revolutionary theoretical and practical implications of ESP if it does exist, it is clear that a sufficiently strong prima facie case has been made for its existence to justify a major research effort to achieve this objective.

Such a program, unfortunately, will need to be a long-term affair. Parapsychology is in a very primitive stage of development compared to most of the other sciences. Although there is some testing of theory-based hypotheses (e.g., Stanford, 1973; Schmidt, 1975), much of the "hypothesis testing" in parapsychology involves the cross-validation of post hoc effects found in preliminary experiments. The parapsychological literature consists primarily of one huge and rather unwieldy data base. What I will attempt to do in the remainder of this chapter is to integrate that data base and to reveal some consistent trends that emerge from it. These trends may not be strong or reliable enough to deserve the title of "scientific laws," but they may point the way toward the further development of methods for improving the reliability of ESP data and the construction and elaboration of testable theories.

More specifically, I will attempt to review in the remainder of this chapter the great majority of valid, published experiments that, more than simply demonstrating ESP, have contributed, or attempted to contribute, some understanding of its properties and its relationship to other variables. The logic of this admittedly ambitious undertaking is predicated on the assumption that a great deal of weight should not be placed on the results of any one experiment or experimental series in this field, regardless of the apparent elegance of the methodology or the apparent impressiveness of the results. To state the point positively, reliable knowledge is most likely to derive from the convergence of the results of several experiments on a common conclusion. While I could have lightened my burden by reviewing only those experiments I consider "important," such a strategy would merely add my own prejudice to whatever biases already exist in the literature itself. Although space limitations will prevent me from reviewing the literature as critically as I would like, I can take some comfort in knowing that the fair-minded and critical reader will want to consult the original reports before drawing final conclusions, regardless of how thoroughly critical is my own treatment.

The sources I have drawn from consist primarily of the major professional journals in the field (*Journal* and *Proceedings of the American Society for Psychical Research*, *Journal of Parapsychology*, *Journal* and *Proceedings of the Society for Psychical Research*, *International Journal of Parapsychology*, *European Journal of Parapsychology*, and *Parapsychological Monographs*). The second major source will be abstracts of papers referred and approved for presentation at the Parapsychological Association conventions since 1967 but not yet published at length in the journals. The published abstracts of these papers, while not the equivalent of journal articles, are rather substantive, especially since 1971 when the series *Research in Parapsychology* was initiated. Other abstracts, most of which were published in the *Journal of Parapsychology* and reviewed by their staff if not published elsewhere, will only be cited if they involve replication attempts or reflect on the generality of findings from more fully reported experiments. In cases where my information about a paper is derived exclusively from the abstract but a more detailed report is presumably available, both will be listed in the references.*

Any published scientific literature tends to provide a somewhat biased representation of all experiments actually conducted, especially with regard to the proportion of significant findings. In the following pages, I will be interested primarily in exploring consistency with respect

---

*The chapter includes journal articles published before the fall of 1976. I have also cited about half the papers presented at the 1976 Parapsychological Association convention. These are now published in *Research in Parapsychology 1976*, and some have already appeared in journal form.

to the *direction* of experimental relationships across studies rather than their *significance* per se. In this former respect it is my opinion, based on some knowledge of the publication policies of my sources, that the literature is not seriously biased.

I have tried to describe the experiments reviewed in the rest of this chapter such that the reader may assume that a difference between groups or experimental conditions is nonsignificant unless it is stated as being significant or its significance is obvious from the context (e.g., significant hitting in one group and significant missing in the other). The same principle applies to the significance with respect to MCE of overall ESP means in an experiment and the means of particular groups or conditions. While I have tried to apply these criteria consistently, readers who require detailed information on particular topics are urged to consult the original reports.

2. ESP and the Experimental Situation

Whenever a parapsychologist wants to test subjects in an ESP experiment, he must make numerous decisions about how the experiment should be conducted. Does it matter how far away the targets are from the subject? What kind of targets should he use? Should he offer incentives for high scores? Should he employ an agent to "send" the targets? Might it help to hypnotize the subject or attempt to put him in a state of consciousness maximally conducive to receiving psi impressions? The purpose of this section is to examine what parapsychologists have learned about the effects of various experimental manipulations on ESP scores.

2.1. Transcending Space and Time: Beyond the Fourth Dimension

2.1.1. ESP and Distance: From Rock Concerts to Moon Rocks

If one accepts the possibility that a person can obtain information about distant events without use of the known senses, it is tempting to speculate that some transmission of physical energy is involved, even though that energy may have yet to be discovered by scientists. One probable implication of most theories of ESP that assume such transmission is that receptivity should decrease as physical distance between the subject and the target stimulus increases.

2.1.1a. Long-Distance Experiments. A large number of experiments have shown that significant ESP scores can occur when subjects and targets are separated by long distances. Perhaps the first substantial long-distance experiment was by Carington (1940a, b), who had subjects in other countries, including the United States, attempt to duplicate freehand drawings located in his home in England. The results were highly significant, but his statistical methods were of questionable validity. A subsequent "replication" attempt gave results of comparable significance (Schmeidler and Allison, 1948), but the significance was based on one subseries where the subjects and target drawings were located in the same building.

J. B. Rhine considered the distance question in the early Duke experiments (Rhine, 1934/1973). The Pearce–Pratt experiment, described earlier, provides strong evidence that ESP can occur over moderate distances of 100 to 250 yards with the targets and percipient in separate buildings. Other experiments from the early Duke period provided significant evidence of ESP over distances ranging from hundreds to thousands of miles (Gibson, 1937; J. B. Rhine, 1937). In the latter article, Rhine reported that over 4,000 runs from published and unpublished experiments involving distances from 70 to 3,000 miles resulted in a mean ESP score that was significantly above chance.

Subsequent demonstrations of ESP occurring over long distances have primarily involved subjects who had achieved high scores in preliminary testing or reported frequent spontaneous psi experiences. Undoubtedly the most extensively tested of these was a physician named Carlo Marchesi, who recorded his responses in Yugoslavia and mailed them to Duke, where the targets had been located (McMahan and Bates, 1954; McMahan and Rhine, 1947; Rhine and Humphrey, 1942). The results for all three experiments combined were significantly positive, but the magnitude of the effect was not impressive given the large number of runs (1,352) completed. A number of shorter card-guessing experiments with selected subjects also produced significant results involving psi-hitting (Anderson, 1959a; Mangan, 1957; Nielsen, 1956a), psi-missing (Osis, 1955), psi-hitting and psi-missing (Osis and Pienaar, 1956), and replicated displacement effects (Mangan, 1955, 1957). A South African subject was repeatedly able to wake himself up at times randomly selected by a friend 900 miles away (Bleksley, 1963).

A transcontinental card-guessing experiment with a selected subject that produced chance results was reported by Osis (1956), and we do not know how many other nonsignificant results simply were never published. Distance experiments with groups of subjects have produced mixed results (e.g., Fisk and West, 1957; Green, 1965; Kahn, 1952; Michie and West, 1957; J. B. Rhine, 1962; Skibinsky, 1950). Nonetheless, the success of long-distance card-guessing experiments in the published literature compares quite favorably in terms of significant outcomes to the success of short-distance experiments from the same literature.

The number of long-distance free-response experiments is relatively small. The only long-distance drawing experiments, outside of Carington's and Schmeidler's work discussed above, were successful endeavors by Rush and Jensen (1949) and the recent experiments in "remote viewing" (e.g., Puthoff and Targ, 1976). Probably the most exotic of the significant distance series was a dream study where the agents were the audience at a rock concert being held several miles from the percipients (Krippner, Honorton, and Ullman, 1973; see also Krippner, Honorton, Ullman, Masters, and Houston, 1971). However, a transcontinental dream experiment with a single sender submitted to "sensory bombardment" was less successful (Foulkes, Belvedere, Masters, Houston, Krippner, Honorton, and Ullman, 1972).

The most ambitious attempt to transcend the distance barrier through ESP was by astronaut Edgar Mitchell on the Apollo 14 moon flight (Mitchell, 1971). During six rest periods, Mitchell was to send random sequences of 25 ESP symbols to four persons on earth, all of whom had been preselected for psychic ability. Unfortunately, Mitchell was not always able to send at the proper time, and two of the transmissions were missed entirely. This threw off the time correspondences between sending and receiving, and it required some arbitrary decisions to be made about which guess sequences to match with which target sequences for analysis. The precise analyses decided upon are too complex to describe here. Suffice it to say that matching in terms of sequence, e.g., first guess sequence with first target sequence, produced marginally significant psi-hitting, while analyses based more upon the temporal proximity of the sequences produced significant psi-missing. These results, being of a highly post hoc nature, must be interpreted with even greater than usual caution.

2.1.1b. Comparison of Distances. Although ESP may or may not be a possible means of future communication for space voyagers, the evidence does indicate that ESP can function over long distances. However, this does not mean that ESP functions equally well at all distances. The more interesting question of whether ESP effects are attenuated with distance has yet to be addressed in this chapter.

Generally speaking, the early Duke work revealed little evidence of decline with distance (J. B. Rhine, 1937). In the Pearce–Pratt series, however, the mean ESP score was significantly lower at 250 yards than at 100 yards, but outstanding single run scores were obtained at both distances (Rhine and Pratt, 1954). Also, Gibson (1937), who gave GESP tests to three unselected subjects in the same building and at distances up to 2,000 miles, reported substantial declines with distance in all three cases.

In the nonsignificant transoceanic experiment reported by Osis (1956), the subject, who was located in Germany, achieved very high scores on control runs he conduct by himself at home. While having subjects test themselves without supervision is not accepted procedure in parapsychological research, Osis defended the validity of these results by citing a significant negative correlation between the daily scores on the short-distance and long-distance runs. Since the subject did not know his long-distance scores when he completed the corresponding short-distance runs, the attenuation-with-distance interpretation retains some plausibility, although this reasoning implies that some psi was operating at the long distance.

In a more sophisticated experiment, Osis and Fahler (1965) manipulated distance and time (precognition vs. clairvoyance) in a 2 × 2 factorial design. Subjects were members of a Finnish psychical research society. Multivariate analysis of variance was used to evaluate not only direct hits but also +1 and −1 displacements. The result was a complicated interaction affecting primarily the −1 scores. None of the simple effects suggested a straightforward decline of scoring level with distance. Some kind of decline with distance was also reported by Turner (1965), but I was only able to find an abstract of the report.

Of the experiments discussed above, those of Gibson (1937), Osis (1956), Rhine and Pratt (1954), and Turner (1965) reveal a significant decline with distance. All involved research with selected subjects. No studies reveal comparable incline effects. However, in each experiment where a significant decline effect was found, other uncontrolled variables could have been responsible for the effect. Perhaps the most important of these factors was that subjects were aware of the target locations. This procedure allows psychological effects to be confounded with distance effects, e.g., the subject may lose confidence if he thinks the target is far away from him, and the decline effect may be attributable to this loss of confidence. Karlis Osis attempted to circumvent this problem in an elaborate series of card-guessing experiments with subjects restricted to persons who had shown evidence of ESP ability in previous testing (Osis and Turner, 1968; Osis, Turner, and Carlson, 1971). In the first experiment, senders were located in New York, Los Angeles, and Sydney, Australia, with the percipients scattered throughout the United States, but mostly in the East. Subjects did not know which target location they were aiming for on any particular run. Complex multivariate techniques again were used to evaluate the results. The only evidence of significant decline effects were on two measures of +1 displacement (see p. 198).

Recognizing that this post hoc finding required replication, Osis undertook two confirmatory experiments. In each of these, a sender traveled from New York to Sydney and back, with intermediate stops in Paris and New Delhi. Again, subjects were kept "blind" as to the location of the sender on any particular run. In the first replication experiment, the decline effect was replicated on one of the two +1 measures, while in the second experiment it was replicated in neither. Given the large number of potential relationships from which this one finding was selected, support for the decline-with-distance hypothesis was marginal at best in the Osis–Turner experiments.

2.1.1c. Conclusion. Generally speaking, the experimental evidence indicates that ESP can occur at great distances and does not decline with distance. These findings do not fit well with most hypotheses that physical energies mediate the transmission of extrasensory information. Indeed, the information transmission model itself may be erroneous, a point I will return to at the end of the chapter.

On the other hand, it would be unwise to form any final conclusions at this point. Despite their methodological shortcomings, some studies have shown a significant decline with distance and none have shown a significant incline. A possible reason for the failure of the Osis–Turner experiments was that all the distances were so long that there was not enough variability to allow significant distance effects to consistently occur above the noise abundant in all ESP data. Another possibility is that ESP information triggers neural receptors in an "all-or-none" fashion provided that a critical threshold level of physical energy is received, in which case we *might* not expect a decline of scores with distance, even though there is a continuous decline in the strength of the carrier energy. There are a number of conceptual problems not discussed in this section that any physical theory of extrasensory transmission would have to solve before we could take it seriously, but the best attitude at present is still an open mind.

2.1.2. Precognition: ESP of the Future

It seemed natural to Rhine that since ESP could overcome distance it could overcome time as well. Instances of such "precognition" frequently were recorded in the spontaneous case literature, and informal testing with some of his star subjects further convinced Rhine that ESP could transcend the time barrier.

2.1.2a. Evidence for Precognition. The first formal experiment to provide evidence for precognition was again the drawing experiment of Carington (1940a,b), who found that his subjects often would draw pictures closely corresponding to targets for later sessions, targets that had not yet been chosen. Tyrrell (1936) tested a highly talented subject who had shown success in previous clairvoyance experiments with a mechanical box device. In the precognition experiment, the subject opened one of five lids immediately before Tyrrell activated a circuit that randomly selected a target and caused a light to appear in the corresponding box. After 2,255 trials, she accumulated a rate of success giving odds of several hundred thousand to one against chance.

In 1938, Rhine reported results of a series of experiments with 49 subjects, 32 of whom were grade school children (Rhine, 1938b). Variations of the basic DT and matching tests were used. In the DT tests, for example, subjects recorded their guesses on record sheets. Immediately thereafter, the experimenter shuffled a deck of ESP cards to determine the target order. Although the mean score per run was only 5.14, this result was highly significant for the total of 4,523 runs completed by the subjects.

A concern that has continued to plague precognition researchers to the present day is that the experimenter might be using some other form of psi (either ESP in the present time or psychokinesis [PK]) to determine the target order in such a way that it will significantly match the percipient's guesses. When target orders were generated by shuffling decks of cards, this became known as the "psychic shuffle." One likely mechanism of the "psychic shuffle" in precognition tests is that the experimenter uses unconscious ESP to stop shuffling at the time when the order of cards most closely corresponds to the subject's pattern of calling the symbols. The plausibility of the "psychic shuffle" as a counterexplanation of precognition results was demonstrated in an experiment where subject and experimenter both shuffled decks of cards and found the resulting sequences to be significantly related (Rhine, Smith, and Woodruff, 1938). In a later precognition experiment, Rhine (1941a) attempted to circumvent this problem by having target orders determined by mechanical shuffling of the cards. Although today this procedure would not be considered a very good way of ruling out PK, it did have the advantage of assuring a more random target sequence than likely was obtained by hand shuffling. A matching test was chosen for this experiment, so only the order of the 5 key cards had to be rigorously randomized. The subjects were 19 adults and 5 children, who completed a total of 2,108 runs. Prior testing had indicated that the children tended to score above chance and the adults below chance on precognition tests. This pattern was significantly confirmed for each group.

Unfortunately, not all precognition experiments had been this successful. Nevertheless, in the appendix to his 1941 report, Rhine summarized the results of all known precognition experiments conducted at his laboratory and elsewhere up to June 1939. Despite the psi-missing in some experiments, he found the overall results were significantly above chance. Using a statistical test that treats the results of individual experimental groups in terms of their mean deviation from chance regardless of sign, the probability was 10^{-12}. For a discussion of the early precognition work, see Rhine (1945a).

Since 1940, parapsychologists have continued to use the precognition technique for ESP testing, albeit rarely in experiments as massive as those described above. Impressive results have continued to appear in these shorter experiments when testing was restricted to preselected subjects. A number of such experiments began to appear in the literature in the 1950s, specifically those referred to in the last section on distance effects. By this time, a more advanced method, which made use of random number tables, had been developed at Rhine's laboratory for generating target sequences (see Chapter 1). Significant results were obtained with this technique by several selected subjects (Anderson, 1959a; Mangan, 1955, 1957; Nielsen, 1956a; Osis, 1955).

Highly significant results with selected subjects have been obtained more recently by Helmut Schmidt using a machine that generates random target sequences through the principle of decay of a radioactive source (Schmidt, 1969b; Schmidt and Pantas, 1972; see Chapter 1 for a discussion of this apparatus). A possible alternate interpretation for some of these results is that the subjects might have been using PK to influence the target generation of the machine to coincide with their guesses, and Schmidt (1969b) presents supplementary data suggesting that this may have happened with at least one subject. Significant precognitive psi-hitting by selected subjects with one of Schmidt's machines also has been reported by Haraldsson (1970), Honorton (1971a) and by Kelly and Kanthamani (1972).

The use of the precognition technique in free-response testing has been less frequent but equally successful. In two eight-night dream experiments, the British psychic Malcolm Bessent was asked to dream about events or slides he would experience the next day. He was awakened during the night to give dream reports, but the target was never selected until the following morning. In each experiment, outside judges were able to match target and dream reports for the eight nights to a degree significantly better than chance (Krippner, Ullman, and Honorton, 1971; Krippner, Honorton, and Ullman, 1972).

Puthoff and Targ (1976) asked a professional photographer named Hella Hammid, who previously had been successful in clairvoyance tests with the "remote-viewing" technique, to try it precognitively. Only four trials were completed, but an outside judge was able to correctly match all targets and descriptions. The correspondences were qualitatively quite impressive, somewhat more so than those obtained with the clairvoyance procedure. Successful precognitive remote viewing also was found with two female college students (Bisaha and Dunne, 1977).

As might be expected, precognition experiments with unselected subjects have been less consistent in providing significant overall deviations from chance, although many of the studies I will cite later in which significant relationships were found between ESP scores and predictor variables employed precognition procedures. In perhaps the largest precognition experiment with unselected subjects, close to 30,000 readers of *Maclean's* magazine completed a ten-trial precognition test by filling out and mailing back postcards placed in the magazine (J. B. Rhine, 1962). Separate random target orders were generated for each subject by computer. The overall mean score was significantly *below* chance.

2.12b. Precognition versus Clairvoyance. Of the several studies where precognition and clairvoyance tests have been systematically compared within subjects, only three provided significant differences, two of which favored precognition. Freeman (1962) gave seven college students alternate DT and precognition runs over several sessions. They scored significantly above chance on precognition and close to chance on DT. The difference was significant, although it is unclear how consistent the effect was across subjects. Furthermore, demand characteristics favoring precognition were introduced for other purposes, and these may have been responsible for the effect. The British psychologist Robert Thouless (1949) tested himself with DT and precognition methods in counterbalanced order over several sessions. Contrary to his initial expectation, he scored significantly above chance on one of two precognition tests and significantly below chance on a DT test. He attributed this result to the greater novelty of the precognition tests which sustained his interest longer than the DT method; he had practiced DT extensively in the past. Buzby (1963) reported significant positive scoring on clairvoyance but not precognition among a group of 33 college students, the difference being significant. Overall results for a second group, reported in more detail later (Buzby, 1967b), showed no significant difference.

A number of other experiments have shown no significant within-subject differences between the two methods nor any consistent directional trends (Beloff and Bate, 1970; Dean, 1972; Fahler, 1957; Freeman, 1969a; McMahan and Rhine, 1947; Nash and Nash, 1968; Osis and Fahler, 1965; Zenhausern, Stanford, and Esposito, 1977). However, only the Beloff, Osis, and Zenhausern experiments controlled the order of clairvoyance and precognition trials within sessions. Zenhausern *et al.*

(1977) did find a significant interaction between type of test and sex, with females scoring significantly higher on clairvoyance than on precognition. Comparisons using between-subjects designs simply have not been reported in the literature.

2.1.2c. Comparison of Time Intervals. Just as it was meaningful to ask whether ESP scores decline with distance, it is meaningful to ask if scores on precognition tests decline as the time interval between the actual test and target selection increases. Hutchinson (1940) reported significantly lower scores on runs checked 10 days after the test than on runs checked 1 day after the test. Scoring on the 1-day runs was significantly positive. However, the 10-day runs were usually the last runs subjects completed in the session, so the results might reflect nothing more than a within-session decline effect. Also, subjects knew in advance which runs would be checked at which time, introducing possible demand characteristics. In an earlier series where 1-day and 10-day intervals were compared and some effort was made at counterbalancing the design, no significant difference was found, and the means in both conditions were close to chance. Turner (1965) found no significant differences among precognition scores checked 1, 2, or 3 weeks after the test.

The only other studies where time intervals have been compared in any systematic way were correspondence experiments with individual subjects. Osis (1955) found no significant difference between scores on runs checked within 1 week of testing and those checked 1 month after testing. How many days he waited was decided arbitrarily for each run. Overall scores in this experiment were significantly below chance. A subject tested by Anderson (1959a) actually scored better on runs checked 1 year later than on those checked only 5 days later. The difference was not quite significant, but significant psi-hitting was restricted to the 1-year runs. In neither of these studies were subjects informed at the time of testing which runs would be scored when.

2.1.2d. Conclusion. Research with selected subjects provides a strong case in support of the conclusion that ESP under certain circumstances can provide information about events that do not yet exist at the time of the response. The philosophical implications of precognition are obviously rather mind-boggling, but a discussion of these is beyond the already ubiquitous scope of this chapter. The evidence for precognition is particularly impressive methodologically, because by definition there is no way that the subject can be guided by sensory cues, since the target sequence does not exist at the time he makes his responses. The possibility that all precognition data can be explained by other forms of psi such as PK has not been completely ruled out, but it is rather strained in those experiments where target orders were derived from random number tables and entry points were determined in a complex manner. Precognition procedures have been no less successful than clairvoyance procedures in group experiments with nongifted subjects. There is no evidence that precognition scores decline as the time interval between testing and target generation increases, but more research on this topic with high-scoring subjects is needed. Other data relevant to the precognition issue are discussed in section 6.1.1.

2.2. Forced-Choice Target Material: Variety Is the Spice of Psi

2.2.1. Type of Target: It's All a Matter of Preference

Parapsychologists have revealed no lack of creativity in selecting types of target material for forced-choice ESP experiments. Not surprisingly, a number of experimenters have systematically compared scores on two types of targets using within-subject designs. Although subjects frequently score quite differently on these target types, the nature of these trends by no means has been clear or consistent, at least on the surface.

2.2.1a. Physical Dimensions. Size of the target stimulus is a case in point. Pratt and Woodruff (1939) found that subjects scored significantly above chance on an STM test when the ESP symbols were made very small, but close to chance when the symbols were of normal size. However, this effect could not be replicated significantly in a second experiment. In both experiments, subjects knew which type of symbol was being used on some runs but not others, and this variable had no significant effect on the results. In another matching experiment L. E. Rhine (1937) found that grade school children scored equally well on various sizes of symbols. To complete the cycle, the French biologist Chauvin (1961) found that in a clairvoyance guessing game where targets were the numbers 1 and 2, he and four children from his family scored significantly below chance when the numbers were very small and near chance when they were of normal size. Subjects did not know the size of symbol on particular trials, although they knew symbol size was a variable in the design.

Pratt and Woodruff were able to explain the findings from their first experiment as a tendency for subjects to score significantly only on targets they had not responded to in previous testing. Many of Pratt's subjects in his first series had prior experience with normal-sized ESP symbols, while Rhine's subjects apparently had not. Chauvin and his children had been tested before with numerical stimuli, but the microscopic stimuli were probably new to them. This pattern of results suggests that, at least as far as stimulus size is concerned, novelty has the effect of increasing the magnitude of ESP scoring, but the direction of the effect depends upon other factors. However, in an experiment designed to systematically manipulate subjects' familiarity with type of target (symbol or position of symbol in a row of five spaces), novelty was found to have no effect (Hallett, 1952).

Other variations of target type where the emphasis has been on the physical attributes of the targets as opposed to their meaning or impact for the subjects have produced mixed results which so far have contributed little to our understanding of the ESP process. MacFarland and George (1937) found that significant psi-hitting among 13 college students was not adversely affected when the ESP symbols were distorted in shape. In a series of classroom GESP experiments in which grade school children also achieved significant positive scoring overall, Van Busschbach (1956) initially found higher scoring when the targets were colors or symbols as opposed to words, but this effect vanished when the order of run types was counterbalanced. Differences in target type (generally words vs. symbols) entered into complex interactions in classroom ESP tests of grade school and high school students conducted by Freeman (1963, 1965, 1966b, 1967, 1968, 1969b, 1970a, b, 1972b), but no significant main effects were reported.

In an experiment involving numerical stimuli, Nash and Nash (1959) reported nonsignificant scoring when the targets were addition problems that subjects had to solve (e.g., the target is "1 + 2" and the correct response is "3"), while significant psi-missing occurred when the targets were the numbers themselves (e.g., "3"). The difference is significant by a C.R. analysis computed by the reviewer. Subjects were unaware that addition problems were included in the target sequence. A possible explanation of the less significant scoring on the addition problems is that subjects were picking up on the actual numbers rather than their sum, but no direct evidence of this is reported. Translation also may have been a factor in an experiment reported by Krippner (1966). Children who were asked to respond by circling the appropriate word on a clairvoyance test scored significantly above chance when the targets were words but nonsignificantly when the targets were pictures representing the words.

2.2.1b. Psychological Dimensions. There are some indications from the literature that subjects may be more sensitive to the personal meaning of target stimuli than to their physical form. Perhaps the most compelling single illustration of this point is an experiment with a single subject in which targets consisting of descriptions or pictures of people were compared with blank cards onto which images of these people had been hallucinated by a hypnotized person. Untreated blank cards served as control targets. Significant positive scoring occurred on the treated blank cards and on the three experimental types of stimuli combined. Unfortunately, no comparisons with the control stimuli were possible (Lucas and Roll, 1973).

Meaningful stimuli do not always produce psi-hitting, however. Skibinsky (1950) found in three GESP distance series that overall significant psi-missing occurred on runs where the targets were names of the subjects' family members as compared to slightly above-chance scoring with normal ESP symbols. The difference was significant in the three series pooled. Unfortunately, subjects probably filled out the name run first in all sessions, introducing a confounding order effect. Van de Castle (1953) found that a single subject scored very significantly above chance on conventional types of targets (e.g., ESP symbols and numbers) but slightly below chance on drawings that she made herself and that were meaningful to her. Nash and Nash (1968) found that male college students scored significantly above chance on word targets that they selected by group vote as representing "favorite things" and significantly below chance on number targets selected by the experimeter. Freeman (1961), however, found no mean difference among college students between scores on ESP symbols and target objects they selected themselves as having emotional significance for them. (We will return to this study later.) Other experiments in which target material of an emotional nature was used without the subject's knowledge have revealed appropriate effects on ESP scoring. These experiments will be discussed in section 5.1.2.

Rao conducted a series of experiments in which subjects were asked to select five symbols to which they had a "favorable emotional attachment." Scoring on these symbols was then compared to scoring on conventional ESP symbols in the same session. In the first experiment, six female subjects selected on the basis of high scores in preliminary testing scored above chance on "choice" symbols and below chance on ESP symbols, the difference being significant (Rao, 1962). However, in a second experiment using the STM technique, five unselected subjects produced a significant reversal of this effect (Rao, 1963a).* Unlike the earlier experiment, subjects did not know which type of target they were guessing on any given trial. Two further STM experiments failed to produce any overall difference, but post hoc analyses revealed a reversal of the trend between the first and second runs of the session in each case (Rao, 1963c). The reversal was significant in the second experiment and approached significance in the first.

---

*Here and elsewhere in the chapter, "significant reversal" means that the second effect was independently significant, not necessarily that it differed significantly from the first effect.

Another series of experiments that has continued this pattern of inconsistent within-subject differences involved comparisons of targets composed of English words and words in a foreign language (Hindi or Telugu) unknown to the subjects. Kanthamani (1965b) found that subjects scored above chance on English words and below chance on Hindi words. The difference was significant in two of three experiments and approached two-tailed significance in the third. However, subjects scored significantly higher on Hindi than on English words when she attempted to adopt a different method of presenting targets to the subjects (Kanthamani, 1965a).

Rao (1964b), on the other hand, found in an STM test that his male subjects scored significantly higher on Telugu than on English words in each of two experiments, while females reversed the trend. The effect was strongest when the target and key cards were in the same language. An earlier experiment produced mixed results (Rao, 1963b). Seventy-five high-school students completed two standard clairvoyance runs, one with each type of target. The initial analysis produced results generally in line with those of his later experiments described above. However, Rao noted that while his subjects had always completed the Telugu run first (a procedure that he recognized had confounded target type and order), he had always selected targets for the English run first. When he went back and compared the Telugu responses with the English targets, and vice versa, the results confirmed Kanthamani's finding (i.e., overall higher scores on English words) to a significant degree. Another experiment, however, produced a nonsignificant trend in the opposite direction from the previously found pattern (Rao, 1965a). Finally, Sailaja (1965) reported in abstract form an experiment with five subjects of unspecified sex who scored significantly higher on Telugu than on English targets, but an additional subject later failed to confirm the effect.

Two other experiments involving major procedural variations produced no differences in scoring on English and Telugu words. In one of these, the subjects were Indian students who knew both languages (Sailaja and Rao, 1973). In the other, ordinary ESP symbols were compared to ESP symbols incorporated into artistic drawings of African masks. Subjects scored significantly higher on the mask targets, suggesting that targets which are aesthetically pleasing to subjects may facilitate psi-hitting (Rao, 1964a). Ten of the subjects in this experiment were given a language ESP test in addition to the symbol test. Scores on the two tests were negatively correlated to a very high degree across subjects. It is unclear whether the order of the tests was counterbalanced. Freeman (1961), in a study mentioned earlier, found a similar significant negative correlation, in this case between scores on ESP symbols and on emotionally toned objects.

2.2.1c. The "Preferential Effect." These last two findings illustrate, perhaps more clearly than any we have discussed so far, the tendency for subjects to score differentially on two types of target material when they are combined in a single experiment. In these two experiments, subjects were not consistent with respect to which target type was associated with psi-hitting, in contrast to those experiments where one target type produced a significantly higher mean score than the other. In both cases, the customary finding is for psi-hitting to occur on one target type and a comparable degree of psi-missing on the other, a phenomenon that Rao (1965a) called the "differential effect." He earlier had labeled this the "preferential effect," assuming that the psi-hitting occurred on whichever target type the subject preferred. However, the fact that subjects sometimes scored higher on ESP symbols than their "choice" symbols (e.g., Rao, 1963a) caused him to introduce the more neutral term. It should be mentioned that only in Rao's first experiment (Rao, 1962) was the subject aware what type of card he was aiming for on a particular trial, so only in this experiment would we expect the psychological consequences of preference to vary as a function of target type. In this experiment, subjects scored significantly higher on the supposedly preferred target type. Also, in most of the studies where emotional and "choice" targets were compared, there was no check to see if subjects actually *preferred* the "choice" targets.

Sanders (1962) tested the preferential hypothesis directly by alternating runs in which subjects responded by calling out their guesses with runs in which they wrote down their guesses. There was no main effect for type of response, but in each of two series the subjects scored significantly higher with the method they preferred. Schmeidler (1946b) had subjects alternately guess symbol and color of ESP cards in a clairvoyance test. She found that subjects scored significantly better on calls representing the particular symbols or colors they claimed to prefer. In a later experiment, the target pool consisted of pictures that varied on four attributes, and subjects were asked to guess on each trial which attributes were present in the target (Schmeidler and Lewis, 1969). On the first four trials, subjects had to guess all four attributes, while on the second four they were told two of them and were asked to guess the other two. Afterward, they were asked which procedure they preferred. Subjects scored significantly higher on the preferred procedure than on the nonpreferred procedure, the scores on the latter actually falling significantly below chance. An interesting secondary finding was that subjects scored significantly higher on the nonpreferred targets when the results were analyzed for +1 displacements. Schmeidler suggested that "impatient" subjects may have been looking ahead while engaged in the nonpreferred task, causing them to direct their psi-hitting tendencies toward the next trial in the sequence. Finally, Hebda, Velissaris, and Velissaris (1974) reported that subjects scored significantly higher with a deck composed of cards of a type (e.g., ESP cards, animal cards) they preferred than with a type they did not prefer.

2.2.1d. Conclusion. Evidence is beginning to accumulate which supports the perfectly reasonable proposition that when subjects are allowed to choose which of two methods of response they prefer in an ESP experiment, they will score better on the one they prefer. Although this "preferential hypothesis" has been validated primarily with respect to response type rather than target type, it offers our best hope to date of integrating a very messy and inconsistent body of data concerning the effect of target type on ESP scoring in forced-choice experiments. So far, the applicability of the preferential hypothesis has only been demonstrated in situations where subjects each completed two types of tasks. The hypothesis that sensitivity to subject preferences can help guarantee overall psi-hitting in single-task experiments, although plausible, remains a question for further research.

2.2.2. Multiple Aspect Targets: Getting the Whole Picture

Several experiments in the parapsychological literature have involved targets that differ simultaneously on two or more attributes. An example of such target material is a deck of ordinary playing cards, which differ in terms of suit and number. The most interesting question raised by the use of multiple-aspect targets is whether subjects tend to score more total or exact hits than would be predicted from their scoring rates on the component elements. In other words, do subjects respond to such targets as wholes or as a series of independent parts?

Foster (1952) reviewed five early ESP experiments that achieved overall significantly positive scoring. In four of these series, subjects scored significantly higher on exact hits than would be expected on the basis of their scores on the separate attributes. (This number of expected exact hits, based on scores for separate attributes, hereafter will be called the "adjusted expectancy.") Unfortunately, these experiments were conducted in the early 20th century when controls against sensory cues were not as adequate as they are today, and one of the four experiments showing the effect was by S. G. Soal (see Sec. 1.3.2).

In a more recent series of experiments, the gifted subject Bill Delmore consistently scored a highly significant excess of exact hits compared to the adjusted expectancy on playing cards using both standard clairvoyance and psychic shuffle methods (Kanthamani and Kelly, 1974a, b, 1975). Another subject tested with double-aspect targets (form and color, each with $p = 1/5$) also scored significantly above chance on exact hits but, unlike Delmore, her exact hit total was not quite significant when I compared it to the adjusted expectancy (Mangan, 1957). There was *possibly* evidence of excess exact hits in dual-aspect group experiments by Lancaster (1959) and Warcollier (1962), but the reports I have seen are only brief abstracts. In an experiment with unselected subjects involving triple-aspect targets, Schmeidler and Lewis (1968) found a significantly high number of exact hits, while scoring on the separate attributes was close to chance. This effect was not found in a later experiment with four-aspect targets, however (Schmeidler and Lewis, 1969).

Although the above results provide indirect evidence for holistic "perception" of ESP targets, other explanations cannot be ruled out. When Delmore guessed the cards using ordinary clairvoyance methods, he did not make unitary responses. On the contrary, he tended to guess the number first and then the suit (Kanthamani and Kelly, 1974a). His pattern was to guess the number correctly to a highly significant degree but only to get the suit right if the number had been right. Schmeidler's subjects were required by the nature of the task to guess the attributes successively rather than holistically. Her subjects were given immediate feedback after guessing each attribute, leading her to suggest that the excess of direct hits may have resulted from heightened motivation or positive affect at the time of later guesses if guesses on previous attributes had been successful.

One negative study with respect to exact hits as compared to attribute hits was reported by Hallett (1952), who used double-aspect targets consisting of the identity of ESP symbols and their locations on rows of five spaces. Scoring was positive on position and negative on symbol, the difference reaching significance in each of two experiments. The number of exact hits was close to chance.

2.2.2a. Conclusion. The general pattern among those few studies where multiple-aspect targets were used and appropriate analyses reported is for subjects to score at least as high or higher on the total target than on any of its primary attributes. Such results suggest either that such targets are perceived holistically (even if the overt responses are fragmentary) or that a correct guess on one attribute somehow facilitates correct guesses on other attributes. It may be that both processes occur in different cases, and other factors such as psychological set may also play a role. These issues, of course, must be resolved by future research.

2.3. Test-taking Strategies: In Search of the Magic Formula

Subjects are usually left to their own devices when it comes to the best strategy for successful card guessing. There have been a few experiments, but only a few, where experimenters have attempted to manipulate the manner in which the subject guesses the targets on a particular type of test. Most of these have involved the subject's rate of guessing.

2.3.1. Rate of Responding: The Tortoise and the Hare

Stuart attempted to establish subjects' preferred tempos by having them tap a pencil in three-quarter time. Then a series of trials were administered in which each subject had to make his calls correspond to the beat of a metronome. The metronome was set at different tempos, sometimes at the subjects' preferred tempo and other times either above or below it. In each of three exploratory series involving both BT and STM procedures, subjects scored significantly above chance at the preferred tempo and near chance at the other tempos. In each series, the difference was significant (Stuart, 1938). However, results of a more systematic confirmatory experiment, although in the predicted direction, were not significant (Stuart and Smith, 1942). Hebda et al. (1974) and Nash and Nash (1958) also found no significant correlation between ESP scores and rate of responding with unselected subjects.

Other experiments suggest that slower calling rates may facilitate psi-hitting. Van de Castle (1953) had a subject call each five-trial segment of the run at a different tempo, the order being varied across runs. The intertrial intervals ranged from 30 seconds to 90 seconds or more. Overall scoring was significantly positive, but there was a significant linear decline in scores as response rate increased. Osis and Pienaar (1956) reported the results of GESP tests with two subjects, each tested with two response rates in counterbalanced order. The trials (including intertrial intervals) lasted either 5 seconds or 20 seconds. There was significant psi-hitting at the slow rate and significant psi-missing at the fast rate. Among a group of ten subjects preselected for high ESP ability by screening tests, Tart (1976a) found that those who apparently worked most slowly on a confirmatory GESP test with trial-by-trial feedback obtained the highest scores. The particular agent-experimenter used with the high-scoring subjects in this experiment may be a confounding factor, however. Finally, Stuart (1947) found that students who felt "rushed and inhibited" in a classroom free-response drawing experiment scored significantly above chance on the target for the *next* trial, and significantly higher on this target than did the other subjects in the class. The *overall* results for the class as a whole were below chance on direct targets, but it is not reported how much this was contributed by the subjects who felt rushed. However, Heyman and Schmeidler (1967) found that subjects described as "dynamic–hasty" on a test of one's orientation to time (see Sec. 3.2.3d) scored significantly above chance on +1 displacement when asked to respond *slowly* (one call every ten seconds).

2.3.1a. Conclusion. There is suggestive evidence that slower response rates facilitate psi-hitting in forced-choice ESP tests. But since this evidence comes exclusively from a handful of selected subjects, its generality is quite questionable. Stuart's drawing experiment suggests the hypothesis that lower scores resulting from rushed responses may be a by-product of +1 displacement, although Heyman's results suggest that individual differences must be considered as well.

2.3.2. Being Spontaneous: Impulsivity Pays Off

A strong impression shared by many experienced parapsychologists is that an attitude of spontaneity during an ESP test is conducive to good scoring. Subjects often are instructed to adopt such an orientation toward the ESP test. Is the value of such spontaneity merely a myth energized by the disdain many parapsychologists feel toward the excesses of rationalism, or is there some evidence for it? Fortunately, we have some data that we can turn to for at least a tentative answer.

2.3.2a. Affectability. Stuart (1941) reanalyzed several thousand runs from previous clairvoyance and precognition experiments in which subjects had been asked to predict their scores on a run-by-run basis. He found that when subjects' predictions for the first ten runs of the session were influenced by their scores on the immediately previous run, their scores in the remainder of the session tended to be lower than if their predictions had been more independent. Although such "affectability" in predicting ESP scores does not necessarily reflect a lack of spontaneity in actually making ESP responses, it is symptomatic of a rationalistic cognitive style that ordinarily would not favor spontaneity.

2.3.2b. Spontaneous Card Calling. Ross, Murphy, and Schmeidler (1952) found that children rated as "spontaneous" on the basis of free-play behavior scored suggestively higher on an ESP card test than did less spontaneous subjects. However, the first experiment designed specifically to test the spontaneity hypothesis was by Scherer (1948). In two experiments using two different homemade ESP testing machines, Scherer asked subjects to make one guess at a time and to make such responses only when they had a strong "hunch" that the response would be accurate. Various control conditions were introduced, the most comparable of which had the same subjects make one trial at a time in a "deliberate" manner. On one machine, there was a highly significant difference between results in the experimental condition and the various control conditions, with significant psi-hitting in the former. Results with the second machine were in the predicted direction but not significant.

In exploratory self-testing, Cadoret (1952) consistently found that the first trial with a new technique tended to yield a higher scoring rate than other trials. This kind of result fits in nicely with the spontaneity hypothesis not only because of the novelty element (e.g., Pratt and Woodruff, 1939) but also because the first responses in a calling sequence are the ones least influenced by the development of sequential calling patterns.

The effect of such calling patterns was examined more systematically by Stanford (1966a), who had a group of college students complete two precognition runs. In one run "closed decks" (always five of each symbol) were used, and subjects were urged to call each symbol an equal number of times. In the second run, "open decks" were used, and subjects were urged to make their calls more spontaneously. Mean deviation scores for the two runs did not differ significantly, but run-score variance was significantly higher for the open deck run. Similar results were subsequently found in three other experiments (Stanford, 1966a, 1968), two of which were conducted by experimenters other than Stanford. In one of these experiments, no calling set was given. Another experiment by Stanford providing indirect support for the spontaneity hypothesis is discussed in Sec. 3.3.1b. For an overall review, see Stanford (1975).

Morris and Cohen (1971) gave subjects four DT runs with an "open set." They found that those subjects whose responses showed the most "randomness," as defined by a relatively large number of doubles in the call sequence, scored significantly below chance while the low-doubles group scored significantly above chance.

Schouten (1975) attempted to eliminate calling patterns more directly by training subjects to produce more random sequences. The specific objective of the training was to help subjects avoid response strategies altogether and to make their responses more "free." However, the training was not successful in boosting ESP scores. Among those subjects who met Schouten's criterion for unbiased responding, there was no significant difference between their scores in the first (nonrandom) session and their scores in the session where their calls had been most random, although the latter scores approached significant psi-missing. Unfortunately, no analyses comparable to Stanford's analysis of run-score variance were reported in either the Morris or Schouten experiments.

2.3.2c. Imagery versus Impulse. In two DT clairvoyance experiments, subjects were instructed on some runs to imagine the targets visually and on other runs to "guess the first thing that comes to mind." In neither case did one method or the other prove superior, nor was there any significant interaction with imagery ability as measured by the Betts QMI, despite independent evidence of psi in the data. (Honorton, Tierney, and Torres, 1974; Schechter, Solfvin, and McCallum, 1975).

2.3.2d. Conclusion. The highly consistent results reported by Stanford suggest that a set for spontaneous calling, whether it is imposed by the experimenter or occurs naturally, facilitates both psi-hitting and psi-missing (i.e., high variance) as opposed to chance scoring. The single-trial results of Cadoret and Scherer, although involving psi-hitting only, can readily be interpreted within this framework, while the results of Morris and Cohen are more equivocal. If one assumes that absence of measurable calling biases reflects such spontaneity, it should be a relatively simple matter to verify the generality of Stanford's results by reanalyzing previously collected data. Although there apparently was no analysis for run-score variance, Schouten's experiment suggests that attempts to enforce spontaneity by extensively training subjects to call randomly is unlikely to be a fruitful solution. A possible reason for the failure of this approach is that subjects become so concerned about not responding in a biased manner that genuine spontaneity is sacrificed, despite the experimenter's intention.

Generally speaking, attempting to visualize the targets does not seem to be more effective than more intuitive guessing strategies, even for "good" imagers.

2.4. External Conditions: Manipulating Motivation

2.4.1. Environmental Conditions: Pollution in the Laboratory

It is natural to expect better performance on any mental task if the surroundings are pleasant and free from distraction. Although most parapsychologists consider the test environment to be important, only rarely has it been the object of systematic experimental manipulation.

The first such manipulation I was able to find in the literature was by Bevan (1947a), who had college students complete card-guessing runs with the room either normally light or darkened. Subjects scored above chance in the light and below chance in the dark, the difference being significant. In GESP experiments with cats, positive ESP scores were significantly reduced by introducing unpleasant conditions such as excess light or darkness, increasing the speed of an electric fan aimed at the cats, rubbing the cats' fur the wrong way, or holding them back from food (Osis, 1952; Osis and Foster, 1953).

Less noxious environmental changes seem to have little effect, however. Gibson and Stuart (1942) reviewed seven card-guessing series and found no consistent relationship between ESP scores and average barometric pressure for the day of the test in a nearby city. Barometric pressure also had no discernible effect on ESP scores of the Yugoslav subject Marchesi (McMahan and Rhine, 1947). Eilbert and Schmeidler (1950) and Reed (1959) found that playing different kinds of background music had no significant effect on ESP scores, in experiments where there was other evidence of ESP in the data. Palmer, Bogart, Jones, and Tart (1977) discovered that redecorating a barren-looking laboratory room failed to reverse a psi-missing trend in a free-response ganzfeld experiment.

Pratt (1961) noted that the great majority of high-scoring ESP subjects reported upon in the *Journal of Parapsychology* up to that time did exceptionally well when tested in their own homes, often better than when tested in the laboratory. This observation was significantly confirmed in a more systematic fashion in an experiment with unselected children as subjects (Drucker, Drewes, and Rubin, 1977). However, Eilbert and Schmeidler (1950) found that college students scored significantly higher when tested at the college than when asked to come to the *experimenter's* home to be tested.

Finally, Woodruff (1943) introduced ESP tests into an experiment designed primarily to test the effect of low temperatures and oxygen deprivation on a motor task. College students completed five DT runs before and five after each of eight sessions involving various combinations of stress factors. Stress was not present during the tests themselves, however. A significant decrease in scoring following the session, as compared to before the session, was obtained; but it was entirely attributable to the control condition where the only effective variable apparently was boredom.

2.4.1a. Conclusion. There are a few studies that suggest that adverse environmental conditions lead to decrements in ESP scoring, provided that they are sufficiently extreme. The possibility that ESP scores may be improved by testing subjects in their own homes should be explored further, when the requirements of the experimental design permit.

2.4.2. Incentives: Here Comes the Bribe*

It is almost a religion among many parapsychologists that high ESP scores depend upon the subject being strongly motivated to achieve such scores (e.g., Smith and Gibson, 1941). Incredibly, there are only a few

*This subheading was stolen from Dr. Lawrence Casler.

experiments in the literature where motivational variables have been directly manipulated. They can be broken down into those involving tangible incentives, such as money, and intangible incentives, such as knowledge of results.

2.4.2a. Tangible Incentives. In a precognition experiment with adult and child subjects, Rhine (1941a) offered rewards ranging from candy bars to $100 for high scores on some runs. There was no significant difference between overall scores on these runs and other runs in the experiment, although rewards seemed to lead to somewhat improved scores among the child subjects. Woodruff and Murphy (1943) assigned one group of subjects to a condition where they received 5¢ for each hit obtained in a second set of clairvoyance runs above what they achieved in the first set. Control subjects were offered no rewards. There was an increase in scoring rate from the first to second set of runs in the experimental group, but it was not significant, nor apparently was it significantly different from the change in the control group. Woodruff and George (1937) introduced a manipulation of financial incentive (this time, theater tickets) with two high-scoring subjects, but the results were highly ambiguous. Sprinthall and Lubetkin (1965) offered half of the subjects they tested $100 if they could get a score of 20 or higher on one BT run. Both the experimental and the control groups scored close to chance. Palmer and Miller (1972) found that a significant relationship between ESP scores and an attitude scale was significantly reduced when a $10 reward was offered for the highest score.

2.4.2b. Feedback as Incentive. Participating in an ESP test can have its own intrinsic rewards, provided the subject can learn how well he or she scored. However, as any college student who has to wait weeks and weeks for an exam grade will tell you, a long delay in receiving such feedback can be more frustrating than receiving no feedback at all.

Rhine (1938a) reported the results of close to 5,000 clairvoyance runs completed by 175 subjects in eight experiments by various investigators. Results were positive to a highly significant degree when subjects received immediate feedback of their scores after each run. Less extreme but still significant psi-missing occurred when feedback was delayed several days. The latter were experiments where decks of cards were mailed to subjects who made their guesses and then mailed the cards and record sheets back to Duke for scoring. Sometimes these latter subjects never received their actual scores. Cases where the scores were checked at the end of a session but not after each run produced chance results. Comparable effects were found when an even larger number of precognition runs were broken down in this way (Rhine, 1941a). Although these results could be attributable to any one of a number of procedural differences,

Rhine felt that negativism (possibly unconscious) resulting from the delay in feedback was the most likely interpretation.

A somewhat better test of this hypothesis is provided by the experiment of Woodruff and Murphy (1943). Experimental subjects, who received feedback of their scores after each of four runs and knew beforehand that this would be the case, scored significantly higher than the control subjects, who received no feedback. Although feedback was somewhat confounded with monetary incentive in this experiment, the internal analyses suggest that the feedback was the most powerful factor.

2.4.2c. Feedback as Direct Cause. Schmidt (1975) has theorized that feedback actually may exert a direct causal influence, backward in time, on ESP scores. If he is right, feedback should be psi-facilatory, but not because of its incentive value.

An experiment relevant to this issue was conducted by Schmeidler (1964a, b), who gave her subjects feedback on only one of three runs. She found no significant differences between the mean scores on feedback and nonfeedback runs in each of two series. This finding is not directly relevant to the incentive hypothesis, because subjects did not know in advance on which runs they would receive feedback. However, a mean difference would seem to be a logical prediction from Schmidt's theory. Although Schmidt (1975) argued that feedback to the experimenter may have washed out any effect of differential feedback to subjects, Schmeidler's study still stands as evidence against the applicability of Schmidt's theory to the results of Rhine and of Woodruff discussed above.

A more recent study by Broughton (1977b), however, provided at least a modicum of support for Schmidt's theory. Subjects each completed two runs on an electronic device similar to Schmidt's machine. After these runs were completed, the computer generated a random "hypothesis" as to which run score should be higher. Half of the subjects received feedback of their correct scores, while the other half received pseudoscores generated randomly by the computer. The main finding of the study was a significant confirmation of the computer's "hypotheses," but only with respect to those scores actually reported to the subject, whether they were his own scores or not. (All subjects thought the scores they received were their own.) However, no significant results were obtained in a strict replication attempt of this experiment. Obviously, more research will be needed before a pattern emerges that will allow us to assess the validity of Schmidt's theory as it applies to ESP.

2.4.2d. Conclusion. Tangible incentives such as monetary rewards for high scores do not seem to facilitate ESP, but there is some evidence that providing subjects with immediate feedback of their scores may be more successful. This latter effect can be explained most readily in terms of the incentive value of such feedback, although a physical theory of psi has been proposed which assumes that feedback can have a direct causal influence on ESP scores. Other types of nontangible incentives (e.g., approval of the experimenter) simply have not been investigated experimentally.

2.5. Social Psychological Factors: The Interpersonal Side of ESP

2.5.1. The Telepathic Agent: Vital Cog or Excess Baggage?

To the early psychical researchers, the most prominent form of ESP was telepathy, or direct communication between two minds (Myers, 1903/1975). This imbalance evaporated when Rhine (1934/1973) stressed that his subjects could obtain impressive ESP scores when no one was trying to "send" them the targets, or even when no one knew what the target order was at the time. Although a few successful experiments had been reported in which agents concentrated on target symbols that had not yet been recorded (Rhine, 1934/1973; Soal and Bateman, 1954), there was always the possibility that information about the target orders written down after the session could be acquired by precognitive clairvoyance. These factors caused Rhine (1945b, 1946) to conclude that telepathy as such had not been adequately demonstrated.

2.5.1a. The Status of "Pure" Telepathy. An associate of Rhine devised an ingenious procedure to get around the clairvoyance interpretation (McMahan, 1946). She prepared decks of cards containing numerical stimuli and then memorized an unwritten code translating the numbers to ESP symbols. She communicated the code orally to another staff member who was responsible for verifying the scoring of results. During the experiment, McMahan picked up the cards one by one and "sent" the appropriate symbol. There was no way the subject could demonstrate ESP unless he could "break" the code telepathically. The code itself was never recorded.

McMahan conducted five separate series with this procedure, all of which used unselected subjects and none of which gave significant positive results. Nevertheless, some indirect evidence of telepathy was obtained in the final series, for which subjects were divided into two groups based upon personality measures and scores on a previous clairvoyance test. The two groups differed significantly on the telepathy test in a direction that confirmed previous findings with the more conventional GESP procedure. Birge (1948) also failed to obtain significant psi-hitting on real-time targets with McMahan's procedure in three separate series, but a post hoc analysis revealed significant psi-hitting on +1 targets.

A similar mental coding technique was adapted by Soal to his standard testing paradigm, the percipient being Gloria Stewart. Three sessions with this procedure yielded highly significant positive scoring. Unfortunately, the controversial status of Soal's research makes it unwise to put much weight on these findings.

2.5.1b. GESP versus Clairvoyance: Subjects Not "Blind." Whatever the status of "pure telepathy," the widespread use of GESP procedures in psi experiments is ample evidence that many experimenters believe the presence of an agent may improve the chances of a successful outcome. Although many significant results have been obtained using the GESP method, the effect of having an agent can only be assessed adequately in those experiments where GESP and clairvoyance (or precognition) procedures are directly compared. Experiments in which the percipients were not informed or were misinformed about whether an agent was sending the targets on a particular run are most valuable as tests of the agent's actual effect on the results. In experiments where percipients were not "blind" in this respect, it is unclear whether significant differences should be attributed to a telepathic component in the psi interaction or to psychological factors associated with the percipient. For example, the percipient might be more relaxed, more confident, or more highly motivated if he thinks someone is sending to him, even if no agent actually exists.

Let us first consider experiments where the percipient was *not* "blind." Among "gifted" subjects, both Shackleton and Stewart (Soal and Bateman, 1954) and the distinguished trance medium Eileen Garrett (Birge and Rhine, 1942) scored significantly better in card tests when a GESP procedure as opposed to a clairvoyance procedure was used.

Group experiments in which GESP and clairvoyance runs were given to the same subjects in the same session have failed to produce significant differences, although in some cases significant relationships were found between pooled ESP scores and other variables (Adcock and Quartermain, 1959; Beloff, 1969; Bevan, 1947a,b; Casper, 1951, 1952; Rivers, 1950; West, 1950). Two experiments using between-groups designs also failed to reveal any significant differences between the two types of test (Altom and Braud, 1976; Casler, 1962). Palmer, Tart, and Redington (1976), however, found that in a screening experiment involving over 1,800 college students tested in a classroom setting, scoring was significantly higher on a GESP run than on a BT run within subjects, the GESP mean being significantly above chance. Agents were partly visible to subjects in this experiment; thus sensory cues were not completely ruled out. Barring such an interpretation, these results suggest that an agent may contribute to higher scoring but that large samples are needed to demonstrate the effect.

   2.5.1c. GESP versus Clairvoyance: Subjects "Blind." In smaller studies, however, significant results actually have occurred more frequently when the subject was "blind" regarding the agent. The "gifted" subject Lalsingh Harribance scored significantly above chance on GESP but close to chance on clairvoyance when the two types of run were alternated (Klein, 1972). Harribance was under the impression that all runs were GESP (Morris, personal communication), the procedure which he preferred (Klein, 1972). However, it should be noted that on other occasions Harribance achieved comparably high scores on clairvoyance tests when this procedure was used exclusively (e.g., Roll and Klein, 1972). MacFarland (1938) found significantly higher scoring among five male college students on GESP than on DT runs, the subjects apparently believing that DT was used throughout. Unfortunately, the GESP runs always were given first, introducing the possibility that the difference reflects nothing more than a decline effect (see Sec. 4.2.1.). This experiment also became the object of a methodological controversy (Kennedy, 1939; Stuart, 1940). Bierman and Camstra (1973) found higher scoring on GESP than on clairvoyance trials in each of two classroom experiments involving 88 and 1,402 high school students, respectively. However, the significance levels of the differences were unclear from the report, as was the method of ordering the two types of trials. Subjects apparently thought all trials were GESP.

   Kreitler and Kreitler (1972, 1973) reported a series of four GESP experiments in which, unbeknownst to the percipient, an agent attempted to influence his or her performance on a relatively unstructured psychological test. In the first of these experiments the percipient's task was to identify letters of the alphabet projected subliminally. The Kreitlers found that the subjects were significantly more successful on those trials where an agent in another room was attempting to transmit the correct letter than on control trials. A successful replication of this finding was reported by Lubke and Rohr (1975).

   In the last of these experiments, which also involved subliminal perception, the Kreitlers varied whether the ESP stimulus supported or contradicted the subliminal stimulus and also whether the agent was actually attempting to transmit the ESP stimulus or simply thinking about it. Both the subliminal and ESP stimuli were components of classical illusions (e.g., the Muller–Lyer illusion), and the percipient's task was to report which of two identical supraliminal lines or circles (the basic stimuli of the illusions) seemed longer or larger. A significant post hoc effect was found, indicating that the ESP stimulus was most effective when it contradicted the subliminal stimulus and was being "transmitted" by the agent. Although the order of the latter variable was not counterbalanced (cf. Child, 1977), the Kreitlers' finding would not seem to correspond to a traditional decline effect.

In the two other experiments, no significant main effect was found using autokinetic perception as the psychological test, but at least a partial confirmation of the effect was found using the Thematic Apperception Test (Kreitler and Kreitler, 1972; Child, 1977).

In a free-response ganzfeld experiment, Raburn and Manning (1977) manipulated both the actual presence of an agent and the subject's information about same in a 2 × 2 factorial design. Both main effects were significant, indicating that the highest scores occurred when an agent was present and the subject was aware that his ESP was being tested. These results seem to suggest that both the presence of an agent and the subjects' awareness of this fact contribute to positive scoring. However, the latter conclusion would be more compelling were control subjects given a clairvoyance set rather than a set that ESP was not involved in the experiment at all.

Not all experiments with "blind" subjects have provided results favoring GESP, however. In an experiment with college students that may not have been adequately controlled against sensory cues, Coover (1917) obtained significant positive scoring when GESP and clairvoyance scores were pooled, but no significant difference between them (Rhine, 1934/1973). Better controlled runs with psychics as subjects produced chance results. Whether or not the agent was to look at the card during the trial was determined randomly on a trial-by-trial basis, and the agent looked at the card immediately after the trial even on clairvoyance trials. In two of her "pure telepathy" experiments, McMahan (1946) conducted a BT clairvoyance test simultaneously with the telepathy test by picking up cards from the two decks at the same time. The same subjects participated in both experiments. In the first experiment, they were told that only telepathy was being tested while in the second they were told it was only clairvoyance. The overall results revealed significant positive scoring on clairvoyance and slightly below chance scoring on telepathy, but the difference was not significant. Note, however, that this design differs appreciably from that of other experiments we have reviewed so far in this section. In three experiments with college students, Schmeidler (1961) divided her subjects into agent–percipient pairs and gave each pair two GESP and two clairvoyance runs. Percipients apparently thought all runs were GESP. There were no overall significant differences as a function of run type, but there were significant internal effects that we will examine shortly. An Argentine psychiatrist scored significantly above chance to about equal degrees with both methods in a free-response experiment. He was led to believe that only a GESP procedure was used. Randall (1974) found no significant GESP–clairvoyance differences in six classroom ESP tests with high school students.

Finally, several ESP experiments with animals have provided data relevant to the topic of GESP in "blind" subjects. In an experiment described in more detail later, Schouten (1972) trained mice to press one of two levers for water reward. Which lever was to be rewarded in each trial was determined by a random number generator. On some trials, another mouse (the "agent") was present in a cage where a discriminable cue stimulus appeared. The "agent" also received water rewards, but only on those trials in which the "percipient" pressed the correct lever. Schouten found no significant difference in mean scores on the GESP and clairvoyance trials, but he did find a significant negative correlation between the individual percipients' scores on the two types of trials, a result reminiscent of Rao's (1965a) "differential effect" (see Sec. 2.2.1c). Follow-up experiments failed to provide significant results, however (Schouten, 1976b). Using a shock-avoidance paradigm, Extra (1972) found in each of two experiments a marginally significant tendency for rats to receive fewer shocks when the experimenter heard a warning stimulus (inaudible to the rat) than when he did not.

2.5.1d. Effect of Different Agents. One possible explanation of the inconsistent results from experiments comparing clairvoyance and GESP is that they depend upon who happens to be selected as the agent. In the large-sample classroom experiment of Palmer *et al.* (1976), for example, there was a significant interaction between type of test and which agent/experimenter team did the testing. The significantly higher scoring on the GESP run was found to be almost entirely attributable to subjects tested by one of the five teams. These subjects scored significantly above chance on GESP and significantly below chance on clairvoyance. Tart (1976a) found that one of the agent/experimenters in his ESP training experiment obtained highly significant scores with most of his subjects, a performance generally not matched by the other agents.

Schmeidler (1961) attempted to predict the GESP scoring trends of her agent–percipient pairs on the basis of their responses on a group Rorschach test. In two of the three experiments, predicted low scorers obtained significant below-chance scores on GESP, in contrast to significantly higher but chance scores obtained on the clairvoyance runs. No significant results were obtained with the predicted high scorers.

Several classroom ESP experiments have examined the question of whether students would score higher when the agent was their teacher or someone they both knew well and liked. Anderson and White (1958a) had two teachers "send" conflicting target sequences simultaneously to a class of high school students. Students got the highest scores on target sequences sent by teachers they had independently ranked as "preferred." White and Angstadt (1963b) obtained comparable results in an experiment where the competing agents were a student nominated by his classmates and his counterpart from another class, but this result could not be significantly replicated (White and Angstadt, 1963a). Louwerens (1960) found that Dutch nursery school children obtained very high scores when their teachers served as agents, but nonsignificant results when the experimenter assumed this role. Unfortunately, the design was such that the session with the experimenter always followed the session with the teacher, so the decline may simply have been due to repeated testing. Van Busschbach (1955) also found significant psi-hitting among grade school children with their teacher as agent, but results were almost as good when the agent was a stranger. Wiesinger (1973) found the teacher's attitude toward parapsychology and the "test atmosphere" to be predictive of ESP scoring, but not the attitudes of teachers and pupils toward each other. Better results overall were obtained when children were the agents rather than the teacher.

Another common procedure is to compose agent–percipient pairs of persons who are closely acquainted with each other or who are fond of each other. Several such studies have employed control groups. In two of these, closely acquainted pairs scored significantly above chance while unacquainted pairs scored significantly below chance (Stuart, 1946a; Rice and Townsend, 1962). Unfortunately, Stuart's study, a free-response drawing experiment, can be criticized because conclusions were based on the results of "non-blind" judging procedures, and the Rice study allowed agents easy opportunities to cheat, were they so inclined. In the third study, agent–percipient pairs were composed of college students who either liked or disliked each other as determined by a peer rating procedure (Casper, 1952). On GESP runs, the incompatible pairs scored significantly *higher* than the compatible pairs. This effect reversed slightly on clairvoyance control runs. In a fourth study, spouses scored significantly above chance and (it would appear) significantly higher than strangers (Beer, 1971). Subjects were aware of the agent's identity in all these experiments. Moss, on the other hand, reports that agent–percipient rapport has consistently failed to be a factor in a series of free-response experiments (e.g., Moss, 1969). In experiments that lacked control groups, null results have been found in GESP experiments where the agent–percipient pairs consisted of "sweethearts" (Beloff, 1969), spouses (Brinkman and Van Hilten, 1972), and persons defined as having "sympathetic relationships" (Van't Hoff, 1972). Finally, Casler (1971) failed in an attempt to improve GESP scoring by creating rapport between agent and percipient through appropriate hypnotic suggestions given to one or the other.

2.5.1e. Conclusion. There is as yet no convincing experimental evidence of direct "mind-to-mind" communication, i.e., telepathy, that adequately controls for clairvoyance or precognition. Nonetheless, indirect support for the telepathy hypothesis comes from several experiments in which significant differences betweeen GESP and clairvoyance scores were found when percipients were "blind" to the type of test. However, these results have not been entirely consistent and some of the positive experiments have weaknesses in design or reporting of results. Other evidence indicates that some of this inconsistency may be attributable to the fact that different agents often affect percipients' scores in different ways. Attempts to demonstrate that persons well known or well liked by percipients make the most successful agents have produced conflicting results, although the general trend is confirmatory.

Finally, the question of whether telepathy, assuming its existence, is primarily attributable to the agent, the percipient, or some interaction between them has yet to be directly addressed experimentally.

2.5.2. The Experimenter Effect: Psychology or Psi?

In the last section we saw that the agent can have an effect on scoring in ESP tests. In this section we will examine evidence that demonstrates that a person need not be involved in actually "sending" the targets to have such an effect. The person we will be focusing upon predominantly, but not exclusively, is the experimenter. We will consider not only whether or not he or she can influence experimental outcomes but also whether the vehicle of such influence is the method of interacting with subjects, or whether the experimenter's own psi (or potential for activating the subject's psi in the absence of sensory contact) may somehow be a contributing factor.

A number of experiments have been reported in which two experimenters conducting the same experiment with the same or similar subjects have obtained significantly different results. Although not an experimenter effect in the strict sense of the term, a finding of Sharp and Clark (1937) indicated that testing sessions conducted with a skeptical observer present produced significantly below-chance scoring, whereas subjects scored above chance when the observer was sympathetic to ESP. Subjects apparently did not know of the observers' beliefs, but one subject complained that the skeptical observer distracted her. In an experiment where five subjects responded to two competing target sequences handled by two different experimenters, they scored very significantly above chance on one set of sequences and close to chance on the other. The effect occurred with both GESP and DT clairvoyance procedures (MacFarland, 1938). Osis and Dean (1964) reported the results of clairvoyance tests given to eight audiences following 40-minute lectures on ESP. Partway through the experiment, Osis became ill and Dean had to take over the role of lecturer-experimenter. Despite the fact that Dean gave essentially the same lecture and conducted the experiment in the same way as Osis, the groups tested by Osis scored significantly higher than those tested by Dean, the difference being most pronounced among those subjects who indicated the strongest belief in ESP. Although we have no assurance that the groups tested by the two experimenters were truly comparable, the experimenter effect remains the most likely interpretation. Still another experimenter difference was found in classroom testing of British schoolboys by Beloff and Bate (1970).

   2.5.2a. Experimenter Psychology. The most obvious interpretation of such experimenter differences is that different experimenters sometimes create different moods, sets, motivational levels, or psychological "atmospheres," which in turn determine whether ESP will occur and, if so, whether it will manifest as psi-hitting or psi-missing. The first experiment to test this hypothesis directly was by Pratt and Price (1938). Margaret Price, who had a history of being a highly successful experimenter (e.g., Price, 1938; Bates and Newton, 1951), treated some subjects in a friendly, encouraging manner and others in an abrupt, discouraging manner. She found that in both instances her subjects scored around chance. However, scores markedly increased to their usual high level when she returned to her more natural way of relating to subjects. Her natural approach encouraged spontaneity during the test, a factor that seems to facilitate psi (see Sec. 2.3.2b).

   A more systematic attempt to test the above hypothesis was reported by Honorton, Ramsey, and Cabibbo (1975). Subjects were randomly assigned to one of two groups. One group was tested by an experimenter instructed to be friendly and supportive, while the other group was tested by an experimenter given the opposite set. Each subject completed 200 trials on a Schmidt machine. Each of two experimenters tested subjects in each group. As predicted, there was significant psi-hitting in the group tested by a "friendly" experimenter and significant psi-missing in the group tested by an "unfriendly" experimenter.

   Parker (1975a) found that agent–percipient pairs scored significantly higher in a GESP card-guessing experiment when tested by one of three experimenters who believed in ESP than when tested by one of three experimenters who did not. Both sets of experimenters had been given lectures prior to the experiment that supported their biases. Taddonio (1976) chose to manipulate experimenters' expectancies regarding whether the type of ESP test to be employed should produce psi-hitting or psi-missing. Each experimenter tested a separate group of subjects. The results significantly confirmed the experimenters' expectations in both a preliminary experiment and a replication attempt. Other data pertinent to the effect of the beliefs projected by experimenters are discussed in Sec. 3.6.1c.

   2.5.2b. Teacher–Pupil Attitudes. In the above experiments, the behavior of the experimenters was systematically manipulated. However, it is obvious that different experimenters can create different psychological effects on subjects simply by "being themselves," and such effects can still influence ESP scoring.

   Margaret Anderson and Rhea White reasoned that such an effect should be especially pronounced when pupils are tested by their own teachers, with whom they have had close contact for prolonged periods. In the previous section, evidence was cited that some teachers make particularly good agents in GESP tests, but Anderson and White thought they might also make good experimenters in clairvoyance tests, provided teacher–pupil rapport was high. More specifically, they predicted that ESP scores should be most positive when teachers and pupils felt most positive toward each other and most negative when the mutual feeling was negative. In a series of well-designed experiments, they prepared a separate target sequence of ESP symbols for each pupil in the class and sealed them in opaque envelopes. Blank record sheets were pasted on top of the envelopes for the pupils to record their responses. In addition, the pupils were asked to fill out anonymous rating scales evaluating their teachers. The teacher, in turn, was asked to respond yes or no for each student to the question "If you could form your ideal group for this class, would you include this student?" The teacher then administered the ESP test to his or her class and returned all the materials to Anderson for scoring.

   In the first experimental series, the pooled results from seven high school classes confirmed the hypothesis to a highly significant degree (Anderson and White, 1956). A strict replication attempt with a sample consisting of seven new classes was equally successful (Anderson and White, 1957), as was a replication attempt by Deguisne (1959). In each case, student attitudes contributed more strongly to the effect than did teacher attitudes. In an extension of the paradigm, pupils were tested twice, once at the beginning of the school term and once at the end. It was found that scores on the two occasions changed in the same direction as student attitudes toward their teachers (Anderson and White, 1958b). In general, the pattern has been for overall scores to be near chance in the Anderson–White experiments: psi-missing when attitudes are negative canceling out psi-hitting when attitudes are positive.

Unfortunately, a number of experiments with high school students failed to confirm these earlier results (Anderson and White, 1958c; White and Angstadt, 1961, 1965). Rilling, Pettijohn, and Adams (1961) confirmed the hypothesis with respect to pupil attitudes but found a significant reversal with respect to teacher attitudes. Nonetheless, a pooling of the successful and unsuccessful experiments revealed a highly significant confirmation of the original Anderson–White hypothesis, i.e., significant psi-hitting when attitudes were mutually positive and significant psi-missing when they were mutually negative. The relationship was even stronger when student evaluations alone were considered (White and Angstadt, 1965).

Despite one early success (Anderson, 1957), the Anderson–White hypothesis has not been supported with grade school students (Anderson and White, 1958c; Eisenbud, Hassel, Keely, and Sawrey, 1960; Goldstone, 1959; Hall, 1958; Rilling, Adams, and Pettijohn, 1962). Two experiments in which college students were tested by their professors also failed to produce positive results (Anderson and White, 1958c; Rilling *et al.*, 1962), although Rilling reported a perfect positive relationship between his four class means and the estimated attitude of the professors toward the reality of psychic phenomena. Nash (1960b) obtained a significant confirmation of the hypothesis among college students by having classmates take turns testing each other. The attitudes of college students toward the experimenter were associated in more complex ways with ESP scores in other research by this author (Nash, 1964).

In summary, the first Anderson–White experiment has probably spawned more replication attempts than any other experiment in parapsychology. With high school students, the rate of replicability has been high by parapsychological standards, especially with respect to pupil attitudes toward their teachers. It is not clear why the effect does not hold up for grade school and college students. Perhaps passing through the stage of "adolescent rebellion" causes interpersonal relationships between students and teachers to be more dynamic for high school students than for the other groups. If so, the import of these findings might be that relatively powerful feelings may be necessary if attitudes toward the experimenter are to influence ESP scoring.

2.5.2c. Sex of Experimenter. One set of powerful feelings that most of us share concerns sex. Stanford and Associates (1976) attempted to capitalize on this drive in an experiment where the scores obtained by male subjects on a disguised ESP test determined whether they later would get to examine erotic photographs. The authors hypothesized that the female experimenters would be sexually arousing to their male subjects, thereby giving the erotic pictures more incentive value than they possessed for subjects tested by male experimenters, thus leading to higher ESP scores. Subjects tested by female experimenters in fact scored significantly above chance and significantly higher than those tested by male experimenters.

In a more conventional experiment, Woodruff and Dale (1950) took turns testing each of 50 female subjects in different sessions, 20 DT runs per session. Following each session, subject and experimenter both filled out rating scales describing how they felt about each other, the experiment, and their general mood and sense of well-being. In the case of the male experimenter, the surprising result was a significant tendency for higher scores to occur when the two participants felt neutral about each other than when rapport was exceptionally good. No such trend appeared with the female experimenter. A possible interpretation of this post hoc and admittedly tenuous finding is that when subject and experimenter are of the opposite sex, rapport that is too good diverts attention from the ESP test and leads to poorer performance. This interpretation would not be relevant to Stanford's experiment, because the ESP aspect of the test did not require conscious attention (see Sec. 5.1. for a discussion of Stanford's methodology).

2.5.2d. Experimenter Psi. Up to this point, we have been dealing with cases where the subject and experimenter interacted with each other directly. Under such circumstances, it is most reasonable to assume that experimenter effects are mediated by the psychological ramifications of the overt subject–experimenter interaction. However, other data suggest that persons involved with the experiment but not interacting with the subject can also influence scoring in some way.

In a classic but sketchily reported experiment by West and Fisk (1953), 20 subjects were asked to guess the orders of 32 packs of "clock cards" with 12 cards per pack. Half of the packs were prepared by Fisk, who had generally obtained positive results as an experimenter (e.g., Fisk, 1951a, b; Fisk and Mitchell, 1953; Michie and West, 1957). The other half were prepared by West, who obtained chance results with equal consistency (e.g., West, 1950, 1952; Michie and West, 1957). The order in which subjects guessed the packs was systematically varied in a Latin Square design, and the subjects were unaware of the manipulation of experimenters. Despite the fact that the experiment was conducted by correspondence and the experimenter had no direct contact with the subjects, there was highly significant positive scoring on the packs prepared by Fisk and only chance scoring on those prepared by West.

A similar type of effect serendipitously intruded into an experiment by Price (1973b), who discovered that his subjects selectively achieved high scores on certain targets prepared by an experimental assistant who happened to be in a very negative mood at the time. Although post hoc, this finding suggests that experimenters may need to pay attention to such subtle mood factors in the execution of their experiments. Complex experimenter mood effects also have been reported in the work of Osis (Osis and Carlson, 1972; Osis *et al.*, 1971), but capitalization on chance seems a likely explanation for most of these findings.

In a series of experiments intentionally aimed at detecting experimenter psi effects, Feather and Brier (1968) obtained evidence that subjects may be sensitive to who will score the record sheets of an experiment even before that person is designated. In each of three experiments, subjects completed four precognition runs. They were told that the experimenter would score only two of the four runs himself, and that they were to predict which two. Afterwards, the runs to be scored by the experimenter were determined randomly. With respect to these latter runs only, subjects scored significantly higher on those they accurately predicted the experimenter would score than on the other runs. Such an effect did not occur on the runs scored by the other checker. The effect was independently significant in the first two experiments pooled and in the third experiment. Sensitivity to the scorer also might explain the results of the West and Fisk experiment, since each experimenter also checked the results of the packs he prepared.

Only one experiment so far has attempted to discriminate between the psychological and psi interpretations of the experimenter effect (Parker, 1977). Several parapsychologists were cornered at a recent convention and asked to fill out two personality scales, one of which was a disguised ESP test. Independent judges then divided the subjects into two approximately equal groups on the basis of how frequently they reported significant evidence of psi in their experiments. The two groups did not differ significantly on any of the personality traits thought to distinguish successful and unsuccessful experimenters, but the successful experimenters were the only ones to provide significant evidence of psi on the covert ESP test. Thus Parker's results favor the psi interpretation of the experimenter effect.

2.5.2e. Conclusion. To keep things in perspective, it should be pointed out that having more than one experimenter test one's subjects does not automatically guarantee a significant experimenter effect (e.g.,

Broughton and Millar, 1975; Craig, 1975; Musso, 1965; Parker, Millar, and Beloff, 1977; Price and Pegram, 1937; Sailaja and Rao, 1973), although there was some evidence of experimenter effects in the Broughton, the Craig, and the Sailaja experiments. On the other hand, it seems clear that under certain circumstances experimenters can unwittingly make or break their own experiments. There is evidence that how experimenters treat their subjects, their beliefs about ESP and about the outcome of their experiments, how much they are liked by their subjects, and even their sex can influence the results of ESP experiments. Such factors also may explain why some telepathic agents are more successful than others in GESP experiments; in reality, the distinction between agent and experimenter may not be a very important one.

Somewhat harder to swallow is the growing evidence that persons outside the immediate experimental context and whose functions are unknown to the subjects at the time of the test can influence the results. One thing that makes such results so unpalatable is the difficulty in specifying the mechanism involved in producing such effects. One possibility is ESP and/or PK on the part of the experimenter. For example, Fisk might have unwittingly used ESP to decipher the calling biases of his subjects and then used ESP or PK to generate technically random target orders to match these biases. Psi has been known to be capable of such complex feats (e.g., Morris, 1968). A second possibility involves unconscious ESP on the part of the subject. For example, Alan Price's subjects might have unconsciously "picked up" on the distress of the experimental assistant, thus making the targets prepared by her more salient to them. As pointed out by Eisenbud (1963), it is naive to think subjects can use ESP to identify targets and not also use it to identify other aspects of the experimental situation. Note that this interpretation does not assume active psi on the part of the experimenter. At this point, however, both interpretations remain speculative.

A second unpalatable feature of psi-based experimenter effects is that they create monumental complexities for the experimenter who wishes to design a tightly controlled ESP experiment or to replicate such an experiment. Indeed, experimenter effects may be responsible for much of the lack of independent replicability in ESP research. The Heisenberg Uncertainty Principle has invaded parapsychology, as it has all the behavioral sciences. The observer can no longer be considered apart from the observed.

For the reader who wants to delve further into this topic, a number of recent review articles are available (Kennedy and Taddonio, 1976; Thouless, 1976; White, 1976a, b).

2.6. Altered States of Consciousness: Tuning In by Turning On

The idea that ESP abilities can be enhanced by entering a so-called altered state of consciousness (ASC) dates back at least to the Indian sage Patanjali (2nd century B.C.), and it was a dominant concept of 19th-century parapsychology. Although the era of the great trance mediums has largely passed, contemporary parapsychologists have shown a renewed interest in techniques that help one to withdraw attention from the external world. The most extensively studied of such techniques has been hypnosis.

2.6.1. Hypnosis: The Power of Suggestion

The association between hypnotism and psychic phenomena has been proclaimed since the early days of Mesmerism. A number of dramatic examples are reported in the literature of the 18th and 19th centuries, but none of these demonstrations meet modern standards of experimental control (see Dingwall, 1967). The most impressive of these early experiments were those of Gilbert and Janet, who repeatedly succeeded in causing a peasant woman named Leonie to enter hypnosis from a distance of half a mile. More recently, hypnosis at a distance has been demonstrated by a series of experiments in the Soviet Union (Vasiliev, 1962). While these experiments seem to be better controlled than the early French work, fully detailed reports are not available.

2.6.1a. Forced-Choice Experiments. Rhine attempted to use hypnosis in some of the early Duke research but eventually abandoned the technique as unfruitful (Rhine *et al.*, 1940/1966). However, in the 1950s and 1960s a number of experimental reports appeared in the literature which painted a much more optimistic picture. The bulk of these findings were contributed by three experimenters: Jarl Fahler, Lawrence Casler, and Charles Honorton.

Fahler's results were by far the most impressive statistically (Fahler, 1957; Fahler and Cadoret, 1958; Fahler and Osis, 1966). He used standard card-guessing techniques, generally testing the same subjects under both hypnosis and "waking" control conditions, a procedure that unfortunately increases the likelihood of demand characteristics confounding the interpretation of results. It is unclear from the reports whether suggestions of success on the ESP test accompanied the hypnotic inductions. Fahler generally obtained highly significant psi-hitting in the hypnosis conditions and mostly chance results in the control conditions, although in one experiment (Fahler and Osis, 1966) the hitting was restricted to those trials on which the subject expressed confidence that his or her guess was correct (see Sec. 4.1.3).

Casler (1962, 1964, 1967, 1971) also used standard card-guessing methodology, but his experimental designs were somewhat cleaner than those of Fahler. He used college students exclusively as subjects, and each subject was tested under both hypnosis and "waking" conditions. Moderately significant differences favoring hypnosis were reported in four of the five published experiments, although a sixth unpublished experiment briefly mentioned by Casler (1964) failed to achieve significance. In the other nonsignificant experiment, the hypnotic suggestions were oriented toward enhancing agent–percipient rapport rather than ESP scoring per se (Casler, 1971). No suggestions at all regarding the ESP test were given in two other experiments, one of which was successful (Casler, 1964). The fact that subjects predicted higher scores for the hypnosis runs than for the control runs in this experiment indicates that suggestions of success may have been present implicitly. One of the interesting and so far unresolved issues in the hypnosis–ESP area is whether hypnosis facilitates ESP because it induces an ASC, because it creates an expectation or attitude change, or both.

Honorton used hypnosis in an effort to enhance both psi-hitting and psi-missing in subjects preselected for these directional scoring tendencies on the basis of responses on the Stuart Interest Inventory (see Sec. 3.2.4). Standard DT card-guessing techniques were employed throughout, and scores on hypnosis and control runs again were compared within subjects. In the experiments where hypnosis was accompanied by suggestions of success (Honorton, 1964, 1966), hypnosis produced significant psi-missing in the predicted missers but was unsuccessful for the predicted hitters. Matters were further complicated by the failure of the attitude scale to properly predict scoring direction in the control runs. In the third study (Honorton, 1969a), where "waking" suggestions were used without hypnosis, the results were of marginal significance, suggestions having the most pronounced effect this time on the predicted hitters. In the fourth study (Honorton, 1969a), where the suggestions of success were indirect and impersonal, they had no discernible effect on ESP scores.

In summary, hypnotic suggestions of success seemed more effective (at least in producing the predicted effect) in Honorton's experiments than personal "waking" suggestions, which in turn seemed more effective than impersonal "waking" suggestions or no suggestions at all. Likewise, subjects' confidence of success, as inferred from their predictions of scores before each run, declined monotonically across these experimental conditions. This pattern indirectly suggests that hypnosis influenced ESP scoring primarily because of its effect on subjects' expectancies. On the other hand, Van de Castle and Davis (1962) reported somewhat better results with hypnosis when suggestions of success were not included (see also Honorton and Krippner, 1969).

Forced-choice ESP–hypnosis experiments by other experimenters have produced mixed results. The first formal experiment of this type was reported by Grela (1945). He found significant psi-hitting among college students when hypnosis was combined with suggestions of success, but the scores were not significantly higher than those in various control conditions. Rao (1964a) reported a significant difference between the hypnosis and "waking" runs of a single subject, but the difference was contributed largely by psi-missing on the waking runs. In an earlier experiment, the same informal hypnotic induction failed to produce overall significant scoring, but there was no control group (Rao, 1963c). McBain, Fox, Kimura, Nakanishi, and Tirado (1970) incorporated hypnosis in a very carefully conceived GESP experiment in which overall significant psi-hitting was obtained, but again there was no control group. Essentially chance results have been report by Nash and Durkin (1959), Edmunds and Jolliffe, (1965), and Stephenson, (1965).

2.6.1b. Free-Response Experiments—the Hypnotic "Dream." Hypnosis most frequently has been applied to free-response ESP experiments in the guise of the hypnotic "dream." Following a standard hypnotic induction, the subject is given the suggestion to have a dream that will include the content of a randomly selected picture being concentrated upon by an agent. Honorton has reported significant psi-hitting with this procedure among female subjects selected for high susceptibility to hypnosis (Honorton and Stump, 1969; Honorton, 1972b). The latter study incorporated various control conditions involving no hypnosis and/or low-susceptible subjects, all of which produced chance results. Furthermore, ESP scores in the hypnosis groups were significantly and positively related to two measures of subjects' reported change in their states of consciousness during the session. Parker and Beloff (1970) reported two attempted replications of Honorton's work, one of which was successful. Significant psi-hitting was achieved in only the first of two sessions completed by each subject in this experiment, but since Honorton's subjects completed just one session these results are comparable to his.

Glick and Kogen (1972) reported significant psi-hitting among one of two apparently nongifted subjects in another hypnotic dream study similar in design to Honorton's, but Krippner (1968) achieved marginally significant results only in a "waking" control group. Keeling (1972) added the dimension of hypnotizing both members of agent–percipient pairs before each group of trials. The pooled results of ratings submitted by three groups of judges (undergraduate psychology students, clinical psychology graduate students, and students in an adult education course on the occult) yielded significant overall psi-hitting. Only the ratings of the graduate students were independently significant.

Hypnosis of the percipient entered into one final free-response experiment (Moss, Paulson, Chang, and Levitt, 1970). Agents were asked to "send" the contents of emotionally arousing pictorial slides to percipients located in another room. Hypnotized subjects scored significantly above chance while control subjects scored at chance. However, the interpretation of this effect is obscured because subjects were allowed to assign themselves to conditions, and the method of statistical analysis was not specified in the report.

2.6.1c. Hypnotic Training of ESP. A technique for training ESP through hypnosis has been developed by Ryzl (1962). He claims that about 500 persons have been trained using this method, representing a success rate of approximately 10%. However, only one of his trainees, Pavel Stepanek, has gone on to show consistent success as an ESP subject (cf. Pratt, 1973), although it is conceivable that others may have had the ability to do so. It is unclear how much the hypnotic training contributed to the ability of even this subject. Independent attempts to apply Ryzl's technique have not been successful (Beloff and Mandleberg, 1966; Stephenson, 1965), although Honorton and Krippner (1969) question whether the technique was properly applied in these projects.

2.6.1d. Conclusion. Attempts to improve ESP scoring levels on a short-term basis through hypnosis have produced generally consistent results from a number of different laboratories. To illustrate this point, Van de Castle (1969) pooled the results of all forced-choice experiments reported up to that time in which scoring under hypnosis and control conditions were directly compared. He found that the mean score over 1,776 hypnosis runs was 5.51 ($p < 10^{-20}$), while the mean of 1,381 control runs was only 5.03. The record for free-response experiments is equally impressive, although most of the successful studies with this procedure lacked "waking" controls. Clearly, the hypnosis–ESP relationship is one of the more consistent in the parapsychological literature. See Honorton and Krippner (1969) and Van de Castle (1969) for excellent reviews of experimental studies.

It is likely that hypnosis is psi-conducive both because hypnotic suggestions increase one's confidence in one's ESP ability and because the induction procedure produces an altered state of consciousness that either encourages relaxation and withdrawal of attention from the external world or reduces the operation of rational, "left-hemisphere" mental processes that are thought to be inhibiting to psi. Evidence for the "confidence" interpretation comes from those studies in which mean ESP scoring levels were evaluated in relation to subjects' predictions of their run scores following various combinations of hypnosis and suggestions of success. Evidence for the "ASC" interpretation comes primarily from the free-response experiment of Honorton (1972b), who found a positive relationship between ESP scores and verbal state reports among hypnotized subjects. Considerable indirect evidence comes from a growing number of experiments where other consciousness-altering techniques besides hypnosis have been used to boost ESP. We turn to these studies next.

2.6.2. Hypnagogiclike States: ESP in the Twilight Zone

Hypnagogic is a term used by sleep psychologists to refer to the intermediate period between sleep and wakefulness.* From a phenomenological perspective, it can be broadly characterized as consisting of deep physical relaxation, heightened imagery (especially visual imagery), withdrawal of attention from the external world. and a tendency toward "primary process" mental organization. Many parapsychologists suspect that the hypnagogic state, or at least one or more of its associated characteristics, may be particularly well suited for psychic functioning. Much of the recent work on ESP in altered states was inspired by an article by Rhea White (1964) in which she analyzed the techniques used by various sensitives to enhance psychic receptivity. White found that these techniques contained many common elements, among which were relaxation and stilling of the mind preparatory to the emergence of psi-related visual imagery. In the early 1970s, many parapsychologists began to apply such techniques to their experimental subjects and note their effect on ESP scores, especially in free-response tests. Several specific techniques have been tried, and we will examine each separately.

2.6.2a. Progressive Relaxation. An exercise that has been known for a number of years to induce deep muscular relaxation is the progressive relaxation technique of Jacobson (1938/1974). The technique essentially consists of having the subject alternatively tense and relax specific muscle groups and note the contrast between the tension and relaxation. William Braud combined the Jacobson technique with suggestions for mental quietude as a means of inducing a so-called "psi-conducive syndrome" (Braud, 1975b).

---

*The term *hypnopompic* is sometimes used to refer to the transition state upon awakening, but for the sake of simplicity, the term *hypnagogic* will be used to refer to the transitions both into and from sleep.

Braud and his colleagues have consistently obtained significant over-all psi-hitting in experiments where this induction technique immediately precedes a standard free-response GESP test (Altom and Braud, 1976; L. W. Braud, 1977; Braud and Braud, 1974; Braud and Braud, 1973; Braud and Thorsrud, 1976). A control group was employed in only one of these experiments, in which a group receiving straight relaxation sugges-tions was compared to a group receiving straight tension suggestions (Braud and Braud, 1974). As predicted, there was significant psi-hitting in the relaxation group and chance scoring in the tension group. The differ-ence was significant. Differences in relaxation between the two groups were verified by both verbal reports and EMG measures, and the groups reported very similar expectancies of success prior to the induction pro-cedure. (Both techniques had been presented as psi-conducive.) In a pre-liminary experiment where all subjects received the standard progressive relaxation procedure, the psi-hitters were shown to be significantly more relaxed than the psi-missers.

A successful independent confirmation of Braud's results was re-ported by Stanford and Mayer (1974) using a clairvoyance procedure. However, the experiment did not include a control group, and there was no significant relationship between ESP scores and verbal reports of relax-ation during the session. Nonetheless, subjects as a group manifested significant psi-hitting. In contrast, significant results were not obtained in a progressive relaxation experiment by Miller and York (1976).

There is only one experiment in which progressive relaxation was used in conjunction with forced-choice testing (Sandford and Keil, 1975). In this experiment, a single subject scored significantly above chance on control runs but right at chance in runs preceded by progressive relax-ation. The only other chance outcome I am aware of in a free-response experiment using progressive relaxation exclusively to induce an ASC was in the control condition of an experiment by Charlesworth (1975), to be discussed later (Sec. 2.6.2e), where an abbreviated progressive relax-ation induction was utilized.

2.6.2b. Perceptual Deprivation. Honorton has recently become the leading advocate of perceptual deprivation techniques to facilitate psychic receptivity (Honorton, 1974b). He argues that in normal waking con-sciousness the organism is bombarded by external and internally gener-ated sensory stimuli of a patterned or meaningful nature that compete with and drown out low-level ESP stimuli and hinder their detection. Perceptual deprivation techniques have the effect of reducing this "noise," while at the same time causing the mind to compensate for this dearth of patterned stimulation by creating hypnagogic-like imagery (see

West, 1962). This imagery may serve as a vehicle for the transmission of ESP impressions from the unconscious.

Inspired by a non-psi experiment of Bertini, Lewis, and Witkin (1969), Honorton chose the "ganzfeld" technique to create the appropriate state of consciousness. The purpose of this technique, described more fully in Chapter 1, is to eliminate *patterned* external stimulation. The subject remains in the ganzfeld anywhere from 15 to 45 minutes (Honorton recommends the longer intervals), during or after which he or she gives mentation reports that are later matched to target pictures using standard free-response judging procedures.

The first published ganzfeld experiment was by Honorton and Harper (1974), who found significant psi-hitting among 30 unselected subjects. Because of the simplicity of the technique and the qualitative impressiveness of some of the hits, a plethora of ganzfeld experiments soon began to flood the literature. Some were successful in producing overall significant psi-hitting under comparable conditions to those of Honorton (L. W. Braud, 1977; Braud, Wood, and Braud, 1975; Dunne, Warnock, and Bisaha, 1977; Raburn and Manning, 1977; Smith, Tremmel, and Honorton, 1976; Terry and Honorton, 1976; Terry, Tremmel, Kelly, Harper, and Barker, 1976; York, 1977), while others were not (Braud, 1976; Braud and Wood, 1977; Habel, 1976; Palmer and Aued, 1975; Palmer *et al.*, 1977; Palmer and Lieberman, 1975; Parker, 1975b; Parker *et al.*, 1977; Rogo, Smith, and Terry, 1976; Stanford and Neylon, 1975; Terry, 1976a). Of the successful ganzfeld experiments, only two employed nonganzfeld control groups (Braud *et al.*, 1975; Terry *et al.*, 1976). Results in the control conditions were nonsignificant in both of these experiments, but only in the Braud experiment were scores in the ganzfeld and control conditions significantly different.

Some of the "unsuccessful" experiments nonetheless yielded significant internal effects that provide some support for the underlying theoretical rationale of the ganzfeld. Parker (1975b), in an experiment where the overall results were below chance, found a significant negative relationship between ESP scores and a self-report scale measuring alterations of consciousness during the session. In other words, a relatively pronounced alteration in consciousness was associated with significant ESP scoring, but in the negative direction, i.e., persons reporting pronounced ASCs manifested psi-missing. Likewise, Palmer *et al.*, (1977) found significant psi-missing among subjects who reported relatively pronounced ASCs in the ganzfeld, based upon their responses to rating scale items answered immediately after the session. The correlation between ESP scores and the ASC scale was significant. In still another experiment with below-chance scoring overall, Stanford and Neylon (1975) reported a significant negative correlation between ESP scores and changes in body awareness, an item very similar to one that contributed considerable variance to Palmer's ASC scale.

Most other ganzfeld experiments simply did not include state report measures, so their contribution to this trend cannot be assessed. I can report, however, that such trends were not found in two of my own experiments (Palmer and Aued, 1975; Palmer and Lieberman, 1975). However, when results from the latter study (a clairvoyance experiment that included a psychological set for "out-of-body experiences" in one condition) were combined with results from other comparable conditions from other phases of the project, I found a significant *positive* correlation between ESP scores and an ASC scale similar to the one reported in my most recent experiment (Palmer *et al.*, 1977). In this case, however, the overall results were *positive*, indicating that high positive scores were obtained by subjects who experienced the most pronounced ASCs. A report of these findings is in preparation.

The above results strongly suggest that even in "unsuccessful" experiments, significant levels of ESP scoring frequently occur among subjects for whom the ganzfeld succeeds in evoking a relatively pronounced alteration of consciousness, but that the direction of the scoring trend varies from study to study. The reasons for this variability are currently unknown.

A further significant finding in the two ganzfeld experiments where this variable has been examined is a tendency for subjects who, contrary to the norm, either overestimate or do not underestimate the duration of the ganzfeld session to score below chance and significantly lower than other subjects (Palmer *et al.*, 1977; Stanford and Neylon, 1975).

Finally, Honorton, Drucker, and Hermon (1973) used a sensory isolation technique called the witch's cradle to induce an ASC for a free-response experiment. The overall ESP mean was nonsignificantly above chance. Significant positive scoring, however, was evidenced by those subjects who reported above-average alterations in consciousness during the session (in line with the pattern of results from ganzfeld and hypnotic dream studies), but a significant overall relationship between state reports and ESP scores apparently was obtained from only one of several statistical tests.

2.6.2c. Meditation. Four experiments in the literature attempted to use standard meditation techniques to facilitate ESP. Two of these studies were conducted in the context of meditation groups meeting on a weekly basis, so the subjects either had or were in the process of acquiring experience with meditation (Osis and Bokert, 1971; Roll and Solfvin,

1976). Both experiments were extremely complex, and complicated multivariate statistical techniques were used to analyze the results. Roll used a free-response test and Osis both a free-response and a forced-choice test. The report of Roll and Solfvin was simply too short to allow an adequate assessment of their conclusions, but one hopes a more detailed report will follow. The Osis and Bokert report was sufficiently detailed, but this reviewer found it incomprehensible. Both sets of authors interpreted their results as indicating that subjects who had the most pleasant and self-transcending meditation experiences scored most negatively on the ESP test. Provided that the overall scoring level was below chance, this conclusion would fit nicely with the ganzfeld results, since it would imply the strong possibility of significant psi-missing on the part of those with the deepest meditation experiences. Mean ESP scores were not reported in Osis's experiment, while in Roll's it would appear that the mean on the most relevant GESP trials was right at chance.

The other two experiments were simpler and yielded more clearly positive results. Dukhan and Rao (1973) tested Western and Indian students of Yoga in an Indian ashram. Over three separate experiments, there was a generally consistent tendency for subjects to score significantly higher on a BM card-guessing test following a meditation session than before the session. The results represented a shift from psi-missing to psi-hitting. It is unclear from the report how consistent was the effect across subjects. Schmeidler (1970) gave six graduate students one clairvoyance run before and one after listening to a lecture on meditation and practicing a breathing exercise suggested by an Indian Swami. Subjects scored significantly above chance on the run following the exercise, compared to slightly below chance scoring beforehand. The difference, however, was not significant.

2.6.2d. Out-of-Body Experiences. Psychic experiences have often been reported anecdotally in conjunction with a specific ASC in which a person feels that his center of consciousness is located in space outside of his body (e.g., Crookall, 1961). A common characteristic of such out-of-body experiences (OBEs) is that the person "sees" his physical body as if from another point in space.

One of the more dramatic single episodes in the experimental parapsychological literature concerned a woman who correctly identified a five-digit number during an apparent OBE, which took place while her physiology was being monitored in a sleep laboratory (Tart, 1968). Unfortunately, sensory cues were not completely ruled out in this experiment, as the author points out. Another subject, who has written a popular book about his own OBEs (Monroe, 1971), produced more equivocal results in a similar experiment (Tart, 1967). Still another subject claimed to be able to visit his pet cat during OBEs. In one experiment it was found that the cat was significantly less active during these OBEs than during control periods (Morris, 1974).

Another series of experiments was undertaken to induce OBEs in unselected subjects and to assess the effect on free-response ESP performance (Palmer and Lieberman, 1975, 1976; Palmer and Vassar, 1974). Progressive relaxation exercises followed by one of several techniques designed to induce a hypnagogic state were combined with suggestions to imagine leaving the body and traveling to an adjacent room to identify a target picture. Although a significant difference was obtained in only one of four individual experiments (one of which is yet to be published), the pooled results indicated that subjects who reported feeling that they were literally "outside their bodies" during the session were significantly more successful at identifying the target picture than were subjects who did not, but only when the induction procedure was limited to pure sensory isolation techniques such as the ganzfeld. However, OBE reports had a high positive loading on the ASC scale described earlier, suggesting that OBEs in this experiment (and perhaps in other situations as well) may have paranormal elements simply because they tend to occur in psi-conducive hypnagogic states—not because the person has somehow literally left his body as suggested by some occult theories.

2.6.2e. Miscellaneous Techniques. Charlesworth (1975) obtained significant psi-hitting with a guided-imagery technique, in which the subject was guided through a fantasy journey and asked to identify objects along the way. The agent was simultaneously guided through the same fantasy, except that she was told what the objects (i.e., ESP targets) were. Results in two control groups were nonsignificant, and there was no significant difference between experimental and control groups. No significant overall results were obtained in a second experiment where the subject and agent pairs were twins, but there was an interesting interaction that we will discuss later (Sec. 3.5.4).

Finally, there have been two studies in which naturally occurring hypnagogic states were compared to other ASCs. Krippner (1968) compared the success of eight subjects following three different induction techniques in a free-response GESP experiment. Subjects first went through a standard "hypnotic dream" procedure. Later, they were instructed to take a nap and given the posthypnotic suggestion to dream about another picture. This procedure was the most likely of the three to involve a hypnagogic state. Last, it was suggested that subjects' nocturnal dreams during the week would correspond to yet another picture, and they were instructed to keep dream diaries. Eight other subjects went through the same regimen without hypnosis. Based on judges' but not subjects' ratings, hypnotized subjects scored significantly above chance in the hypnagogic condition and control subjects in the dream condition. There apparently were no significant differences between conditions. Although these findings are quite marginal, the trend seems to indicate that alterations of consciousness associated with sleep or presleep states may be more effective than simple hypnosis in facilitating ESP in free-response tasks.

William Braud (1977) evaluated free-response GESP scoring in two conditions methodologically similar to Krippner's nocturnal dream condition. Each subject responded to two targets, one "sent" right before he went to sleep (hypnagogic) and the other "sent" late at night (dream). Significant scoring occurred for the hypnagogic targets but not the dream targets. The difference approached but did not reach significance.

2.6.2f. Conclusion. An impressive number of experiments have produced significant psi-hitting when small samples of unselected subjects were submitted to induction techniques designed to produce hypnagogiclike states. Most of these were free-response studies in which each subject completed only one trial. Although most of these experiments lacked control groups, the ratio of studies reporting significant overall psi-hitting seems much higher than in studies where such induction techniques have not been used. Furthermore, most studies that did use control groups found only chance scoring in these conditions.

Among the small proportion of experiments in which subjects filled out state report scales, the evidence is rather consistent in revealing that the most extreme mean deviation scores occurred among those subjects who experienced the most pronounced ASCs. This evidence comes primarily from the ganzfeld literature, but not exclusively so (e.g., Braud and Braud, 1974; Honorton, 1972b). It would appear from this evidence that ASCs effect the magnitude of the deviation from chance, whereas the direction (i.e., psi-hitting or psi-missing) is determined by other factors that vary across experiments but that seem to be consistent within a given experiment.

Finally, it is conceivable that the induction techniques described in this section are effective not because they produce ASCs but because they introduce demand characteristics that might influence subjects' confidence or orientation toward the task (Rogo, 1976). Although questions concerning subject expectancies have not correlated significantly with ESP scores in those experiments where they have been employed (see Sec. 3.6.2b), such questions themselves are likely to be contaminated by demand characteristics and may reflect response biases more than actual attitudes. Thus the issue raised earlier in the discussion of the ESP–hypnosis research (Sec. 2.6.1d) is also relevant to the research on hypnagogiclike states, although the simplest and most straightforward interpretation of these latter findings, at least, remains the ASC hypothesis. A review critical of the ASC interpretation of the studies reviewed in the section has been published by Rogo (1976).

2.6.3. Dreams: Losing Sleep for Science

The most common ASC to be associated with ESP in everyday life is clearly the nocturnal dream. Ever since biblical times, tales have been recorded of dreams that later came true. In an analysis of more recent reports of psychic experiences mailed to Rhine's laboratory at Duke, Louisa Rhine (1962) found that 65% of them occurred in the dream state and that the dream experiences tended to provide a more complete description of the target event than did waking experiences. Furthermore, psychotherapists began reporting cases in which their patients had dreams about the therapist's life that were related to therapy in dynamically meaningful ways (Eisenbud, 1970; Ullman, Krippner, and Vaughan, 1973).

With the advent of the rapid-eye-movement (REM) monitoring technique, research was initiated at Maimonides Medical Center in New York City to demonstrate under well-controlled laboratory conditions that ESP could occur in dreams. The basic procedure, described more fully in Chapter 1, was to waken subjects from REM periods, record their dream reports, and then assess the correspondence between these reports and randomly selected art prints "sent" by an agent in another room.

In the first Maimonides experiment, each of 12 subjects spent one night in the laboratory. The results of this study were marginally significant, in that subjects but not outside judges were able to "blindly" match the targets and dream reports better than expected by chance. Two agents, one male and one female, were used in the experiment, and the significance was found to be attributable to those nights when the male served as agent (Ullman, Krippner, and Feldstein, 1969).

However, most of the significant results from Maimonides have involved repeated testing of particular individuals selected either through a screening process, such as the experiment described above, or because the experimenters had reason to believe they would be successful in this type of test. Some pilot data possibly notwithstanding (Ullman, Krippner, and Honorton, 1970), the bulk of the significant findings have involved only three individuals: Dr. William Erwin, a psychologist (Ullman and Krippner, 1969; Ullman et al., 1969); Dr. Robert Van de Castle, another psychologist (Hall, 1967; Krippner and Ullman, 1970); and Malcolm Bessent, a professional psychic (Krippner et al., 1971, 1972). Nevertheless, 9 of 12 formal nocturnal dream studies conducted at Maimonides using the

REM monitoring technique have produced significantly positive results (Honorton, 1974a), and a number of individual correspondences have been quite impressive.

On the other hand, two attempted replications of successful Maimonides experiments conducted at the laboratory of a noted dream researcher were unsuccessful (Belvedere and Foulkes, 1971; Foulkes *et al.*, 1972). Another replication attempt with a single subject produced significant results only on those trials where the judges were confident of their ratings (Globus, Knapp, Skinner, and Healey, 1968). Several direct ESP–dream correspondences also were found in the experiment of Hall (1967).

The two experiments referred to at the end of the last section in which unselected subjects recorded their dreams at home produced equivocal results (W. G. Braud, 1977; Krippner, 1968).

2.6.3a. Conclusion. The results of the well-controlled Maimonides experiments have demonstrated that ESP can occur in dreams. An overview of these studies is contained in a semipopular book by Ullman *et al.* (1973). However, the generality of the Maimonides results beyond a select group of individuals is questionable, and the incidence of replication in other laboratories has not been particularly impressive. What little evidence we have comparing ESP in dreams and hypnagogic or related states indicates that the latter is the best place to look, in terms of both economy of effort and yield of ESP.

2.6.4. Drugs: Uppers, Downers, and Outers

Only a handful of experiments have been conducted to assess the effect of psychopharmacological agents on ESP test performance, all using human subjects.

2.6.4a. Stimulants versus Depressants. In the early Duke research, Rhine (1934/1973) noticed that sodium amytal markedly reduced scoring rates in three of his high-scoring subjects, while caffeine caused these subjects' normally high levels of scoring to resume after they had been low. He observed that fatigue and illness likewise depressed scoring rates in these subjects.

Two experiments have incorporated double-blind techniques to compare the effects of stimulants and depressants on ESP scoring. Cadoret (1953) had 11 young adults complete four testing sessions in which they ingested either sodium amytal, dexadrine, lactose placebo, or nothing. They completed five BT runs and four free-response drawing trials before drug administration and again one hour thereafter. Significant treatment main effects were found on the pre- to postdrug change scores on both tests. Amytal produced a decrease in scoring in each case. Dexadrine produced a decrease on the card tests and an increase on the drawing tests. The latter of these dexadrine effects seemed to be attributable primarily to the subjects' associations to their drawings, in contrast to the drawings themselves.

Huby and Wilson (1961) conducted two experiments similar to Cadoret's. In their first experiment, 100 subjects produced marginally significant psi-missing on a two-run symbol guessing test following quinalbarbitone (a depressant). Scores following ingestion of this drug also differed significantly from scores following administration of a lactose placebo. Amphetamines produced nonsignificant psi-missing. These trends were not confirmed in a second experiment with 54 subjects (26 of whom had participated in the first experiment) and twice the number of runs per subject. A possible reason for the difference is that the ESP test was given two hours following drug administration as compared to 45 minutes in the first experiment. Another complicating factor is that subjects in both experiments were restricted to those who scored an average of plus *or minus* one hit from chance on a preliminary two-run card test.

2.6.4b. Anesthesia. In a clock-card experiment with 36 maternity patients, Gerber and Schmeidler (1957) inadvertently tested 6 while they were still under the influence of an unspecified anesthetic. These 6 subjects scored significantly below chance. However, the difference between the drug-influenced and non-drug-influenced subjects was significant only among a subgroup of the sample who had been rated by the experimenter as relaxed and acceptant during the test. The principal analysis of the experiment had confirmed a prediction for nondrugged subjects that those who were relaxed and accepting would score significantly higher than the others, so there is at least some justification in treating this subgroup separately.

2.6.4c. Psychedelic Drugs. Users of psychedelic drugs frequently report psychic experiences while under the influence of these substances (Tart, 1971). However, experimental research on this topic is virtually nonexistent, due in large part to the tight government restriction on the use of psychedelic drugs even for research purposes. The most substantial study was conducted in Holland by van Asperen de Boer, Barkema, and Kappers (1966), who compared the results of 37 subjects on a variety of ESP tests given when they either were or were not under the influence of psilocybin. Unfortunately, the order of sessions was not counterbalanced. Although there was overall significant psi-hitting on standard DT tests, scoring was slightly better in the control conditions. Whittlesey (1960) gave 27 psychiatric outpatients one card-guessing run before and one after ingesting an unspecified dose of LSD. There was significantly below-chance run-score variance overall, but apparently no significant mean differences between the two runs. In a longer series of experiments, Cavanna and Servadio (1964) succeeded primarily in demonstrating that it is difficult to get subjects to attend to an ESP test while having an LSD experience.

    2.6.4d. Conclusion. The evidence is fairly consistent in showing that central nervous system depressants tend to reduce the level of scoring in ESP card tests. The evidence that stimulants have the opposite effect is much less consistent. Too little research with psychedelic drugs has been reported to allow any conclusions whatsoever.

3. The Subject in ESP Experiments

    In section 2, I paid little attention to the characteristics of the subject who happened to be on the receiving end of the experimenter's attempts to elicit ESP. This obviously is not a matter we can afford to ignore for long. First of all, subjects vary in the amount of potential ESP ability they bring with them to an ESP experiment, and a given subject's ESP talent may in turn be related to such things as his (or her) personality, cognitive skills, sex, age, and even species. Secondly, the attitudes and moods a subject brings to the experiment may be expected to influence scoring, and these in turn may be modified by the kinds of experimental manipulations discussed in section 2. This is especially true of manipulations such as hypnosis, which I discussed in the last subsection. The first topic of the upcoming section, physiological predictors, provides a convenient bridge between our studies of induced ASCs and individual differences as they relate to ESP test performance.

3.1. Physiological Predictors: In Search of the Mind–Brain Interface

    Physiological variables have been studied both as predictors of ESP scores and as ESP measures themselves. In this section we will be concerned exclusively with the first of these functions.

3.1.1. EEG Studies: The Hard-Headed Approach to Altered States

    The only physiological variable that has been studied to any appreciable extent as a predictor of ESP scores is the electroencephalograph (EEG), and this research has dealt almost exclusively with brain waves in the "alpha" band, i.e., 8–13 Hz. The reason why parapsychologists became so interested in alpha is that it is often associated with a relaxed, passive state of mind, which has long been considered psi-conducive (e.g., White, 1964). Although a few alpha–ESP studies were reported in the early experimental literature (e.g., Wallwork, 1952), interest in the possible relationship between these variables was slight until about 1970, when evidence began to appear in the psychological journals suggesting that alpha could be increased in human subjects through biofeedback training (e.g., Nowlis and Kamiya, 1970). Such findings suggested to some parapsychologists that "alpha training" might be useful in training ESP; if a person were taught to increase his or her alpha, ESP performance might improve as well. Training people to increase their alpha production substantially above optimal baseline levels proved to be easier said than done, as parapsychologists themselves soon discovered (Honorton and Carbone, 1971; Lewis and Schmeidler, 1971). Nevertheless, an extensive body of data has surfaced that, while not always consistent, does suggest some kind of relationship between ESP scores and whatever it is that EEG recording techniques measure.

3.1.1a. Alpha Density—Between Subjects. Percent-time alpha (or alpha density) has been studied as a predictor both between subjects and within subjects. In some studies, between-subjects and within-subjects effects have been confounded. Let us look first at the between-subjects effects.

The first sign of a positive relationship between alpha and ESP came from a single-session card-guessing experiment by Honorton (1969b), who found a significant correlation of +.72 between these two measures. The subjects were ten high school students selected on the basis of high ESP scores in a pretest. In a follow-up experiment with a new sample of ten older subjects, the correlation was −.63, also significant (Honorton and Carbone, 1971). However, the ESP scores that entered into this correlation were pooled over ten sessions, nine of which occurred after subjects had been exposed to alpha feedback training. When only the results of the first session are considered, the correlation is positive (+.17), although nonsignificant.

Stanford and Lovin (1970) reported a significant negative correlation between alpha density and ESP in a single-session card-guessing experiment not involving feedback. The authors noted that both they and Honorton (1969b) used a scoring method of the EEG records that gave relatively little weight to alpha bursts of short duration. Alpha density failed to significantly predict ESP scores between subjects in three other ESP experiments (Morris and Cohen, 1971; Stanford, 1971; Stanford and Palmer, 1975). The latter experiment used a free-response procedure.

3.1.1b. Alpha Density—Within Subjects. Honorton and Carbone (1971) computed alpha–ESP correlations for each of their subjects across ten sessions and found no more of them to be significant than expected by chance, although they were predominantly negative in direction. Cadoret (1964), on the other hand, found significantly higher ESP scores on "trials accompanied by slow EEG" than on "relatively fast" EEG trials. Although between-subjects and within-subject effects apparently were confounded in this experiment (a brief abstract is all we have to go on), the trend was relatively consistent across his seven subjects. No straightforward differences between mean ESP scores on trials made simultaneously with attempts to respectively generate or suppress alpha were found in either of two biofeedback experiments with unselected subjects (Honorton, Davidson, and Bindler, 1971; Pleshette, 1975).

In another experiment where between-subjects and within-subject effects were confounded, Stanford and Stanford (1969) examined changes of alpha density within the run in relation to card-guessing performance. They failed to confirm their prediction that the half run showing the most alpha would yield the greater number of ESP hits. However, a post hoc analysis revealed significantly higher run-score variance in runs with an above average increase in alpha density from the first to the second half of the run. These high-change runs also were significantly associated with a tendency for subjects to avoid calling an equal number of each symbol on each run. This result gave the initial post hoc finding a measure of construct validity, because previous research had shown a relationship between unbalanced calling sequences and high run-score variance (Stanford, 1966a,b). Apparently, increases in alpha within the run reflect a tendency not to try to balance calling probabilities at the end of the run.

A number of experimenters have tested single subjects selected for outstanding ESP talent or for proficiency in controlling their alpha. Three forced-choice experiments with the psychic Harribance included EEG monitoring. In the first two, Harribance's overall scoring rate was significantly and substantially above chance (Morris *et al.*, 1972). The highest scoring runs were selected for comparison with chance runs, and in each experiment significantly more alpha was present in the high-scoring runs. Analyses using alpha to predict ESP scores were not reported. In the third experiment, Harribance's overall score was slightly below chance (Kelly and Lenz, 1976b). Spectral analysis was used to compare individual hit and miss trials. The only significant effect was an excess of power in the 12- to 13-Hz range on the missing trials, a finding not predicted in advance. The only other forced-choice experiment with a selected subject was by Wallwork (1952), who simply classified GESP trials as concurrent with strong, average, or no alpha. Overall ESP scores were near chance, and there were no significant alpha–ESP relationships.

Turning to free-response experiments, Rao and Feola (1973) tested an experienced meditator who also had gained proficiency in controlling his alpha through feedback training. Alternate trials with instructions to generate or suppress alpha during the image-reception period revealed significantly higher ESP scoring on the generation trials. In a correlational study with another experienced meditator, no significant relationship was found between ESP scores and alpha density either during the reception periods or during pretest mind-clearing periods (Stanford and Stevenson, 1972).

Finally, Tart (1968) found an unusual slow alpha pattern during the apparent time a subject reporting an out-of-body experience correctly identified a five-digit number (see Sec. 2.6.2d).

3.1.1c. Alpha Density and ASCs. Studies examining the relationship between alpha density and ESP clearly have yielded inconsistent results. An experiment that may shed some light on the matter is a complex study by Honorton *et al.* (1971). This experiment, the main purpose of which was to examine card-guessing performance in relation to alpha feedback training, differed from the EEG experiments described so far in that subjects were asked to give periodic verbal reports of their "states of consciousness" during the ESP test. Although several significant relationships were uncovered, the analyses reported are not the most appropriate for documenting the point the authors wish to make. Nevertheless, it is clear from the overall pattern of results that positive ESP scores occurred most often when generation of alpha was combined with verbal reports of an alteration of consciousness. Although demand characteristics might have been a contributing factor to the results, it nonetheless would appear that alpha was a necessary but not sufficient condition for high scores. Indirect support for this latter proposition comes from a free-response experiment (Stanford and Palmer, 1975). Although subjects in this experiment who produced high percentages of alpha did not necessarily get high ESP scores, above-chance scoring subjects produced significantly more alpha during the reception period than did below-chance scoring subjects. Unfortunately, no state report measures were included in this experiment.

The hypothesis that *both* alpha and a concomitant ASC are needed to boost ESP scoring levels blends well with the ASC–ESP results from nonphysiological experiments discussed earlier in the chapter, and it may help to explain the inconsistent results from EEG experiments where the ASC factor was not taken into account. Evidence from the nonphysiological ASC literature that pronounced ASCs produce psi-missing in some experiments *might* help to explain the significant negative correlations between alpha density and ESP found in some of the EEG experiments.

If alpha is only psi-conducive to the degree it reflects an alteration of consciousness, one would not expect it to be a consistently successful predictor of ESP scoring rates. Conversely, requiring that state reports be accompanied by physiological indices may weed out invalid reports (e.g., those influenced by demand characteristics) and thereby lead to a strengthening for the evidence for an ASC–ESP relationship. A cogent argument for the "convergent operations" approach in ASC research has been made by Stoyva and Kamiya (1968).

  3.1.1d. Alpha Frequency. While most parapsychologists have restricted the EEG analyses to the study of alpha density, Rex Stanford has examined the frequency of the EEG (i.e., cycles per second) within the alpha band. In each of three experiments, he found ESP scores to be positively and significantly correlated with the net increase in alpha frequency from a pretest mind-clearing period to the test period itself (Stanford, 1971; Stanford and Lovin, 1970; Stanford and Stevenson, 1972). In two of these experiments, there was also a significant negative correlation between ESP scores and pretest alpha frequency (Stanford and Lovin, 1970; Stanford and Stevenson, 1972).

  Neither of these relationships was found in a free-response experiment where subjects listened to Indian flute music along with a mental set designed to stimulate visual imagery during the pretest period (Stanford and Palmer, 1975). Moreover, no correlation between ESP scores and alpha frequency in a pretest meditation period was found in an experiment where the psychic Malcolm Bessent was asked to give "readings" about subjects' personal lives (Stanford and Palmer, 1973). No EEG recordings could be taken during the readings themselves in this experiment.

  Neither of these latter experiments undermines the consistency of the relationship between ESP scores and pretest to test increase in alpha frequency, provided the pretest involves a simple mind-clearing exercise. Stanford interprets this finding to mean that successful subjects achieve an initial state of relaxation and mental quietude but then become more aroused during the ESP test. Unfortunately, this interpretation depends solely on inferences from physiological data, although its plausibility is reinforced by data from research bearing on the relationship between ESP and alpha density.

  3.1.1e. Conclusion. There is no simple relationship between EEG alpha density and ESP scoring levels. There is some evidence that alpha is a facilitater of psi only if other factors are present, and the results of Honorton *et al.* (1971) suggest that one such factor may be some kind of ASC. Stanford has consistently found a significant relationship between changes in mean alpha frequency and ESP scores under certain conditions. Surprisingly, no other experimenters have attempted to replicate this work.

If, as suggested in an earlier section, hypnagogiclike states may be psi-conducive, one might expect theta rather than alpha to be the brain wave pattern most closely associated with high ESP scores, especially in those experiments where visual mediation of ESP responses is encouraged. This, of course, remains to be seen. Alpha, on the other hand, may be most desirable prior to the test, when a preparatory period of mind clearing may be useful.

3.1.2. Hemispheric Specialization: Which Hand Has the ESP?

A series of behavioral experiments not involving physiological measurements are included in this section because of their relevance to recent data disclosing different primary cognitive functions of the two hemispheres of the brain. This research suggests that spatial, holistic functions are characteristic of the right hemisphere, while verbal, analytic functions are more characteristic of the left hemisphere (Dimond and Beaumont, 1974). Given this dichotomy, ESP would appear to be primarily a "right-hemisphere" process (Braud, 1975b).

Braud and Braud (1975) compared the activation of these so-called right- and left-hemisphere processes on immediately subsequent performance in a free-response ESP test. One group of subjects was asked to solve logic and math problems while the other group listened to sounds suggesting depth and imagery. The former, "left-hemisphere" group scored significantly below chance on the ESP test while the "right-hemisphere" group's scores were at chance. The difference was significant. Stanford and Castello (1977) gave their subjects an ESP test disguised as a word association test (see Sec. 5.1.1). Half of the subjects were given a mental set to produce abstract associations characteristic of left-hemisphere functioning, and the other half were given a set to produce concrete associations characteristic of right-hemisphere functioning. The ESP scores were near chance for both groups.

Richard Broughton hypothesized that ESP should function best when the ESP response is mediated as much as possible by the right hemisphere while the left hemisphere is occupied with a competing task. In the first three experiments, subjects were asked to make their ESP responses by lifting one of five wooden objects (each representing one of the five ESP symbols) with either their right or left hands. For half the trials the left hemisphere was occupied with a mental task (Broughton, 1976). In two of the three experiments, significant results were obtained suggesting that the most ESP occurred when the response was made with the left hand (right hemisphere) and the left hemisphere was engaged in the distracting task. However, the specific effects in the two experiments were not the same, and the support provided for the hypothesis by the first experiment was rather indirect.

In the second series of experiments, a reaction time task was used (Broughton, 1977a). The idea was to determine whether having an agent listen to a tone would influence subjects' reaction time to that tone when they made their responses with their left hand (right hemisphere) but not their right hand. A significant interaction consistent with this hypothesis was found only when the subjects were engaged simultaneously in a "left-hemisphere" reading task.

On the other hand, Maher and Schmeidler (1977) found significant ESP performance only in a condition where a "verbal" type of discrimination response was made with the right hand while the left hand was engaged in a pattern-tracing task. This result suggested that successful ESP performance was being mediated by the left hemisphere, although the failure to find any significant differences between conditions renders the finding marginal. The authors suggest that either hemisphere is capable of showing ESP on a task related to its inherent skills but that results are enhanced if the other hemisphere is agreeably occupied with an irrelevant task.

3.1.2a. Conclusion. More research will be needed before a distinctive pattern of results emerges from this paradigm. The findings so far do suggest, however, that dissociative states (in a more literal sense of that term than one usually finds in the altered states area) might be particularly psi-conducive. If so, it follows that persons with a natural aptitude for performing two competing tasks simultaneously may prove to be good ESP subjects. For theoretically oriented discussions of hemispheric specialization in relation to psi, see Broughton (1975) and Stanford and Castello (1977).

3.1.3. Other Physiological Predictors: Slim Pickings

A few experiments have explored autonomic variables as predictors of ESP scoring. Woodruff and Dale (1952) found no relationship between GSR and ESP scores in two experiments where a shock paradigm was used in an unsuccessful effort to reinforce correct responses. In another experiment, a single subject completed four BT runs in each of 37 sessions, alternating between a relaxed and concentrating mental set either within sessions or between sessions (Otani, 1955). A significant interaction between set and within-run change in GSR was reported, the principal deviation consisting of significant psi-missing in the relaxed runs when GSR did not increase during the run. According to Tart (1963), an unpublished replication of this experiment was unsuccessful (cf. Otani, 1958).

Finally, Price (1973a) reported a negative correlation ($N = 5$) between the heart rate variability of five female "psychics" while giving free-response "readings" of anonymous target persons and a measure of the accuracy of their statements.

A review of the relationship between ESP and physiological variables has been written by Beloff (1974).

3.2. The "Psychic Personality": Profiling the High Scorer

Although performances on ESP tests can fluctuate widely in any given individual, the existence of exceptional subjects such as those described at the beginning of this chapter document the fact of individual differences in psychic ability. Although clinical approaches sometimes have been used to study psychic ability (e.g., Pratt, 1973; Tenhaeff, 1962), by far the most common approach has been to correlate ESP scores with various paper-and-pencil tests of personality. In fact, this literature has become quite extensive.

In this section, I will restrict myself to an examination of the relationship between ESP scores and behavioral dispositions or tendencies that are relatively stable over time. Most personality–ESP experiments can be classified according to the two broad trait clusters of neuroticism and extraversion that frequently emerge in factor-analytic studies of personality (e.g., Cattell, 1965; Eysenck, 1960), so I will begin with these two categories.

3.2.1. Neuroticism: ESP Test Anxiety

I will use the term *neuroticism* to refer broadly to tendencies toward maladaptive behavior caused either by anxiety or by defense mechanisms against anxiety. "Objective" personality inventories meeting this criterion that have been used in ESP experiments include the Taylor Manifest Anxiety Scale (Carpenter, 1971; Freeman and Nielsen, 1964; Honorton, 1965; Nielsen and Freeman, 1965; Rao, 1965b; Roll and Solfvin, 1976; Sailaja and Rao, 1973; Schmeidler and Lindemann, 1966), the Maudsley or Eysenck Personality Inventory (Brodbeck, 1969; Freeman, 1972a; Green, 1966b; Nielsen, 1972b, c; Osis *et al.*, 1971; Randall, 1974), Cattell's 16PF or HSPQ (Kanthamani and Rao, 1973a; Kramer and Terry, 1973; Nicol and Humphrey, 1953, 1955), the Minnesota Multiphasic Personality Inventory (Nash, 1966), Guilford's personality scales (Crumbaugh, 1958; Nash and Nash, 1967; Nicol and Humphrey, 1953, 1955), Maslow's Security–Insecurity Questionnaire (Smith and Humphrey, 1946; Stuart, Humphrey, Smith, and McMahan, 1947), Spielberger's State–Trait Anxiety Inventory (Ballard, 1977), the Bernreuter Personality Inventory (Humphrey, 1945b; McElroy and Brown, 1950), the Heston Personal Adjustment Inventory (Kahn, 1952), the Mental Health Analysis (Rivers, 1950), the Mosher Sex Guilt Scale (Carpenter, 1971), and a composite measure of openness versus defensiveness (L. W. Braud, 1976, 1977). Only the experiments by Braud and by Roll and Solfvin used free-response methods.

Projective measures that have been correlated with ESP scores include the Rorschach (Schmeidler, 1958, 1960, 1961; Schmeidler and LeShan, 1970), the Blacky Test (Schmeidler, 1962a), and Kragh's Defense Mechanisms Test (Carpenter, 1965; Johnson, 1974; Johnson and Kanthamani, 1967; Miller and York, 1976). Only Miller and York used free-response methodology.

Discounting experiments where significance was based on post hoc classification of subjects or analysis of extreme scorers only, just a handful of experiments have yielded significant simple relationships between ESP and neuroticism (L. W. Braud, 1977; Carpenter, 1965; Kahn, 1952; Johnson and Kanthamani, 1967; Kanthamani and Rao, 1973a; Nicol and Humphrey, 1953; Rao, 1965b). All of these significant relationships, however, have been in the direction of the least anxious or defensive subjects getting the highest ESP scores. The most successful predictors have been Cattell's scales and the Defense Mechanisms Test, especially the latter.

The pattern between neuroticism and ESP becomes more consistent when one eliminates from consideration those experiments where subjects were tested in a group or classroom setting. Of the remaining experimental series where the direction of the effect could be determined from the report, the less neurotic subjects scored higher in 20 series (Carpenter, 1965; Humphrey, 1945b; Johnson and Kanthamani, 1967; Kanthamani and Rao, 1973a; Miller and York, 1976; Nash, 1966; Nash and Nash, 1967; Nicol and Humphrey, 1953, 1955; Sailaja and Rao, 1973; Stuart *et al.*, 1947), while the more neurotic subjects scored higher in only six series (Carpenter, 1971; Green, 1966b; Nash and Nash, 1967; Nielsen and Freeman, 1965; Rivers, 1950). A more detailed discussion of a similar breakdown is published elsewhere (Palmer, 1977).

Interactions between neuroticism and other variables, discussed elsewhere in the chapter, have been reported by Carpenter (1971) and Schmeidler (1960). Randall (1974) found significantly high between-subjects variance in three of six classroom experiments among high school students who scored above average on the Junior Eysenck Personality Inventory.

3.2.1a. Conclusion. There is a clear trend in the data indicating that persons whose responses on personality tests indicate relatively good emotional adjustment score more positively on standard ESP tests than do more "neurotic" subjects. The results of Randall notwithstanding, the effect seems to be on the direction of the deviation (hitting versus missing), rather than on its magnitude per se. The fact that the relationship is more consistent when subjects are tested individually may be because neurotic tendencies do not become engaged in relatively nonthreatening group testing situations, where a subject can "lose himself in the crowd." Differences in *predispositions* to anxiety (which is what these personality inventories measure) would be expected to have their greatest influence when subjects must face a strange experimenter alone and have their performances singled out for evaluation. A possible boundary condition of the neuroticism–ESP relationship is discussed in Sec. 3.7.2a.

3.2.2. Extraversion: Neuroticism's Siamese Twin?

The second major personality variable to be correlated with ESP scores is extraversion. Relationships have been reported involving Cattell's scales (Kanthamani and Rao, 1972; Nicol and Humphrey, 1953, 1955), Eysenck's scales (Aström, 1965; Brodbeck, 1969; Green, 1966a,b; Haraldsson, 1972; Nielsen, 1972a; Osis *et al.*, 1971; Randall, 1974), Guilford's scales (Nash and Nash, 1967; Nicol and Humphrey, 1953, 1955), the Bernreuter scale (Humphrey, 1945b, 1951a; Casper, 1952; McElroy and Brown, 1950; Nielsen, 1970), the MMPI (Nash, 1966; Szyczygielski and Schmeidler, 1975), a ten-item scale of unspecified origin (L. W. Braud, 1976, 1977), experimenter ratings (Kanthamani, 1966), and clinical ratings of "withdrawal" in emotionally disturbed children (Shields, 1962). Only a handful of these authors reported significant simple relationships between ESP and extraversion, but all were in the direction of more positive ESP scores among extraverts (Aström, 1965; L. W. Braud, 1976; Casper, 1952; Humphrey, 1951a; Kanthamani and Rao, 1972; Nash, 1966; Shields, 1962). A significant relationship in the same direction was also reported by Marsh (1962) in a free-response experiment, but I lack access to the full report, which presumably described the measure of extraversion used. Charlesworth (1975) suggested that a significant difference favoring fraternal as opposed to identical twins in a free-response experiment may have been attributable to the fact that the fraternal twins were significantly more extraverted, but no measure of extraversion was described in the published report. Again, the great majority of all experiments where the direction of the effect could be determined from the report revealed higher scores for extraverts, but there have been exceptions (Nash, 1966; Nash and Nash, 1967; Randall, 1974; Szyczygielski and Schmeidler, 1975). Whether subjects were tested individually or in groups had less effect on the extraversion–ESP relationship than on the neuroticism–ESP relationship, so the trends reported in this paragraph are based on studies of both types. For a more detailed analysis, the reader again is referred to Palmer (1977).

3.2.2a. Conclusion. There is a clear trend in the data indicating a positive relationship between social extraversion and scores on standard ESP tests. The trend is similar to that between neuroticism and ESP; in fact, the evidence for the two relationships often comes from the same experiments. There is a high degree of correlation between the extraversion and neuroticism scales that have been used in ESP research, especially in those "objective" scales that have been most successful as predictors of ESP scores. This obviously introduces interpretational problems. The only attempt to partial out these effects was by Kanthamani (1968), who found that her significant neuroticism–ESP relationship with Cattell's HSPQ survived the partialing out of extraversion but not vice versa.

In my judgment, the most reasonable and parsimonious conclusion that can be drawn from the data is that there is a weak but generally consistent tendency for the highest ESP scores (at least on initial testing) to be obtained by subjects with superior social adjustment, especially as this affects their ability to adapt to and be comfortable in social situations such as psychology experiments. A stronger interpretation of the ESP–extraversion relationship is presented by Eysenck (1967).

3.2.3. Other Personality Measures: Place Your Bets and . . .

Several other personality variables have been used as predictors in ESP experiments, but their use has been too infrequent to allow clear trends to emerge.

3.2.3a. Aggression. Some significant negative relationships between ESP scores and externally directed aggressiveness have been reported using the Rosenzweig Picture Frustration Study (Eilbert and Schmeidler, 1950; Schmeidler, 1950, 1954) and Cason's Test of Annoyance (Nicol and Humphrey, 1953, 1955). Osis found complex and inconsistent effects with the Rosenzweig that do not support the generality of these earlier findings (Osis and Fahler, 1965; Osis and Turner, 1968; Osis *et al.*, 1971). Schmeidler's results suggested that the relationship only holds for subjects who are "moderately annoyed" at the test, and this factor may be responsible for the inconsistent results.

3.2.3b. Hypnotic Susceptibility. Using a within-subject design, Stanford (1972b) found that susceptibility to hypnosis as measured by the Barber Suggestibility Scale was positively related to ESP scores in a conventional card test but negatively related to scores in an "augury" test more relevant to PK. Both trends were significant, based on the pooled results of two series. Honorton (1969a) also found a positive (but nonsignificant) correlation between the BSS and card-guessing scores. In a GESP experiment involving a restricted range of scores on the Stanford Hypnotic Susceptibility Scale, McBain *et al.* (1970) found a significant positive correlation between ESP scores and the agents' scores on the SHSS, but not the percipients'. Hypnotic susceptibility has not proven to be significantly related to ESP scores in free-response experiments (Palmer and Lieberman, 1976; Roll and Solfvin, 1976). For other data relevant to hypnotic susceptibility, see Sec. 2.6.1.

3.2.3c. Self-Concept. In each of two experiments, Stanford (1964a, 1965) found that subjects who believed in ESP and who scored above chance on an ESP card test with multiple calls (see Chapter 1,) had a significantly greater difference between their self- and ideal-self-concepts, as measured by a Semantic Differential technique, than did believers who scored below chance. Unfortunately, it could not be determined whether the mean self–ideal discrepancy of the high scorers indicated realistic self-perception or feelings of inferiority.

3.2.3d. Perception of Time. Several experiments have employed a projective technique called the Time Metaphor Test. Designed to directly assess subjects' preferred ways of viewing time, it has been shown to correlate with measures of need for achievement. The test does not seem to relate to ESP card-guessing scores in any simple way, but some complex effects have been reported (Goldberg, Sondow, and Schmeidler, 1976; Heyman and Schmeidler, 1967; Mihalsky, 1972; Osis *et al.*, 1971; Schmeidler, 1964c; Taetzsch, 1965).

3.2.3e. Values. Nash (1958) reported a significant positive correlation between ESP card-guessing scores and the religion subscale of the Allport–Vernon Scale of Values, but a nonsignificant relationship was reported by Buzby (1963). The subscale measuring a theoretical value orientation was not found to relate significantly to ESP scores (Schmeidler and McConnell, 1958).

3.2.3f. Other Scales. Roll and Solfvin (1976) found a significant positive correlation between clairvoyance but not GESP scores and the Time Competence Scale of the Personal Orientation Inventory in a free-response experiment. In another free-response experiment, Palmer and Lieberman (1975) reported a significant negative correlation between ESP scores and a projective measure of articulation of body concept. Carpenter (1973) found a significant interaction between belief in ESP and the California *F* Scale of authoritarianism as predictors of card-guessing performance. McGuire, Percy, and Carpenter (1974) found that scales from the California Psychological Inventory contributed to a multiple regression equation predicting ESP scores. Stanford (1965) found among subjects who believed in ESP a significant negative correlation between ESP scores and an item concerning the pleasure derived from touching and fingering physical objects. Other scales used in only one experiment that have failed to correlate significantly with ESP scores include Allport's Ascendance–Submission Scale (Kanthamani, 1966), Rotter's Internal–External Control of Reinforcement Scale (Stanford, 1972a), Rokeach's Dogmatism Scale (Schmeidler and Lindemann, 1966), and the need–achievement subscale of the Edwards Personal Preference Schedule (Schmeidler and Lindemann, 1966).

3.2.3g. Conclusion. Among these other personality variables, aggressiveness and self-concept appear to be the most promising. More research with these variables will be needed, however, before any conclusions can be drawn.

3.2.4. The Stuart Interest Inventory: A Case of Raw Empiricism

Another approach to the prediction of ESP scores is represented by the Stuart Interest Inventory, a scale designed exclusively for ESP research on which subjects express their degree of liking for 60 objects and events on five-point scales (Stuart, 1946b). Because of earlier research suggesting a relationship between ESP and "affectability" (Stuart, 1941), scores on the scale were based upon extremity of attitude rather than direction. Although the specific scoring scheme Stuart used did not prove to be a very valid measure of affectability, a significant difference in favor of midrange scorers on the SII was found in the pooled results of 32 card-guessing series including 900 subjects (Humphrey, 1949, 1951b). Casper (1951), however, was unable to significantly replicate the effect with a sample of 146 subjects.

Using a more empiricist approach, Humphrey (1950) submitted the SII to item analysis, selecting the 14 items that best discriminated high and low ESP scores in three previous experiments in terms of the percentages of subjects choosing each response alternative. The new scale was successfully cross-validated in 13 subsequent series but not in still later series (Humphrey, 1951b). However, its predictive utility was significantly confirmed in a more recent experiment (Carpenter, 1969). Honorton (1964, 1966) found that the scale successfully predicted direction of scoring following hypnotic induction, but not in control runs.

3.2.4a. Conclusion. The new version of the Stuart scale shows some promise as a predictor of ESP scoring direction, but I wouldn't bet my money on it. The old version is longer, certainly no better, and may be outdated. No research has been reported attempting to provide either version with any construct validity, and neither has much face validity as a measure of underlying dispositions that might be conceptually related to psi. In other words, even if the SII–ESP relationship is genuine, we have no idea what it means.

3.3. Cognitive Variables: From Substance to Style

In this section, we will take a look at how individual differences in cognitive abilities and styles are related to ESP test performance. All the experiments in this section used forced-choice testing procedures unless otherwise indicated.

3.3.1. Intelligence and Scholastic Ability: IQ and Psi Q

A number of experimenters have correlated ESP scores with scores on standard intelligence tests. However, sample sizes have usually been small and representative of a limited range of intellectual ability, e.g., college students. Most of these correlations have been nonsignificant, although predominantly in the positive direction (Bond, 1937; Drucker *et al.*, 1977; Eason and Wysocki, 1965; Humphrey, 1945a, 1948; Kanthamani and Rao, 1971; Nash and Nash, 1964; Nicol and Humphrey, 1953, 1955; Rivers, 1950; Shields, 1965; Vasse and Vasse, 1958). The few significant relationships have been exclusively positive (Humphrey, 1945a; Nash and Nash, 1958; Schmeidler, 1962a). Although this pattern suggests a positive relationship between ESP and intelligence in the population sampled, the fact that highly significant psi-hitting has been found among mentally retarded children (Bond, 1937; Drake, 1938) suggests caution in making any broad generalizations.

A related variable that has been studied as a predictor of ESP scores is school grades. Anderson (1959b) reported a significant relationship between ESP scores and class grades among 1,228 high school and junior college students. Schmeidler (1960) likewise found a significant positive relationship between these variables in a large sample of college students, but only among those who believed ESP was possible under the conditions of the experiment. Other experiments, however, produced nonsignificant relationships (Anderson and Gregory, 1959; Nash and Nash, 1964; White and Angstadt, 1961).

As far as interactions are concerned, Freeman (1967, 1968, 1970a) conducted a series of complex experiments suggesting a relationship between type of target and relative spatial and verbal aptitude. These complex effects were not entirely consistent.

3.3.1a. Conclusion. Correlational studies have shown a weak but fairly consistent positive relationship between ESP and intelligence test scores within restricted samples. However, the crucial predictor variable may not be intelligence. For example, Anderson's finding of a positive relationship between ESP scores and grades was highly confounded with the relationship described previously between ESP scores and teachers' attitudes toward their pupils (see Sec. 2.5.2b). One interpretation of this pattern of results is that the brighter students feel more comfortable in the classroom situation than do their less intelligent counterparts, and this is why they score better on ESP tests. In Schmeidler's (1960) research, a measure of personal adjustment produced the same pattern of results as described above for class grades. Although no correlation between personal adjustment and class grades was reported in Schmeidler's article, measures of intelligence and personal adjustment are often positively correlated. In the context of other research findings described in the last section, it seems most reasonable to conclude that the positive relationship between ESP and intelligence, assuming its validity, is the by-product of a more fundamental relationship between ESP and personal adjustment.

3.3.2. Short-Term Memory: Not Much to Remember

Only a handful of experiments have considered individual differences in short-term memory in relation to ESP scoring. In a series of four preliminary experiments, Feather (1965) gave subjects 15 or 20 seconds to memorize a list of 25 ESP symbols or digits. In between memorization and recall the subjects completed a conventional ESP card test. Results for the four series pooled indicated a significant positive relationship between the ESP and memory scores, and a significantly high proportion of subjects with "low" memory scores scored below chance on the ESP test. A significant confirmation of the memory–ESP correlation was obtained in the pooled results of three confirmatory experiments of similar design (Feather, 1967). However, subjects in all these experiments were given so little time to memorize the lists that the "memory" test may have functioned merely as a second ESP test, a point made by K. R. Rao (personal communication).

Kanthamani and Rao (1975c) found a significant positive correlation between ESP scores and recall of paired associates with low association strength. In this case, subjects with above-median memory scores scored significantly above chance on the ESP test. On the other hand, Parker (1976) found a significant negative relationship between ESP and a measure of digit-memory span, but only in one of two experiments. The overall mean in this experiment was very close to chance. In both sets of experiments, the memory test was incorporated in the ESP test.

Other research pertinent to the memory–ESP relationship is discussed in section 4.1.2d.

3.3.2a. Conclusion. The few studies relating ESP to short-term memory have yielded inconsistent results.

3.3.3 Creativity: A Creative Interpretation Needed

An important aspect of intelligence that psychologists have found very difficult to quantify is creativity. In each of two experiments with college students, Schmeidler (1962b, 1964d) found negative correlations between ESP scores and two measures of creativity: a "classes-of-use" test and Barron's Independence of Judgment Scale. Only one of the four correlations was significant. The overall negative scoring in both experiments suggests that the results should be interpreted as psi-missing on the part of the *more* creative subjects.

Honorton (1967) tested high school students and found significant positive correlations between ESP scores and scores on a classes-of-use test and Torrance's Social-Motivation Inventory. This time the more creative subjects averaged close to chance while the *less* creative subjects manifested significant psi-missing. McGuire *et al.* (1974) reported a positive correlation between ESP and scores on the Welsh Figure Preference Test in an unspecified population, but the relationship apparently was not significant.

Anderson (1966) reported the results of a classroom experiment with 591 grade school children in which the ESP test was presented as a rocket-launching game. Teachers rated each pupil's creativity on a three-point scale. The most creative students scored significantly above chance and the middle group significantly below chance. The mean of the least creative group was nonsignificant. Group means and the method of statistical analysis were not reported. Levine and Stowell (1963) reported nonsignificant correlations between clairvoyance scores and classes-of-use tests in each of two experiments.

Finally, Moss found that pairs of subjects at least one of whom was engaged in an artistic profession had significantly more hits than other pairs in two free-response GESP experiments (Moss, 1969; Moss and Gengerelli, 1968). In a later study, the relationship was in the predicted direction but nonsignificant, perhaps due to the smaller sample size (Moss *et al.*, 1970). In the first two experiments, the artistic pairs scored significantly above chance. A chi-square analysis, which I computed of results reported by Gelade and Harvie (1975) in an attempted replication of Moss' experimental procedure, again revealed significantly more hits in pairs composed of two artists than in other pairs. However, in a card-guessing experiment, music majors were found to score no higher than other subjects (Jackson, Franzoi, and Schmeidler, 1977).

   3.3.3a. Conclusion. Integrating this disparate set of findings is left as an exercise for readers more creative than this reviewer. It is likely that the relationship between creativity and ESP depends on the particular measure of creativity used, the type of ESP test, and the nature of the experimental situation. Until such factors are systematically studied, conclusions in this area will continue to be hard to come by.

   The one consistent finding discussed in this section is a tendency for agent–percipient teams to be most successful in Moss's free-response GESP paradigm if both members of the team are artists. Although profession is only an indirect measure of creativity, it may be at least as valid as the direct measures currently available. Again, however, social psychological variables cannot be ruled out as possible mediators of this relationship.

3.3.4. Mental Imagery: Still More Confusion

   Because of indications that ESP responses are frequently mediated by visual imagery (e.g., Honorton and Harper, 1974; McCallam and Honorton, 1973), a number of experimenters have recently examined ESP scores in relation to one of the few objectively scored measures of imagery, Sheehan's (1967) version of the Betts QMI. The test requires the subject to generate images of various objects and events and to rate the vividness of each image on a seven-point scale.

   Honorton *et al.* (1974) found that above-average imagers on the Betts scored significantly above chance and below-average imagers significantly below chance on a six-run DT test. In a strict replication attempt, Schechter *et al.* (1975) obtained a significant reversal of Honorton's finding, with the below-average imagers scoring significantly above chance. A significant negative correlation between ESP and Betts scores also was found by Pleshette (1975) in an ESP test completed simultaneously with efforts at brain wave control, but the mean ESP score was not reported. No significant nonartifactual relationships between ESP and Betts scores have been found in free-response experiments (Palmer and Lieberman, 1975; Roll and Solfvin, 1976; Smith *et al.*, 1976).

   A companion scale to the Betts is the Gordon Test of Visual Imagery Control, in which subjects are asked how well they can manipulate images. When he combined the results of two experiments using this scale,

Price (1973b) found in a post hoc analysis that the scores of "autonomous" imagers were significantly more variable (i.e., between-subjects) than those of "controlled" imagers. The effect was independently significant in the first experiment and approached significance in the second. The two types of imagers also manifested significantly different run-score position effects (see Sec. 4.1.1) in each experiment, but the two interactions were not the same.

3.3.4a. Conclusion. The Betts has been shown to be heavily influenced by subtle variations in testing conditions (Marks, 1972; Palmer and Lieberman, 1975; Sheehan and Neisser, 1969), and such factors conceivably could be responsible for the inconsistent results with this measure. For a review, see Honorton (1975). More research will be needed to see if the Gordon scale is a more consistent predictor.

3.3.5. Dream Recall: A Dream Yet to Come True

A variable of possible relevance to the ability to evoke vivid visual imagery is the frequency with which persons recall their dreams. Honorton (1972a) found that adult education students who reported recalling their dreams at least once a week scored significantly above chance on a card-guessing test and significantly higher than the other members of the class. According to Honorton, a significant relationship between ESP scores and dream recall briefly reported by Johnson (1968) also was positive. However, Haraldsson (1975, 1976) twice failed to find significant relationships between these variables among large samples of Icelandic high school, vocational school, and college students. The trend in the first study, at least, would seem to be inconsistent with that found by Honorton. Two classroom card-guessing experiments with British high school children likewise yielded no significant relation between ESP and dream recall (Randall, 1972).

3.3.5a. Conclusion. A significant positive relationship between ESP and dream recall has been reported in two of six experiments. More data will be needed to determine if this indicates a genuine trend.

3.3.6. Field Dependence: A Merging of Present and Future?

Several tests have been devised to assess a person's ability to differentiate a figure in space from its surrounding environment or "ground." Persons who are relatively unsuccessful at making this discrimination are called "field-dependent" (Witkin, Dyk, Faterson, Goodenough, and Karp, 1962). A prominent measure of field dependence, the Embedded Figure Test (EFT), has related significantly to precognition scores in two experiments (Buzby, 1967a; Nash and Nash, 1968). In each case, the precognition scores of field-dependent subjects deviated from chance in either direction to a significantly greater degree than those of field-independent subjects. A measure of articulation of the body concept derived from the Draw-a-Person (DAP) test, which is positively correlated with the EFT, significantly differentiated subjects in the same direction as the EFT in the Nashes' experiment; but it would appear that a reversal occurred in the research of Buzby (1968a), inasmuch as significantly high variance was restricted to subjects who were both field-dependent on the EFT and field-independent on the DAP.

Relationships between clairvoyance scores and both the EFT and DAP test have consistently produced only chance results overall (Buzby, 1967a, 1968a, b; Nash and Nash, 1968, 1971). In an experiment with grade school children, however, Schmeidler (1962a) found a significant positive correlation between clairvoyance scores and scores on a test similar to the EFT, a trend indicating more psi-hitting among field-independent subjects.

3.3.6a. Conclusion. There is some preliminary evidence of a positive relationship between field dependence, as measured by the EFT, and the magnitude of precognition deviation scores, regardless of sign. Why this apparent relationship only holds for precognition is unclear; an admittedly metaphorical interpretation might be that field-dependent persons, who perceive more "globally," have a less rigid psychological boundary between the present and future that makes them more open to precognitive stimuli that more field-independent subjects tend to block out. Tart (1977a) proposes a somewhat similar interpretation to account for some precognitive displacement effects (see Sec. 6.1.1c).

3.4. Disabilities: ESP among the Less Fortunate

3.4.1. Mental Illness: Psi in the Psychically Disturbed

In medieval times and even in colonial America, psychic powers were considered to be a form of mental illness. The infamous Salem witch trials bear witness to the brutality sometimes suffered by those who were considered to be psychic. In our now more enlightened era, ESP no longer is considered a mark of insanity, but the question remains whether those diagnosed as mentally ill on what we hope are more rational grounds have more or less ESP ability than the population at large.

3.4.1a. Noninstitutionalized Patients. Hudesman and Schmeidler (1971) gave ESP clock-card tests to three outpatients following psychotherapy sessions. ESP scores were significantly above chance in sessions independently rated "good," and they were significantly better than scores following sessions rated "mediocre" or "poor." A follow-up experiment with two new patients failed to confirm these results, but a third patient showed a significant tendency to avoid both the target and its diametric opposite on the clock face (Hudesman and Schmeidler, 1976). The authors concluded that individualized hypotheses must be formulated for particular patients.

Jampolsky and Haight (1975) gave various forced-choice ESP tests to ten hyperkinetic children and a control group. The groups did not differ significantly in their performance, although nine of the ten hyperkinetic children had scores above chance.

3.4.1b. Institutionalized Patients. Shulman (1938) gave ten or more STM runs to each of 141 psychotic patients with various diagnoses. Overall results were at chance, but he did find significant and consistent psi-hitting among 12 manic-depressives in the depressed state and significant psi-missing (by t test) among 9 patients afflicted with involutional melancholia. If valid, these findings may reflect in part the generally superior performance of extraverted as compared to introverted subjects. Shulman states that melancholia patients are considered to be more withdrawn than depression patients, and he noted this difference manifested in the test situation. Randall (1974) found that high school males who reported depression on a questionnaire had card-guessing scores that deviated significantly from chance in either direction, i.e., significant "between-subjects variance." Combined with the findings of Shulman, these results suggest that depression may contribute to the magnitude of ESP effects, while direction is influenced by other factors such as extraversion.

Bates and Newton (1951) reported an experiment conducted 13 years earlier in which 95 patients were given a variety of forced-choice ESP tests. The overall results were highly significant, but there were no clear differences as a function of diagnostic category. Since the experimenter, Margaret Price, consistently obtained highly significant results with a variety of populations (see Pratt and Price, 1938), these results tell us nothing about the psychic ability of psychotics relative to other groups. West (1952), who has the reputation of being an unsuccessful experimenter, did nothing to damage his reputation in three DT series with psychotic patients, nor did 15 patients tested by Zorab (1957) show any evidence of ESP.

Finally, Humphrey (1954) tested 28 patients before and after electroshock therapy and 11 others before shock only. No pre-to-post-shock differences were found, but post hoc analyses revealed significant preshock psi-hitting among those patients diagnosed as schizophrenic. Humphrey found the schizophrenics to be unusually cooperative for patients with this diagnosis.

3.4.1c. Conclusion. There is little evidence that mentally ill patients have any more or less psychic ability than anyone else. However, only Jampolsky's experiment systematically compared such patients to a control group. The possibility that depression may enhance the bidirectional magnitude of ESP effects should be explored further. The discussion of ESP and mood (section 3.7) will be relevant to this issue. For a more extensive review of the literature on psi and psychosis, see Rogo (1975).

3.4.2. Physical Disabilities: Could the Thyroid Be the Key?

3.4.2a. Brain Injury. Since ESP must be at least mediated by the brain, one might expect its manifestation to be affected by brain injury. Unable to find subjects with localized brain lesions, Schmeidler gave a ten-trial card-guessing test to 18 concussion patients and 11 controls who either had recently recovered from concussion or who were hospitalized for fractures of regions other than the head (Schmeidler and McConnell, 1958). The concussion patients scored significantly above chance and significantly higher than the controls. Schmeidler noted that in comparison to the controls, the concussion patients were extremely passive, and the ones who got the highest scores, in addition, were cooperative during the test. Smythies and Beloff (1965) found no significant card-guessing performance in patients suffering from Parkinson's disease tested either before or after stereotactic surgery.

3.4.2b. Blindness. Price achieved her usual highly positive scores with a group of blind subjects, mostly adolescents, and a partially matched group of orphanage children, but no significant differences between them (Price, 1938; Price and Pegram, 1937).

3.4.2c. Thyroid Conditions. A number of persons with hyperthyroid conditions have seemed to possess unusual psi abilities (Taves, 1944). A young hyperthyroid woman tested by Reiss (1937, 1939) achieved the incredibly high average score of 18.24 hits per run over 1,850 trials in a GESP distance experiment. Following an unspecified treatment, the mean plummetted to 5.30. Almost as impressive a scoring rate was obtained by an 11-year-old mentally retarded boy in GESP runs with his mother as agent (Drake, 1938). This child apparently had hypothyroidism, and his scores declined following injections of thyroxin. Unfortunately, as the author was aware, some of the most successful runs with this subject were completed with less than adequate controls for auditory cues.

In neither of these two cases can the decline in scoring be clearly attributed to the thyroid condition (e.g., Reiss's subject suffered an emotional breakdown in between the two testing periods) and things obviously would be clearer if both subjects had the same type of thyroid imbalance. Nevertheless, the fact that two of the highest scoring card-guessing subjects in the history of parapsychology both had thyroid conditions points to an area of research that has been neglected far too long.

3.4.2d. Conclusion. All we have from the limited research on physical disabilities in relation to ESP are leads. However, the lead involving thyroid disturbances, in particular, could prove to be a very important one. Brain damage also may be worth a second look.

3.5. Biological Variables: ESP in the Life Cycle

Although our personalities and intellectual skills are conditioned to a large degree by the environment, certain other characteristics are for the most part fixed at birth. Whether an organism comes into the world as a human or an infrahuman species, male or female, firstborn or later born, has a profound and irreversible impact on his or her life experience. All organisms pass through the life cycle from birth, through childhood and adolescence, and into adulthood and old age. How is ESP ability affected by these biologically determined individual differences and life processes?

3.5.1. Sex Differences: Females Are More Intuitive, Sometimes

It is a common belief in our society that women are more intuitive than men. If intuition is any way connected to ESP, one also might expect women to be more psychic than men and thus to obtain higher scores on ESP tests.

3.5.1a. GESP Classroom Experiments. For some reason, analyses of sex differences have been reported most faithfully when the experiments involved the testing of primary or secondary school students in a classroom setting. Van Busschbach (1959) found that girls in the first and second grades of Dutch schools scored significantly higher than boys. However, other samples of Dutch and American school children did not reveal significant sex differences (Van Busschbach, 1955, 1956, 1961), and in some cases the boys scored better. Overall scoring generally was above chance in these experiments.

Louwerens (1960) found that when the teachers served as agents in a GESP experiment with 684 Dutch nursery school children, the girls scored significantly above chance and significantly higher than the boys. When some of these students were retested later, however, with the experimenter serving as agent, exactly the opposite result occurred. This time, however, the sex difference was not significant. Such reversals are common in ESP experiments when the same subjects are tested under two different conditions (Rao, 1965a), so the identity of the agent may not be a crucial variable. However, it is worth mentioning that the teachers served as agents in most of Van Busschbach's experiments.

In a more recent GESP experiment with 1,402 Dutch school children and the teacher serving as agent, girls again scored significantly higher than boys (Bierman and Camstra, 1973). An earlier pilot study failed to yield a significant difference, however. White and Angstadt (1963a, b) failed to find any significant sex differences in two experiments where the agents were classmates of the subjects, but the sample sizes were much smaller than those of the Dutch investigators, and the latter of White's experiments produced no significant evidence of psi whatsoever.

Finally, Van de Castle (1971) gave GESP card tests with the experimenter as agent to two groups of adolescent Cuna Indians, a tribe inhabiting islands off the coast of Panama. Pooled results for the 285 subjects revealed that girls again scored significantly higher than boys, but the result was primarily attributable to a significantly high proportion of the boys (62%) scoring below chance.

3.5.1b. Other GESP Experiments. In GESP experiments where subjects are tested individually, a common approach is to create a number of agent–percipient pairs. Sometimes the scores of these pairs are analyzed in terms of their sexual composition. McBain *et al.* (1970) found that same-sex pairs scored significantly higher than mixed-sex pairs in an experiment with significant overall positive scoring. However, in four GESP experiments in which senders attempted to bias the responses of naive subjects on various unstructured psychological tests (e.g., perception of the autokinetic effect, awareness of subliminal stimuli), sexual composition of the agent–percipient pairs had no significant effect (Kreitler and Kreitler, 1972, 1973).

In a review of the Maimonides dream experiments, Krippner (1970) reported that only the pooled results of male subjects were significant, and the results were not affected by the sex of the agent. However, it must be remembered that much of these data were contributed by a handful of highly selected subjects. In a modified ganzfeld experiment, Habel (1976) found significant psi-missing among all-male pairs and nonsignificant psi-hitting among all-female pairs, with mixed pairs scoring close to chance. No overall analysis comparing these groups was reported.

3.5.1c. Clairvoyance and Precognition Experiments. Experiments without an agent, including those conducted in a classroom setting, have consistently failed to yield any significant main effects for sex. I was able to find 34 experiments of this type in the literature where sex breakdowns were mentioned, and in only two of these was there a significant main effect for sex (Freeman, 1963; Rao, 1963b). The boys scored highest in each of these experiments, although Freeman's conclusion was based on analyses that used the trial rather than the subject as the unit of analysis.

However, sex has occasionally been shown to interact with other variables as predictors of ESP scores. These variables, discussed elsewhere in the chapter, include type of target symbol and arrangement (Freeman, 1963, 1964, 1965, 1966b, 1967, 1968, 1970a,b, 1972b), language of ESP target words (Rao, 1963b, 1964b), belief in ESP (Layton and Turnbull, 1975; Schmeidler, 1960), and precognition versus clairvoyance (Zenhausern *et al.*, 1977).

3.5.1d. Sexual Dominance. Two experimenters examined the sexual composition of intact groups, each predicting that scoring would be influenced by whether the group was dominated by males or by females. Mihalasky (1972) reported that some kind of complex interaction involving sex of subject, whether the leadership of the group was male or female, and a homemade personality scale measuring "dynamism" was found to be in the predicted direction in 12 of 15 groups tested. In a simpler experiment, Friedman, Schmeidler, and Dean (1976) defined sexual dominance in terms of the relative numbers of each sex in the group. Results of a card-guessing test given to 1,100 subjects in 11 intact groups revealed that in groups where sexual dominance was evident, subjects of the dominant sex scored significantly higher than subjects of the nondominant sex, when the groups were pooled for analysis. Finally, Wiklund (1977) found on the basis of a post hoc analysis that 15 of 16 subject triads scored highest when the experimenter was of the opposite sex from the majority of the triad members.

3.5.1e. Conclusion. There is evidence that among Dutch school children, females tend to score more positively than males in GESP card tests conducted in a classroom setting, at least when the agent is their teacher. Outside of this limited context (and with the exception of the psi-missing of Van de Castle's male Cuna Indians), sex of subject seems to have no direct effect on ESP scoring, although it occasionally has been shown to interact with other predictor variables. The sexual composition of agent–percipient pairs in more individualized GESP experiments has been shown to affect scoring in some experiments, but the patterns have been inconsistent and probably interact with other aspects of the test situation. Sexual dominance may be a useful variable to examine further in experiments with certain intact groups.

3.5.2. Age Differences: The Power of Youth

It is especially difficult to study age differences in ESP test performance, particularly over a large age range, because of the problems in finding a test procedure suitable for all ages. Until very recently, the only attempt to systematically compare the performance of children and adults were Rhine's early precognition experiments. In the first of three series, involving 19 adults, 5 children, and over 2,000 runs, the children scored significantly above chance and the adults significantly below chance (Rhine, 1941a). Two subsequent series of similar extent yielded results that were in the same direction but not significant (Rhine, 1942). In these latter experiments, the children were always tested in groups with a "party" atmosphere, while the adults were tested individually. Thus testing conditions were not very comparable for the two age groups.

In his classroom GESP experiments, Van Busschbach (1953, 1955, 1956) found that primary school children (ages 10 to 12) scored significantly above chance, while secondary school students (ages 12 to 20) scored at chance. Several thousand students were tested, and the differences were significant. Bierman and Camstra (1973), on the other hand, failed to find such a difference in their classroom GESP experiments.

Both Rhine and Van Busschbach relied exclusively on statistical techniques that indiscriminately pooled hits across subjects. Therefore, we have no firm basis of knowing how uniformly the effects were distributed among the subjects in their samples. Practically speaking, this does not introduce a serious bias in Van Busschbach's case, but it may well be a factor in Rhine's, where the number of runs per subject was quite large.

The most ambitious attempt to compare ESP test results in different age groups was a recent GESP experiment by Spinelli (1977). He tested 150 children of ages 3 to 8 and 50 adults of ages 19 to 21. Subjects were tested in pairs, each member alternating as sender and receiver. The children scored above chance to a highly significant degree, while the adults scored close to chance. An earlier experiment with a wider range of ages produced comparable results, but the agents in this experiment were allowed to choose which target to send on each trial, a methodological no-no that conceivably could have biased the results. In this experiment, subjects from 3 to 8 scored significantly above chance while those 14 or older scored at chance. Van Busschbach (1959) also found significant scoring among children aged 6 to 8 in classroom GESP experiments conducted in Holland, but comparable series conducted in the United States yielded only chance results, a fact he attributed to poor testing conditions (Van Busschbach, 1961).

The significant age differences that have been found all involved comparing subjects before and after puberty. Experiments comparing age ranges within these broader categories have failed to yield significant main effects (Anderson and Gregory, 1959; Anderson and McConnell, 1961; Green, 1965; Musso, 1965; Shields, 1962; Spinelli, 1977; Van Busschbach, 1961; White and Angstadt, 1963a, b), with one exception (Van Busschbach, 1959). However, White and Angstadt (1963b) found an interaction suggesting that younger subjects were most successful in discriminating between two competing target sequences in the predicted direction.

3.5.2a. Conclusion. There is some evidence that children score more significantly and positively on forced-choice ESP tests than do adolescents or adults. Puberty seems to be the crucial cutoff point. However, the failure of fifth and sixth grade students to score any better than high school students in the large-scale Anderson–White clairvoyance experiments (see Sec. 2.5.2b) and the weakness of design of some of the confirmatory experiments suggest caution in drawing conclusions. Conceivably age, like sex, has a straightforward effect on scoring only in GESP experiments. More and better research on the relationship between age and ESP is needed.

3.5.3 Birth Order: Shall the First Be First?

In a correspondence experiment involving over 6,000 readers of a magazine or newspaper, Green (1965) reported a post hoc effect indicating that magazine readers who had been only children scored below chance on -1 displacement, eldest children above chance, and younger children at chance. The groups differed by one-way analysis of variance to a highly significant degree. No such effect was found with the newspaper readers, whom Green considered to be of generally lower economic status than the magazine readers. Eastman (1967) reported significant psi-hitting among firstborn college students, who apparently scored significantly higher than later born or only children. No significant birth order effects were found in two other experiments (Brodbeck, 1969; Schmeidler and Lindemann, 1966).

3.5.3a. Conclusion. Despite some suggestive evidence that psi-hitting may be more prevalent among eldest children, a clear trend has yet to be established between birth order and ESP.

3.5.4. Twins: Togetherness Outside the Womb

Twins often have been considered potentially ideal subjects for GESP experiments in which one twin would try to "send" a target to the other. It is tempting to speculate that twins might be particularly able to "tune in" to each other telepathically because of their common biological origin. Although such twin studies are frequently talked about, very few have been published in the serious literature.

Kubis and Rouke (1937) tested six pairs of twins by having them respond simultaneously to cards looked at by the experimenter. Informal testing with two of these pairs involved having the twins take turns sending to each other. Results were essentially of a chance nature, as were the results of a GESP experiment by Rogers (1960). Duane and Behrendt (1965) reported remote driving of the EEG in 2 of 15 pairs of identical twins. The report was very sketchy, but it would appear that alpha waves evoked in one twin by photic driving spontaneously and simultaneously appeared in the EEG of the other twin located in another room. In a similar experiment where an effort was made to induce plethysmographic reactions in a percipient by showing emotional verbal stimuli to the agent, friends or spouses achieved somewhat better results than did twins (Esser, Etter, and Chamberlain, 1967). Barron and Mordkoff (1967) found suggestive evidence of autonomic responses in one twin coincident with arousal in his counterpart, but three other pairs of identical twins produced null results. Nash and Buzby (1965) tested 25 pairs of twins ranging in age from 5 to 13. Each twin completed six DT clairvoyance runs. Overall results were nonsignificant, but a post hoc analysis revealed that 10 of the 11 pairs of identical twins had overall scores of the same algebraic sign (i.e., either above or below chance) as compared to only 5 of 12 pairs of fraternal twins suitable for this analysis. The difference was significant. In another clairvoyance experiment, however, France and Hogan (1973) found no evidence of similar hit patterns between members of pairs of identical twins, pairs of fraternal twins, or pairs of ordinary siblings.

The best of the twin studies was a recent experiment by Charlesworth (1975). Pairs of identical and fraternal twins were tested in a free-response GESP experiment presented in the context of an imaginary dream (see Sec. 2.6.2e). Each twin was sender once and receiver once. The fraternal twins had significantly more hits than expected by chance and significantly more than obtained by the identical twins, although the twin types apparently differed also on extraversion, a possible confounding variable.

3.5.4a. Conclusion. There is no evidence that twins have any special aptitude for "telepathic" exchange. However, more research on the topic is needed, especially studies comparing twins and ordinary siblings.

3.5.5. ESP in Animals: The Carrot and the Stick

The suggestive evidence that children may have greater psychic ability than adults seems to indicate that advanced brain activity may be inhibitory to psi. If this is the case, infrahuman species might be expected to manifest considerable ESP. There have been numerous anecdotal reports of ESP in animals, the best documented being so-called psi-trailing cases, in which pets left behind by a family when they move eventually turn up at the family's new residence, often after traversing considerable distances (Rhine and Feather, 1962).

ESP experiments involving animals have been and will be discussed in other sections of the chapter where appropriate. The purpose of this section is to briefly review these "anpsi" experiments from the standpoint of the evidence they provide that animals do in fact have ESP abilities.

3.5.5a. Experiments with Cats. The first systematic attempt to demonstrate ESP in animals under experimental conditions was by Osis. In the first set of experiments, the experimenter attempted to exert a telepathic influence over which of two food cups kittens would approach first (Osis, 1952). In the second set, a clairvoyance procedure was adopted, the cats being required to choose which of two doorways at the end of an alley would lead to a food reward. Significant evidence of psi was obtained in both sets of experiments (Osis and Foster, 1953). Although controls against sensory cues were probably adequate, I would not go so far as to say they were ruled out. Furthermore, results of the first set of experiments could just as easily be attributable to the agent's PK as to ESP on the part of the kittens, a possibility that exists in any GESP experiment with human or animal percipients. I also am not convinced that experimenter knowledge of the target was ruled out in the second set, rendering telepathy or "agent" PK as possibilities there as well. ESP and PK are also alternate interpretations of an experiment by Morris (1974), who demonstrated that the activity level of a kitten was altered when his master "visited" him during out-of-body experiences. Unfortunately, results of later experiments when the cat was older were less consistent (Roll, Morris, Harary, Wells, and Hartwell, 1975).

3.5.5b. The Shock-Avoidance Paradigm. One of the more elegant approaches to testing psi in animals was the shock-avoidance paradigm of Duval and Montredon (1968a, b). A random number generator controlled the delivery of brief shocks to one or the other side of an electrified grid floor divided by a low barrier. The animal could avoid shock by precognizing on which side the shock would be delivered next and positioning himself on the opposite side. The procedure was completely automated and could be run in the experimenter's absence, thereby reducing, if not entirely eliminating, the possibility of experimenter PK confounding the interpretation of results.

Duval made the a priori decision to evaluate only what he called "random behavior trials" (RBTs), which he defined as trials during which the animal crossed the barrier once without the stimulus of a previous shock.* Cases where the animal simply stayed on the same side or crossed in response to shock were considered instances of stereotyped

---

*Duval's criterion for RBTs did not account for double jumps within a single trial, which some might consider to be instances of "random behavior."

behavior not likely to be psi-mediated. In each of two experiments involving four and ten mice, respectively, Duval demonstrated that the mice crossed the barrier to avoid shock significantly more often than they crossed into shock. Morris (1970) examined the target sequences used in these experiments and found them to be satisfactorily random. Such a test had not been reported by Duval.

An impressive series of apparent replications and extensions of Duval's work was invalidated when the experimenter, Walter J. Levy, was caught manipulating data by his associates (Rhine, 1974). A subsequent series of replication attempts at Rhine's laboratory only yielded spotty evidence of significance in nine experiments (Levin, 1975; Terry, 1976b), the average number of trials per experiment being roughly comparable to that reported by Duval.

Eysenck (1975) reported the results of two shock-avoidance series with rats, the series differing only in the intensity of the shock administered. In the low-shock (0.1 mA) series, the animals *approached* the shock to a degree significantly greater than chance; in the higher-shock (0.2 mA) series, only chance results were obtained. Eysenck tentatively interpreted his results as supporting the applicability of optimal level theories of arousal to psi research. Duval, unfortunately, did not report the level of shock he used, so Eysenck's results cannot be integrated with this previous work.

Finally, Extra (1972) reported no overall significant scoring in two shock-avoidance experiments with rats, but in each case he found significantly greater avoidance under GESP than under clairvoyance conditions.

3.5.5c. Positive-Reinforcement Paradigms. Duval's research also led to attempts to see whether ESP could be demonstrated in positive-reinforcement paradigms. Schouten (1972) trained ten mice in a brightness-discrimination task. The mice were to press a black or a white lever for water reward when a buzzer and light came on in a corresponding black or white portion of the chamber. For test trials, the light stimulus was removed to a corresponding cage in another room and only the buzzer remained as a (nondiscriminable) cue stimulus. Thus the animal had to use psi to determine which lever would yield reward.

The overall results revealed a marginally significant tendency for animals to receive reward more frequently than expected by chance. However, an extensive series of follow-up experiments yielded virtually no evidence of psi (Schouten, 1976b).

Nevertheless, other experimenters have reported significant results with positive reinforcement. In a precognition experiment otherwise similar to Schouten's, Terry and Harris (1975) trained five rats to make a brightness discrimination in a Skinner box for water reward. The rats scored significantly above chance in the subsequent ESP test, but only on RBTs. (Schouten's significant results in 1972 also were attributable to such trials.) In another precognition experiment, this time with gerbils, Parker (1974) reported a significant excess of correct choices on all trials combined, but nonsignificant results were obtained in each of two independent replication attempts (Broughton and Millar, 1975).

3.5.5d. The "Russian Roulette" Paradigm. In a third approach to testing ESP in animals, which I call the Russian Roulette paradigm, the behavior of the animals at a particular time is noted. Subsequently, some of the animals are randomly selected to receive a noxious stimulus (usually resulting in death) while the other animals are spared. Differences in the preselection behavior of the two groups are interpreted as evidence for precognition.

The first exploratory experiments of this type were undertaken by Morris (1970), who found encouraging results with both rats and goldfish, the behavioral measures being the amount of free-field activity. As expected, the targeted rats were less active than controls (i.e., "freezing") and the targeted goldfish were more active than controls.

A series of systematic attempts to provide further evidence of ESP with this paradigm have been reported by James Craig. Craig and Treurniet (1974) found that rats scheduled to be killed immediately after the experiment were *more* active than rats to be killed at least three weeks later. However, the effect was significant on only one of three activity measures, and no significant effects were found in a later experiment (Treurniet and Craig, 1975). In a related series of experiments, the behavioral measure was which direction rats would turn at the end of a T-maze (Craig, 1973, 1975). For some of the rats, the decision as to whether death would be imminent or delayed was partly contingent on their choices, while for other rats it was not. In each of three experiments, there was no significant tendency for rats in the contingent condition to make choices that would postpone their deaths. There were significant post hoc effects in most of Craig's experiments, but these tended to be inconsistent across experiments.

3.5.5e. "Clever" Animals. Numerous accounts have appeared in the popular literature describing animals who seem to be able to perform mental feats beyond their presumed intellectual capacities, the most famous perhaps being the horse Clever Hans (Pfungst, 1911/1965). It sometimes is suggested that such abilities may have a psi component, although responses to intentional or unintentional cues by the trainer seems to be the preferred explanation in most cases (Rhine, 1951).

The only experiment where ESP in such an animal has been tested under reasonably well-controlled conditions involved a dog named Chris, whose forte was answering mathematical questions by pawing an appropriate number of times on his master's arm. Chris was trained to make ESP responses in this way by means of a numerical code and then tested on several occasions with standard card-guessing procedures (Wood and Cadoret, 1958). Results were significantly positive and quite impressive when only the trainer and/or his friends or family were present during the test. Less impressive but still significant psi-missing occurred when Cadoret, a parapsychologist, was present as an observer.

   3.5.5f. Conclusion. Although some significant evidence of ESP has been found in experiments with animals, the results are not noticeably superior to those obtained with humans. The possibility of experimenter or agent psi clouds the interpretation of several animal experiments. The positive-reinforcement paradigm seems to be slightly more promising than the shock-avoidance paradigm and substantially more promising than the Russian Roulette paradigm, trends that certainly should be greeted with joy by the world's rodent population. Research with "clever" animals is only likely to pay off if the animal can perform in the absence of its trainer and other persons who might give sensory cues. An excellent review of most of the "anpsi" research has been written by Robert Morris (1970).

3.6. Attitudes toward ESP: Faith Conquers All

3.6.1. Belief in ESP: Speaking of Animals . . .

   Parapsychological jargon contains its share of colorful terms, but none are better known than Gertrude Schmeidler's labels of "sheep" and "goats," which she applied to believers and nonbelievers in ESP. This "sheep–goat effect" has become perhaps the most thoroughly studied relationship in the field of parapsychology. Interpretation of this deluge of data is not as simple and straightforward as one might expect, and to make sense of it we will need to introduce certain distinctions that are often overlooked by the experimenters themselves.

   3.6.1a. Belief in ESP—in the Test Situation. In a detailed summary of her early research on the sheep–goat effect, Schmeidler reported the results of 18 separate card-guessing series (excluding 3 that were arbitrarily stopped when the results reached significance), 14 of which were conducted in a classroom setting (Schmeidler and McConnell, 1958). A total of 1,248 subjects were tested in these series. Subjects were asked whether they believed ESP to be possible *under the conditions of the experiment.* Those who totally rejected this possibility were labeled goats and all others were labeled sheep, even those who were doubtful about it. When the results for both the individual and classroom series were separately pooled, a highly significant difference was found in each case, the sheep scoring significantly above chance and the goats scoring significantly below chance. However, the effect was an extremely weak one in terms of the magnitude of the deviations; the high significance levels were the result of the large sample sizes.

Because the sheep–goat hypothesis is so easy to test, belief questions have been included in a large number of forced-choice ESP experiments (although not, surprisingly, in free-response experiments). However, many experimenters have claimed to be testing this hypothesis using questions and/or classification criteria that differed substantially from Schmeidler's. In particular, investigators often overlook the fact that Schmeidler did *not* ask her subjects whether ESP exists but only whether it can occur in the test situation. Any experienced investigator knows that there are many people with strong beliefs in ESP who don't believe that it can be manufactured on demand in a laboratory, especially by means of "sterile" card tests.

Considering only those experiments where Schmeidler's procedure was replicated essentially, if not precisely, we find several significant confirmations of the sheep–goat hypothesis (Bevan, 1947b; Carpenter, 1971; Eisenbud, 1965; Palmer, 1973; Schmeidler, 1971; Wilson, 1964). Carpenter's and Eisenbud's effects reached significance only by a one-tailed test, and Eisenbud's belief question could be interpreted as referring to the subject's confidence in his own scoring ability rather than his belief in the utility of the procedure. Another significant confirmation was reported by Schmeidler (1962b), but only on the basis of a secondary post hoc analysis. Finally, the effect was confirmed in two experiments where classification was based on a multiple-item scale heavily loaded with items reflecting Schmeidler's criterion (Bhadra, 1966; Ryzl, 1968b).

On the other hand, a large number of studies have produced nonsignificant results with this type of breakdown (Adcock and Quartermain, 1959; Beloff and Bate, 1970; Friedman *et al.*, 1976; Honorton, 1972a; Kahn, 1952; Nash, 1965; Nash and Nash, 1967; Schmeidler, 1964e, 1968; Schmeidler and Craig, 1972; Schmeidler and Lewis, 1968, 1969; White and Angstadt, 1961; Wilson, 1964). Thus we see that only about a third of these replication attempts have been successful, and even this figure is probably too high if one takes into account publication biases. However, the important point is that all the significant sheep–goat differences have been in the predicted direction; none of the reversals has even approached significance. In fact, the overall pattern of results is strikingly similar to that of Schmeidler's original research, where significant effects (all in the proper direction) were found in only 4 of the 18 separate series (Schmeidler and McConnell, 1958).

3.6.1b. Belief in ESP—in the Abstract. Questions asking subjects simply whether or not they believe in ESP have produced a pattern of results not too different from the pattern based on Schmeidler's question. In these experiments, the usual procedure is either to divide subjects into approximately equal groups or to use correlational methods of analysis; classification criteria are not as precisely defined as those suggested by Schmeidler. Believers scored significantly higher than nonbelievers in four of these experiments (Barrington, 1973; Eilbert and Schmeidler, 1950; Haraldsson, 1976; Moss and Gengerelli, 1968). In three other experiments, a question of this type contributed to a multiple-item scale that significantly discriminated these two groups in the expected direction (Bhadra, 1966; Palmer and Miller, 1972; Ryzl, 1968b). One significant reversal has been reported (Moss *et al.*, 1970), but this finding is not particularly meaningful because the goats were preselected on the basis of high ESP scores in previous testing. All other experiments have yielded essentially chance differences (Casper, 1951; Haraldsson, 1975; Harary, 1976; Kahn, 1952; Nash, 1958; Nash and Nash, 1967; Osis and Dean, 1964; Palmer, 1973; Palmer *et al.*, 1976; Rhine, 1968; Roll and Solfvin, 1976; Schmeidler and Lindemann, 1966; Smith and Canon, 1954; Woodruff and Dale, 1950). An indirect projective measure of belief in ESP has also yielded generally nonsignificant results so far as ESP deviation scores are concerned (Osis and Dean, 1964; Van de Castle, 1957; Van de Castle and White, 1955).

This pattern is not quite as strong as the previous one, but it does seem to be nonrandom. The question then becomes whether belief in ESP is an independent correlate of ESP scores, or whether its discriminating power depends upon its confounding with Schmeidler's criterion. Questions regarding belief in ESP in the abstract and belief in ESP in the test situation have been directly compared in only three experiments (Kahn, 1952; Nash and Nash, 1967; Palmer, 1973). Only Palmer's experiment yielded a significant attitude effect. In this case, the sheep–goat hypothesis was significantly confirmed using a slightly modified version of Schmeidler's classification, while the abstract belief question resulted in a nonsignificant reversal.

There also have been a number of experiments that I have seen only in abstract form where sheep–goat questions were included in the design and the results of the relevant analyses were either reported as nonsignificant (Banham, 1968; Crumbaugh, 1958; Gerstein and Merker, 1964; Jackson *et al.*, 1977; McGuire *et al.*, 1974; Peterson, 1972; Taetzsch, 1964, 1965) or not reported at all (Carpenter, 1973; Dean and Taetzsch,

1963; Nash, 1964; Rogers, 1967c). It would appear likely from the abstracts that most if not all of these authors defined the sheep–goat variable in terms of belief in ESP in the abstract.

At this point, the most reasonable conclusion would seem to be that abstract belief in ESP is not an independently valid predictor of ESP scores.

3.6.1c. Manipulating Belief. Some experimenters have sought not only to measure already existing belief in ESP but to manipulate such beliefs experimentally. Layton and Turnbull (1975) instructed an experimenter to tell one group of subjects that the existence of ESP had been scientifically verified and that he expected it to be demonstrated in this test, but to give a second group the opposite information. Although the manipulation was apparently effective in creating the appropriate beliefs, a straightforward confirmation of the sheep–goat hypothesis was not obtained in either of two experiments.

Taddonio (1975), on the other hand, obtained significant confirmations of the hypothesis in each of two experiments of similar design to Layton's, the effect in each case being strongest among subjects who were undecided about their own ability to score well on ESP tests before the session began. Perhaps Taddonio's experiments were more successful than Layton's because her belief manipulation stressed the adequacy of the test for measuring ESP, whereas Layton stressed the existence of ESP per se.

Two other experimenters also attempted to manipulate subjects' beliefs by identifying themselves with attitudes either favorable or unfavorable to the ESP hypothesis (Alkokar, 1968; Waldron, 1959). Both experiments yielded significant results, but they were more complex than those of Taddonio.

3.6.1d. Variance Effects. Several experimenters have examined belief in ESP in relation to ESP variance measures. Although Schmeidler and McConnell found no significant difference between the scores of sheep and goats with respect to run-score variance (Schmeidler and McConnell, 1958), three other investigators reported results that generally indicated higher run-score variance among goats and conflicted subjects than among sheep (Nash and Nash, 1958; Osis and Dean, 1964; Van de Castle, 1957).

Van de Castle and Osis in their experiments also examined the variance of subjects' total scores, where the finding was that such variance was greater among extreme sheep and conflicted subjects than among goats and less enthusiastic sheep. Buzby (1967b) found significantly higher between-subjects variance among sheep who were "vitally" interested in ESP than among sheep whose interest was only "casual." The effect was significant in two independent series, but it only appeared in precognition (in contrast to clairvoyance) runs, and the effect could not be replicated by Nash and Nash (1968). Finally, Jones and Feather (1969) found consistently higher between-subjects variance among persons who reported a variety of psychic experiences than among less "psychic" individuals. It is usually safe to assume that persons who have had a variety of psychic experiences believe strongly in ESP, although Jones reported no data on this point.

In a tentative attempt to integrate the results of the variance studies, Palmer (1972) suggested that extreme sheep, and perhaps others who are strongly involved emotionally with the issue of ESP, produce the strongest and most reliable scores on ESP tests, but that some of these subjects score above chance and others below. This inference was based primarily on trends that indicate high between-subjects variance and low run-score variance among extreme sheep.

This factor conceivably could explain a tendency noted in some sheep–goat data for the highest scoring subjects to be those who think a positive outcome in the experiment to be possible but not likely (Friedman et al., 1976; Palmer and Miller, 1972; Schmeidler, 1968; Schmeidler and McConnell, 1958). In other words, there is a tendency for the mean of the more extreme sheep to regress back to chance, a tendency that might be attributable to a cancellation of high- and low-scoring subjects. An alternative interpretation of this regression is suggested by an experiment of Stanford (1964b), who found that scores of extreme sheep declined within the run, while scores of other subjects inclined. Stanford only gave his subjects one run, but if the decline of his extreme sheep is the kind of thing that can continue beyond one run, it could lead to mean differences between extreme and moderate sheep in multirun experiments. However, it should be emphasized that evidence for lower mean scores among extreme than moderate sheep is only suggestive, and there is at least one significant exception (McBain et al., 1970).

3.6.1e. Interaction Effects. Because of the fragility of the sheep–goat effect, it is fortunate that several investigators have looked for interactions between belief in ESP and other variables as predictors of ESP scores. The other predictor that has recieved the most attention so far is sex differences. In secondary analyses of her original series of sheep–goat experiments, Schmeidler (1960) found a significant interaction indicating that the sheep–goat effect was strongest for females. Layton and Turnbull (1975) found a similar interaction favoring females in the first of two experiments in which belief was experimentally manipulated, but the effect did not reappear in the replication attempt. These results prompted me to look for this interaction in data I had recently reported (Palmer *et al.*, 1976). I also found a significant interaction ($F = 4.77$, $df = 1/1708$, $p <$ .05), but this time the predicted effect occurred only for males.

Another set of secondary analyses caused Schmeidler to conclude that the sheep–goat effect in her original studies did not appear for subjects who showed signs of maladjustment on the Rorschach (Schmeidler, 1960). Carpenter (1971) found a complex interaction between belief in ESP, a measure of sex guilt, and whether ESP targets were accompanied by erotic photographs (see Sec. 5.1.2). In an experiment devoid of goats, Nielsen (1970) reported that sheep scored significantly above chance and significantly higher than "open-minded" subjects, but only in sessions where they rated their moods as either extremely positive or extremely negative. Finally, Palmer and Miller (1972) found a significant interaction indicating that the sheep–goat effect was eliminated when a monetary reward was offered for the highest score.

3.6.1f. Conclusion. Research described by Schmeidler and McConnell (1958) provides strong evidence that subjects who believe ESP to be possible under the conditions of the experiment score more positively on card-guessing tests than subjects who do not. Although most smaller-scale replication attempts have failed to produce significant confirmations of this finding, the fact that all the significant effects have been in the predicted direction reinforces Schmeidler's conclusion. Still further support comes from experiments in which the sheep–goat question was phrased in terms of belief in ESP in the abstract, although the results suggest that Schmeidler's classification scheme is the most effective. Attempts to influence ESP scoring by manipulating belief in ESP have produced mixed results.

The results of variance studies suggest, among other things, that strong or emotionally involved believers in ESP have a tendency to score reliably above or below chance on ESP tests, possibly contributing to a suggestive tendency for extreme sheep to average closer to chance on ESP card tests than moderate sheep. Evidence of within-run decline effects among extreme sheep suggests an alternate explanation of this apparent regression.

Belief in ESP has shown a tendency to interact with other variables such as sex, mood, and emotional adjustment as predictors of ESP scoring. However, the direction of such interactions may depend on situational factors not now understood.

3.6.2. Questions Related to Belief: Wolves in Sheep's Clothing

Sheep–goat experiments frequently include questions that are related to belief in ESP, but deal with other aspects of subjects' cognitions about this topic.

3.6.2a. Psychic Experiences. One such question concerns whether the subject has ever had a psychic experience or belives that he is "psychic." In only two cases have subjects admitting such experiences or talent scored significantly higher than other subjects (Alkokar and Deshpande, 1966; Moss and Gengerelli, 1968), the latter being a free-response experiment. Such a question was included in the successful composite scales of Bhadra (1966) and Palmer and Miller (1972), but in the latter, at least, its contribution to the scale's success was considerably less than the contribution of the abstract belief question. Beloff and Bate (1970) found that subjects who believed they had psychic ability scored differently from other subjects to a significant degree across seven samples, but the direction of the effect differed from sample to sample. Also, Jones and Feather (1969) found significantly higher between-subject variance among subjects who reported a relatively wide range of psychic experiences. Otherwise, this question has failed to yield significant discriminations (Casper, 1951; Gelade and Harvie, 1975; Harary, 1976; Moss, 1969; Osis and Dean, 1964; Palmer, 1973; Roll and Solfvin, 1976; Schmeidler, 1964e, 1968, 1971; Schmeidler and Lindemann, 1966; Woodruff and Dale, 1950).

3.6.2b. Confidence of Success. Sheep–goat experiments often include a question asking how well the subjects themselves think they will score or have just scored on the ESP test. The only experiment I can find in the literature where such predictions proved to be accurate involved Argentine grade school children (Musso, 1965), although Eisenbud's (1965) experiment may also qualify if the belief question is interpreted as a confidence question. Nash (1958) found a significant *negative* relationship between predictions of success and actual ESP scores. A confidence item was included in two of the successful composite scales (Bhadra, 1966; Palmer and Miller, 1972), but its contribution to the success of the latter experiment, at least, was negligible. Schmeidler (1971) found that subjects who predicted above-chance scores revealed a significantly different relationship between a composite mood scale and ESP run-score variance than did subjects who did not predict above-chance scores.

Confidence items have failed to yield significant discriminations in numerous other forced-choice experiments (Eilbert and Schmeidler, 1950; Friedman *et al.*, 1976; Kahn, 1952; Michie and West, 1957; Osis and Dean, 1964; Palmer, 1973; Ryzl, 1968a; Schmeidler, 1964e, 1971; Schmeidler and Craig, 1972; Woodruff and Dale, 1950). Schmeidler (1964e) found that her subjects could make significantly accurate predictions on a run-by-run basis, but subjects tested by Nash (1960a) were not so successful. Expectancy of success has also been a poor predictor in free-response experiments (Braud and Braud, 1974; Braud *et al.*, 1975; Parker *et al.*, 1977; Stanford and Mayer, 1974), although complex curvilinear effects were found in two experiments where subjects were given the mental set to have out-of-body experiences during the session (Palmer and Lieberman, 1975; Palmer and Vassar, 1974).

To keep things in perspective, it should be pointed out that simple questions asking a person how well he expects to perform on a test, because they get into the area of personal competence, are very susceptible to response biases. Genuine confidence, a rather rare commodity in ESP tests, may yet prove to be helpful. In fact, the creation of such confidence is one explanation of why hypnosis seems to facilitate ESP (see Sec. 2.6.1a).

3.6.2c. Attitude toward ESP. Finally, several experiments have included questions addressing subjects' "attitudes" toward ESP as distinct from their "beliefs" about its existence (see Fishbein and Raven, 1967). In other words, these questions refer to whether the subject would *like* for ESP to exist. The results can be succinctly summarized by saying that no significant or consistent relationship between attitudes toward ESP and ESP scores has been uncovered (Kahn, 1952; Layton and Turnbull, 1975; Ryzl, 1968a; Schmeidler and Lindemann, 1966).

3.6.2d. Conclusion. Neither previous psychic experiences nor predictions of ESP scores nor attitude toward ESP have been shown to correlate with ESP test performance in a straightforward manner, although any or all of them may interact with other variables in this capacity.

For a detailed review of the sheep–goat literature and studies on related questions, see Palmer (1971, 1972).

3.7. Spontaneous Transient States: Good Days and Bad Days

3.7.1. Mood and Emotional Variables: The Effect of Affect

Personality traits and attitudes are less likely to influence ESP performance directly than through the mediation of dispositions that are present at the time of the test itself. Spielberger (1966) has operationalized this notion with his "state–trait" theory of anxiety. If this reasoning is valid, one might expect measures of a subject's mood, anxiety, or other emotional states to be associated with ESP scores, perhaps to an even greater degree than underlying trait measures.

Two classes of ESP experiments are relevant to this issue. The first group of studies deal with what might be called the subject's mood, i.e., how good or bad he or she feels, or how much he or she feels like taking the test. The second group of studies have sought to define these affective states more precisely, dealing with predictor variables such as state anxiety, surgency, and social affection.

3.7.1a. General Mood. One of the first mood studies was a correspondence experiment conducted in England by Fisk and West (1956). Fisk displayed three clock-card targets in his home each day, which subjects were asked to identify from their homes. There were 162 subjects who completed at least the minimum of 96 trials, and most of these filled out a simple scale rating their moods at each session on a continuum from "elation" to "depression." Sessions where subjects' moods were classified as "pleasureable" were associated with significantly positive scoring, while the outcomes with other moods depended upon how the results were analyzed.

The bulk of subsequent mood studies have been conducted by three investigators: Winnifred Nielsen, David Rogers, and James Carpenter. The most elaborate approach has been that of Nielsen, who has attempted to explore the interaction between mood and personality variables. In her first experiment (Nielsen, 1956b), eight subjects completed 20 sessions, each of which included five precognition runs and a three-part mood scale measuring physical, mental, and emotional vitality. Because a precognition procedure was used, subjects could complete the sessions at home anytime they wished. The results indicated that significant above-chance scoring was restricted to subjects who rated their moods consistently across all three subscales within the session, regardless of whether the mood was pleasant or unpleasant. Nielsen interpreted this as a relationship between ESP scores and extremeness of mood. In a follow-up experiment (Nielsen, 1970), the same effect was found using the same mood scale scored in a way that more directly measured extremeness rather than consistency of mood. However, the effect reversed for a small subsample who were not believers in ESP.

Secondary analyses of these two experiments, plus a third experiment briefly discussed by Nielsen (1970), revealed another interaction. This one indicated the relationship between ESP scores and extremity of mood consistently appeared only for subjects classified as introverted on the Bernreuter Personality Inventory. Nielsen explored this interaction further in a series of 12 experiments with high school and college students tested in a classroom setting (Nielsen, 1972a, 1972b). The Eysenck Personality Inventory was substituted for the Bernreuter, and subjects' responses were scored against both their own individual target orders and a single target order for the whole group. Unfortunately, the reports of this research are quite sketchy. In general, though, the results seem to confirm the previously reported interaction between introversion and extremity of mood for individual targets. In one experiment, however, it was the relatively neurotic (rather than introverted) subjects on the EPI who showed the mood effect (Nielsen, 1972b), and a complex interaction generally consistent with this latter finding also was reported by Freeman (1972a).

Since the Bernreuter "introversion" scale is as much a measure of neuroticism as of introversion, perhaps the best way to summarize Nielsen's overall results is to say that anxious, introverted subjects tended to obtain positive ESP scores when they were in extremely pleasant or extremely unpleasant moods, in marked contrast to their usual tendency to obtain negative scores (see Sec. 3.2.2).

Both Rogers and Carpenter found that mood was related to the variability of ESP run scores (regardless of direction) around MCE. Effects involving the more common ESP deviation scores were either not significant or not reported.

The simpler of these two paradigms was that of Rogers (1967b), whose subjects were asked to complete standard precognition runs at times when they were either in a good mood (and really wanted to take the test) or in a bad mood. This stipulation probably led to more variability on the mood dimension than occurred in Nielsen's experiments. Both in this experiment and in an earlier experiment where Rogers tested himself (Rogers, 1966), there was significantly below-chance variance (i.e., run scores consistently close to five) in the negative mood state, and nonsignificant above-chance variance in the positive mood state. In each experiment, the variances in the two conditions differed significantly.

Carpenter had his subjects complete precognition runs (four or five per session) at their leisure. His subjects also filled out at each session a mood scale consisting of items selected from Nowlis's mood adjective checklist. In each of three experiments, an interaction was found between pleasantness and extremity of mood in relation to ESP run-score variance (Carpenter, 1968, 1969). Variance was consistently higher in moderately pleasant than in moderately unpleasant moods (this subeffect was independently significant in two of the three experiments), but in sessions where moods were rated as extreme, unpleasant moods were associated with the higher variance.

Carpenter (1973) briefly reported on five subsequent experiments of similar design, using a truncated mood scale that consisted only of items that were significant predictors of ESP scores in his previous experiments. In two of the five experiments, this new scale significantly replicated the effect found previously, and there were clear trends in the predicted direction in two others. Two experiments revealed interactions between this effect and attitude or personality variables, suggesting that a systematic multivariate approach might result in greater predictability.

Carpenter's results are similar to those obtained by Rogers, but only if one assumes that Rogers' subjects were in "moderate" moods when they completed their ESP runs. As mentioned before, the instructions Rogers gave his subjects would seem to encourage them to do their runs when they were in "extreme" moods. Also, the effect with Rogers's subjects was contributed primarily by low variance in negative moods. On the other hand, the effect in Carpenter's moderate-mood sessions consisted predominantly of high variance in positive moods (at least in the earlier experiments, where mean scores were reported).

Mood questions have occasionally been included as secondary variables in other experiments. In forced-choice experiments, simple mood questions have failed to correlate significantly with ESP deviation scores (Banham, 1974; Mussig and Dean, 1967; Nash, 1958; Palmer et al., 1976; Pleshette, 1975; Woodruff and Dale, 1950), but the more substantive research discussed above suggests that such simple effects should not be expected.

Simple relationships between mood and ESP scores also have not been found in free-response experiments (Braud and Braud, 1974; Braud et al., 1975; Palmer and Vassar, 1974; Parker et al., 1977; Stanford and Mayer, 1974). Stanford and Mayer found the best scoring among subjects who were not in the mood to take the test but in a good mood generally. However, such an effect has not been reported (or looked for) in other free-response experiments.

3.7.1b. Discrete Affective States. Schmeidler's approach to the mood–ESP question has been to examine ESP scores in relation to subjects' self-ratings of more precisely defined affective states, based on Nowlis's adjective checklist. In her first series of three experiments (Schmeidler, 1971), a complex but consistent relationship was found between ESP run-score variance and a composite mood index including the sum of "concentration," "surgency," and social affection in one of the two groups tested. Generally speaking, this index correlated negatively with the variance scores for subjects who predicted high scores for themselves on the ESP test; among the remaining subjects, the correlation was positive. The correlations from the two subgroups differed significantly in each of the two experiments where the scoring predictions were requested, the results of the first experiment providing the hypothesis for the second. These latter two experiments involved group testing of the same high school students.

This pattern of results did not appear to a significant degree in any of three subsequent group experiments representing highly divergent subject populations (Schmeidler and Craig, 1972). A somewhat similar pattern appeared for the only group that was composed of students, but only in the first of two sessions. Having anticipated that the affect–ESP relationship would differ for different groups, Schmeidler's strategy again was to use each group's results in a first session to predict that group's results in a second session. This strategy was successful for only one of the three groups. In this group, which consisted of young businessmen, a positive correlation between ESP deviation scores and a mood index of egotism minus the sum of aggression and anxiety was independently significant in both sessions.

In a more recent experiment, Hudesman and Schmeidler (1976) gave a clock-card ESP test and the Nowlis checklist to a psychotherapy patient at the beginning and end of a series of therapy sessions. The results indicated that high ESP scores were associated with hostility and low scores with depression. Given the obsessive-compulsive nature of the patient's neurosis, these findings suggest that ESP scores were highest when the patient's defenses were being successfully mobilized. The authors speculate that ESP tests may have value as a projective technique in psychotherapy.

Whereas Schmeidler depended upon "eyeball" detection of patterns within a matrix of bivariate correlations, other investigators have employed multivariate statistical techniques to study the relationship between ESP scores and discrete affective states (Friedman et al., 1976; McGuire et al., 1974; Osis and Bokert, 1971; Osis and Turner, 1968; Osis et al., 1971). While all of these reports claimed to have demonstrated some kind of significant relationship between ESP and affect, the effects were predominantly post hoc and directional trends were consistently inconsistent (to coin a phrase) across samples.

A handful of experiments have focused more exclusively on what might be called "state anxiety." In two of three experiments with Indian college students, Sailaja and Rao (1973) found that subjects rated as "nervous" during a job interview scored significantly higher than subjects rated as "confident." In both cases, I computed t tests that indicated that the nervous subjects scored significantly above chance. The ESP test had been presented to subjects as one criterion for employment. This finding is puzzling in the context of studies with trait measures that suggest that low-anxious subjects score best on ESP tests. In fact, results with the Taylor Manifest Anxiety Scale indicated slightly better performance among Sailaja's less anxious subjects, contrary to the "nervousness" ratings. The authors suggest that nervousness may reflect strong motivation to get the job, rather than anxiety. Finally, Ballard (1977) reported a post hoc effect indicating that subjects who showed the greatest decrease in "state anxiety" (as measured by Spielberger's scale) following a pretest relaxation exercise scored significantly higher on ESP targets clandestinely matched with erotic photographs than did other subjects. Other findings discussed in section 2.6 on altered states are also relevant, especially those that demonstrated a relationship between ESP scores and subjective reactions to induction techniques.

3.7.1c. Conclusion. No simple statement that has any generality can be made regarding the relationship between ESP and affective states, except for the highly nonspecific comment that the magnitude of the affect seems to be at least as important as its hedonic tone. The pattern among simple "mood" studies seems to be for one experimenter to consistently obtain a certain complex effect that differs from the consistent complex effect obtained by another experimenter using superficially similar procedures. There is some similarity, however, in the patterns of results obtained by Rogers and Carpenter. Results from studies attempting to look at more discrete affective states can only be described as chaotic. Nevertheless, it is evident that mood variables can influence ESP scoring, but they do so by interacting with other variables in complex ways that we are only beginning to understand. Such interactions may well provide the key for unlocking the mystery of how to make ESP more reliable. From a more cynical point of view, these complex results suggest that experimenters make an effort to either control affective states (if this is possible) or at least measure them, if for no other reason than to partial out their confounding effects on more tractable relationships.

3.7.2. Graphic Expansiveness: State or Trait?

A projective personality test that I did not include in the section on personality traits involves ratings of the graphic expansiveness of freehand drawings. Because of evidence that such drawing tendencies often change from session to session and can be influenced by the test situation (see Humphrey, 1946b; West, 1950), I have included this discussion in the section on transient states. Although the transient state reflected by these drawings has never been specified, one might speculate that "expansive" drawings (i.e., those made in a free-and-easy style using a large amount of the sheet) reflect a more positive and uninhibited mood or response set than do "compressive" drawings.

Graphic expansiveness has been incorporated in a number of ESP drawing experiments by having the ESP responses themselves rated on this dimension. Generally speaking, results have revealed a tendency for expansive drawings to yield higher ESP scores than compressive drawings in clairvoyance tests, but a reversal of this trend in GESP tests (Bevan, 1947a, b; Humphrey, 1946a, b; Stuart *et al.*, 1947). A minority of studies have shown nonsignificant reversals of this pattern, however (Nash and Richards, 1947; West, 1950). Graphic expansiveness has also been used as a predictor of performance in card-guessing tests conducted at the same session. These experiments have yielded the same pattern as the drawing experiments, although not quite as strongly (Bevan, 1947a; Casper 1951; Kahn, 1952; Kanthamani and Rao, 1973b; McMahan, 1946; Smith and Humphrey, 1946; Stuart *et al.*, 1947; West, 1950). For both types of ESP tests, the results suggest that graphic expansiveness affects the direction of scoring rather than the absolute magnitude of the deviation from chance. A more detailed analysis of the above trends is presented elsewhere (Palmer, 1977).

Further evidence that a "compressive" attitude may facilitate hitting in GESP tests comes from a classroom experiment that provided data for some of Humphrey's analyses referred to in the previous paragraph (Stuart, 1945). Stuart manipulated mental set directly by having subjects make half of their drawings in an "unrestricted" manner (either "automatically" or by means of "free association") and the other half in a "limited" manner (by concentrating on either the agent or an object). Significant psi-missing occurred with the "unrestricted" set, while the "limited" set produced nonsignificant psi-hitting. The difference was significant. However, this effect could not be repeated in a follow-up experiment also considered by Humphrey, possibly because subjects were given less time to make their drawings (Stuart, 1947). There is indirect evidence that psi-hitting was transformed into +1 displacement among subjects who felt "rushed" in this latter experiment (see Sec. 2.3.1). Unfortunately, in neither experiment is it reported whether the induced sets influenced the actual expansiveness of the drawings.

3.7.2a. Conclusion. Although systematic within-experiment or within-session comparisons are generally lacking, there is a quite consistent tendency for expansiveness of freehand drawings to be associated with relatively positive ESP scoring in clairvoyance experiments and relatively negative scoring in GESP experiments. The reason for the interaction is unclear, although Humphrey (1946b) has speculated that "compressiveness" in the GESP situation may indicate social responsiveness to the agent that might be helpful in this type of test.

Despite the deficiencies of expansiveness ratings as a trait measure, they do possess some construct validity as a measure of emotional adjustment (Elkisch, 1945; Humphrey, 1946a). Interpreted as such, they support my previously stated conclusion of a positive relationship between ESP scores and trait measures of emotional adjustment only with respect to clairvoyance tests. Since most of the experiments supporting this relationship that I discussed in the section on personality traits (Sec. 3.2) also used clairvoyance (precognition) procedures, the findings on graphic expansiveness raise the possibility that the relationship should not be generalized to GESP tests. More research will be needed to shed light on this matter.

4. Toward More Reliable ESP

A major concern of most thoughtful parapsychologists is how to make ESP more reliable. I have really been addressing this question indirectly all along. Experimenters customarily choose the procedures they will adopt and the kinds of subjects they will test with precisely this goal in mind. Any knowledge they gain about the effects of manipulations and individual differences on ESP scores contributes to our understanding of how to make ESP more reliable.

I have set aside for special consideration in this section two topics whose relevance to this issue is somewhat more direct than that of topics discussed so far. The first has to do with attempts to segregate particular responses or sets of responses that are likely to be ESP hits. The second has to do with attempts to actually increase the incidence of these "psi-prone" trials by means of training.

4.1. Psi-Prone Trials: Separating the Wheat from the Chaff

When a subject makes a series of responses on a forced-choice ESP test, it is quite possible that some responses will be more likely to be influenced by ESP than other responses. If these psi-prone trials could be identified independently of the actual scores, the information yield of ESP data could be increased, perhaps substantially. In this section, I will examine three approaches parapsychologists have utilized in their efforts to define psi-prone trials.

4.1.1. Position Effects: The Salience of U

This first approach attempts to designate psi-prone trials in terms of their position in the run. Its use has been restricted almost exclusively to standard card tests using the five ESP symbols. In his first monograph, Rhine (1934/1973) reported that when DT procedures were used, most of his star subjects produced U curves, defined as the highest scoring on the first and last five-trial segments of the run. However, one subject produced an inverted U function, indicative of better scoring in the middle of the run. When procedures such as BT were used that required the subject to make his calls more slowly and deliberately, a decline effect (i.e., above-chance scoring declining to chance as the run proceeded) was the most common tendency.

4.1.1a. The "DT Curve." Rhine attributed this U curve (or DT curve, as it was often called) to a kind of "salience" of the end points of the run, which was only apparent when the structure of the run as a unit of 25 trials was clear to the subject. He argued that such structure was more evident with the DT procedure than with other procedures, hence the preponderance of U curves with this method. He suggested that ESP was concentrated at the beginning and end of DT runs because it is at these stages that spontaneity would be at a maximum and mechanical guessing patterns least operative (Rhine, 1969a).

A large-scale experiment in which 30 adult and child subjects completed a total of 1,114 DT runs reinforced Rhine's earlier observation (Rhine, 1941b). Overall scoring was significantly below chance, and a plot of the deviation scores on the five segments of the run, pooled over subjects, revealed an inverted U function, i.e., the most extreme psi-missing in the first and last segments. Furthermore, a similar curve was apparent within the segments, i.e., the most extreme scoring on the first and fifth trials of the segments. These two functions (i.e., within the run and within the segments) were shown to be significantly similar by a special correlation technique called the "covariation of the salience ratios."

Some internal effects in these data fit in nicely with Rhine's reasoning. Among the adult subjects, U curves were most prevalent in those conditions where subjects wrote their responses on paper instead of calling them out, and also when brief interruptions were introduced following each segment of the run. In other words, salience was most prevalent under those conditions in which the structure of the run was most evident and among those subjects who would most likely be sensitive to such structuring.

In three additional series of approximately 1,000 runs each using precognitive DT (PDT) procedures, the U curve for the segments of the run and the significant covariation of salience ratios were confirmed (Humphrey and Rhine, 1942; Rhine, 1942). However, in these experiments the overall results were close to chance, so the deviation scores did not differ more from chance in the middle segments than in the outer segments. The U curve was much clearer within the run than within the segments.

Searching for position effects within segments has not been in vogue since the 1940s. Rhine himself argued that segment salience is not likely to be observed unless the run segments are clearly demarcated (Rhine, 1941b), which often is not the case even in DT experiments. The covariation ratio thus fell into disuse as well. Before it died, however, significant ratios were reported in a group experiment (Humphrey and Rhine, 1944) and the first of several experiments with the "gifted" subject Marchesi (Rhine and Humphrey, 1942). The ratio was not significant in subsequent research with this subject (McMahan and Rhine, 1947; McMahan and Bates, 1954).

However, simple U curves within the run have frequently been reported in experiments using DT or similar procedures with both selected subjects (Gibson, 1937; Osis, 1955; Pegram, 1937; Rhine and Humphrey, 1942; Rogers, 1967a) and unselected groups of subjects (Anderson and Gregory, 1959; Dean, 1972; Joesting and Joesting, 1970; Martin and Stribic, 1940; Pratt, 1961; Schmeidler, 1944; Sharp and Clark, 1937; Taetzsch, 1964). In a somewhat related experiment where the targets were numbers of various lengths, Nash and Durkin (1959) found that the most hits occurred on the first and last digits. The salience was reported as statistically significant only in the experiments of Dean, Nash, Osis, Pratt, and Schmeidler (as reported by Humphrey and Rhine, 1944).

This level of repeatability is not as impressive as it might appear on the surface. While most of the curves were U-shaped (more or less), some investigators reported inverted Us (Anderson and Gregory, 1959; Rogers, 1967a). Of more concern is the fact that the most significant scoring sometimes occurred in the middle segments (Anderson and Gregory, 1959; Martin and Stribic, 1940; Osis, 1956).

Finally, U curves of any type are far from universal in DT-type experiments. The star subject of Martin and Stribic (1938a,b) showed significant decline effects within the run when tested with DT or UT procedures, as did a subject tested by Anderson (1959a) using a precognition procedure. Another high-scoring subject, Harribance, revealed both highly significant decline (Stump et al., 1970) and incline (Roll and Klein, 1972) effects in runs consisting of 10 or 12 trials, but no clear pattern in a series of 25-trial runs (Child and Kelly, 1973). One parapsychologist who tested himself with a DT procedure found a significant decline effect (Cadoret, 1952), while another found a decline in variance, i.e., regression to chance from either above- or below-chance scoring early in the run (Carpenter, 1966; Carpenter and Carpenter, 1967). U curves also have failed to show up in other experiments with selected subjects (McMahan and Rhine, 1947; McMahan and Bates, 1954; Osis, 1956; Steilberg, 1971).

Disconfirming instances are harder to document in experiments with groups of subjects, although many undoubtedly exist that have not been reported or were reported inadequately. One disconfirming experiment yielded a rather clear-cut decline effect (Humphrey and Pratt, 1941), while the results from two others could best be summarized as incline effects

(MacFarland, 1938; Schmeidler, 1964b), the latter a regression to chance from psi-missing. None of these effects were reported as significant.

Although one might argue that U curves are more likely than some other kind of function to occur in group DT experiments, the precise nature of this effect is far from clear. As usual, the problem is the penchant of parapsychologists to pool results over subjects. While the overall U curves reported in these experiments might be composed of U curves contributed by the individual subjects, they just as easily could be composed of individual incline and decline effects. Indeed, this latter interpretation seems somewhat easier to reconcile with the curves of individual subjects described above.

Both Martin and Stribic (1940) and Rhine (1941b) noted tendencies in their data for U curves to be most prevalent among those subjects and conditions that yielded the least significant overall scoring. This also may help explain the relative lack of U curves among selected individuals, many of whom are "selected" because they generally achieve very high scores.

Testing procedures such as GESP and BT that involve longer trial durations have provided U curves (Humphrey, 1943; Mitchell, 1971; Rose, 1955; Rose and Rose, 1951), decline effects (Estabrooks, 1927/1961; Humphrey, 1943; Humphrey and Pratt, 1941), and incline effects (Keil, 1965; Steilberg, 1971). Only the effects of Rose (1955) and Estabrooks were reported as significant. There is not much of a pattern here, except that, contrary to what was found with DT procedures, all of the experiments that yielded U curves, with the exception of Humphrey (1943), involved testing of "gifted" subjects. The only one of the other experiments falling into this category was that of Steilberg.

4.1.1b. Individual Differences. Given the inconsistency of position effects, surprisingly little research has been done examining individual differences in this area. Stanford (1964b) found evidence of a decline effect among above-chance-scoring subjects who had a strong belief in ESP and an incline effect among disbelievers and subjects whose belief was more equivocal. In another sheep–goat experiment where both hitters and missers were included in the analysis, Schmeidler (1944) reported that her overall U curve (which may have involved a combination of inclines and declines) was attributable to the extreme goats. Carpenter found that his decline of variance effect did not hold up when he adopted special expansive or compressive response sets (Carpenter and Carpenter, 1967).

4.1.1c. The Cancellation Effect. Position effects have been used to explain another unusual effect in parapsychology: cases where run-score variance around mean chance expectation is significantly below chance.

(An extreme example of this would be a series of consecutive scores of five.) It was suggested that such low variance would result if positive scoring in one part of the run were to be "cancelled" by negative scoring in the other part. Stanford (1966b), in fact, found in each of two experiments significant position effects (i.e., differences between the first 10 and last 15 trials) in runs from a condition with significantly low run-score variance which he failed to find in runs from a condition completed by the same subjects at the same session where variance was significantly high. Suggestive position effects in low-variance runs also were found by Rogers (1967a). Variance analyses were not introduced into the parapsychologist's repertoire until the mid-1960s, so unless some raw data can be reanalyzed we will not know whether low run-score variance characterized earlier experiments where significant position effects were found.

4.1.1d. Conclusion. There is some evidence, predominantly from the early Duke period, indicating that ESP hitting and missing tends to be concentrated in the first and last segments of the run, provided that DT or other techniques with short trial durations are used which encourage the subject to perceive the run as a unit. However, it is clear that many individual subjects do not conform to this pattern, and the U curves often reported in group studies may in fact represent the pooling of individual incline and decline effects. Slower procedures such as BT and GESP have produced no consistent position effects in group experiments, although some relatively recent experiments with selected subjects have revealed U curves. Although position effects seem to be influenced by individual and situational differences, very little systematic research has been undertaken to elucidate such differences. A theory that position effects may be the cause of significantly low run-score variance around mean chance expectation has received some support from preliminary research.

Although position effects may be real, they are too inconsistent to have much value as a basis for defining psi-prone responses, even in the limited contexts where they are applicable. If the card-guessing paradigm continues to wane in parapsychology, interest in position effects as such will probably continue to decline. For a review of the literature on position effects see Rhine (1969a).

4.1.2. Response Bias: Turning a Liability into an Asset

Although the promise held out by early research on position effects has not been realized in later work, a second approach to detecting what might be called psi-prone trials has been more successful. Earlier in the chapter, evidence was presented which suggested that elimination of systematic calling biases in forced-choice tests might improve scoring levels, provided that responding indeed became more spontaneous. However, eliminating such biases is easier said than done. Some relatively recent research suggests that response biases may actually have some positive value by providing a frame of reference against which more spontaneous responses can be more readily detected. This section will be devoted to an examination of such research.

4.1.2a. Response Bias in High-Scoring Subjects. In reanalyzing five extensive card-guessing series completed by Gloria Stewart (one of the two "outstanding" subjects of S. G. Soal), Pratt (1967b) found highly nonrandom patterns with respect to pairs of calls. In the first four series, this nonrandomness was reflected primarily in Stewart's tendency to undercall "doubles" (i.e., pairs of the same symbol), and Pratt found a significant excess of hits on the second trials of these undercalled doubles. In other words, when Stewart violated her normal bias against calling doubles, her rate of hitting was significantly higher on the doubled responses than on other trials. Perhaps when the ESP "message" was strong enough to cause her to break her normal calling pattern, it also was strong enough to cause her to choose the correct target.

Because of the questions raised about Soal's integrity, the above results must be evaluated cautiously, even though Soal had never to my knowledge predicted this effect and it was not discovered until about 20 years after the data had been collected.

Regardless of its validity, Pratt's finding has had considerable heuristic value. Stanford (1967) noted that in two card-guessing series completed by a high-scoring subject (Martin and Stribic, 1938a,b), there was a significant tendency for the subject to obtain the largest percentage of hits on the symbols he called least frequently. Ryzl and Pratt (1963) found that their star subject, Pavel Stepanek, revealed a comparable scoring tendency in a two-choice task, as did Harribance using standard ESP cards (Morris, 1972). In neither case, however, is it clear whether this was a general characteristic of the subject's performance over his career.

Neither Martin nor Ryzl reported the data in a way that would allow the response bias hypothesis to be tested for pairs of calls, as was the case with Stewart. Morris reported that Harribance had a bias in *favor* of calling doubles, but it is unlikely one could argue that avoiding doubles constituted a genuine response bias in this case. In any event, scoring rates on doubles and nondoubles were not significantly different in this research.

Finally, no response bias effect is evident in data from Rhine's subject Hubert Pearce (Greenwood and Stuart, 1937), but neither was there any clear evidence of response bias in Pearce's calls.

4.1.2b. Response Bias in Unselected Subjects. All the results discussed so far were obtained with subjects who revealed highly significant overall psi-hitting and (with the exception of Pearce and, possibly, Harribance) highly significant response biases on the unit of analysis where the scoring differences were found. The first study to report a response bias effect in subjects not preselected for ESP ability was a number-guessing GESP experiment with retarded children (Bond, 1937). Bond found that the children often would fall into very routinized calling patterns (e.g., calling the numbers in order), and on runs where they did so, their otherwise significant level of positive scoring was reduced to chance.

While Bond's finding is not especially profound, more subtle response biases also have been shown to interact with scoring rates in unselected subjects. Stanford found support for the response bias hypothesis in two modified forced-choice experiments in which response biases were built into the tests themselves. In the first of these experiments, subjects were asked to answer a series of multiple-choice questions based on a dream transcript they had just read (Stanford, 1970). Unbeknownst to the subjects, one of the answers to each question had been randomly selected as an ESP target. As predicted, when subjects gave answers that were wrong in terms of the transcript, they obtained significantly more ESP hits than when they gave "correct" answers. Furthermore, this effect was strongest for those subjects who obtained the highest scores on an independent test of incidental memory. Thus, when subjects with relatively good memory ability went against their natural tendency (or "response bias") to accurately recall the content of the dream, they scored significantly above chance on the covert ESP test. This study will be discussed from a point of view relevant to its covert aspects later on.

In the second experiment, subjects' ESP scores were determined by whether they gave primary or secondary responses to items on a word-association test (Stanford, 1973). The list was limited to words with high-commonality primary associates, and either the primary or the secondary associate was randomly selected as the ESP target for each trial. Two measures of response bias, the number of primary responses given on the tests and the shortness of the response latencies, both correlated significantly with the difference between the percentages of ESP hits on primary and secondary responses. In other words, subjects who had the strongest bias to give primary responses were the ones who scored *relatively* high when they violated that bias and gave secondary responses. However, there apparently was no tendency for these subjects to score significantly above chance on their secondary responses, or even to score higher in the absolute sense than they did on their primary responses. This outcome was attributable in part to a significant tendency among all subjects for significantly higher scores on primary than on secondary responses. Stanford had predicted this latter result on the basis of Roll's (1966) theory that responses that depend upon "well established associative connections" (Stanford, 1973, p. 150) are most likely to be psi-mediated.

The results so far suggest that response bias effects only occur among subjects who have strong response biases to begin with, as we would expect, given the underlying rationale of response bias theory (which is closely related to signal detection theory in psychology). In a somewhat different experiment, Stanford (1967) found that subjects who designated a smaller-than-average number of segments on a mock "radar screen" as containing ESP targets obtained significantly more hits on segments actually containing targets than did subjects who designated a larger number of segments.

Two experiments have dealt with response bias effects in the context of a paper-maze test (Glidden, 1974; Child and Singer, 1977). The mazes consist of concentric circles, and the subject's task is to move from the center to the periphery of the maze while avoiding barriers, some of which are knowable only by ESP. (See Chapter 1 for a more complete description.) In both experiments, attempts were made to define violations of response biases as moves other than those leading most directly out of the maze. In neither case were such counterbias responses found to be significantly associated with more psi-hitting than other responses. However, the proper way to define counterbias responses in this paradigm is unclear, and such responses may simply represent naturally based strategies no more spontaneous than the "biased" responses.

Finally, in a test where subjects had to choose either a word or a nonsense syllable as the ESP response, Kanthamani and Rao (1975d) found that subjects who had a bias toward choosing words scored significantly higher overall than subjects with the opposite bias in each of three experiments. There was no evidence that any of the subjects had *significant* response biases, or that there was any relationship between the *degree* of bias and scoring on *counterbias* responses. Thus Kanthamani's experiment is irrelevant to the response bias hypothesis as subsequently stated by Stanford, although the main effect they uncovered may be indirectly relevant to this hypothesis in ways that are at present unclear.

4.1.2c. Response Bias in Animals. A number of the animal experiments discussed earlier (Sec. 3.5.5.) provided data relevant to the response bias issue. In an experiment in which cats had to choose one or the other side of a T-maze for food reward, scoring rates were significantly lower when the cat had chosen the same side on three or more previous trials than when such severe side biases were not present (Osis and Foster, 1953). In a conceptually similar experiment with rodents using a Skinner-box format, Schouten (1972) found significant psi-hitting only on trials where the animals violated their normal habit of pressing the same bar that had given reward on the previous trial. (I computed a chi-square test on Schouten's data which demonstrated that scoring rate was significantly higher on nonbiased than on biased responses.) Although follow-up research failed to yield significant evidence of ESP on either kind of response (Schouten, 1976b), a similar experiment by Terry and Harris (1975) revealed significant psi-hitting restricted to trials where their rats changed response bars for no apparent reason. Parker (1974) found significant positive scoring on both kinds of trials, although scoring rates were somewhat higher on counterbias responses for two of his three gerbils. (In the other experiments described in this section, it is unclear how uniformly the effect was distributed among the animals.) In two nonsignificant replication attempts of Parker's experiment, there was no appreciable difference between scoring on biased and counterbiased responses (Broughton and Millar, 1975).

In the research of Duval and Montredon (1968a,b), avoidance of shocks would appear to be restricted to "random behavior trials," but some parapsychologists question the relevance of this particular concept to response bias theory (e.g., Schouten, 1972).

4.1.2d. Related Paradigms. Two other research paradigms, both involving human subjects, are indirectly related to the response bias question. The relationship can only be considered indirect because, in contrast to Stanford's research, the responses evaluted for bias are not the ESP responses. Thus the relevance of these studies to the response bias issue must be considered limited.

The first of these is more directly concerned with the relationship between ESP and memory on a trial-by-trial basis. Kanthamani and Rao (1974) gave three groups of high school students a word-association test, the ESP score being determined by the manner in which the subject recorded his or her response (e.g., in capital or lower-case letters). In each case, subjects scored significantly above chance on those trials where the associate was correctly recalled, but below chance on the other trials. The difference was only significant in one of the three series, but it was significant for the three series pooled. Two additional studies where subjects were tested in groups produced more equivocal results (Kanthamani and Rao, 1975a), and significant psi-missing was found for correctly recalled pairs in a third study (Gambale, Margolis, and Crucci, 1976). Kreiman (1975) found psi-missing on incorrectly recalled trials and chance scoring on correctly recalled trials in each of two experiments. Generally nonsignificant results were found in a study by O'Brien (1976).

Parker (1976) attempted to obtain a comparable effect using a digit-span test instead of a word-association test and succeeded in one of two experiments.

In the second stage of their research with the word-association technique, Kanthamani and Rao (1975b) manipulated the association strength of paired associates. In each of two series they found a significant difference in ESP scoring between correctly and incorrectly recalled words, but only for low-association pairs. Scoring was above chance on correctly recalled words and below chance on incorrectly recalled words, and both of these effects differed significantly from chance for the two series pooled. These results are consistent with the authors' earlier studies in which low-association pairs were used. However, this effect was not confirmed in three other experiments (Gambale, 1976; Harary, 1976; Lieberman, 1976).

As pointed out by Lieberman (1976), the research described in the preceding paragraph is relevant to the response bias hypothesis in the sense that correct responses should be more consonant with built-in response biases for high-association pairs than for low-association pairs. Thus Kanthamani's results are consistent with the notion that ESP should be most prevalent when the subject is forced to give a low-commonality (i.e., counterbias) response. However, her results are not consistent with the memory theory of Roll (1966), who I expect would predict high-association pairs to be the most psi-facilitory. Still another possibility is that low-association words create a more challenging memory test, and this kind of mental attitude is relatively psi-conducive.*

The second paradigm involves having subjects indicate whether they like or dislike a particular word by placing an L or a D on one of five lines, the choice of line constituting the ESP response. Using the simple version of this test called the Word Reaction Test, Freeman (1964, 1969b) found in each of two group experiments that subjects scored significantly higher on trials where the response (L or D) was consistent with the subject's general response tendency than they did on other trials. For example, subjects who made more D responses than the group average scored higher on D responses than on L responses.

Although it is questionable whether the L/D responses provide a valid measure of response bias in Stanford's sense, these results seem to suggest that subjects obtained the most ESP hits on responses that were consistent with their biases. However, Feather (1967a) reported a significant reversal of this effect using Freeman's test. Furthermore, Freeman's effect generally has not occurred in experiments with a later

*This possibility was suggested by Dr. K. R. Rao.

version of the Word Reaction Test (called the Word Feeling Test) in which subjects were asked to express *degree* of like and dislike for the words on an expanded scale (Freeman and Nielsen, 1964; Nielsen and Freeman, 1965).

Finally, Freeman (1973) developed a related testing technique in which subjects answered questions similar to those on intelligence tests by indicating the answer in one of five ways. He found that subjects who scored above the class average got more ESP hits on the questions they missed, whereas the other subjects reversed this trend. The overall pattern was statistically significant, this time in a direction consistent with response bias theory.

4.1.2e. Conclusion. Experiments with both humans and animals support the hypothesis that responses on forced-choice ESP tests that violate strong nonrandom response tendencies of the subject are more likely to be correct than are responses consistent with such biases. Although such effects are by no means universal, all significant trends have been in the predicted direction.

Response bias research may provide a valuable means for detecting psi-prone responses, but only among subjects who have such biases and whose overall scores may suffer because of them. For subjects who either respond more spontaneously or whose biased patterns are not identifiable, other methods will need to be found.

4.1.3. Confidence Calls: Letting the Subject Do It

Earlier in the chapter, I pointed out that subjects were not very good at predicting their total scores on ESP tests (see Sec. 3.6.2b). However, this does not preclude the possibility that they might be more successful at picking out particular trials where something told them that their response was more than a mere guess. This possibility provides yet another potential source for designating psi-prone trials in ESP experiments.

The most striking evidence of successful confidence calling was provided by the high-scoring subject Bill Delmore (Kanthamani and Kelly, 1974a). Pooling the results of three series using psychic shuffle and BT-like techniques, the authors found that Delmore completely identified playing cards on 91% of his confidence calls as compared to only 4% of his other calls. (Even the 4% was significantly above chance.) Delmore made confidence calls on only 8% of his trials. Another "high-scoring" subject, Carlo Marchesi, failed to reveal significant ESP scoring on confidence calls distributed over 180 DT runs, but his overall scoring at this stage of his career was nonsignificant (McMahan and Bates, 1954).

Fahler instructed two subjects under hypnosis to indicate trials they thought were likely to be correct or that felt "different" in some way (Fahler and Osis, 1966). The results revealed not only significant psi-hitting on the "marked" trials but also significant psi-missing on the unmarked trials.

Humphrey and Nicol (1955) reported the results of two card-guessing experiments in which subjects were asked to make five to ten confidence calls per run. In each experiment, those subjects who followed the instruction scored significantly higher on checked than on unchecked trials, but only on those runs where they did *not* receive trial-by-trial feedback of the correctness of their guesses. Combining the two series revealed that significant psi-hitting on the checked calls was balanced by significant psi-missing on the unchecked calls, the same pattern reported by Fahler.

Two experiments by Nash reveal that significant scoring on confidence calls can occur under conditions where scoring on other trials remains close to chance. In the first experiment the checked calls yielded significant psi-hitting (Nash and Nash, 1958) while in the other it was psi-missing (Nash, 1960a). In both cases, the difference between the checked and unchecked trials was significant. Kreiman and Ivnisky (1973b) reported significant psi-missing on runs where confidence calls were requested in a GESP experiment, the effect being mostly attributable to trials where emotional targets were used. No significant difference between checked and unchecked trials was reported in the abstract (my only source for this experiment), but results on unchecked trials would appear to have been close to chance.

In his second experiment, Nash asked his subjects to predict on a run-by-run basis how they expected to score. He found that the psi-missing on confidence calls was primarily attributable to those runs on which subjects in fact predicted below-chance scoring. Schmeidler (1964e) obtained the same effect in a precognition experiment, except that checked and unchecked trials did not differ significantly for all runs combined. Perhaps those subjects who predicted below-chance scores desired at some level to confirm their predictions, in which case the confidence calls reflected a correct "awareness" of the target which somehow got manifested by an incorrect response.

Nash and Nash (1963) found a significant excess of confidence call hits in the first of two sessions, but this was followed by a significant decline to chance scoring on confidence calls in the second session. Such declines were not reported in Nash's earlier experiments, which also involved more than one session. In an experiment where subjects were not given the usual set to give about five confidence calls per run, Schmeidler (1964e) found that confidence calls produced significantly more positive scores than other trials only for subjects who averaged fewer than one confidence call per run. Schmeidler (1961), in an earlier set of experiments, found significant psi-hitting on such infrequent confidence calls, but no difference test was reported.

A number of other forced-choice experiments have failed to yield any significant differences between the proportion of hits on checked and unchecked calls (Honorton, 1970, 1971b, 1972a; Honorton et al., 1974; Jackson, Franzoi, and Schmeidler, 1977; Kreiman and Ivnisky, 1973; McCallam and Honorton, 1973; Schechter et al., 1975) although several obtained significant relationships involving confidence calls (Sec. 4.2.2a). These experiments generally involved fewer total trials than those discussed previously, and this may have something to do with the nonsignificant differences.

In the only free-response experiment to incorporate confidence calls, agents attempted to "send" the content of pictorial slides to percipients in another room (Gelade and Harvie, 1975). Following each of five trials, the percipient was asked to pick out the correct slide from a pair of slides and to rate his or her confidence on a four-point scale. Subjects scored significantly above chance on trials where they rated themselves as either "fairly confident" or "very confident," while they scored below chance to an almost significant degree on the remaining trials. Unlike the confidence calls in the forced-choice experiments, however, these confidence calls could have been (and likely were) influenced by subjects' sensory knowledge of the degree of correspondence between calls and targets.

4.1.3a. Conclusion. The literature on confidence calls provides its share of significant effects, but their directions have not been consistent and significance sometimes has depended upon selecting out portions of the data post hoc. There is some evidence that the direction of scoring on confidence calls may depend upon subjects' expectations regarding their total run scores, at least when low scores are expected. The puzzling tendency found in three experiments for psi-hitting on confidence calls to be balanced by psi-missing on other trials may be an example of Rao's (1965a) "differential effect."

It has been customary in analyzing confidence call effects to pool trials over subjects. This procedure led one observer to suggest that such effects could occur artifactually if the subjects who had the highest total ESP scores also made the most confidence calls (Thouless, 1956). While the "guilty" experimenters have generally countered this criticism by demonstrating that this precondition was not met by their data (e.g., Humphrey and Nicol, 1956), it is not always clear in these reports how uniformly confidence call effects are distributed among subjects. This makes it difficult to judge the generality of the effects.

Confidence calls nevertheless show some promise as a vehicle for identifying psi-prone responses, but more research will be needed to tease out the conditions under which they will be most effective and whether they will expose psi-hitting or psi-missing. Individual differences in ability to make accurate confidence calls, in particular, need some study. A first step in this direction was provided by McCallam and Honorton (1973), who found that subjects who showed the greatest increase in percentage of correct confidence calls following feedback training were those who based their confidence calls on a multiplicity of internal cues.

4.2. Effects of Repeated Testing: Monotony and Monotonicity

4.2.1. Decline Effects: Too Much of a Good Thing

Ask any parapsychologist what is the most consistent finding in parapsychology, and he or she is likely to tell you that it is the decline effect, which means that subjects' scores are likely to get lower the more they are tested. Although decline effects indeed are common in parapsychology, some species are more common than others. As usual, we are going to have to make a few distinctions if we are to avoid overly simplistic conclusions.

4.2.1a. Long-Term Declines—"Gifted" Subjects. When a subject comes along with outstanding ESP ability, it is natural for the enterprising parapsychologist to want to collect large amounts of data. It is not uncommon for such benevolent souls to complete hundreds and even thousands of card-guessing runs over periods ranging from several weeks to several years. It is not surprising that many of these subjects eventually "burn out."

The list of cases where high-scoring subjects sooner or later lost their ability is a long one (Banham, 1966; Brugmans, 1922; Drake, 1938; Freeman, 1966a; Mangan, 1957; McMahan and Bates, 1954; Mitchell, 1953; Pratt, 1937, 1974b; Rhine, 1934/1973, 1938b; Riess, 1937; Rose, 1955; Soal and Bateman, 1954). Even this survey is probably not exhaustive. Although one might expect scores of preselected high-scoring subjects to decline simply as a result of regression artifact, the initial scoring levels of these subjects were too high and/or maintained for too long for this to be a viable explanation.

The length of time subjects maintain their talents is quite variable. Some declined after only a few runs (e.g., Banham, 1966; Mitchell, 1953), while others endured for much longer periods (e.g., Pratt, 1973; Rhine, 1934/1973). The star subject of Martin and Stribic (1940) maintained a scoring rate of 6.85 hits per run through 3,659 card-guessing runs administered over a three-year period. I have seen no reports that this subject's ability ever declined, although he has not been formally tested in many years. However, the endurance record goes to the Czech subject Pavel Stepanek, who maintained his card-guessing ability for ten years before finally dropping off (Pratt, 1973). However, the nature of his scoring tendencies changed over the years, and his ability still may exist in some as yet undetected form. In fact, this may be true of other subjects who seemingly have lost their abilities. Furthermore, subjects who have lost the ability to achieve high scores may later regain this talent. An Australian Aborigine whose initial scoring level was quite high saw her scores decline markedly over a course of 68 runs (Rose and Rose, 1951). When retested several years later, she temporarily regained her initial scoring rate but again declined sharply (Rose, 1955).

Although a number of contemporary "gifted" subjects, such as Harribance and Delmore, have as yet to evidence decline (perhaps because they haven't been tested long enough), I am aware of only one experiment in which a subject's scores increased significantly during a period of repeated testing, outside of a "training" context (Anderson, 1959a). This subject completed 90 precognition runs over a nine-month period.

4.2.1b. Between-Sessions Declines—Unselected Subjects. Subjects who lack outstanding psychic ability are not tested as extensively as those who have such abilities, for obvious reasons. Nevertheless, it is not too uncommon for such subjects to participate in more than one session. The first investigators to report significant decline effects under these circumstances were Taves and Dale (1943), but others have reported them from time to time (Honorton and Carbone, 1971; Humphrey, 1945c; Osis, 1952; Osis and Turner, 1968; Parker and Beloff, 1970). In most cases, the decline was from psi-hitting to chance scoring. However, the effect reported by Honorton and Carbone was a shift from psi-hitting to psi-missing, and Osis and Turner did not report their means. The only (apparently) significant incline effect I could find was in a free-response experiment, where significant psi-hitting was restricted to the second of two sessions (Keeling, 1972).

4.2.1c. Within-Session Declines. Significant declines or inclines of scoring rate within one experimental session are a potential effect in almost all ESP experiments, but they have been reported in only a handful. While there is obviously no way to tell how many effects of this type have gone undetected, it is safe to assume that they are quite rare. Among the significant findings however, decline effects are somewhat more prevalent than incline effects. Significant declines have been reported with both selected subjects (Osis, 1956; Roll and Klein, 1972) and unselected subjects (Dean and Taetzsch, 1963; Freeman, 1962; Humphrey, 1945c; Kahn,

1952; McMahan and Lauer, 1948; Parker and Beloff, 1970; Schmeidler, 1968; Schmeidler, Friedenberg, and Males, 1966; Van Busschbach, 1959). All except Dean and Taetzsch's results involved a decline from psi-hitting to chance scoring. Schmeidler (1964b) reported a significant incline effect, but it was from significant psi-missing to chance scoring. I could find only one experiment that produced an overall significant increase from chance scoring to psi-hitting (Palmer *et al.*, 1976). In a third experiment where subjects completed both card and drawing tests in the same session, a significant incline was reported for the drawing trials only. Overall scores were slightly above chance (Stuart *et al.*, 1947). I could find no consistent directional trend among the nonsignificant studies, nor could I find any relationship between scoring trends and the number of runs per session.

A potentially more reliable finding comes from a series of experiments in which declines of run-score variance were found within sessions (Carpenter, 1966, 1968, 1969; Carpenter and Carpenter, 1967; Rogers and Carpenter, 1966). In other words, run scores started out either high or low at the beginning of the session but approached chance as the session progressed. The decline was significant in three of five experiments, and in one other experiment the run-score variance was significantly high in the first half of the experiment. Length of session in the significant series varied from 4 to 36 runs. In the one experiment with a single subject, a significant decline was found in sessions consisting of 16 to 36 runs but not in longer sessions (Carpenter and Carpenter, 1967).

When factors are operating in an experiment that tend to produce psi-hitting in one condition or group of subjects and psi-missing in another, Carpenter's findings indirectly suggest that difference scores might be more prevalent early in a session that later in a session, i.e., the difference scores will decline automatically as the psi-hitting and psi-missing both regress to MCE as the session proceeds. Such a trend was found very consistently in a series of experiments by Sailaja and Rao (1973), and it conceivably could have influenced the results of countless other experiments in which overall decline effects were not found.

4.2.1d. Experimenter Declines. A few post hoc analyses have been reported which suggest that scoring levels in experiments with multiple subjects declined during the course of the experiment (Casper, 1951; Taddonio and O'Brien, 1977; Taves and Dale, 1943). Such results have been attributed to waning interest or enthusiasm on the part of the experimenter. It is much too early to draw even tentative conclusions on this topic, but experimenter decline effects clearly deserve more systematic investigation.

4.2.1e. Conclusion. It is clear that most high-scoring ESP subjects sooner or later lose their ability to achieve high scores, some considerably sooner than others. However, spontaneous recovery has been noted in at least one case, and it is possible that "loss of ability" may really reflect a diversion of scoring to other modes, such as those I will discuss later in the chapter.

Decline effects are considerably less prevalent among less talented subjects. Of course, one would not expect decline effects unless the scoring level were initially high, and significant declines are somewhat more frequent than significant inclines, both within and between sessions. Decline of run-score variance is a potentially more reliable within-session effect, but it needs to be validated by other investigators.

4.2.2. Immediate Feedback: Can ESP Be Learned?

There are several possible explanations for decline effects in ESP testing, a discussion of which is beyond the scope of this chapter. However, most parapsychologists would attribute them to declining motivation on the part of the subject (Rhine, 1964). Another interpretation has been stated by Tart (1966), who compared decline effects to extinction effects in learning. When an animal in a learning experiment is no longer given a reward for a correct response, the rate of emission of the response declines. Likewise, if high-scoring ESP subjects are not rewarded after each *trial* by knowledge of the outcome, their rate of emitting psi-mediated ESP responses also will go down, until their percentage of hits is no greater than that expected by chance. In the ESP case, the decline of scoring is seen by Tart as not being entirely due to a decline in motivation. Testing makes subjects self-conscious about their manner of using psi, and unless guided by immediate feedback, this self-consciousness merely upsets the delicate balance of mental processes that control psi, thus creating confusion (Tart, personal communication). Although ESP subjects receive such feedback at the end of the session, and sometimes after each run, Tart considers this delay too long to prevent extinction.

The other side of this coin is that subjects cannot learn to improve their ESP performance without the information provided by immediate feedback. Such feedback is necessary if subjects are to learn to identify subtle internal cues that might differentiate a psi-mediated response from a wild guess. However, Tart was careful to point out that learning could only be accomplished by subjects who had a fairly high level of ESP talent to begin with. Subjects lacking such talent would not make enough psi-mediated responses spontaneously to allow them to discriminate cues associated with psi-mediated hits (which are inevitably mixed with some "chance" hits) from irrelevant cues. On the other hand, immediate feedback would have some information value for subjects with moderate levels of talent, so moderately high levels of scoring would not be likely to decline during the course of testing. Thus, at a minimum, immediate feedback should eliminate most decline effects.

A relatively large number of ESP experiments providing subjects with immediate feedback have been reported, especially since the introduction of automated testing devices such as the Schmidt machine. Let us now take a look at these studies.

4.2.2a. Unselected Subjects. Among experiments using subjects not selected for initial ESP talent, the results have been mixed. Among studies with humans where temporal trends could be deduced from the reports, quite a few have reported negative results as far as learning is concerned (Beloff, 1969; Beloff and Bate, 1971; Dale, Taves, and Murphy, 1944; Haraldsson 1970; Jampolsky and Haight, 1975; McElroy and Brown, 1950; Taves, Dale, and Murphy, 1943; Thouless, 1971) McElroy supplemented informational feedback with electric shock for incorrect guesses in some runs, and he found not only that there was no learning but also that there was a significant decline effect across the shock runs. None of the reports of the animal experiments discussed in section 3.5.5 mentioned temporal trends, so one may assume that significant learning effects most likely were absent here as well.

The picture is not all negative, however. A young girl tested by Targ and Hurt (1972) improved dramatically on clairvoyance and then on precognition tests using a machine similar to Schmidt's. In a later experiment, 6 out of 147 subjects showed significant increases in performances as compared to none who showed significant decreases (Targ and Cole, 1975). Although none of these subjects had been preselected for ESP talent, it cannot be ruled out that they had such talent.

This latter possibility is more remote in experiments where conclusions are based on the results of all members of a group of unselected subjects. In an experiment with young children, Drucker *et al.* (1977) found a significant increase in performance from the first to the second run. Subjects were asked to guess on each trial the color of an *M & M* candy the experimenter would "blindly" pick from the bag. Subjects received an *M & M* of that color from another source for each correct response. The incline effect was primarily attributable to those subjects who scored above the group mean on an intelligence test, despite a rather restricted range of intelligence in the sample. However, no incline effect was reported in an earlier experiment of similar design reported in the same article.

Dagel and Puryear (1971) gave subjects 200 trials on an ESP testing machine, half of which were with feedback and half without. The order was counterbalanced across subjects. Neither the methodology nor the results were reported in adequate detail, but it would appear that subjects scored significantly higher on feedback than nonfeedback trials only when the nonfeedback trials were given first. If the significant difference involved a shift from chance scoring to psi-hitting, these results are consistent with a learning interpretation.

The most extensive series of learning studies with unselected subjects used a card-guessing procedure (Honorton, 1970, 1971b; Jackson *et al.*, 1977; Kreiman and Ivnisky, 1973a; McCallam and Honorton, 1973). The typical procedure in these studies was for subjects to complete three practice runs with trial-by-trial feedback sandwiched between two sets of three standard DT runs without feedback. Subjects in control conditions received either false feedback during the practice runs or no feedback during the "practice" runs, or the practice runs were omitted entirely. (This varied from experiment to experiment.) During the test runs, subjects were asked to make confidence calls on about five trials per run.

In three of the five experiments, there was a significant increase in overall scoring from the prefeedback to the postfeedback runs when the practice period consisted of no more than three runs (Honorton, 1970; Kreiman and Ivnisky, 1973a; McCallam and Honorton, 1973). Three experiments also yielded a significant increase in the proportion of correct confidence calls (Honorton, 1970, 1971b; McCallam and Honorton, 1973). Significant increases were never obtained in control conditions. However, there is a respect in which these results do not fit a learning interpretation. In one of the successful experiments, the significant increase in overall scores was from significant psi-missing on the pretest to a mean just slightly above chance on the posttest (Honorton, 1970). This looks more like regression to the mean than learning. Jackson *et al.* (1977) found significant psi-missing on pretest confidence calls in their feedback group as compared to only chance scoring on the posttest. Confidence call means exhibited this same pattern in two of Honorton's three experiments (Jackson *et al.*, 1977). Kreiman and Ivnisky (1973a) do not report their means in the abstract of their full report (to which I do not have access), but they shy away from interpreting their own results as evidence of learning.

Braud and Wood (1977) attempted to adapt Honorton's paradigm to a free-response situation using the ganzfeld to facilitate a psi-conducive state. The four practice sessions consisted of tonal feedback indicating the accuracy of individual mentation reports during the session. According to one of the two measures of ESP the authors used, ESP scores for the feedback group were significantly above chance in the posttraining ganzfeld sessions and significantly higher than their scores in the pretraining sessions. No such difference was found in the control group. The only significant effect by the second measure was the regression effect found in the feedback group in two of the card-guessing studies described above: significant psi-missing in the pretest followed by chance scoring in the posttest, but in this case the effect appeared in the control group only.

The only significant decline effect I could find in an experiment with immediate feedback was by Banham (1973), and this involved a contrast between the first and last 10 trials of a 100-trial test. It is doubtful that this effect would have been significant had the author used the more conventional procedure of analyzing data from all the trials.

4.2.2b. Selected Subjects. The crucial test of Tart's theory is whether subjects who have demonstrated ESP talent before training show increases in scoring rate as a result of training. Several studies using Schmidt machines with talented subjects were not reported in such a way that the learning hypothesis could be evaluated (Haraldsson, 1970; Schmidt, 1969a, b; Schmidt and Pantas, 1972), although we may assume that any obvious scoring increments would have been reported. There was no evidence that any of these subjects declined in performance, however. Delmore, on the other hand, increased his scoring dramatically between the first and second series of a card-guessing experiment with immediate feedback on most trials, an effect that might conceivably reflect learning (Kanthamani and Kelly, 1974b).

The most direct attempt so far to test Tart's theory has been by Tart himself (Tart, 1976a). He screened over 1,500 college students for ESP ability with simple card tests and invited those who scored significantly above chance to complete six additional runs on two electronic ESP testing machines. The machines provided immediate feedback and were adapted for testing in the GESP mode. Subjects who continued to score significantly were assumed to have genuine talent, and they were graduated to the training phase of the experiment, which consisted of 20 runs on the machine of their choice.

Ten of the 25 subjects who completed the training phase scored significantly above chance, most to an extreme degree. Only one of these subjects evidenced a significant increase in scoring across the 20 runs, but there were no significant decline effects. The most encouraging finding from the standpoint of Tart's theory, however, was a significant positive correlation for one of the machines between the individual performance curves in the training study (the measure of "learning") and the total number of hits on that machine in the second phase of the screening (the measure of initial talent). In other words, the most talented subjects were the ones who showed the most stable ESP performance over the 20 runs. The correlation for the other machine was in the opposite direction but not significant. Finally, the one subject who increased her scoring rate significantly during training had the highest score of any subject on her machine during the screening phase. The validity of Tart's conclusions has been the subject of an extensive debate in the literature (Stanford, 1977a, c; Tart, 1977b).

4.2.2c. Conclusions. Although trial-by-trial feedback does not produce changes in ESP scoring rate over time with a high degree of consistency, the changes it does produce are much more likely to be incline effects than decline effects. As we saw in the last section, just the opposite is the case in experiments where immediate feedback is not employed. This pattern suggests that such feedback does indeed have a tendency to stabilize ESP scoring and perhaps to enhance it in some cases.

Whether the incline effects that have been found really represent learning is an open question. Such increases by themselves are not sufficient to verify learning; for example, they might reflect nothing more than heightened motivation as scoring continues to be positive. More secondary effects such as the suggestive interaction between scoring increases and intelligence reported by Drucker will be needed before the validity of the learning hypothesis can be clearly established, although a learning interpretation of their experiment is questionable due to the small number of runs. Tart's finding that his most talented subjects were the ones whose performance slopes during training were most positive holds promise that more clear-cut scoring increases might be found with more extensive training than Tart was able to provide, particularly if subjects are given aids for detecting internal cues. Biofeedback could prove to be a useful tool in this connection.

5. Short-Circuiting the Ego

Tart's training procedure involves the activation of what might be called ego processes toward the goal of enhancing ESP. That is, the subject uses conscious, intellectually guided effort to make correct responses. While recognizing the potential value of this approach, many parapsychologists also believe that ego processes may at the same time inhibit ESP by reducing spontaneity or mobilizing psychological defenses. Furthermore, an ESP message simply may not reach a level of consciousness where it can be dealt with by ego processes. Such considerations have led to the development of testing techniques that do not require the subject to make any conscious, intentional ESP responses at all, thereby effectively bypassing these ego functions. The findings generated by the use of such techniques are the topic of this section.

5.1. Covert ESP Tests: Keeping Subjects in the Dark

5.1.1. PMIR: ... But I Thought You Were Testing My Memory!

ESP is clearly an unconscious process that functions primarily outside the voluntary control of the organism. Generally speaking, subjects are unaware on which particular trial an ESP message is getting through, or even if it is getting through at all. It is tempting to carry this logic one step further and speculate that ESP may sometimes function at times when we are not trying to use it or may not even want to use it, and in such a way that we are completely unaware of its operation. Rex Stanford (1974) has proposed an elaborate scientific model that assumes that ESP functions in just this way in order to fulfill the organism's needs. He refers to goal-directed behavior governed by the operation of psi as "psi-mediated instrumental response" or PMIR.

5.1.1a. The Word-Association Paradigm. The unintentional operation of psi can be demonstrated most clearly in a laboratory setting by experiments where the subject is not consciously aware that the experiment involves ESP at all. A number of such experiments have recently been conducted by Stanford himself in the guise of word-association tests (Stanford and Associates, 1976; Stanford and Castello, 1977; Stanford and Rust, 1977; Stanford and Stio, 1976; Stanford and Thompson, 1974). All these experiments were intended to test an assumption of the model that states that PMIR can function through an "unconscious timing mechanism," and their designs were basically similar. Subjects were each given a ten-item word-association test in a context supposedly unrelated to ESP. One of the ten trials was randomly designated as the crucial trial. If the subject's response latency on that trial met a certain criterion (e.g., the fastest of the ten trials), he subsequently experienced a pleasant task, such as rating *Playboy* photographs. (Stanford has exclusively tested male subjects in this paradigm.) If the subject did not meet the criterion, he experienced a tedious and boring task, such as crossing out letters in a manuscript. Thus the subject's performance on a covert ESP test was instrumental in determining whether he experienced a pleasant or unpleasant task later.

None of the above experiments produced overall significant positive scoring on the main dependent variable, which was a function of the mean difference in reaction time between the crucial trial and the average of all ten trials. However, in one experiment, significantly more persons entered the favorable condition than expected by chance (Stanford and Rust, 1977). This experiment differed from the others in that the person who experienced the consequences of the subject's ESP performance was someone other than himself. Whether or not a significantly large number of subjects entered the favorable condition in Stanford's earlier experiments could not be precisely evaluated because timing of the response latencies was too insensitive to eliminate ties within subjects for the words with the shortest latencies. Stanford and Rust (1977) eliminated this problem by timing within $1/100''$ instead of $1/10''$.

Two of the experiments obtained results that supported specific predictions from the PMIR model. Stanford and Associates (1976) found that female experimenters obtained significantly higher ESP scores from their subjects than did male experimenters, the subsequent "pleasant" task having a sexual theme. Presumably the sexual arousal engendered by males interacting with female experimenters increased the need-relevance of the pleasant task such that it provoked more ESP than it would otherwise. The "need strength" hypothesis was not confirmed in another experiment (Stanford and Stio, 1976), but there is some independent evidence that the arousal manipulation was not effective in this experiment.

A second prediction derived from the model is that "PMIR occurs in part through psi-mediated facilitation or triggering of otherwise ready or available responses" (Stanford, 1974, pp. 45–46). This hypothesis had received support from an earlier word-association experiment not specifically designed to test the PMIR model (Stanford, 1973). Through a complicated logic, Stanford deduced from this hypothesis that PMIR should be more effective when the criterion for the crucial trial is a short response latency than when it is a long one. This prediction was confirmed by Stanford and Stio (1976). However, in two other experiments designed to test other hypotheses, both criteria nonetheless were incorporated. In one of these experiments there was a nonsignificant reversal of the effect found by Stanford and Stio (Stanford and Thompson, 1974), while data from the other are not at present available for reanalysis (Stanford and Associates, 1976).*

A third hypothesis involving the subject's self-concept was not confirmed (Stanford and Associates, 1976), but only a weak manipulation of self-concept was used for ethical reasons.

5.1.1b. The Academic-Exam Paradigm. The PMIR model has received additional support from a procedure developed by Martin Johnson (1973). On short-answer essay exams given to three college classes, he provided answers to half the questions in sealed envelopes to which the exams were attached. The targeted questions were randomly selected for each student individually. For two classes the answers were correct,

---

*Dr. Stanford kindly supplied me with this information in the course of reviewing the first draft of the chapter.

while for the third they were incorrect. In each case where the answers were correct, the students scored significantly higher on the targeted questions than on the control questions. However, when the enclosed answers were incorrect, they scored significantly higher on the control questions. It would appear that students who were unaware that ESP was involved with the exams used the concealed information to improve their scores in the first two experiments. However, in the third experiment their ESP presumably did not tell them that the answers were wrong and the "strategy" backfired. Although the scale used to score the answers was different in this experiment from that in the first two, it would appear that the *overall* scores in the first two experiments were higher, even when the scaling is taken into account.

The results of Johnson's first two experiments were successfully replicated twice by Braud (1975a), who also found that the subjects who used psi most effectively got the lowest scores on the part of the exam where answers were not supplied. However two attempted "replications" based on multiple-choice rather than essay questions failed to yield any significant results (Willis, Duncan, and Udofia, 1974).

An earlier experiment by Stanford (1970) is conceptually related to Johnson's paradigm and will be discussed in this section. In this case, subjects were asked to listen to the transcript of a bogus dream report and then to answer questions about its content. Unbeknownst to them, one of the four possible answers to each question was randomly selected as an ESP target. Thus, in contrast to Johnson's procedure, the correctness of the ESP responses bore no systematic relationship to the correctness of responses on the cognitive test. Among other things, Stanford found that when subjects gave answers that contradicted the transcript, they made significantly more hits than expected by chance. It would appear that designating an incorrect answer on the memory test as an ESP hit actually distorted subjects' recall of the transcripts without their awareness.

5.1.1c. PMIR and Overt ESP. Although the PMIR model stresses the role of unintentional psi as a mediator of instrumental responses, it assumes that intentional psi can serve this function as well. The hypothesized relationship between intentional and unintentional psi was supported by Stanford and Thompson (1974), who found a significant positive correlation between ESP scores derived from their word association test and scores from an orthodox card-guessing test administered immediately before.

Perhaps the best example of a case where intentional psi could be used to fulfill strong needs is a series of experiments in which subjects were led to believe that their scores on an ESP test would help to determine whether or not they would be allowed to enroll in a university course or receive employment in the university library (Sailaja and Rao, 1973). An interview was sandwiched between the two ESP tests. Overall scores were nonsignificant, but in each experiment scoring was higher after the interview than before. The difference was significant in two experiments and approached significance in the other. Subsequent research suggested that the difference was primarily due to the fact that the first ESP test caught subjects by surprise, while by the second test they were able to develop a more appropriate mental set.

5.1.1e. Conclusion. There is evidence from a number of experiments that subjects can use ESP unconsciously and unintentionally to fulfill their own needs or the needs of others. The academic exam paradigm has so far been the most successful in producing significant overall ESP effects, at least with essay-type questions. Since multiple-choice items are scored in an all-or-none fashion, it is conceivable that procedures based on such scores are simply too insensitive to demonstrate the effect. Although support for the specific predictions of Stanford's PMIR model has been inconsistent, all significant relationships have been in the predicted direction.

5.1.2. Covert Target Impregnation: X-Rated Parapsychology

A number of more traditional ESP experiments in which subjects made intentional ESP responses that were not instrumental in achieving some other end nevertheless had covert elements. These experiments were designed to demonstrate that subjects can respond to emotionally relevant target stimuli, of whose nature they are consciously unaware, in ways that are relevant to their own needs.

5.1.2a. Anxiety and Emotional Stimuli. In a variation of the standard BM card test, Carpenter (1971) included erotic photographs (e.g., couples engaging in sexual acts) inside half of the envelopes containing ESP cards that subjects were supposed to match to the key cards. The subjects, who were high school students, were unaware that erotic photographs were involved in the experiment. Carpenter found a significant interaction between target type and trait anxiety as measured by the Taylor Manifest Anxiety Scale. As expected, high-anxious subjects scored higher on the neutral targets and low-anxious subjects scored higher on the targets associated with the erotic pictures.

In an experiment quite similar to Carpenter's except that college students were tested with a BT procedure and the pictures were somewhat less risqué, Ballard (1975) found a significant negative relationship between scores on Spielberger's Trait Anxiety Scale and ESP scores on erotic targets, but only for females. This relationship was not confirmed in a follow-up experiment (Ballard, 1977), but his female subjects had an unusually high mean score on the anxiety scale, suggesting a possible restriction of range problem. He did find, however, that scoring on erotic targets was highest among subjects who reported the greatest decrease in *state* anxiety following a pretest relaxation exercise. These results fit in with the general pattern of better scoring on erotic targets among the least anxious subjects.

Carpenter (1971), in a second experiment with college males, used the Mosher Sex Guilt Scale and belief in ESP as predictors in an ESP experiment otherwise identical to his first endeavor described above. Among believers in ESP (who scored significantly lower on sex guilt than did nonbelievers) he found significantly higher ESP scores on erotic than on neutral targets. Among the more guilt-prone goats, he found generally chance scoring on the erotic targets, but there was a significant tendency for these goats to score lower on the neutral targets than the less guilt-prone goats. These findings are complex, but they show that psi-hitting on erotic targets was restricted to subjects who both believe in ESP and have relatively little sex guilt as measured by the Mosher scale. To the extent that "sex guilt" represents a kind of anxiety, these findings are consistent with those described above.

Finally, Johnson and Nordbeck (1972) tested a woman with frequent psychic experiences who also revealed signs of neuroticism on the Defense Mechanisms Test. A BM procedure was used, and the target cards (unknown to the subject) consisted of words having positive or negative emotional import for her, as deduced from personality tests and a clinical interview. She scored above chance on the positive words and below chance on the negative words, the difference being significant. A second experiment was unsuccessful, but in between experiments the subject had learned the nature of the target cards and expressed displeasure at the previous deception. Thus the psychological conditions were drastically altered in this second experiment.

5.1.2b. Other Experiments With Covert Emotional Stimuli. Rogers (1967c) found in each of two experiments that subjects who believed in ESP and reported sexual arousal after reading an erotic passage scored significantly higher on targets that consisted of provocative words from the passage than on ESP symbol targets. The difference was only significant when the word runs were given after subjects had read the passage and the symbol runs before, not vice versa.

Wiklund (1975) used pictures of beautiful or gruesome scenes as targets in two blind matching experiments. Subjects were unaware of the identity or nature of the pictures. In the first experiment, the overall mean was significantly below chance, and there was a signficiant interaction between target type and perceptual response on a spiral aftereffect test. "Intraceptive" (subjectively oriented) subjects concentrated their psi-missing on the gruesome targets, while "extraceptive" (objectively oriented) subjects concentrated their psi-missing on the beautiful targets. Results in the replication attempt were nonsignificant, despite a larger sample size. Price (1973b) generally found that supplementing ESP symbols with erotic symbols had no significant effect on ESP scores, but the erotic symbols he used (the first letters of erotic words) would not be expected to have much emotional impact.

5.1.2c. Conclusion. The overall pattern of results from studies using covert emotional stimuli suggests that subjects who are relatively anxious tend to avoid responding correctly to targets associated with emotionally arousing or potentially threatening stimuli when they are not informed of the presence of such stimuli. Carpenter's experiment with the Mosher scale and Johnson's experiment are the most convincing in this respect, because the target material was related in relatively specific ways to the psychodynamics of the subjects.

5.2. Physiological Response Indices: ESP's Body Language

In the designs we examined in the last section, the ESP message was always mediated by a verbal or quasi-verbal response; i.e., the message still required some representation in consciousness. But what if a psychic impression is either too weak or too heavily censored to achieve even this secondary representation in consciousness? Such an impression could still influence the organism at an even more primitive level that might be detected by examining unconscious and/or unintentional physiological responses to the remote ESP stimulus. As was the case in the PMIR experiments described in the previous section, the subject need not be trying to make an ESP response or even know that he or she is in an ESP experiment. In this section I will discuss those experiments where physiological responses were used not as predictors of ESP responses but as ESP responses themselves.

5.2.1. Autonomic Responses: Let Your Finger Do the Talking

5.2.1a. Plethysmograph. The majority of studies have examined autonomic reactions, and the most common of these has been blood volume of the finger as measured by the plethysmograph. The first systematic attempt to use the plethysmograph as an ESP index was by Figar (1959), who simultaneously recorded subjects in the same room separated by a heavy curtain. At various times, one subject would silently perform mental arithmetic while the physiological responses of the other subject were noted. Responses coincident with the agent's mental arithmetic were detected on a large number of trials, accompanied by a large number of spontaneous deflections occurring simultaneously in the two subjects. Statistical analyses of these results proved to be highly significant (West, 1959). However, Dalton (1960) pointed out that the spontaneous synchronicities of response could be due to common reactions to environmental stimuli, while Nash and Nash (1962) found errors in the statistical analysis of Figar's results which reduced the other effect to nonsignificance. The Nashes also replicated Figar's experiment with the participants seven miles apart and failed to obtain significant results. Sanjar (1969) likewise failed to achieve significance with a similar design, although he included a third subject who was not to receive an ESP message as a control for environmental effects. The design of this study has been criticized by Dean (1970).

A better experimental design than Figar's would be to compare autonomic reactions on experimental trials to reactions on control trials where the stimulus presented to the agent is not expected to evoke a response. Such an approach was pioneered by Dean and his co-workers (Dean, 1962, 1966a, b, 1971a, b; Dean and Nash, 1967; Dean and Otani, 1972). Dean used as target material cards with names that were emotionally meaningful to the percipient or to the agent, names selected at random from the phone book, and blank cards. The cards were looked at by the agent, in random order and with random intertrial intervals, while the reactions of the remote percipient were recorded. The principal method of analysis was to compare the magnitude of the pen deflection during trials where a name was presented to that of trials where a blank card was presented.

Dean reported generally significant results using this method with three percipients, including himself, although in only one case was a detailed experimental report published (Dean and Nash, 1967). Although the effect was generally strongest with names known to the percipient, trends approaching significance also appeared for other names, especially in the Dean and Nash experiment. In one case, a reversal (more response to blank cards) occurred when the student was tested around exam time (Dean, 1966b). However, a successful replication of the primary finding with a single subject was reported by Barry (1968).

In an experiment of a design similar to Dean's, Esser et al. (1967) found that 7 of 12 percipients made more responses to emotional stimuli presented to the agent than to neutral stimuli, while only one subject reversed this trend. However, a larger replication attempt by Haraldsson (1972) produced only chance results on the relationship of interest.

Two experiments employing methodology somewhat different from

Dean's have yielded significant results with plethysmographic measures. Tart (1963) examined percipients' responses on occasions when a remotely located agent received painful electric shocks randomly interspersed with other occasions when the shock was "sent" but, instead of being received by the agent, was diverted to a resistor. Compared to matched control periods, percipients evidenced significantly more plethysmographic responses on each type of experimental trial, the effect actually being somewhat stronger on those trials where the agent did not receive the shock. Percipients were asked to press a telegraph key when they felt that a "subliminal stimulus" had been presented to them during the session, but these conscious ESP responses were unrelated to any of the experimental manipulations.

In a more complex experiment, Schouten (1976a) used both name cards (of the various types employed by Dean) and loud tones to stimulate the agent at random intervals. Using numbers of responses as the dependent variable, significant results with the plethysmograph were obtained only with names. Although only names known to the percipient produced independently significant results, effects of comparable magnitude were found with names supplied by the agents and with neutral names.

5.2.1b. Skin Resistance. Skin resistance has been used almost as frequently as plethysmograph with this paradigm, but the results have been less encouraging. Woodruff and Dale (1952) used electric shock to condition a GSR to one of three ESP symbols. When the symbols were later presented in random sequence under conditions of sensory shielding, there was no evidence of discriminating GSR responses, despite periodic reinforcement to prevent extinction. Beloff, Cowles, and Bate (1970) obtained chance results using names or photos of the percipients as the crucial stimuli supplied to the agent.

A better comparison of skin resistance and plethysmograph is provided by those experiments in which both recording techniques were used. Tart's (1963) results with GSR were in the same direction as with plethysmograph but nonsignificant. Schouten (1976a) found that name stimuli had no effect on his skin resistance measure, but he did find that when sound stimuli were used, there were significantly *fewer* GSRs when the agent was being stimulated than during control periods. Schouten interprets this result as an increase of basal skin resistance (BSR) during the sending periods, indicative of lower sensitivity to *sensory* stimulation during periods of extrasensory stimulation. Why such an effect did not appear with name stimuli remains obscure. Sanjar (1969) used both measures only in a preliminary experiment. Although GSR seemed somewhat more effective than plethysmograph, the results were not impressive and controls were lax.

5.2.1c. Conclusion. Autonomic responses to remote stimuli of emotional salience to agent and/or percipient have been demonstrated with a fair degree of consistency in properly designed experiments when the measure is the plethysmograph, but not when it is the GSR. Although I am by no means an expert in autonomic physiology, I know of no physiological reason to expect different results with these two measures. Experimenter effects may be responsible for some of the difference, but this explanation cannot readily account for the relatively superior results with plethysmographs in Tart's and Schouten's experiments.

The failure of Schouten to find significant plethysmograph results with tone stimuli suggests that stimuli must have either emotional valence or cognitive meaning to be effectively transmitted. On the other hand, the tendency of neutral names to be almost as effective as emotional names in the work of Schouten and of Dean and Nash, and the apparent transmission of information on pseudoshock trials in Tart's experiment, suggests that a stimulus need not have emotional impact to get through. Perhaps there is a generalization effect involved; i.e., if *some* of the stimuli in an experimental condition are of an emotional nature, neutral stimuli interspersed among them take on at least some of this emotional quality themselves and are also transmitted. Schouten's sound stimuli would not be predicted to be effective by this hypothesis because they were not interspersed with the name stimuli and (apparently, at least) did not arouse a specific emotion themselves.

5.2.2. EEG: Show Me Your Sine

A smaller number of experiments have attempted to influence central as opposed to autonomic nervous system responses by means of remote stimulation. The first substantial effort to determine whether the EEG could be influenced in this way was Tart's (1963) experiment discussed above. Using period analysis, he found a general desynchronization of the EEG during experimental (shock and pseudoshock) trials as compared to control trials, but the difference was significant only on the variable that measured EEG activity superimposed on the basic waveform. This is the most sensitive of the measures provided by period analysis.

5.2.2a. Stroboscopic Stimulation. The most common procedure for testing remote EEG effects has been to drive the agent's EEG with a strobe device and to determine whether comparable changes simultaneously appear in the brain waves of a sensorially isolated percipient. The first report I could find of such an experiment was by Duane and Behrendt (1965), who claimed remote driving of EEG alpha with 2 of 15 pairs of identical twins.

In a more sophisticated experiment, Targ and Puthoff (1974) randomly interspersed 12 trials of 6Hz and 16-Hz stimulation, respectively, with 12 control trials. Although no photic driving was demonstrated in any of the six percipients, alpha blocking was observed in one of them during the experimental trials. Confirmatory research with this subject revealed continued significant alpha blocking with 16-Hz stimulation of the agent, and the same trend approached significance with 6-Hz stimulation. An attempted independent replication with one subject and omission of the 6-Hz condition yielded some significant effects based on post hoc analyses of EEG spectra, but the pattern of results differed from session to session and thus cannot be considered a clear confirmation of Targ's findings (Kelly and Lenz, 1976a).

5.2.2b. Evoked Potentials. Lloyd (1973) reported a pilot study in which an average evoked response (AER) occasionally was elicited in response to a single flash of light presented to a remote agent. However, the design of this experiment was criticized by Millar (1976), who proceeded to conduct his own experiment under better controlled conditions. He found no evidence of remote AER when the agent was repeatedly submitted to .5-Hz photic stimulation during a 75-second period.

5.2.2c. Conclusion. Attempts to influence EEG by remote stimulation so far have been less successful than attempts to influence blood volume, but the presence of some positive findings should encourage further research. Some of the EEG experiments discussed in section 3.1.1 that were primarily designed to find correlates of ESP behavioral responses could also be construed as involving EEG responses to ESP stimuli. Studies where EEG–ESP relationships are examined on a trial-by-trial basis are particularly relevant (Kelly and Lenz, 1976b; Wallwork, 1952).

6. The Ubiquity of It All

In the preceding sections we have seen a wide range of ESP effects: psi-hitting, psi-missing, variance effects, position effects, precognition, etc. However, all of these effects involve the relationship between each ESP call and the target designated for that trial. In this section, we will examine instances where ESP calls seem to be related in systematic ways to stimuli other than the target, or to patterns in the target sequences.

Results of this type present perhaps the clearest illustration yet of the ubiquity of psi. Almost every conceivable form of psi manifestation has been demonstrated at one time or another. This ubiquity must be taken into account when we finally confront the question of how we can best make sense of the experimental results we have considered in this chapter.

6.1. Displacement Effects: ESP Off Target

In most ESP tests, the subject is trying to use ESP to acquire information about a particular target as distinct from other potential targets. However, it is not uncommon for ESP to miss the target and pick up one or more of these other stimuli, the subject being completely unaware that this is happening. Such "displacement" represents one of the major barriers to the reliable application of psi.

6.1.1. Between-Trials Displacement: Expanding the Space–Time Frame

Between-trials displacement refers to scoring a hit on a target occurring either before or after the real-time target in a sequence of targets. Interest traditionally has been focused on the targets occurring immediately before or after the real-time target, and hitting on such targets is referred to as −1 and +1 displacement, respectively. The +1 displacement may provide evidence of precognition in cases where targets are selected randomly on a trial-by-trial basis, but this perspective will not be our primary concern in this section.

6.1.1a. Evidence for Between-Trials Displacement. If we can accept its credibility, the strongest evidence for between-trials displacement effects in the parapsychological literature comes from the extensive testing of Basil Shackleton (Soal and Bateman, 1954). In a screening experiment, Shackleton scored significantly above chance on both +1 and −1. He continued to score significantly above chance on +1 throughout most of his career while scoring nonsignificantly on the actual target and −1. With one sender, however, he reverted to his original habit of scoring significantly on both +1 and −1. Most of this latter effect subsequently was found to be attributable to cases where the +1 and −1 targets were the same symbol, thus giving him both a +1 and −1 hit on the same response. This was called the "reinforcement effect" (Pratt, 1951).

Significant displacement effects have occasionally been found with other subjects, but not nearly as frequently as direct hitting. Russell (1943) found no clear evidence of between-trials displacement in the results of eight major experiments conducted at Rhine's laboratory up to that time. Six of these involved single subjects. However, Mangan (1955, 1957) found a woman who consistently scored significantly above chance on +1, while her scoring on real-time targets was inconsistent.

The strongest evidence of displacement in research with unselected subjects comes from "home-testing" experiments organized by G. W. Fisk (Fisk, 1951a, b; West, 1953). Fisk mailed packs of standard ESP cards to 235 correspondents, who tested each other on varying numbers of runs using a GESP format. The experiment was intended as a screening device to select talented subjects for additional testing under better controlled conditions. A significantly positive overall mean score in the actual targets in this experiment could not have been taken seriously, but scoring on these targets was not significant, although positive. The main finding of interest, which it would be somewhat harder to attribute to experimental error, was highly significant psi-missing on both +1 and −1. Evidence of "reinforcement" was also found in these data. Significant between-trials displacements have occasionally been reported in other forced-choice and free-response experiments, some of which have been described elsewhere in the chapter. However, they form no consistent pattern.

   6.1.1b. Between-Trials Displacement in High-Scoring Direct Hitters. Tart (1977a) recently reported that all five of the high-scoring subjects on the ten-choice machine in his GESP learning experiment (Tart, 1976a) showed significant psi-missing on +1 and −1. Although the −1 effect was at least partly an artifact due to the immediate feedback, Tart cited internal evidence possibly suggesting a genuine bilateral psi-missing effect on the +1 and −1 targets. Very similar bilateral psi-missing on +1 and −1 was found in GESP tests with a high-scoring Aborigine woman (Rose and Rose, 1951). Pratt and Foster (1950) found significant evidence of psi-missing on +1 in the DT results of one of Martin and Stribic's high-scoring subjects. This analysis was based only on pairs of trials that included no direct hits. Pairs containing a direct hit revealed a significant excess of +1 hits, but Pratt later concluded that analysis of such pairs for displacement effects was inappropriate (Pratt, Martin, and Stribic, 1974). A comparable anlaysis of pairs of misses contributed by Martin and Stribic's best subject, C. J., revealed different displacement effects for different types of DT or UT tests (Pratt *et al.*, 1974). Two of the three effects involved significant psi-missing on either +1 or −1, while the other involved significant psi-hitting on −1. Analysis of pairs of misses from Gloria Stewart, one of Soal's high-scoring subjects, revealed a significant excess of +1 and −1 hits (Pratt, 1967a). Other high-scoring subjects such as Pearce have failed to show significant displacement (Russell, 1943).

   6.1.1c. Conclusion. In the literature as a whole, significant scoring on displacement targets is reported much less frequently than on real-time targets. How much of this is attributable to the fact that displacement effects are analyzed less often than real-time effects is unclear. No consistent relationships have been found between displacmement scores and psychological variables.

   A number of subjects who have evidenced strong hitting on real-time targets have shown secondary displacement effects. The nature of such effects have been inconsistent, but most seem to involve psi-missing on either +1, −1, or both. If one ignores the controversial Stewart data, this type of pattern is most evident in GESP experiments, including, perhaps, Fisk's experiment with unselected subjects.

Tart (1977a) labeled the effect he found as "transtemporal inhibition," likening it to the secondary inhibition of stimuli immediately adjacent to the focal stimulus in all known sensory systems. Since +1 effects in his experiment were most likely precognitive because targets were generated on a trial-by-trial basis, he argued that his results suggested an expanded primary perception forward in time. In other experiments, the expansion of perception could be interpreted either spatially or temporally.

6.1.2. Within-Trial Displacement: Confusing Kings with Queens

A second kind of displacement occurs within a particular trial. In forced-choice experiments, it involves the tendency to consistently call a particular incorrect symbol when missing a particular target, e.g., consistently calling "circle" every time the target is "star." Parapsychologists refer to this effect as "consistent missing." In certain free-response experiments, within-trial displacement involves the evocation of imagery related to control pictures to be used in the judging process.

6.1.2a. Consistent Missing. Significant evidence of consistent missing in card-guessing experiments has been reported by Cadoret and Pratt (1950) and by Timm (1969). However, the most impressive evidence of consistent missing comes from a recent experiment with Bill Delmore, who reports strong visual imagery associated with his ESP responses (Kelly *et al.*, 1975). This "gifted" subject made 10,350 calls of ordinary playing cards concealed by heavy black paper. In addition, he made 1,875 guesses of playing cards projected tachistoscopically at a rate likely to induce mistakes of identification. The subject's overall positive score on the ESP runs was highly significant, and there was significant evidence of consistent missing concentrated in the runs with the highest scores. The most interesting aspect of the data was the fact that the particular errors the subject made were the same on the high-scoring ESP runs as on the visual task, for example, confusion among picture cards (e.g., calling a king a queen) and confusion among colors (e.g., calling a heart a diamond). As expected, such consistent missing effects were not found in high-scoring runs using a "psychic shuffle" procedure where visual mediation was not relevant (Kanthamani and Kelly, 1975). The results of these two experiments together strongly suggest that, at least for this one subject, ESP information is encoded in the same way as visual information in relevant types of ESP tests.

Consistent missing effects have also been found with a between-subjects design. In a correspondence experiment, Fisk and West (1957) invited subjects who were situated in their own homes to guess a common sequence of 12 clock cards displayed at Fisk's home, the order being rerandomized for each test. There was a significant tendency for particular cards to receive the same call regardless of their locations in the sequence. Although no formal statistical test of consistent missing was applied, for none of the 12 targets was the most frequent call the correct one. This kind of consistent missing effect seems to suggest that particular targets "pull" particular responses that may not be accurate.

6.1.2b. Free-Response Experiments. Within-trial displacement to control pictures in free-response experiments can occur, especially when the subject is asked to pick out a target picture from a group of pictures soon after the reception period. Such displacements are frequently reported anecdotally (e.g., Stanford and Neylon, 1975), and some statistical evidence of their occurrence has recently been found in a ganzfeld experiment (Palmer et al., 1977).

6.1.2c. Conclusion. Within-trial displacement effects have never evoked much interest among parapsychologists, but they have been shown to occur in both forced-choice and (more equivocally) free-response experiments. In forced-choice experiments, at least, consistent missing has as much potential information value as direct hitting, and subjects who manifest this aberration possibly could be trained to compensate for it and become outstanding psi-hitters.

6.1.3. Focusing and Holistic Effects: Microscope and Macroscope

The kinds of displacement analyses we have looked at so far assumed that all targets in the sequence are equivalent as sources of ESP information. In this section, I will consider two opposite kinds of situation where this assumption does not hold.

6.1.3a. The Focusing Effect. The "focusing effect" refers generally to the tendency for psi-mediated responses to be focused on particular physical targets in a sequence. The term was coined as a label for a unique scoring tendency found in the data of the "gifted" subject Stepanek (Pratt, 1973). This subject, you may recall (Sec. 1.2.), specialized in guessing which side of a card concealed in an opaque envelope was facing upward. It later was discovered that Stepanek had developed a tendency to make the same call each time certain sides of *some* of the envelopes were presented to him, regardless of the status of the enclosed cards. This finding became of parapsychological interest when the envelopes were enclosed in cardboard covers and focusing on the same envelopes continued. Then *sensory* focusing began to appear on some of the covers, and this new effect continued when the covers were concealed. The focusing effect began soon after the containers were first introduced in the research and were consistent across different experimental series. Stepanek does not "focus" intentionally, and he claims his attention is always concentrated on the cards.

Pratt (1973) suggests that Stepanek unconsciously utilizes subtle sensory cues to classify exposed containers into two categories, which are responded to extrasensorially when the containers are concealed. However, ESP *might* be involved even when the containers are visible.

No evidence of focusing effects has yet been discovered with other high-scoring subjects. It was not found with Harribance when the targets were ten male or female photographs (Roll and Klein, 1972). Lucas and Roll (1973) asked a subject to repeatedly guess four decks of cards of different types, each card being concealed in an opaque envelope. The subject apparently did not know which deck she was guessing on a particular run. Results indicated a significant tendency *not* to repeatedly call the same symbol on a given card. This looks like the diametric opposite of the focusing effect demonstrated by Stepanek. However, the relevance of this finding to the focusing effect is limited by the fact that there was no evidence of the effect being concentrated on particular cards.

The closest thing I could find to a replication of the focusing effect was the experiment of Fisk described in the last section. West (1953) noted that the consistent missing effect found in Fisk's data was concentrated on 3 of the 12 target envelopes, although no statistical test was reported to back up this assessment.

6.1.3b. Holistic Effects. In an ingenious experiment with Harribance as subject, Child and Kelly (1973) created "unbalanced decks," which consisted of nine, seven, five, three, and one replications of the standard ESP symbols in random permutation. For example, a deck might consist of nine circles but only one star. Harribance was aware of this manipulation in general terms only. His scoring was significantly above chance, but the result was attributable at least partly to a significant tendency to unbalance his calls in the direction of the deck's composition. In other words, if a deck contained large numbers of stars and crosses he would tend to call large numbers of stars and crosses on that run. This effect was not simply an artifact of direct hitting, because it was independently significant when only misses were analyzed. These results suggest that Harribance responded holistically to the deck more than he did to the particular sequence of targets.

6.1.3c. Conclusion. The focusing effect clearly applies to Stepanek, but its generality to other subjects is questionable. Fisk's results with unselected subjects offer some hope in this regard, however, and they suggest further that particular targets may engender identical calling biases in different individuals. The generality of Child's holistic effect is completely indeterminate because only one unbalanced deck experiment has been reported. This procedure certainly should be tried with other subjects.

6.2. Summary and Conclusion: What Does It All Mean?

It is now time to bring the chapter to a close and take stock of where we have been. How can we further integrate the over 700 references reviewed so far in the chapter and what guidelines can be suggested for the next stages of inquiry?

6.2.1. The Unreliability of ESP Scores: A Nemesis Revisited

Early in the chapter I made the point that ESP scores are quite unreliable, even by the standards of reliability customary in the social and behavioral sciences. The signal-to-noise ratio is very low, and one must endure a great deal of static to hear any message that may be present.

The implications of this fact can hardly be understated. Many psychologists, for example, are simply unwilling to study unreliable variables because of the problems they present. The willingness of parapsychologists to accept the challenge such variables offer is one of the major characteristics that distinguishes them from most other scientists.

In practice, the unreliability of ESP scores means that a large amount of data must be collected to obtain a small amount of information. Much dirt must be panned before any gold is discovered. At the level of relationships between ESP and other variables, we saw that almost never have such relationships appeared consistently in different experiments. As Rao (1977) has recently pointed out, it is unclear whether the null results in some cases is evidence against the validity of the relationship or whether the "ESP scores" in these experiments simply did not reflect any ESP. In the beginning of the chapter, subtle differences in methodology and sampling variability were cited as other plausible reasons for the inconsistency. However, the ability to explain this unreliability does not make it go away or make it any less frustrating to the theoretically minded researcher.

Nevertheless, our cloud has an important silver lining. Low or inconsistent reliability is not the same as no reliability. We saw numerous instances throughout the chapter where researchers were successful in replicating the results of their own previous experiments. Independent replications have also been reported from time to time, although not as frequently as "in-house" replications. (This ratio is not surprising, given the greater opportunity for subtle methodological differences to intrude into independent replication attempts). In short, what this reliability means is that *trends* frequently emerge in the data. For example, we saw that some variables are better predictors of ESP scores than are other variables. We saw several instances where relationships which were usually not significant almost always occurred in the same direction when they were significant. These patterns are the elusive gold nuggets we have been seeking amidst the debris. They are what justify the tedium of our expedition into the kingdom of the unreliable.

On the other hand, I would be remiss not to point out the dangers of such a strategy. The human mind has a natural and irresistible urge to abstract order out of chaos, even when there is no order to be abstracted. Occasionally, relationships are significant simply by chance, the infamous "type 1 error" that statisticians talk about. Might not we find "meaningful" patterns of relationship between psychological variables and "scores" taken from a random number table? On a couple of occasions I have generated such relationships myself as a kind of control condition for an ESP experiment, and I have always found that the ESP scores provided more, and more meaningful, relationships (meaningful, at least, to me).

There really is no definitive way at present to resolve the issue raised in the previous paragraph, but that does not mean we should not be keenly aware of it. Like many things in life, the proof of the pudding will be in the eating. Some of the patterns I have pointed out in this chapter will collapse as more data are collected. Others, I am confident, will survive, although I would not wish to speculate which ones they will be. Thus, as the process of research continues, it will become clearer and clearer where the gold is. Such knowledge, in turn, will teach us how to make ESP scores more reliable so we can find still more gold.

Parapsychology has traditionally found itself in a vicious circle: We can't get reliable ESP scores until we discover and then "understand" the functional relationships between ESP and other variables; but we can't discover these functional relationships without reliable ESP scores. By capitalizing on the admittedly low reliability we already have, the cycle can be reversed. What we are seeing in contemporary parapsychology is the beginning of this shift in equilibrium: The vicious circle is gradually turning into a snowball.

6.2.2. ESP and Predictor Variables: The Pattern of the Patterns

Throughout the chapter, but especially in sections 2 and 3, I commented upon certain patterns of relationships (or "gestalts," if you will) that seemed to emerge from an examination of several experiments that addressed similar research questions. I even went so far as to suggest possible interpretations of some of these relationships, although I never meant to imply that they were the only interpretations possible. What I plan to do in this section is carry the process to one higher level of abstraction. Do the patterns themselves fall into patterns that may further our understanding of the factors that influence scoring in ESP tests and thus guide future research? Again, I wish to stress that the interpretations I will propose are not the only ones possible, although they are the most reasonable ones to me.

In a methodological paper (Palmer, 1975), I stressed the importance of distinguishing between factors that influence the magnitude of psi (represented by the absolute deviation of the score from MCE) and the direction of psi (hitting versus missing). I will apply this distinction in the following discussion.

6.2.2a. Factors Affecting Magnitude: Cognitive Processing. In studying the patterns described in the chapter, I got the impression that the variables that most clearly seemed to affect the magnitude as opposed to the direction of psi had something to do with the manner in which subjects' cognitive processes were functioning during the test. The two most successful predictors of magnitude seemed to be spontaneity in the test (Sec. 2.3.2.) and the presence of a hypnagogiclike state of consciousness (2.6.2.). Spontaneity seems to be the primary variable here. Hypnagogiclike states may be expected to encourage spontaneity insofar as they are associated with a breakdown of rationalistic or "linear" (to adopt the current cliché) patterns of mentation.

Spontaneity appeared to facilitate ESP primarily through the vehicle of run-score variance. Most ASC experiments involved free-response procedures with only one or a very small number of trials per subject, so run-score variance could not be computed. What seemed to be happening in these experiments was that the subjects who reported relatively pronounced ASCs were responsible for most of the significant scores, but these scores tended to be all in the same direction in a given experiment. Thus it would seem that situational factors overrode individual differences as determinants of directional trends in these experiments. This is not surprising, because situational factors are more powerful in ASC experiments than in most experiments where subjects' minds are not being "tampered with."

The finding that significant psi-hitting is most likely to occur when subjects violate response biases (4.1.2.) also would seem to support the spontaneity hypothesis, since counterbias responses would appear to be more spontaneous than probias responses. Although there is no experimental evidence of psi-missing on counterbias responses (thus rendering the assumption that this is a magnitude rather than a deviation effect somewhat equivocal), this is due to the fact that the response-bias hypothesis has simply not been evaluated in experiments where the overall scoring deviation was negative. Rhine's salience effect (4.1.1.) is more clearly a magnitude effect, although it has appeared less consistently than the response bias effect. Rhine speculatively interpreted the greater evidence of psi at the beginning and end of the test unit as attributable to greater spontaneity of response on these trials.

There is also some evidence that the magnitude of ESP scoring is greatest on confidence calls, when they are allowed (4.1.3.). It is reasonable to assume that such calls reflect to a large degree the subject's assessment of his or her cognitive processes during the trial, but the relation of this assessment to spontaneity remains a question for future research. There also is some evidence that "extreme sheep," or persons emotionally involved with the issue of psi, tend to score significantly on ESP tests, some as hitters and some as missers (3.6.1d.). The relevance of this finding to spontaneity is not nearly so obvious as those cited above, but neither is it contradictory.

Finally, one piece of evidence that might be cited against the above interpretation is the fact that graphic expansiveness (a test with face validity as a measure of spontaneity, at least in free-response tests) does not seem to predict the magnitude of ESP scoring (3.7.2.).

   6.2.2b. Factors Affecting Direction: Social Psychological Variables. The variables that seemed to most consistently discriminate hitting and missing tendencies were almost exclusively social psychological in nature. The most obvious of these are the effect of the experimenter (2.5.2.) and the identity of the agent (2.5.1.). The effect of providing or depriving subjects of knowledge of their results (2.4.2.), strongly adverse environmental conditions (2.4.1.), and attractiveness of the targets and/or experimental procedure (2.2.1.) also fit into this category. A number of individual difference variables were also interpreted as reflecting the capacity of the subject to be comfortable in the test situation. These included neuroticism (3.2.1.), extraversion (3.2.2.), intelligence (3.3.1.), and the belief that ESP can occur in the test (3.6.1). The idea that psi-missing can be encouraged by adverse psychological conditions is by no means a new one (e.g., Rhine, 1969b), but it draws support from the data presented in this chapter.

A variable that reflects both social psychological factors (induction of a confident attitude) and cognitive state factors (induction of an ASC) is hypnosis (2.6.1.). Generally speaking, hypnosis seems to affect direction more than magnitude, but some studies also suggest an effect on magnitude per se (e.g., Honorton, 1964, 1966; Honorton and Krippner, 1969).

Another variable that seems clearly related to ESP scoring but that is somewhat difficult to classify in one category or the other is age (3.5.2). Rhine's (1941a, 1942) precognition research, where he generally found psi-hitting in children and psi-missing in adults, could well reflect social psychological factors, especially since in at least some of this research special efforts were made to create a positive social environment for the children but not the adults. In most other research, younger subjects scored significantly above chance and older subjects near chance. Thus magnitude and direction effects cannot be distinguished in these studies. Since people tend to become less spontaneous as they grow older, I would expect this to prove to be a magnitude effect rather than a direction effect, but that remains to be seen.

6.2.2c. Some Equivocal Patterns. A third set of predictor variables have yielded significant results with relatively great frequency, but the results have either been contradictory or have made little psychological sense. These include mood or affective state variables (3.7.), EEG alpha density (3.1.1.), and "cognitive style" variables such as creativity (3.3.3.), imagery ability (3.3.4.), and field dependence (3.3.6.). In some cases, especially creativity, imagery ability, and EEG alpha, part of the problem may be inadequate measuring techniques or the inability to adequately define the underlying variables being measured. It is also likely that these variables interact with other, uncontrolled variables in determining ESP performance. The plausibility of this latter point is reinforced by the fact that some interactions have been demonstrated in ESP experiments between these variables and other predictors that have been treated systematically. Mood has been shown to interact with personality variables in the research of Nielsen (3.7.1a), and field dependence and graphic expansiveness were shown to interact with types of ESP test in the research of Buzby (3.3.6) and Humphrey (3.7.2), respectively.

6.2.2d. Physical Variables: Nothing Cooking. Among those variables that seem to show little or no relationship of any kind to ESP scores, the most apparent cluster consists of physical variables. ESP scores do not seem to be affected by the distance of the target from the percipient either in space (2.1.) or in time (2.2.), the physical characteristics of forced-choice targets (2.3.1.). Physical variables only seem to influence psi insofar as they have secondary psychological effects.

6.2.3. The Ubiquity of It All: Is ESP Really ESP?

Throughout the chapter I have been making certain implicit assumptions about the nature of the psi process. These assumptions are in part an outgrowth of the term *extrasensory perception*, which implies a kind of analogy between ESP and known sensory processes. More specifically, we have been conceptualizing ESP as the ability to acquire information from sources not available to our known senses. This, in turn, implies transmission of information through some kind of channel from a source to a receiver.

At first glance, it seems perfectly reasonable to postulate such a model. After all, what a significant score on an ESP test seems to tell us is that information has been acquired, in much the same way that a student getting a certain proportion of the questions correct on a history exam tells us that he or she has acquired information about history. The problem is that in the case of the history course, or in any other case where sensory modes of information acquisition are operative, we have highly predictive theories that clearly specify how the information gets from the source to the receiver—physical theories of light, sensory physiology, etc. We have theories of this type in parapsychology, but they are very poorly developed and have little or no empirical support. We simply do not know how psi information is transmitted from source to receiver, and until we do, it is hazardous to take it for granted that such transmission occurs at all.

Another factor that should give us pause in prematurely embracing transmission models of ESP is the failure to detect any real limits to the manner of its manifestation. Subjects can score above chance, below chance, both, or neither. Their responses can relate to the intended target or to some other target in the sequence. It matters little whether the target exists in the past, present, or future, or how far away it is from the percipient. ESP can occur without the percipient's intent (as in Stanford's PMIR) or even without the subject making any voluntary response (as in studies of physiological ESP responses).

Given all this ubiquity, is it really that much of an inferential leap to add to our list synchronistic correspondences in nature (i.e., so-called meaningful coincidences) that do not involve the participation of a living mind or brain at all? In fact, wouldn't it really be more parsimonious to do so? While it is true that such synchronistic phenomena have not been as well verified as ESP, might this be simply because we have been so brainwashed by our transmission models that we have not sought to study them? There certainly is enough anecdotal evidence to justify such an examination.

Other anomalies in ESP data, although potentially explainable in terms of a transmission model, nonetheless strain that model. Rao's (1965a) differential effect looks more like some homeostatic principle in nature than the reflection of some psychological process affecting the processing of extrasensory information. In a similar vein, Nash and Nash (1963) have pointed out that the magnitude of psi-missing tends to match the magnitude of psi-hitting in so-called high aim–low aim ESP tests with more than two response alternatives, despite the fact that more psi (so to speak) would seem to be necessary to produce a given negative deviation than the same positive deviation in such a test. Significantly low run-score variance (e.g., Rogers and Carpenter, 1966) does not follow readily from a transmission model, despite some evidence for a "cancellation effect" (see Sec. 4.4.1c). Finally, the provocative findings subsumed under the heading of "experimenter psi" (2.5.2d) burden the transmission model with some assumptions that can at best be called unwieldly.

My intent here is not to suggest that we perfunctorily abandon the transmission model, but only that we keep our options open and our construct systems flexible. Indeed, synchronistic theories of psi are showing signs that they may be coming of age. The most visible proponent of this viewpoint has been Koestler (1972). The skeleton of a synchronistic theory of psi has recently been proposed by Lila Gatlin (1977), and Rex Stanford (1977b) seems to be moving in this direction with his new "conformance theory."

I could elaborate further on these points, but this is a chapter on research findings, not theory. I will leave it to Dr. Rao to carry the ball from here!

7. Acknowledgments

This chapter was written while I was employed as assistant research psychologist in the Department of Psychology, University of California, Davis. I wish to acknowledge with appreciation the est Foundation and the Parapsychology Foundation, Inc., who funded my position. I am also grateful to my senior colleague, Dr. Charles Tart, who provided me with the freedom and encouragement to pursue this project.

A number of individuals have read the first draft of the chapter and provided me with comments and suggestions. They include Dr. T. X. Barber, Dr. Irvin Child, Mr. Charles Honorton, Mr. James Kennedy, Dr. Robert Morris, Dr. Rex Stanford, and Ms. Debra Weiner. The chapter is much improved because of their efforts, but any deficiencies that remain are, of course, the responsibility of the author.

8. References

Adcock, C. J., and Quartermain, D. Some problems in group testing of ESP. *Journal of Parapsychology*, 1959, *23*, 251–256.
Alkokar, V. V. Experimentally induced shifts in attitude to ESP and their effects on scoring. *Journal of Parapsychology*, 1968, *32*, 63. (Abstract)

Alkokar, V. V., and Deshpande, V. D. Paranormal perceptivity and ESP test performance. *Journal of Parapsychology*, 1966, *30*, 131. (Abstract)

Altom, K., and Braud, W. G. Clairvoyant and telepathic impressions of musical targets. In J. D. Morris, W. G. Roll, and R. L. Morris (Eds.), *Research in parapsychology 1975*. Metuchen, New Jersey: Scarecrow Press, 1976. Pp. 171–174.

Altrocchi, J. Experiments with Lalsingh Harribance: Psychological studies. In W. G. Roll, R. L. Morris, and J. D. Morris (Eds.), *Proceedings of the Parapsychological Association No. 6, 1969*. Durham, North Carolina: Parapsychological Association, 1971. Pp. 68–70.

Anderson, M. Clairvoyance and teacher–pupil attitudes in fifth and sixth grades. *Journal of Parapsychology*, 1957, *21*, 1–12.

Anderson, M. A precognition experiment comparing time intervals of a few days and one year. *Journal of Parapsychology*, 1959, *23*, 81–89. (a)

Anderson, M. The relationship between level of ESP scoring and class grade. *Journal of Parapsychology*, 1959, *23*, 1–18. (b)

Anderson, M. The use of fantasy in testing for extrasensory perception. *Journal of the American Society for Psychical Research*, 1966, *60*, 150–163.

Anderson, M., and Gregory, E. A two year program of tests for clairvoyance and precognition with a class of public school pupils. *Journal of Parapsychology*, 1959, *23*, 149–177.

Anderson, M., and McConnell, R. A. Fantasy testing for ESP in a fourth and fifth grade class. *Journal of Psychology*, 1961, *52*, 491–503.

Anderson, M., and White, R. Teacher–pupil attitudes and clairvoyance test results. *Journal of Parapsychology*, 1956, *20*, 141–157.

Anderson, M., and White, R. A further investigation of teacher–pupil attitudes and clairvoyance test results. *Journal of Parapsychology*, 1957, *21*, 81–97.

Anderson, M., and White, R. ESP score level in relation to students' attitude toward teacher-agents acting simultaneously. *Journal of Parapsychology*, 1958, *22*, 20–28. (a)

Anderson, M., and White, R. The relationship between changes in student attitude and ESP scoring. *Journal of Parapsychology*, 1958, *22*, 167–174. (b)

Anderson, M., and White, R. A survey of work on ESP and teacher–pupil attitudes. *Journal of Parapsychology*, 1958, *22*, 246–268. (c)

Aström, J. *GESP and MPI measures*. Paper presented at the Eighth Annual Convention of the Parapsychological Association, New York, 1965. (Abstract in *Journal of Parapsychology*, 1965, *29*, 292–293.)

Ballard, J. A. *A psi task with hidden erotic and neutral stimuli*. Paper presented at the meeting of the Southeastern Regional Parapsychological Association, Durham, North Carolina, 1975. (Abstract in *Journal of Parapsychology*, 1975, *39*, 34.)

Ballard, J. A. Unconscious perception of erotic, non-erotic and neutral stimuli on a psi task. In J. D. Morris, W. G. Roll, and R. L. Morris (Eds.), *Research in parapsychology 1976*. Metuchen, New Jersey: Scarecrow Press, 1977. Pp. 159–162.

Banham, K. M. Temporary high scoring by a child subject. *Journal of Parapsychology*, 1966, *30*, 106–113.

Banham, K. M. The imaginary quiz as a technique. *Journal of Parapsychology*, 1968, *32*, 64. (Abstract)

Banham, K. M. Feedback, learning, and guessing. *Journal of Parapsychology*, 1973, *37*, 72–73. (Abstract)

Banham, K. M. Mood and guessing. *Journal of Parapsychology*, 1974, *38*, 344. (Abstract)

Barrington, M. R. A free response sheep/goat experiment using an irrelevant task. *Journal of the Society for Psychical Research*, 1973, *47*, 222–245.

Barron, F., and Mordkoff, A. M. An attempt to relate creativity to possible extrasensory empathy as measured by physiological arousal in identical twins. *Journal of the American Society for Psychical Research*, 1967, *62*, 73–79.

Barry, J. [Telepathy and plethysmography.] *Revue Métapsychique* (No. 4, Nouvelle Serie), 1967, 56–74. (Abstract in *Journal of Parapsychology*, 1968, *32*, 144.)

Bates, K. E., and Newton, M. An experimental study of ESP capacity in mental patients. *Journal of Parapsychology*, 1951, *15*, 271–277.

Beer, D. A correlational study to determine the effects of marital status on "telepathy" (GESP) between individuals. *Journal of Parapsychology*, 1971, *35*, 157. (Abstract)

Beloff, J. The "sweethearts" experiment. *Journal of the Society for Psychical Research*, 1969, *45*, 1–7.

Beloff, J. ESP: The search for a physiological index. *Journal of the Society for Psychical Research*, 1974, *47*, 403–420.

Beloff, J., and Bate, D. Research report for the year 1968–69. *Journal of the Society for Psychical Research*, 1970, *45*, 297–301.

Beloff, J., and Bate, D. An attempt to replicate the Schmidt findings. *Journal of the Society for Psychical Research*, 1971, *46*, 21–31.

Beloff, J., and Mandleberg, I. An attempted validation of the "Ryzl technique" for training ESP subjects. *Journal of the Society for Psychical Research*, 1966, *43*, 229–249.

Beloff, J., Cowles, M., and Bate, D. Autonomic reactions to emotive stimuli using sensory and extrasensory conditions of presentation. *Journal of the American Society for Psychical Research*, 1970, *64*, 313–319.

Belvedere, E., and Foulkes, D. Telepathy in dreams: A failure to replicate. *Perceptual and Motor Skills*, 1971, *33*, 783–789.

Bertini, M., Lewis, H., and Witkin, H. Some preliminary observations with an experimental procedure for the study of hypnagogic and related phenomena. In C. T. Tart (Ed.), *Altered states of consciousness*. New York: Wiley, 1969.

Bevan, J. M. ESP tests in light and darkness. *Journal of Parapsychology*, 1947, *11*, 76–89. (a)

Bevan, J. M. The relation of attitude to success in ESP scoring. *Journal of Parapsychology*, 1947, *11*, 296–309. (b)

Bhadra, B. H. The relationship of test scores to belief in ESP. *Journal of Parapsychology*, 1966, *30*, 1–17.

Bierman, D. J., and Camstra, B. GESP in the classroom. In W. G. Roll, R. L. Morris, and J. D. Morris (Eds.), *Research in parapsychology 1972*. Metuchen, New Jersey: Scarecrow Press, 1973. Pp. 168–170.

Birge, W. R. A new method and an experiment in pure telepathy. *Journal of Parapsychology*, 1948, *12*, 273–288.

Birge, W. R., and Rhine, J. B. Unusual types of persons tested for ESP: I. A professional medium. *Journal of Parapsychology*, 1942, *6*, 85–94.

Bisaha, J. P., and Dunne, B. J. Precognitive remote viewing in the Chicago area: A replication of the Stanford experiment. In J. D. Morris, W. G. Roll, and R. L. Morris (Eds.), *Research in parapsychology 1976*. Metuchen, New Jersey: Scarecrow Press, 1977. Pp. 84–86.

Bleksley, A. E. H. An experiment on long-distance ESP during sleep. *Journal of Parapsychology*, 1963, *27*, 1–15.

Blom, J. G., and Pratt, J. G. A second confirmatory ESP experiment with Pavel Stepanek as a "borrowed" subject. *Journal of the American Society for Psychical Research*, 1968, *62*, 28–45.

Bond, E. M. General extrasensory perception with a group of fourth and fifth grade retarded children. *Journal of Parapsychology*, 1937, *1*, 114–122.

Braud, L. W. Openness versus closedness and its relationship to psi. In J. D. Morris, W. G. Roll, and R. L. Morris (Eds.), *Research in parapsychology 1975*. Metuchen, New Jersey: Scarecrow Press, 1976. Pp. 155–159.

Braud, L. W. Openness vs. closedness and its relationship to psi. In J. D. Morris, W. G. Roll, and R. L. Morris (Eds.), *Research in parapsychology 1976*. Metuchen, New Jersey: Scarecrow Press, 1977. Pp. 162–165.

Braud, L. W., and Braud, W. G. Further studies of relaxation as a psi-conducive state. *Journal of the American Society for Psychical Research*, 1974, *68*, 229–245.

Braud, W. G. Conscious vs. unconscious clairvoyance in the context of an academic examination. *Journal of Parapsychology*, 1975, *39*, 277–288. (a)

Braud, W. G. Psi-conducive states. *Journal of Communication*, 1975, *25*, 142–152. (b)

Braud, W. G. Long-distance dream and presleep telepathy. In J. D. Morris, W. G. Roll, and R. L. Morris (Eds.), *Research in parapsychology 1976*. Metuchen, New Jersey: Scarecrow Press, 1977. Pp. 154–155.

Braud, W. G., and Braud, L. W. Preliminary exploration of psi-conducive states: Progressive muscular relaxation. *Journal of the American Society for Psychical Research*, 1973, *67*, 26–46.

Braud, W. G., and Braud, L. W. The psi-conducive syndrome: Free-response GESP performance following evocation of "left-hemispheric" vs. "right-hemispheric" functioning. In J. D. Morris, W. G. Roll, and R. L. Morris (Eds.), *Research in parapsychology 1974*. Metuchen, New Jersey: Scarecrow Press, 1975. Pp. 17–20.

Braud, W. G., and Thorsrud, M. Psi on the tip of the tongue: A pilot study of the influence of an "incubation period" upon free response GESP performance. In J. D. Morris, W. G. Roll, and R. L. Morris (Eds.), *Research in parapsychology 1975*. Metuchen, New Jersey: Scarecrow Press, 1976. Pp. 167–171.

Braud, W. G., and Wood, R. The influence of immediate feedback upon free-response GESP performance during ganzfeld stimulation. In J. D. Morris, W. G. Roll, and R. L. Morris (Eds.), *Research in parapsychology 1976*. Metuchen, New Jersey: Scarecrow Press, 1977. Pp. 43–45.

Braud, W. G., Wood, R., and Braud, L. W. Free-response GESP performance during an experimental hypnagogic state induced by visual and acoustic ganzfeld techniques: A replication and extension. *Journal of the American Society for Psychical Research*, 1975, *69*, 105–113.

Brinkman, W., and Van Hilten, W. [An experimental investigation on the effects on ESP of stimulus contents variance.] *Spiegel der Parapsychologie*, 1972, *2*, 25–34. (Abstract in *Journal of Parapsychology*, 1972, *36*, 179.)

Brodbeck, T. J. ESP and personality. *Journal of the Society for Psychical Research*, 1969, *45*, 31–32.

Broughton, R. S. Psi and the two halves of the brain. *Journal of the Society for Psychical Research*, 1975, *48*, 133–147.

Broughton, R. S. Brain hemisphere specialization and its possible effects on ESP performance. In J. D. Morris, W. G. Roll, and R. L. Morris (Eds.), *Research in parapsychology 1975*. Metuchen, New Jersey: Scarecrow Press, 1976. Pp. 98–102.

Broughton, R. S. An exploratory study on psi-based subject and experimenter expectancy effects. In J. D. Morris, W. G. Roll, and R. L. Morris (Eds.), *Research in parapsychology 1976*. Metuchen, New Jersey: Scarecrow Press, 1977. Pp. 173–177.

Broughton, R. S. Brain hemisphere differences in psi-influenced reaction time. In J. D. Morris, W. G. Roll, and R. L. Morris (Eds.), *Research in parapsychology 1976*. Metuchen, New Jersey: Scarecrow Press, 1977. Pp. 86–88. (b)

Broughton, R., and Millar, B. An attempted confirmation of the rodent ESP findings with positive reinforcement. *European Journal of Parapsychology*, 1975, *1*, 15–35.

Brugmans, H. J. F. W. Une communication sur des experiences télépathiques au Laboratoire de Psychologie à Groninque faites par M. Heymans, Docteur Weinberg, et Docteur H. J. F. Brugmans. In *Le Compte Rendu Officiel du Premier Congrès International des Researches Psychiques*. Copenhagen: 1922.

Buzby, D. E. *Clairvoyance, precognition, and religious values*. Paper presented at the Sixth Annual Convention of the Parapsychological Association, New York, 1963. (Abstract in *Journal of Parapsychology*, 1963, *27*, 271.)

Buzby, D. E. Precognition and a test of sensory perception. *Journal of Parapsychology*, 1967, *31*, 135–142. (a)

Buzby, D. E. Subject attitude and score variance in ESP tests. *Journal of Parapsychology*, 1967, *31*, 43–50. (b)

Buzby, D. E. Precognition and clairvoyance as related to the Draw-A-Man Test. *Journal of Parapsychology*, 1968, *32*, 244–247. (a)

Buzby, D. E. Precognition and psychological variables. *Journal of Parapsychology*, 1968, *32*, 39–46. (b)

Cadoret, R. J. Effect of novelty in test conditions on ESP performance. *Journal of Parapsychology*, 1952, *16*, 192–203.

Cadoret, R. J. The effect of amytal and dexadrine on ESP performance. *Journal of Parapsychology*, 1953, *17*, 259–274.

Cadoret, R. J. An exploratory experiment: Continuous EEG recordings during clairvoyant card tests. *Journal of Parapsychology*, 1964, *28*, 226. (Abstract)

Cadoret, R. J., and Pratt, J. G. The consistent missing effect in ESP. *Journal of Parapsychology*, 1950, *14*, 244–256.

Carington, W. W. Experiments on the paranormal cognition of drawings. *Journal of Parapsychology*, 1940, *4*, 1–129. (a)

Carington, W. W. Some observations on the experiments with drawings. *Journal of Parapsychology*, 1940, *4*, 130–134. (b)

Carpenter, J. C. An exploratory test of ESP in relation to anxiety proneness. In J. B. Rhine (Ed.), *Parapsychology: From Duke to FRNM*. Durham, North Carolina: Parapsychology Press, 1965.

Carpenter, J. C. Scoring effects within the run. *Journal of Parapsychology*, 1966, *30*, 73–83.

Carpenter, J. C. Two related studies on mood and precognition run-score variance. *Journal of Parapsychology*, 1968, *32*, 75–89.

Carpenter, J. C. Further study on a mood adjective check list and ESP run-score variance. *Journal of Parapsychology*, 1969, *33*, 48–56.

Carpenter, J. C. The differential effect and hidden target differences consisting of erotic and neutral stimuli. *Journal of the American Society for Psychical Research*, 1971, *65*, 204–214.

Carpenter, J. C. Validating research on a mood-adjective scale for predicting run-score variance. In W. G. Roll, R. L. Morris, and J. D. Morris (Eds.), *Research in parapsychology 1972*. Metuchen, New Jersey: Scarecrow Press, 1973. Pp. 145–148.

Carpenter, J. C., and Carpenter, J. C. Decline of variability of ESP scoring across a period of effort. *Journal of Parapsychology*, 1967, *31*, 179–191.

Casler, L. The improvement of clairvoyance scores by means of hypnotic suggestion. *Journal of Parapsychology*, 1962, *26*, 77–87.

Casler, L. The effects of hypnosis on GESP. *Journal of Parapsychology*, 1964, *28*, 126–134.

Casler, L. Self-generated hypnotic suggestions and clairvoyance. *International Journal of Parapsychology*, 1967, *9*, 125–128.

Casler, L. Hypnotically induced interpersonal relationships and their influence on GESP. In W. G. Roll, R. L. Morris, and J. D. Morris (Eds.), *Proceedings of the Parapsychological Association No. 6, 1969*. Durham, North Carolina: Parapsychological Association, 1971. Pp. 14–15.

Casper, G. W. A further study of the relationship of attitude to success in GESP scoring. *Journal of Parapsychology*, 1951, *15*, 139–145.

Casper, G. W. Effect of receiver's attitude toward sender in ESP tests. *Journal of Parapsychology*, 1952, *16*, 212–218.

Cattell, R. B. *The scientific analysis of personality*. Baltimore: Penguin Books, 1965.

Cavanna, R., and Servadio, E. *ESP experiments with LSD-25 and psilocybin (Parapsychological Monographs No. 5)*. New York: Parapsychology Foundation, 1964.

Charlesworth, E. A. Psi and the imaginary dream. In J. D. Morris, W. G. Roll, and R. L. Morris (Eds.), *Research in parapsychology 1974*. Metuchen, New Jersey: Scarecrow Press, 1975, Pp. 85–89.

Chauvin, R. ESP and size of target symbols. *Journal of Parapsychology*, 1961, *25*, 185–189.

Child, I. L. Statistical regression artifact in parapsychology. *Journal of Parapsychology*, 1977, *41*, 10–22.

Child, I. L., and Kelly, E. F. ESP with unbalanced decks: A study of the process in an exceptional subject. *Journal of Parapsychology*, 1973, *37*, 278–297.

Child, I. L., and Singer, J. D. Exploration of the paper maze technique for experimental study of psi. In J. D. Morris, W. G. Roll, and R. L. Morris (Eds.), *Research in parapsychology 1976*. Metuchen, New Jersey: Scarecrow Press, 1977. Pp. 177–179.

Coover, J. E. *Experiments in psychical research (Psychical Research Monograph No. 1)*. Stanford: Stanford University, 1917.

Craig, J. G. The effect of contingency on precognition in the rat. In W. G. Roll, R. L. Morris, and J. D. Morris (Eds.), *Research in parapsychology 1972*. Metuchen, New Jersey: Scarecrow Press, 1973. Pp. 154–156.

Craig, J. G. The effect of the experimenter on precognition in the rat. In J. D. Morris, W. G. Roll, and R. L. Morris (Eds.), *Research in parapsychology 1974*. Metuchen, New Jersey: Scarecrow Press, 1975. Pp. 97–100.

Craig, J. G., and Treurniet, W. C. Precognition in rats as a function of shock and death. In W. G. Roll, R. L. Morris, and J. D. Morris (Eds.), *Research in parapsychology 1973*. Metuchen, New Jersey: Scarecrow Press, 1974. Pp. 75–78.

Crookall, R. *The study and practice of astral projection*. London: Aquarian Press, 1961.

Crumbaugh, J. C. Are negative ESP results attributable to traits and attitudes of subjects and experimenters? *Journal of Parapsychology*, 1958, *22*, 294–295. (Abstract)

Dagel, L. T., and Puryear, H. B. The effect of immediate reinforcement in a two-choice general ESP test. In W. G. Roll, R. L. Morris, and J. D. Morris (Eds.), *Proceedings of the Parapsychological Association No. 6, 1969*. Durham, North Carolina: Parapsychological Association, 1971. Pp. 18–19.

Dalton, G. F. Correspondence. *Journal of the Society for Psychical Research*, 1960, *40*, 266–267.

Dale, L. A., Taves, E., and Murphy, G. A short report on a series of exploratory studies. *Journal of the American Society for Psychical Research*, 1944, *38*, 160–170.

Damgaard, J. Recent research with Lalsingh Harribance: A summary of additional research with Lalsingh Harribance. In W. G. Roll, R. L. Morris, and J. D. Morris (Eds.), *Proceedings of the Parapsychological Association No. 8, 1971*. Durham, North Carolina: Parapsychological Association, 1972. Pp. 74–76.

Dean, E. D. The plethysmograph as an indicator of ESP. *Journal of the Society for Psychical Research*, 1962, *41*, 351–353.

Dean, E. D. Plethysmograph recordings as ESP responses. *International Journal of Neuropsychiatry* (Special Issue No. 5), 1966, 439–447. (a)

Dean, E. D. *Psi-missing during examination time as measured by the plethysmograph*. Paper presented at the Ninth Annual Convention of the Parapsychological Association, New York, 1966. (Abstract in *Journal of Parapsychology*, 1966, *30*, 275–276.) (b)

Dean, E. D. A procedural postscript to Dr. Manson Sanjar's "A study of coincident autonomic activity in closely related persons." *Journal of the American Society for Psychical Research*, 1970, *64*, 237–240.

Dean, E. D. Attempts to use plethysmograph recordings in communications. In W. G. Roll, R. L. Morris, and J. D. Morris (Eds.), *Proceedings of the Parapsychological Association No. 5, 1968*. Durham, North Carolina: Parapsychological Association, 1971. Pp. 65–67. (a)

Dean, E. D. Long-distance plethysmograph telepathy with agent under water. In W. G. Roll, R. L. Morris, and J. D. Morris (Eds.), *Proceedings of the Parapsychological Association, No. 6, 1969*. Durham, North Carolina: Parapsychological Association, 1971. Pp. 41–42. (b)

Dean, (E.) D. Can subjects differentiate clairvoyance from precognition? In W. G. Roll, R. L. Morris, and J. D. Morris (Eds.), *Proceedings of the Parapsychological Association, No. 7, 1970*. Durham, North Carolina: Parapsychological Association, 1972. Pp. 31–32.

Dean, E. D., and Nash, C. B. Coincident plethysmograph results under controlled conditions. *Journal of the Society for Psychical Research*, 1967, *44*, 1–14.

Dean, (E.) D., and Otani, S. Long and short distance plethysmographic telepathy tests. In W. G. Roll, R. L. Morris, and J. D. Morris (Eds.), *Proceedings of the Parapsychological Association No. 8, 1971*. Durham, North Carolina: Parapsychological Association, 1972. Pp. 80–82.

Dean, (E.) D., and Taetzsch, R. *An ESP test for speakers using computer scoring*. Paper presented at the Sixth Annual Convention of the Parapsychological Association, New York, 1963. (Abstract in *Journal of Parapsychology*, 1963, *27*, 275–276.)

Deguisne, A. Two repetitions of the Anderson–White investigation of teacher–pupil attitudes and clairvoyance test results: Part I. High school tests. *Journal of Parapsychology*, 1959, *23*, 196–207.

Dimond, S., and Beaumont, J. G. *Hemisphere function in the human brain*. New York: Wiley, 1974.

Dingwall, E. J. (Ed.). *Abnormal hypnotic phenomena: A survey of nineteenth-century cases* (4 vols.). New York: Barnes & Noble, 1967–1968.

Drake, R. M. An unusual case of extrasensory perception. *Journal of Parapsychology*, 1938, *2*, 184–198.

Drucker, S. A., Drewes, A. A., and Rubin, L. ESP in relation to cognitive development and IQ in young children. *Journal of the American Society for Psychical Research*, 1977, *71*, 289–298.

Duane, D. T., and Behrendt, T. Extrasensory electroencephalographic induction between identical twins. *Science*, 1965, *150*, 367.

Dukhan, H. Experiments with Lalsingh Harribance: Experiments in Trinidad. In W. G. Roll, R. L. Morris, and J. D. Morris (Eds.), *Proceedings of the Parapsychological Association No. 6, 1969*. Durham, North Carolina: Parapsychological Association, 1971. Pp. 65–66.

Dukhan, H., and Rao, K. R. Meditation and ESP scoring. In W. G. Roll, R. L. Morris, and J. D. Morris (Eds.), *Research in parapsychology 1972*. Metuchen, New Jersey: Scarecrow Press, 1973. Pp. 148–151.

Dunne, B. J., Warnock, E., and Bisaha, J. P. Ganzfeld techniques with independent rating for measuring GESP and precognition. In J. D. Morris, W. G. Roll, and R. L. Morris (Eds.), *Research in parapsychology 1976*. Metuchen, New Jersey: Scarecrow Press, 1977. Pp. 41–43.

Duval, P., and Montredon, E. ESP experiments with mice. *Journal of Parapsychology*, 1968, *32*, 153–166. (a)

Duval, P., and Montredon, E. *Further psi experiments with mice*. Paper presented at the autumn review meeting of the Institute for Parapsychology, FRNM, 1968. (Abstract in *Journal of Parapsychology*, 1968, *32*, 260.) (b)

Eason, M. J. C., and Wysocki, B. A. Extrasensory perception and intelligence. *Journal of Parapsychology*, 1965, *29*, 109–114.

Eastman, M. *The relationship of ESP scores to knowledge of target location, and to birth order and family size*. Unpublished master's thesis, City University of New York, 1966. (Abstract in *Journal of Parapsychology*, 1967, *31*, 168–169.)

Edmunds, S., and Jolliffe, D. A GESP experiment with four hypnotized subjects. *Journal of the Society for Psychical Research*, 1965, *43*, 192–194.

Eilbert, L., and Schmeidler, G. R. A study of certain psychological factors in relation to ESP performance. *Journal of Parapsychology*, 1950, *14*, 53–74.

Eisenbud, J. Psi and the nature of things. *International Journal of Parapsychology*, 1963, *5*, 245–273.

Eisenbud, J. Perception of subliminal visual stimuli in relation to ESP. *International Journal of Parapsychology*, 1965, *7*, 161–181.

Eisenbud, J. *Psi and psychoanalysis*. New York: Grune and Stratton, 1970.

Eisenbud, J., Hassel, L., Keely, H., and Sawrey, W. A further study of teacher–pupil attitudes and results in clairvoyance tests in the fifth and sixth grades. *Journal of the American Society for Psychical Research*, 1960, *54*, 72–80.

Elkisch, P. Children's drawings in a projective technique. *Psychological Monographs*, 1945, *58*, 1–31.

Esser, A. H., Etter, T. L., and Chamberlain, W. B. Preliminary report: Physiological concomitants of "communication" between isolated subjects. *International Journal of Parapsychology*, 1967, *9*, 53–56.

Estabrooks, G. H. A contribution to experimental telepathy. *Journal of Parapsychology*, 1961, *25*, 190–213. (Originally published, 1927.)

Extra, J. F. M. W. ESP in the rat. *Journal of Parapsychology*, 1972, *36*, 294–302.

Eysenck, H. J. *The structure of human personality* (2nd ed.). London: Methuen, 1960.

Eysenck, H. J. Personality and extrasensory perception. *Journal of the Society for Psychical Research*, 1967, *44*, 55–71.

Eysenck, H. J. Precognition in rats. *Journal of Parapsychology*, 1975, *39*, 222–227.

Fahler, J. ESP card tests with and without hypnosis. *Journal of Parapsychology*, 1957, 179–185.

Fahler, J., and Cadoret, R. J. ESP card tests of college students with and without hypnosis. *Journal of Parapsychology*, 1958, *22*, 125–136.

Fahler, J., and Osis, K. Checking for awareness of hits in a precognition experiment with hypnotized subjects. *Journal of the American Society for Psychical Research*, 1966, *60*, 340–346.

Feather, S. R. A comparison of performance in memory and ESP tests. In J. B. Rhine (Ed.), *Parapsychology from Duke to FRNM*. Durham, North Carolina: Parapsychology Press, 1965.

Feather, S. R. *Influence of response preference on group precognition scores*. Paper presented at the Tenth Annual Convention of the Parapsychological Association, New York, 1967. (Abstract in *Journal of Parapsychology*, 1967, *31*, 321.) (a)

Feather, S. R. A quantitative comparison of memory and psi. *Journal of Parapsychology*, 1967, *31*, 93–98. (b)

Feather, S. R., and Brier, R. The possible effect of the checker in precognition tests. *Journal of Parapsychology*, 1968, *32*, 167–175.

Figar, S. The application of plethysmography to the objective study of so-called extrasensory perception. *Journal of the Society for Psychical Research*, 1959, *40*, 162–174.

Fishbein, M., and Raven, B. H. The AB Scales: An operational definition of belief and attitude. In M. Fishbein (Ed.), *Readings in attitude theory and measurement*. New York: Wiley, 1967.

Fisk, G. W. Home-testing ESP experiments: A preliminary report. *Journal of the Society for Psychical Research*, 1951, *36*, 369–370. (a)

Fisk, G. W. Home-testing ESP experiments: Second report. *Journal of the Society for Psychical Research*, 1951, *36*, 518–520. (b)

Fisk, G. W., and Mitchell, A. M. J. ESP experiments with clock cards: A new technique with differential scoring. *Journal of the Society for Psychical Research*, 1953, *37*, 1–14.

Fisk, G. W., and West, D. J. ESP and mood: Report of a "mass" experiment. *Journal of the Society for Psychical Research*, 1956, *38*, 320–329.

Fisk, G. W., and West, D. J. Towards accurate predictions from ESP data. *Journal of the Society for Psychical Research*, 1957, *39*, 157–162.

Foster, E. B. Multiple aspect targets in tests of ESP. *Journal of Parapsychology*, 1952, *16*, 11–22.

Foulkes, D., Belvedere, E., Masters, R., Houston, J., Krippner, S., Honorton, C., and Ullman, M. Long-distance "sensory-bombardment" ESP: A failure to replicate. *Perceptual and Motor Skills*, 1972, *35*, 731–734.

France, G. A., and Hogan, R. A. Thought concordance in twins and siblings and associated personality variables. *Psychological Reports*, 1973, *32*, 707–710.

Freeman, J. (A.). An ESP test involving emotionally-toned objects. *Journal of Parapsychology*, 1961, *25*, 260–265.

Freeman, J. A. An experiment in precognition. *Journal of Parapsychology*, 1962, *26*, 123–130.

Freeman, J. (A.). Boy–girl differences in a group precognition test. *Journal of Parapsychology*, 1963, *27*, 175–181.

Freeman, J. (A.). A precognition test with a high-school science club. *Journal of Parapsychology*, 1964, *28*, 214–221.

Freeman, J. A. Differential response of the sexes to contrasting arrangements of ESP target material. *Journal of Parapsychology*, 1965, *29*, 251–258.

Freeman, J. A. A sequel report on a high-scoring child subject. *Journal of Parapsychology*, 1966, *30*, 39–47. (a)

Freeman, J. A. Sex differences and target arrangement: High-school booklet tests of precognition. *Journal of Parapsychology*, 1966, *30*, 227–235. (b)

Freeman, J. A. Sex differences, target arrangement, and primary mental abilities. *Journal of Parapsychology*, 1967, *31*, 271–279.

Freeman, J. A. Sex differences and primary mental abilities in a group precognition test. *Journal of Parapsychology*, 1968, *32*, 176–182.

Freeman, J. A. A precognition test with science teachers. *Journal of Parapsychology*, 1969, *33*, 307–310. (a)

Freeman, J. A. The psi-differential effect in a precognition test. *Journal of Parapsychology*, 1969, *33*, 206–212. (b)

Freeman, J. A. Sex differences in ESP response as shown by the Freeman Picture-Figure Test. *Journal of Parapsychology*, 1970, *34*, 37–46. (a)

Freeman, J. A. Ten-page booklet tests with elementary-school children. *Journal of Parapsychology*, 1970, *34*, 192–196. (b)

Freeman, J. A. Mood, personality, and attitude in precognition tests. In W. G. Roll, R. L. Morris, and J. D. Morris (Eds.), *Proceedings of the Parapsychological Association No. 7, 1970*. Durham, North Carolina: Parapsychological Association, 1972. Pp. 53–54. (a)

Freeman, J. A. Sex differences in precognition tests with seventh grade students. In W. G. Roll, R. L. Morris, and J. D. Morris (Eds.), *Proceedings of the Parapsychological Association No. 8, 1971*. Durham, North Carolina: Parapsychological Association, 1972. Pp. 63–65. (b)

Freeman, J. A. The psi quiz: A new ESP test. In W. G. Roll, R. L. Morris, and J. D. Morris (Eds.), *Research in parapsychology 1972*. Metuchen, New Jersey: Scarecrow Press, 1973. Pp. 132–134.

Freeman, J. (A.), and Nielsen, W. Precognition score deviations as related to anxiety levels. *Journal of Parapsychology*, 1964, *28*, 239–249.

Friedman, R. M., Schmeidler, G. R., and Dean, E. D. Ranked-target scoring for mood and intragroup effects in precognitive ESP. *Journal of the American Society for Psychical Research*, 1976, *70*, 195–206.

Gambale, J. *Word frequency and associative strength in memory–ESP interaction: A failure to replicate*. Unpublished master's thesis, The City College of the City University of New York, 1976. (Abstract in *Journal of Parapsychology*, 1976, *40*, 339–340.)

Gambale, J., Margolis, F., and Crucci, K. The relationship between ESP and memory—an attempted replication with modifications. *Journal of Parapsychology*, 1976, *40*, 340. (Abstract)

Gatlin, L. L. Meaningful information creation: An alternative interpretation of the psi phenomenon. *Journal of the American Society for Psychical Research*, 1977, *71*, 1–18.

Gauld, A. *The founders of psychical research*. New York: Schocken, 1968.

Gelade, G., and Harvie, R. Confidence ratings in an ESP task using affective stimuli. *Journal of the Society for Psychical Research*, 1975, *48*, 209–219.

Gerber, R., and Schmeidler, G. R. An investigation of relaxation and of acceptance of the experimental situation as related to ESP scores in maternity patients. *Journal of Parapsychology*, 1957, *21*, 47–57.

Gerstein, P., and Merker, P. Attitudes toward ESP and choice of target as related to ESP performance. *Journal of Parapsychology*, 1964, *28*, 226. (Abstract)

Gibson, E. P. A study of comparative performance in several ESP procedures. *Journal of Parapsychology*, 1937, *1*, 264–275.

Gibson, E. P., and Stuart, C. E. Atmospheric pressures and ESP score averages. *Journal of Parapsychology*, 1942, *6*, 95–100.

Glick, B. S., and Kogen, J. Clairvoyance in hypnotized subjects: Positive results. In W. G. Roll, R. L. Morris, and J. D. Morris (Eds.), *Proceedings of the Parapsychological Association No. 8, 1971*. Durham, North Carolina: Parapsychological Association, 1972. Pp. 58–59.

Glidden, S. H. A random-behavior maze test for humans. *Journal of Parapsychology*, 1974, *38*, 324–331.

Globus, G., Knapp, P., Skinner, J., and Healey, G. An appraisal of telepathic communication in dreams. *Psychophysiology*, 1968, *4*, 365. (Abstract)

Goldberg, J., Sondow, N., and Schmeidler, G. Psi and the experience of time. In J. D. Morris, W. G. Roll, and R. L. Morris (Eds.), *Research in parapsychology 1975*. Metuchen, New Jersey: Scarecrow Press, 1976. Pp. 152–155.

Goldstone, G. Two repetitions of the Anderson–White investigation of teacher–pupil attitudes and clairvoyance test results: Part II. Grade-school tests. *Journal of Parapsychology*, 1959, *23*, 208–213.

Greely, A. M. *The sociology of the paranormal: A reconnaissance*. Beverly Hills: Sage Publications, 1975.

Green, C. E. The effect of birth order and family size on extrasensory perception. *Journal of the Society for Psychical Research*, 1965, *43*, 181–191.

Green, C. E. Extra-sensory perception and the extraversion scale of the Maudsley Personality Inventory. *Journal of the Society for Psychical Research*, 1966, *43*, 337. (a)

Green, C. E. Extrasensory perception and the Maudsley Personality Inventory. *Journal of the Society for Psychical Research*, 1966, *43*, 285–286. (b)

Greenwood, J. A., and Stuart, C. E. Mathematical techniques used in ESP research. *Journal of Parapsychology*, 1937, *1*, 206–225.

Grela, J. J. Effect on ESP scoring of hypnotically induced attitudes. *Journal of Parapsychology*, 1945, *9*, 194–202.

Gurney, E., Myers, F. W. H., and Podmore, F. *Phantasms of the living* (Vol. 1). Gainesville, Florida: Scholars' Facsimiles and Reprints, 1970. (Originally published, 1886.)

Habel, M. M. Varying auditory stimuli in the ganzfeld: The influence of sex and overcrowding on psi performance. In J. D. Morris, W. G. Roll, and R. L. Morris (Eds.)., *Research in parapsychology 1975*. Metuchen, New Jersey: Scarecrow Press, 1976. Pp. 181–184.

Hall, C. [Experiments with telepathically influenced dreams.] *Zeitschrift für Parapsychologie und Grenzgebiete der Psychologie*, 1967, *10*, 18–47.

Hall, J. A. *GESP tests with fourth-and-fifth grade pupils*. Paper presented at the First Annual Convention of the Parapsychological Association, New York, 1958. (Abstract in *Journal of Parapsychology*, 1958, *22*, 301.)

Hallett, S. J. A study of the effect of conditioning on multiple-aspect ESP scoring. *Journal of Parapsychology*, 1952, *16*, 204–211.

Hanlon, J. Uri Geller and science. *New Scientist*, 1974, *64*, 170–185.

Hansel, C. E. M. A critical review of experiments with Mr. Basil Shackleton and Mrs. Gloria Stewart as sensitives. *Proceedings of the Society for Psychical Research*, 1960, *53*, 1–42.

Hansel, C. E. M. *ESP: A scientific evaluation*. New York: Scribners, 1966.

Haraldsson, E. Subject selection in a machine precognition test. *Journal of Parapsychology*, 1970, *34*, 182–191.

Haraldsson, E. Psychological variables in a GESP test using plethysmograph recordings. In W. G. Roll, R. L. Morris, and J. D. Morris (Eds.), *Proceedings of the Parapsychological Association No. 7, 1970*. Durham, North Carolina: Parapsychological Association, 1972. Pp. 6–7.

Haraldsson, E. Reported dream recall, precognitive dreams, and ESP. In J. D. Morris, W. G. Roll, and R. L. Morris (Eds.), *Research in parapsychology 1974*. Metuchen, New Jersey: Scarecrow Press, 1975. Pp. 47–48.

Haraldsson, E. Reading habits, belief in ESP, and precognition. In J. D. Morris, W. G. Roll, and R. L. Morris (Eds.), *Research in parapsychology 1975*. Metuchen, New Jersey: Scarecrow Press, 1976. Pp. 28–29.

Haraldsson, E., Gudmundsdottir, A., Ragnarsson, A., Loftsson, J., and Jonsson, S. National survey of psychical experiences and attitudes toward the paranormal in Iceland. In J. D. Morris, W. G. Roll, and R. L. Morris (Eds.), *Research in parapsychology 1976*. Metuchen, New Jersey: Scarecrow Press, 1977. Pp. 182–186.

Harary, S. B. A study of psi, memory and expectancy. In J. D. Morris, W. G. Roll, and R. L. Morris (Eds.), *Research in parapsychology 1975*. Metuchen, New Jersey: Scarecrow Press, 1976. Pp. 121–126.

Hebda, H. C., Velissaris, C. R., and Velissaris, C. N. The effects of target preference on the scoring of fast and slow subjects. *Journal of Parapsychology*, 1974, *38*, 346. (Abstract)

Heyman, S., and Schmeidler, G. R. *Attitudes toward time and the impatience effect*. Paper presented at the Tenth Annual Convention of the Parapsychological Association, New York, 1967. (Abstract in *Journal of Parapsychology*, 1967, *31*, 316.)

Hodgson, R. A further record of observations of certain phenomena of trance. *Proceedings of the Society for Psychical Research*, 1897–98, *13*, 284–582.

Honorton, C. Separation of high- and low-scoring ESP subjects through hypnotic preparation. *Journal of Parapsychology*, 1964, *28*, 251–257.

Honorton, C. *The relationship between ESP and manifest anxiety*. Paper presented at the Eighth Annual Convention of the Parapsychological Association, New York, 1965. (Abstract in *Journal of Parapsychology*, 1965, *29*, 291–292.)

Honorton, C. A further separation of high- and low-scoring ESP subjects through hypnotic preparation. *Journal of Parapsychology*, 1966, *30*, 172–183.

Honorton, C. Creativity and precognition scoring level. *Journal of Parapsychology*, 1967, *31*, 29–42.

Honorton, C. A combination of techniques for the separation of high- and low-scoring ESP subjects: Experiments with hypnotic and waking-imagination instructions. *Journal of the American Society for Psychical Research*, 1969, *63*, 69–82. (a)

Honorton, C. Relationship between EEG alpha activity and ESP card-guessing performance. *Journal of the American Society for Psychical Research*, 1969, *63*, 365–374. (b)

Honorton, C. Effects of feedback on discrimination between correct and incorrect ESP responses. *Journal of the American Society for Psychical Research*, 1970, *64*, 404–410.

Honorton, C. Automated forced-choice precognition tests with a "sensitive." *Journal of the American Society for Psychical Research*, 1971, *65*, 476–481. (a)

Honorton, C. Effects of feedback on discrimination between correct and incorrect ESP responses: A replication study. *Journal of the American Society for Psychical Research*, 1971, *65*, 155–161. (b)

Honorton, C. Reported frequency of dream recall and ESP. *Journal of the American Society for Psychical Research*, 1972, *66*, 369–374. (a)

Honorton, C. Significant factors in hypnotically-induced clairvoyant dreams. *Journal of the American Society for Psychical Research*, 1972, *66*, 86–102. (b)

Honorton, C. Psi-conducive states of awareness. In J. White (Ed.), *Psychic exploration: A challenge for science*. New York: Putnam's, 1974. (a)

Honorton, C. States of awareness factors in psi activation. *Journal of the American Society for Psychical Research*, 1974, *68*, 246–256. (b)

Honorton, C. Psi and mental imagery: Keeping score on the Betts scale. *Journal of the American Society for Psychical Research*, 1975, *69*, 327–332.

Honorton, C., and Carbone, M. A preliminary study of feedback-augmented EEG alpha activity and ESP card-guessing performance. *Journal of the American Society for Psychical Research*, 1971, *65*, 66–74.

Honorton, C., and Harper, S. Psi-mediated imagery and ideation in an experimental procedure for regulating perceptual input. *Journal of the American Society for Psychical Research*, 1974, *68*, 156–168.

Honorton, C., and Krippner, S. Hypnosis and ESP: A review of the experimental literature. *Journal of the American Society for Psychical Research*, 1969, *63*, 214–252.

Honorton, C., and Stump, J. P. A preliminary study of hypnotically-induced clairvoyant dreams. *Journal of the American Society for Psychical Research*, 1969, *63*, 175–184.

Honorton, C., Davidson, R., and Bindler, P. Feedback-augmented EEG alpha, shifts in subjective state, and ESP card-guessing performance. *Journal of the American Society for Psychical Research*, 1971, *65*, 308–323.

Honorton, C., Drucker, S. A., and Hermon, H. Shifts in subjective state and ESP under conditions of partial sensory deprivation: A preliminary study. *Journal of the American Society for Psychical Research*, 1973, *67*, 191–196.

Honorton, C., Ramsey, M., and Cabibbo, C. Experimenter effects in extrasensory perception. *Journal of the American Society for Psychical Research*, 1975, *69*, 135–150.

Honorton, C., Tierney, L., and Torres, D. The role of mental imagery in psi-meditation. *Journal of the American Society for Psychical Research*, 1974, *68*, 385–394.

Huby, P. M., and Wilson, C. W. M. The effects of centrally acting drugs on ESP ability in normal subjects. *Journal of the Society for Psychical Research*, 1961, *41*, 60–67.

Hudesman, J., and Schmeidler, G. R. ESP scores following therapeutic sessions. *Journal of the American Society for Psychical Research*, 1971, *65*, 215–222.

Hudesman, J., and Schmeidler, G. R. Changes in ESP scores after therapy sessions. *Journal of the American Society for Psychical Research*, 1976, *70*, 371–380.

Hume, D. An enquiry concerning human understanding. In R. M. Hutchins and M. Adler, (Eds.), *Great books of the western world* (Vol. 35). Chicago: Encyclopedia Britannica, 1952. (Originally published, 1748.)

Humphrey, B. M. Patterns of success in an ESP experiment. *Journal of Parapsychology*, 1943, *7*, 5–19.

Humphrey, B. M. ESP and intelligence. *Journal of Parapsychology*, 1945, *9*, 7–16. (a)

Humphrey, B. M. An exploratory correlation study of personality measures and ESP scores. *Journal of Parapsychology*, 1945, *9*, 116–123. (b)

Humphrey, B. M. Further position effects in the Earlham College series. *Journal of Parapsychology*, 1945, *9*, 26–31. (c)

Humphrey, B. M. Success in ESP as related to form of response drawings: I. Clairvoyance experiments. *Journal of Parapsychology*, 1946, *10*, 78–106. (a)

Humphrey, B. M. Success in ESP as related to form of response drawings: II. GESP experiments. *Journal of Parapsychology*, 1946, *10*, 181–196. (b)

Humphrey, B. M. A further study of ESP and intelligence. *Journal of Parapsychology*, 1948, *12*, 213–217.

Humphrey, B. M. Further work of Dr. Stuart on interest test ratings and ESP. *Journal of Parapsychology*, 1949, *13*, 151–165.

Humphrey, B. M. A new scale for separating high- and low-scoring subjects in ESP tests. *Journal of Parapsychology*, 1950, *14*, 9–23.

Humphrey, B. M. Introversion–extraversion ratings in relation to scores in ESP tests. *Journal of Parapsychology*, 1951, *15*, 252–262. (a)

Humphrey, B. M. The relation of some personality ratings to ESP scores. *Journal of the Society for Psychical Research*, 1951, *36*, 453–466. (b)

Humphrey, B. M. ESP tests with mental patients before and after electroshock treatment. *Journal of the Society for Psychical Research*, 1954, *37*, 259–266.

Humphrey, B. M., and Nicol, J. F. The feeling of success in ESP. *Journal of the American Society for Psychical Research*, 1955, *49*, 3–37.

Humphrey, B. M., and Nicol, J. F. An answer to the "examination." *Journal of the American Society for Psychical Research*, 1956, *50*, 39–44.

Humphrey, B. M., and Pratt, J. G. A comparison of five ESP test procedures. *Journal of Parapsychology*, 1941, *5*, 267–292.

Humphrey, B. M., and Rhine, J. B. A confirmatory study of salience in precognition tests. *Journal of Parapsychology*, 1942, *6*, 190–219.

Humphrey, B. M., and Rhine, J. B. The evaluation of salience in Dr. Schmeidler's ESP data. *Journal of Parapsychology*, 1944, *8*, 124–126.

Hutchinson, L. Variations of time intervals in pre-shuffle card-calling tests. *Journal of Parapsychology*, 1940, *4*, 249–270.

Investigating the Paranormal. *Nature*, 1974, *251*, 559–560.

Jackson, M., Franzoi, S., and Schmeidler, G. R. Effects of feedback on ESP: A curious partial replication. *Journal of the American Society for Psychical Research*, 1977, *71*, 147–155.

Jacobson, E. *Progressive relaxation* (3rd rev. ed.). Chicago: University of Chicago Press, 1974.

Jampolsky, G. G., and Haight, M. J. A pilot study of ESP in hyperkinetic children. In J. D. Morris, W. G. Roll, and R. L. Morris (Eds.), *Research in parapsychology 1974*. Metuchen, New Jersey: Scarecrow Press, 1975. Pp. 13–15.

Joesting, R., and Joesting, J. Position effects and target material in ESP. *Psychological Reports*, 1970, *26*, 75–78.

Johnson, M. *Relationship between dream recall and scoring direction*. Paper presented at the winter review meeting of the Institute for Parapsychology, FRNM. (Abstract in *Journal of Parapsychology*, 1968, *32*, 56–57.)

Johnson, M. A new technique of testing ESP in a real-life, high-motivational context. *Journal of Parapsychology*, 1973, *37*, 210–217.

Johnson, M. ESP and subliminality. In W. G. Roll, R. L. Morris, and J. D. Morris (Eds.), *Research in parapsychology 1973*. Metuchen, New Jersey: Scarecrow Press, 1974. Pp. 22–24.

Johnson, M., and Kanthamani, B. K. (H.) The Defense Mechanism Test as a predictor of ESP scoring direction. *Journal of Parapsychology*, 1967, *31*, 99–110.

Johnson, M., and Nordbeck, B. Variations in the scoring behavior of a "psychic" subject. *Journal of Parapsychology*, 1972, *36*, 122–132.

Jones, J. N., and Feather, S. R. Relationship between reports of psi experiences and subject variance. *Journal of Parapsychology*, 1969, *33*, 311–319.

Kahn, S. D. Studies in extrasensory perception: Experiments utilizing an electronic scoring device. *Proceedings of the American Society for Psychical Research*, 1952, *25*, 1–48.

Kanthamani, B. K. (H.) The experimenter's role in language ESP tests. *Journal of Parapsychology*, 1965, *29*, 279–280. (Abstract) (a)

Kanthamani, B. K. (H.) A study of the differential response in language ESP tests. *Journal of Parapsychology*, 1965, *29*, 27–34.

Kanthamani, B. K. (H.) ESP and social stimulus. *Journal of Parapsychology*, 1966, *30*, 31–38.

Kanthamani, B. K. (H.) *The ESP subject: An inquiry into the personality patterns of psi-*

hitters and missers. Unpublished doctoral dissertation. Andhra University, Waltair, India, 1968.

Kanthamani, H. (B. K.) Psi in relation to task complexity. *Journal of Parapsychology*, 1974, *38*, 154–162.

Kanthamani, H. (B. K.), and Kelly, E. F. Awareness of success in an exceptional subject. *Journal of Parapsychology*, 1974, *38*, 355–382. (a)

Kanthamani, H. (B. K.), and Kelly, E. F. Card experiments with a special subject: I. Single-card clairvoyance. *Journal of Parapsychology*, 1974, *38*, 16–26. (b)

Kanthamani, H. (B. K.), and Kelly, E. F. Card experiments with a special subject: II. The shuffle method. *Journal of Parapsychology*, 1975, *39*, 206–221.

Kanthamani, H. (B. K.), and Rao, H. H. A study of memory–ESP relationships using linguistic forms. *Journal of Parapsychology*, 1974, *38*, 286–300.

Kanthamani, H. (B. K.), and Rao, H. H. Response tendencies and stimulus structure. *Journal of Parapsychology*, 1975, *39*, 97–105. (a)

Kanthamani, H. (B. K.), and Rao, H. H. Response tendencies and stimulus structure. In J. D. Morris, W. G. Roll, and R. L. Morris (Eds.), *Research in parapsychology 1974*. Metuchen, New Jersey: Scarecrow Press, 1975. Pp. 154–157. (b)

Kanthamani, H. (B. K.), and Rao, H. H. The role of association strength in memory–ESP interaction. *Journal of Parapsychology*, 1975, *39*, 1–11. (c)

Kanthamani, H. (B. K.), and Rao, H. H. A study of the memory–ESP relationship using linguistic forms. In J. D. Morris, W. G. Roll, and R. L. Morris (Eds.), *Research in parapsychology 1974*. Metuchen, New Jersey: Scarecrow Press, 1975. Pp. 150–154. (d)

Kanthamani, B. K. (H.), and Rao, K. R. Personality characteristics of ESP subjects: I. Primary personality characteristics and ESP. *Journal of Parapsychology*, 1971, *35*, 189–207.

Kanthamani, B. K. (H.), and Rao, K. R. Personality characteristics of ESP subjects: III. Extraversion and ESP. *Journal of Parapsychology*, 1972, *36*, 198–212.

Kanthamani, B. K. (H.), and Rao, K. R. Personality characteristics of ESP subjects: IV. Neuroticism and ESP. *Journal of Parapsychology*, 1973, *37*, 37–50. (a)

Kanthamani, B. K. (H.), and Rao, K. R. Personality characteristics of ESP subjects: V. Graphic expansiveness and ESP. *Journal of Parapsychology*, 1973, *37*, 119–129. (b)

Keeling, K. R. Telepathic transmission in hypnotic dreams: An exploratory study. In W. G. Roll, R. L. Morris, and J. D. Morris (Eds.), *Proceedings of the Parapsychological Association No. 8, 1971*. Durham, North Carolina: Parapsychological Association, 1972. Pp. 55–58.

Keil, H. H. J. A GESP test with favorite music targets. *Journal of Parapsychology*, 1965, *29*, 35–44.

Kelly, E. F., and Kanthamani, B. K. (H.) A subject's efforts toward voluntary control. *Journal of Parapsychology*, 1972, *36*, 185–197.

Kelly, E. F., and Lenz, J. EEG changes correlated with a remote stroboscopic stimulus: A preliminary study. In J. D. Morris, W. G. Roll, and R. L. Morris (Eds.), *Research in parapsychology 1975*. Metuchen, New Jersey: Scarecrow Press, 1976. Pp. 58–63. (a)

Kelly, E. F., and Lenz, J. EEG correlates of trial-by-trial performance in a two-choice clairvoyance task: A preliminary study. In J. D. Morris, W. G. Roll, and R. L. Morris (Eds.), *Research in parapsychology 1975*. Metuchen, New Jersey: Scarecrow Press, 1976. Pp. 22–25. (b)

Kelly, E. F., Kanthamani, H. (B. K.), Child, I. L., and Young, F. W. On the relation between visual and ESP confusion structures in an exceptional ESP subject. *Journal of the American Society for Psychical Research*, 1975, *69*, 1–32.

Kennedy, J. E., and Taddonio, J. L. Experimenter effects in parapsychological research. *Journal of Parapsychology*, 1976, *40*, 1–33.

Kennedy, J. L. A critical review of "Discrimination shown between experimenters by subjects," by J. D. MacFarland. *Journal of Parapsychology*, 1939, *3*, 213–225.

Klein, J. L. Recent research with Lalsingh Harribance: A comparison of clairvoyance and telepathy. In W. G. Roll, R. L. Morris, and J. D. Morris (Eds.), *Proceedings of the Parapsychological Association No. 8, 1971*. Durham, North Carolina: Parapsychological Association, 1972. Pp. 71–72.

Koestler, A. *The roots of coincidence*. London: Hutchinson, 1972.

Kramer, J. K., and Terry, R. L. GESP and personality factors: A search for correlates. *Journal of Parapsychology*, 1973, *37*, 74–75. (Abstract)

Kreiman, N. [Relationships between ESP and memory.] *Cuadernos de Parapsicologia*, 1975, *8* (2), 1–13. (Abstract in *Journal of Parapsychology*, 1975, *39*, 362–363.)

Kreiman, N., and Ivnisky, D. [Effects of feedback on ESP responses.] *Cuadernos de Parapsicologia*, 1973, *6* (2), 1–10. (Abstract in *Journal of Parapsychology*, 1973, *37*, 369.) (a)

Kreiman, N., and Ivnisky, D. [An experiment using targets of different affective contents.] *Cuadernos de Parapsicologia*, 1973, *6* (1), 1–14. (Abstract in *Journal of Parapsychology*, 1973, *37*, 369.) (b)

Kreitler, H., and Kreitler, S. Does extrasensory perception affect psychological experiments? *Journal of Parapsychology*, 1972, *36*, 1–45.

Kreitler, H., and Kreitler, S. Subliminal perception and extrasensory perception. *Journal of Parapsychology*, 1973, *37*, 163–188.

Krippner, S. *Coded and non-coded material in a clairvoyance test*. Paper presented at the Ninth Annual Convention of the Parapsychological Association, New York, 1966. (Abstract in *Journal of Parapsychology*, 1966, *30*, 281–282.)

Krippner, S. Experimentally-induced telepathic effects in hypnosis and non-hypnosis groups. *Journal of the American Society for Psychical Research*, 1968, *62*, 387–398.

Krippner, S. Electrophysiological studies of ESP in dreams: Sex differences in seventy-four telepathy sessions. *Journal of the American Society for Psychical Research*, 1970, *64*, 277–285.

Krippner, S., and Ullman, M. Telepathy and dreams: A controlled experiment with electroencephalogram–electro-oculogram monitoring. *Journal of Nervous and Mental Disease*, 1970, *151*, 394–403.

Krippner, S., Honorton, C., Ullman, M., Masters, R., and Houston, J. A long-distance "sensory bombardment" study of ESP in dreams. *Journal of the American Society for Psychical Research*, 1971, *65*, 468–475.

Krippner, S., Honorton, C., and Ullman, M. A precognitive dream study with a single subject. *Journal of the American Society for Psychical Research*, 1971, *65*, 192–203.

Krippner, S., Honorton, C., and Ullman, M. A second precognitive dream study with Malcolm Bessent. *Journal of the American Society for Psychical Research*, 1972, *66*, 269–279.

Krippner, S., Honorton, C., and Ullman, M. A long-distance ESP dream study with the "Grateful Dead." *Journal of the American Society of Psychosomatic Dentistry and Medicine*, 1973, *20*, 9–17.

Kubis, J. F., and Rouke, F. L. An experimental investigation of telepathic phenomena in twins. *Journal of Parapsychology*, 1937, *1*, 163–171.

Lancaster, J. B. A ESP experiment with a dual (color-symbol) target. *Journal of Parapsychology*, 1959, *23*, 281. (Abstract)

Layton, B. D., and Turnbull, B. Belief, evaluation, and performance on an ESP task. *Journal of Experimental Social Psychology*, 1975, *11*, 166–179.

Levin, J. A series of psi experiments with gerbils. *Journal of Parapsychology*, 1975, *39*, 363–365. (Abstract)

Levine, F., and Stowell, J. *The relationship between creativity and clairvoyance.* Paper presented at the Sixth Annual Convention of the Parapsychological Association, New York, 1963. (Abstract in *Journal of Parapsychology*, 1963, *27*, 272.)

Lewis, L., and Schmeidler, G. R. Alpha relations with non-intentional and purposeful ESP after feedback. *Journal of the American Society for Psychical Research*, 1971, *65*, 455–467.

Lieberman, R. Role of varied time interval and association strength in memory–ESP interaction for group and individual testing. In J. D. Morris, W. G. Roll, and R. L. Morris (Eds.), *Research in parapsychology 1975*. Metuchen, New Jersey: Scarecrow Press, 1976. Pp. 126–129.

Lloyd, D. H. Objective events in the brain correlating with psychic phenomena. *New Horizons*, 1973, *1*, 69–75.

Louwerens, N. G. ESP experiments with nursery school children in the Netherlands. *Journal of Parapsychology*, 1960, *24*, 75–93.

Lubke, C., and Rohr, W. Psi and subliminal perception: A replication of the Kreitler and Kreitler study. In J. D. Morris, W. G. Roll, and R. L. Morris (Eds.), *Research in parapsychology 1974*. Metuchen, New Jersey: Scarecrow Press, 1975. Pp. 161–164.

Lucas, D., and Roll, W. G. Testing the psi association hypothesis. In W. G. Roll, R. L. Morris, and J. D. Morris (Eds.), *Research in parapsychology 1972*. Metuchen, New Jersey: Scarecrow Press, 1973. Pp. 27–28.

MacFarland, J. D. Discrimination shown between experimenters by subjects. *Journal of Parapsychology*, 1938, *2*, 160–170.

MacFarland, J. D., and George, R. W. Extrasensory perception of normal and distorted symbols. *Journal of Parapsychology*, 1937, *1*, 93–101.

Maher, M., and Schmeidler, G. R. Cerebral lateralization effects in ESP processing. *Journal of the American Society for Psychical Research*, 1977, *71*, 261–271.

Mangan, G. L. Evidence of displacement in a precognition test. *Journal of Parapsychology*, 1955, *19*, 35–44.

Mangan, G. L. An ESP experiment with dual-aspect targets involving one trial a day. *Journal of Parapsychology*, 1957, *21*, 273–283.

Marks, D. F. Individual differences in the vividness of visual imagery and their effect on function. In P. W. Sheehan (Ed.), *The function and nature of imagery*. New York: Academic Press, 1972.

Marsh, M. C. Three ESP experiments using drawings as target material. *Publications of South African Society for Psychical Research* (No. 5), 1962, 4–15. (Abstract in *Journal of Parapsychology*, 1963, *27*, 219–220.)

Martin, D. R., and Stribic, F. P. Studies in extrasensory perception: I. An analysis of 25,000 trials. *Journal of Parapsychology*, 1938, *2*, 23–30. (a)

Martin, D. R., and Stribic, F. P. Studies in extrasensory perception: II. An analysis of a second series of 25,000 trials. *Journal of Parapsychology*, 1938, *2*, 287–295. (b)

Martin, D. R., and Stribic, F. P. Studies in extrasensory perception: III. A review of all University of Colorado experiments. *Journal of Parapsychology*, 1940, *4*, 159–248.

McBain, W. N., Fox, W., Kimura, S., Nakanishi, M., and Tirado, J. Quasi-sensory communication: An investigation using semantic matching and accentuated affect. *Journal of Personality and Social Psychology*, 1970, *14*, 281–291.

McCallam, E., and Honorton, C. Effects of feedback on discrimination between correct and incorrect ESP responses: A further replication and extension. *Journal of the American Society for Psychical Research*, 1973, *67*, 77–85.

McElroy, W. A., and Brown, W. R. K. Electric shocks for errors in ESP card tests. *Journal of Parapsychology*, 1950, *14*, 257–266.

McGuire, K., Percy, E., and Carpenter, J. C. A multivariate approach to the prediction of ESP performance. In W. G. Roll, R. L. Morris, and J. D. Morris (Eds.), *Research in parapsychology 1973*. Metuchen, New Jersey: Scarecrow Press, 1974. Pp. 34–35.

McMahan, E. A. An experiment in pure telepathy. *Journal of Parapsychology*, 1946, *10*, 224–242.

McMahan, E. A., and Bates, E. K. Report of further Marchesi experiments. *Journal of Parapsychology*, 1954, *18*, 82–92.

McMahan, E. A., and Rhine, J. B. A second Zagreb–Durham ESP experiment. *Journal of Parapsychology*, 1947, *11*, 244–253.

Medhurst, G. The origin of the "prepared random numbers" used in the Shackleton experiments. *Journal of the Society for Psychical Research*, 1971, *46*, 39–55.

Medhurst, R. G., and Scott, C. A re-examination of C. E. M. Hansel's criticism of the Pratt–Woodruff experiment. *Journal of Parapsychology*, *38*, 163–184.

Michie, D., and West, D. J. A mass ESP test using television. *Journal of the Society for Psychical Research*, 1957, *39*, 113–133.

Mihalasky, J. The influence of sex dominance in group precognition experiments on the relationship between hare–tortoise categories. In W. G. Roll, R. L. Morris, and J. D. Morris (Eds.), *Proceedings of the Parapsychological Association No. 7, 1970*. Durham, North Carolina: Parapsychological Association, 1972. Pp. 60–61.

Millar, B. An attempted validation of the "Lloyd effect." In J. D. Morris, W. G. Roll, and R. L. Morris (Eds.), *Research in parapsychology 1975*. Metuchen, New Jersey: Scarecrow Press, 1976. Pp. 25–27.

Miller, S. W., and York, M. S. Perceptual defensiveness as a performance indicator on a free-response test of clairvoyance. In J. D. Morris, W. G. Roll, and R. L. Morris (Eds.), *Research in parapsychology 1975*. Metuchen, New Jersey: Scarecrow Press, 1976. Pp. 162–164.

Mitchell, A. M. J. Home-testing ESP experiments: Special report on one series of tests. *Journal of the Society for Psychical Research*, 1953, *37*, 155–164.

Mitchell, E. D. An ESP test from Apollo 14. *Journal of Parapsychology*, 1971, *35*, 89–107.

Monroe, R. A. *Journeys out of the body*. New York: Doubleday, 1971.

Morris, R. L. Obtaining non-random entry points: A complex psi task. In J. B. Rhine and R. Brier (Eds.), *Parapsychology today*. New York: Citadel, 1968.

Morris, R. L. Psi and animal behavior: A survey. *Journal of the American Society for Psychical Research*, 1970, *64*, 242–260.

Morris, R. L. Recent research with Lalsingh Harribance: Guessing habits and ESP. In W. G. Roll, R. L. Morris, and J. D. Morris (Eds.), *Proceedings of the Parapsychological Association No. 8, 1971*. Durham, North Carolina: Parapsychological Association, 1972. Pp. 72–74.

Morris, R. L. Complex psi and the concept of precognition. In W. G. Roll, R. L. Morris, and J. D. Morris (Eds.), *Research in parapsychology 1972*. Metuchen, New Jersey: Scarecrow Press, 1973. Pp. 95–97.

Morris, R. L. The use of detectors for out-of-body experiences. In W. G. Roll, R. L. Morris, and J. D. Morris (Eds.), *Research in parapsychology 1973*. Metuchen, New Jersey: Scarecrow Press, 1974. Pp. 114–116.

Morris, R. L., and Cohen, D. A preliminary experiment on the relationships among ESP, alpha rhythm and calling patterns. In W. G. Roll, R. L. Morris, and J. D. Morris (Eds.), *Proceedings of the Parapsychological Association No. 6, 1969*. Durham, North Carolina: Parapsychological Association, 1971. Pp. 22–23.

Morris, R. L., Roll, W. G., Klein, J., and Wheeler, G. EEG patterns and ESP results in forced-choice experiments with Lalsingh Harribance. *Journal of the American Society for Psychical Research*, 1972, *66*, 253–268.

Moss, T. ESP effects in "artists" contrasted with "non-artists." *Journal of Parapsychology*, 1969, *33*, 57–69.

Moss, T., and Gengerelli, J. A. ESP effects generated by affective states. *Journal of Parapsychology*, 1968, *32*, 90–100.

Moss, T., Paulson, M. J., Chang, A. F., and Levitt, M. Hypnosis and ESP: A controlled experiment. *American Journal of Clinical Hypnosis*, 1970, *13*, 46–56.

Mussig, G. F., and Dean, E. D. *Mood as a factor in precognition*. Paper presented at the Tenth Annual Convention of the Parapsychological Association, New York, 1967. (Abstract in *Journal of Parapsychology*, 1967, *31*, 319–320.)

Musso, J. R. ESP experiments with primary school children. *Journal of Parapsychology*, 1965, *29*, 115–121.

Musso, J. R., and Granero, M. An ESP drawing experiment with a high-scoring subject. *Journal of Parapsychology*, 1973, *37*, 13–36.

Myers, F. W. H. *Human personality and its survival of bodily death*. New York: Arno Press, 1975. (Originally published, 1903.)

Nash, C. B. Correlation between ESP and religious value. *Journal of Parapsychology*, 1958, *22*, 204–209.

Nash, C. B. Can precognition occur diametrically? *Journal of Parapsychology*, 1960, *24*, 26–32. (a)

Nash, C. B. The effect of subject–experimenter attitudes on clairvoyance scores. *Journal of Parapsychology*, 1960, *24*, 189–198. (b)

Nash, C. B. Comparison of ESP session score averages of subjects with opposed attitudes toward psi. *Psychics International*, 1964, *1*, 56–69. (Abstract in *Journal of Parapsychology*, 1967, *31*, 84.)

Nash, C. B. Opposite scoring direction in ESP. *Journal of Parapsychology*, 1965, *29*, 122–126.

Nash, C. B. Relation between ESP scoring and the Minnesota Multiphasic Personality Inventory. *Journal of the American Society for Psychical Research*, 1966, *60*, 56–62.

Nash, C. B., and Buzby, D. E. Extrasensory perception of identical and fraternal twins. *Journal of Heredity*, 1965, *56*, 52–54.

Nash, C. B., and Durkin, M. G. Terminal salience with multiple digit targets. *Journal of Parapsychology*, 1959, *23*, 49–53.

Nash, C. B., and Nash, C. S. Checking success and the relation of personality traits to ESP. *Journal of the American Society for Psychical Research*, 1958, *52*, 98–107.

Nash, C. B., and Nash, C. S. Coincident vasoconstrictions in pairs of resting subjects. *Journal of the Society for Psychical Research*, 1962, *41*, 347–350.

Nash, C. B., and Nash, C. S. Comparison of responses to ESP and subliminal targets. *International Journal of Parapsychology*, 1963, *5*, 293–307.

Nash, C. B., and Nash, C. S. Correlation between ESP scores and intelligence. *International Journal of Parapsychology*, 1964, *6*, 309–320.

Nash, C. B., and Nash, C. S. Relations between ESP scoring level and the personality traits of the Guilford–Zimmerman Temperament Survey. *Journal of the American Society for Psychical Research*, 1967, *61*, 64–71.

Nash, C. B., and Richards, A. Comparison of two distances in PK tests. *Journal of Parapsychology*, 1947, *11*, 269–282.

Nash, C. S., and Nash, C. B. A test of adding extrasensorially perceived digits. *Journal of Parapsychology*, 1959, *23*, 126–129.

Nash, C. S., and Nash, C. B. Effect of target selection, field dependence, and body concept on ESP performance. *Journal of Parapsychology*, 1968, *32*, 248–257.

Nash, C. S., and Nash, C. B. A test of the relationship between ESP, Gestalt completion, and man drawing. In W. G. Roll, R. L. Morris, and J. D. Morris (Eds.), *Proceedings of the Parapsychological Association No. 6, 1969*. Durham, North Carolina: Parapsychological Association, 1971. Pp. 15–16.

Nicol, J. F., and Humphrey, B. M. The exploration of ESP and human personality, *Journal of the American Society for Psychical Research*, 1953, *47*, 133–178.

Nicol, J. F., and Humphrey, B. M. The repeatability problem in ESP-personality research. *Journal of the American Society for Psychical Research*, 1955, *49*, 125–156.

Nielsen, W. An exploratory precognition experiment. *Journal of Parapsychology*, 1956, *20*, 33–39. (a)

Nielsen, W. Mental states associated with success in precognition. *Journal of Parapsychology*, 1956, *20*, 96–109. (b)

Nielsen, W. Relationships between precognition scoring level and mood. *Journal of Parapsychology*, 1970, *34*, 93–116.

Nielsen, W. Mood, introversion, and precognition scores on individual and group targets. In W. G. Roll, R. L. Morris, and J. D. Morris (Eds.), *Proceedings of the Parapsychological Association No. 8, 1971*. Durham, North Carolina: Parapsychological Association, 1972. Pp. 88–90. (a)

Nielsen, W. Studies in group targets: A social psychology class. In W. G. Roll, R. L. Morris, and J. D. Morris (Eds.), *Proceedings of the Parapsychological Association No. 7, 1970*. Durham, North Carolina: Parapsychological Association, 1972. Pp. 55–56. (b)

Nielsen, W. Studies in group targets: An unusual high school group. In W. G. Roll, R. L. Morris, and J. D. Morris (Eds.), *Proceedings of the Parapsychological Association No. 7, 1970*. Durham, North Carolina: Parapsychological Association, 1972. Pp. 57–58. (c)

Nielsen, W., and Freeman, J. (A.) Consistency of relationship between ESP and emotional variables. *Journal of Parapsychology*, 1965, *29*, 75–88.

Nowlis, D. P., and Kamiya, J. The control of electroencephalographic alpha rhythms through auditory feedback and the associated mental activity. *Psychophysiology*, 1970, *6*, 476–484.

O'Brien, D. P. *Recall and recognition processes in a memory–ESP paired-associate task.* Paper presented at the southeastern regional Parapsychological Association conference, 1976. (Abstract in *Journal of Parapsychology*, 1976, *40*, 57–59.)

Osis, K. A test of the occurrence of a psi effect between man and the cat. *Journal of Parapsychology*, 1952, *16*, 233–256.

Osis, K. Precognition over time intervals of one to thirty-three days. *Journal of Parapsychology*, 1955, *19*, 82–91.

Osis, K. ESP tests at long and short distances. *Journal of Parapsychology*, 1956, *20*, 81–95.

Osis, K., and Bokert, E. ESP and changed states of consciousness induced by meditation. *Journal of the American Society for Psychical Research*, 1971, *65*, 17–65.

Osis, K., and Carlson, M. L. The ESP channel—open or closed? *Journal of the American Society for Psychical Research*, 1972, *66*, 310–319.

Osis, K., and Dean, (E.) D. The effect of experimenter differences and subjects' belief level upon ESP scores. *Journal of the American Society for Psychical Research*, 1964, *58*, 158–185.

Osis, K., and Fahler, J. Space and time variables in ESP. *Journal of the American Society for Psychical Research*, 1965, *59*, 130–145.

Osis, K., and Foster, E. B. A test of ESP in cats. *Journal of Parapsychology*, 1953, *17*, 168–186.

Osis, K., and Pienaar, D. C. ESP over a distance of seventy-five hundred miles. *Journal of Parapsychology*, 1956, *20*, 229–232.

Osis, K., and Turner, M. E. Distance and ESP: A transcontinental experiment. *Proceedings of the American Society for Psychical Research*, 1968, *27*.

Osis, K., Turner, M. E., and Carlson, M. L. ESP over distance: Research on the ESP channel. *Journal of the American Society for Psychical Research*, 1971, *65*, 245–288.

Otani, S. Relations of mental set and change of skin resistance to ESP. *Journal of Parapsychology*, 1955, *19*, 164–170.

Otani, S. Studies on the influence of the mental and physiological conditions upon ESP function. *Journal of Parapsychology*, 1958, *22*, 296. (Abstract)

Palmer, J. Scoring in ESP tests as a function of belief in ESP. Part I: The sheep–goat effect. *Journal of the American Society for Psychical Research*, 1971, *65*, 373–408.

Palmer, J. Scoring in ESP tests as a function of belief in ESP. Part II: Beyond the sheep–goat effect. *Journal of the American Society for Psychical Research*, 1972, *66*, 1–26.

Palmer, J. ESP scoring as predicted from four definitions of the sheep–goat variable. In W. G. Roll, R. L. Morris, and J. D. Morris (Eds.), *Research in parapsychology 1972*. Metuchen, New Jersey: Scarecrow Press, 1973. Pp. 37–39.

Palmer, J. Three models of psi test performance. *Journal of the American Society for Psychical Research*, 1975, *69*, 333–339.

Palmer, J. Attitudes and personality traits in experimental ESP research. In B. B. Wolman (Ed.), *Handbook of parapsychology*. New York: Van Nostrand Reinhold, 1977.

Palmer, J., and Aued, I. An ESP test with psychometric objects and the ganzfeld: Negative findings. In J. D. Morris, W. G. Roll, and R. L. Morris (Eds.), *Research in parapsychology 1974*. Metuchen, New Jersey: Scarecrow Press, 1975. Pp. 50–53.

Palmer, J., and Dennis, M. A community mail survey of psychic experiences. In J. D. Morris, W. G. Roll, and R. L. Morris (Eds.), *Research in parapsychology 1974*. Metuchen, New Jersey: Scarecrow Press, 1975, Pp. 130–133.

Palmer, J., and Lieberman, R. The influence of psychological set on ESP and out-of-body experiences. *Journal of the American Society for Psychical Research*, 1975, *69*, 193–213.

Palmer, J., and Lieberman, R. ESP and out-of-body experiences: A further study. In J. D. Morris, W. G. Roll, and R. L. Morris (Eds.), *Research in parapsychology 1975*. Metuchen, New Jersey: Scarecrow Press, 1976. Pp. 102–106.

Palmer, J., and Miller, A. Monetary incentive and the sheep–goat effect. In W. G. Roll, R. L. Morris, and J. D. Morris (Eds.), *Proceedings of the Parapsychological Association No. 7, 1970*. Durham, North Carolina: Parapsychological Association, 1972. Pp. 11–12.

Palmer, J., and Vassar, C. ESP and out-of-the-body experiences: An exploratory study. *Journal of the American Society for Psychical Research*, 1974, *68*, 257–280.

Palmer, J., Tart, C., and Redington, D. A large-sample classroom ESP card-guessing experiment. *European Journal of Parapsychology*, 1976, *1* (No. 3), 40–56.

Palmer, J. Bogart, D. N., Jones, S. M., and Tart, C. T. Scoring patterns in an ESP ganzfeld experiment. *Journal of the American Society for Psychical Research*, 1977, *71*, 121–145.

Parker, A. ESP in gerbils using positive reinforcement. *Journal of Parapsychology*, 1974, *38*, 301–311.

Parker, A. A pilot study of the influence of experimenter expectancy on ESP scores. In J. D. Morris, W. G. Roll, and R. L. Morris (Eds.), *Research in parapsychology 1974*. Metuchen, New Jersey: Scarecrow Press, 1975. Pp. 42–44. (a)

Parker, A. Some findings relevant to the change in state hypothesis. In J. D. Morris, W. G. Roll, and R. L. Morris (Eds.), *Research in parapsychology 1974*. Metuchen, New Jersey: Scarecrow Press, 1975. Pp. 40–42. (b)

Parker, A. Parapsychologists' personality and psi in relation to the experimenter effect. In J. D. Morris, W. G. Roll, and R. L. Morris (Eds.), *Research in parapsychology 1976*. Metuchen, New Jersey: Scarecrow Press, 1977. Pp. 107–109.

Parker, A., and Beloff, J. Hypnotically-induced clairvoyant dreams: A partial replication and attempted confirmation. *Journal of the American Society for Psychical Research*, 1970, *64*, 432–442.

Parker, A., Millar, B., and Beloff, J. A three-experimenter ganzfeld: An attempt to use the ganzfeld technique to study the experimenter effect. In J. D. Morris, W. G. Roll, and R. L. Morris (Eds.), *Research in parapsychology 1976*. Metuchen, New Jersey: Scarecrow Press, 1977. Pp. 52–54.

Parker, K. A study of immediate memory and ESP. In J. D. Morris, W. G. Roll, and R. L. Morris (Eds.), *Research in parapsychology 1975*. Metuchen, New Jersey: Scarecrow Press, 1976. Pp. 130–134.

Pegram, M. H. Some psychological relations of extrasensory perception. *Journal of Parapsychology*, 1937, *1*, 191–205.

Peterson, C. J. *Relationships among attitude, memory, and extrasensory perception*. Unpublished master's thesis, Wisconsin State University, 1971. (Abstract in *Journal of Parapsychology*, 1972, *36*, 94.)

Pfungst, O. [*Clever Hans*] (R. Rosenthal, Ed.). New York: Holt, Rinehart & Winston, 1965. (First American edition, C. L. Rahn, trans., 1911.)

Pleshette, G. Biofeedback regulation of EEG alpha, mental imagery, and psi guessing performance. In J. D. Morris, W. G. Roll, and R. L. Morris (Eds.), *Research in parapsychology 1974*. Metuchen, New Jersey: Scarecrow Press, 1975. Pp. 23–24.

Pratt, J. G. Clairvoyant blind matching. *Journal of Parapsychology*, 1937, *1*, 10–17.

Pratt, J. G. The reinforcement effect in ESP displacement. *Journal of Parapsychology*, 1951, *15*, 103–117.

Pratt, J. G. Run salience in the Pratt–Woodruff series. *Journal of Parapsychology*, 1961, *25*, 130–135.

Pratt, J. G. Computer studies of the ESP process in card guessing: I. Displacement effects in Mrs. Gloria Stewart's records. *Journal of the American Society for Psychical Research*, 1967, *61*, 25–46. (a)

Pratt, J. G. Computer studies of the ESP process in card guessing: II. Did memory habits limit Mrs. Stewart's ESP success? *Journal of the American Society for Psychical Research*, 1967, *61*, 182–202. (b)

Pratt, J. G. A decade of research with a selected ESP subject: An overview and reappraisal of the work with Pavel Stepanek. *Proceedings of the American Society for Psychical Research*, 1973, *30*.

Pratt, J. G. Comments on the Medhurst–Scott criticism of the Pratt–Woodruff experiment. *Journal of Parapsychology*, 1974, *38*, 185–201. (a)

Pratt, J. G. In search of the consistent scorer. In J. Beloff (Ed.), *New directions in parapsychology*. London: Elek Science, 1974. Pp. 95–121. (b)

Pratt, J. G. Outstanding subjects in ESP. *Journal of the American Society for Psychical Research*, 1975, *69*, 151–160.

Pratt, J. G. New evidence supporting the ESP interpretation of the Pratt–Woodruff experiment. In J. D. Morris, W. G. Roll, and R. L. Morris (Eds.), *Research in parapsychology 1976*. Metuchen, New Jersey: Scarecrow Press, 1977. Pp. 179–182.

Pratt, J. G., and Foster, E. B. Displacement in ESP card tests in relation to hits and misses. *Journal of Parapsychology*, 1950, *14*, 37–53.

Pratt, J. G., and Price, M. M. The experimenter–subject relationship in tests for ESP. *Journal of Parapsychology*, 1938, *2*, 84–94.

Pratt, J. G., and Woodruff, J. L. Size of stimulus symbols in extra-sensory perception. *Journal of Parapsychology*, 1939, *3*, 121–158.

Pratt, J. G., and Woodruff, J. L. Refutation of Hansel's allegation concerning the Pratt–Woodruff series. *Journal of Parapsychology*, 1961, *25*, 114–129.

Pratt, J. G., Martin, D. R., and Stribic, F. P. Computer studies of the ESP process in card guessing. III. Displacement effects in the C. J. records from the Colorado series. *Journal of the American Society for Psychical Research*, 1974, *68*, 357–384.

Price, A. D. ESP, creativity, and heart rate variability: A new methodology for process-oriented token object studies. In W. G. Roll, R. L. Morris, and J. D. Morris (Eds.), *Research in parapsychology 1972*. Metuchen, New Jersey: Scarecrow Press, 1973. Pp. 44–47. (a)

Price, A. D. Subject's control of imagery, "agent's" mood, and position effects in a dual-target ESP experiment. *Journal of Parapsychology*, 1973, *37*, 298–322. (b)

Price, G. R. Science and the supernatural. *Science*, 1955, *122*, 359–367.

Price, G. R. Apology to Rhine and Soal. *Science*, 1972, *175*, 359.

Price, M. M. A comparison of blind and seeing subjects in ESP tests. *Journal of Parapsychology*, 1938, *2*, 273–286.

Price, M. M., and Pegram, M. H. Extra-sensory perception among the blind. *Journal of Parapsychology*, 1937, *1*, 143–155.

Puthoff, H. E., and Targ, R. A perceptual channel for information transfer over kilometer distances: Historical perspective and recent research. *Journal of the Institute of Electrical and Electronic Engineers*, 1976, *64*, 329–354.

Raburn, L., and Manning, R. Sender relaxation and expectation in telepathy. In J. D. Morris, W. G. Roll, and R. L. Morris (Eds.), *Research in parapsychology 1976*. Metuchen, New Jersey: Scarecrow Press, 1977. Pp. 156–158.

Randall, J. (L.) Group ESP experiments with schoolboys. *Journal of Parapsychology*, 1972, *36*, 133–143.

Randall, J. L. Card-guessing experiments with school-boys. *Journal of the Society for Psychical Research*, 1974, *47*, 421–432.

Randi, J. *The magic of Uri Geller*. New York: Ballantine Books, 1975.

Ransom, C. Recent criticisms of parapsychology: A review. *Journal of the American Society for Psychical Research*, 1971, *65*, 289–307.

Rao, K. R. The preferential effect in ESP. *Journal of Parapsychology*, 1962, *26*, 252–259.

Rao, K. R. Studies in the preferential effect. I. Target preference with types of targets unknown. *Journal of Parapsychology*, 1963, *27*, 23–32. (a)

Rao, K. R. Studies in the preferential effect. II. A language ESP test involving precognition and "intervention." *Journal of Parapsychology*, 1963, *27*, 147–160. (b)

Rao, K. R. Studies in the preferential effect. III. The reversal effect in psi preference. *Journal of Parapsychology*, 1963, *27*, 242–251. (c)

Rao, K. R. The differential response in three new situations. *Journal of Parapsychology*, 1964, *28*, 81–92. (a)

Rao, K. R. Studies in the preferential effect. IV. The role of key cards in preferential response situations. *Journal of Parapsychology*, 1964, *28*, 28–41. (b)

Rao, K. R. The bidirectionality of psi. *Journal of Parapsychology*, 1965, *29*, 230–250. (a)

Rao, K. R. ESP and the Manifest Anxiety Scale. *Journal of Parapsychology*, 1965, *29*, 12–18. (b)

Rao, K. R. Some frustrations and challenges in parapsychology, *Journal of Parapsychology*, 1977, *41*, 119–135.

Rao, K. R., and Feola, J. Alpha rhythm and ESP in a free-response situation. In W. G. Roll, R. L. Morris, and J. D. Morris (Eds.), *Research in parapsychology 1972*. Metuchen, New Jersey: Scarecrow Press, 1973. Pp. 141–144.

Reed, B. A comparison of clairvoyance test results under three different testing conditions. *Journal of Parapsychology*, 1959, *23*, 142. (Abstract)

Rhine, J. B. *Extrasensory perception* (Rev. ed.). Boston: Bruce Humphries, 1973. (Originally published, 1934.)

Rhine, J. B. The effect of distance in ESP tests. *Journal of Parapsychology*, 1937, *1*, 172–184.

Rhine, J. B. ESP tests with enclosed cards. *Journal of Parapsychology*, 1938, *2*, 199–216. (a)

Rhine, J. B. Experiments bearing on the precognition hypothesis. *Journal of Parapsychology*, 1938, *2*, 38–54. (b)

Rhine, J. B. Experiments bearing upon the precognition hypothesis: III. Mechanically selected cards. *Journal of Parapsychology*, 1941, *5*, 1–57. (a)

Rhine, J. B. Terminal salience in ESP performance. *Journal of Parapsychology*, 1941, *5*, 183–244. (b)

Rhine, J. B. Evidence of precognition in the covariance of salience ratios. *Journal of Parapsychology*, 1942, *6*, 111–143.

Rhine, J. B. Precognition reconsidered. *Journal of Parapsychology*, 1945, *9*, 264–277. (a)

Rhine, J. B. Telepathy and clairvoyance reconsidered. *Journal of Parapsychology*, 1945, *9*, 176–193. (b)

Rhine, J. B. A digest and discussion of some comments on "Telepathy and clairvoyance reconsidered." *Journal of Parapsychology*, 1946, *10*, 36–50.

Rhine, J. B. The present outlook on the question of psi in animals. *Journal of Parapsychology*, 1951, *15*, 230–251.

Rhine, J. B. The precognition of computer numbers in a public test. *Journal of Parapsychology*, 1962, *26*, 244–251.

Rhine, J. B. Special motivation in some exceptional ESP performances. *Journal of Parapsychology*, 1964, *28*, 41–50.

Rhine, J. B. Position effects in psi test results. *Journal of Parapsychology*, 1969, *33*, 136–157. (a)

Rhine, J. B. Psi-missing re-examined. *Journal of Parapsychology*, 1969, *33*, 136–157. (b)

Rhine, J. B. Comments: A new case of experimenter unreliability. *Journal of Parapsychology*, 1974, *38*, 215–225.

Rhine, J. B., and Feather, S. J. The study of cases of "psi-trailing" in animals. *Journal of Parapsychology*, 1962, *26*, 1–22.

Rhine, J. B., and Humphrey, B. M. A transoceanic ESP experiment. *Journal of Parapsychology*, 1942, *6*, 52–74.

Rhine, J. B., and Pratt, J. G. A review of the Pearce–Pratt distance series of ESP tests. *Journal of Parapsychology*, 1954, *18*, 165–177.

Rhine, J. B., Smith, B. M., and Woodruff, J. L. Experiments bearing on the precognition hypothesis: II. The role of ESP in the shuffling of cards. *Journal of Parapsychology*, 1938, *2*, 119–131.

Rhine, J. B., Pratt, J. G., Stuart, C. E., Smith, B. M., and Greenwood, J. A. *Extrasensory perception after sixty years.* Boston: Bruce Humphries, 1966. (Originally published 1940.)

Rhine, L. E. Some stimulus variations in extrasensory perception with child subjects. *Journal of Parapsychology*, 1937, *1*, 102–113.

Rhine, L. E. Psychological processes in ESP experiences: Part I. Waking experiences. *Journal of Parapsychology*, 1962, *26*, 88–111.

Rhine, L. E. Note on an informal group test of ESP. *Journal of Parapsychology*, 1968, *32*, 47–53.

Rice, G. E., and Townsend, J. Agent–percipient relationship and GESP performance. *Journal of Parapsychology*, 1962, *26*, 211–217.

Riess, B. F. A case of high scores in card guessing at a distance. *Journal of Parapsychology*, 1937, *1*, 260–263.

Riess, B. F. Further data from a case of high scores in card guessing. *Journal of Parapsychology*, 1939, *3*, 79–84.

Rilling, M. E., Adams, J. Q., and Pettijohn, C. A summary of some clairvoyance experiments conducted in classroom situations. *Journal of the American Society for Psychical Research*, 1962, *56*, 125–130.

Rilling, M. E., Pettijohn, C., and Adams, J. Q. A two-experimenter investigation of teacher–pupil attitudes and clairvoyance test results in the high school classroom. *Journal of Parapsychology*, 1961, *25*, 247–259.

Rivers, O. B. An exploratory study of the mental health and intelligence of ESP subjects. *Journal of Parapsychology*, 1950, *14*, 267–277.

Rogers, D. P. Negative and positive affect and ESP run-score variance. *Journal of Parapsychology*, 1966, *30*, 151–159.

Rogers, D. P. An analysis for internal cancellation effects on some low-variance ESP runs. *Journal of Parapsychology*, 1967, *31*, 192–197. (a)

Rogers, D. P. Negative and positive affect and ESP run-score variance: Study II. *Journal of Parapsychology*, 1967, *31*, 290–296. (b)

Rogers, D. P. *Some explorations in affective arousal and ESP.* Paper presented at the Tenth Annual Convention of the Parapsychological Association, New York, 1967. (Abstract in *Journal of Parapsychology*, 1967, *31*, 318.) (c)

Rogers, D. P., and Carpenter, J. C. The decline of variance of ESP scores within a testing session. *Journal of Parapsychology*, 1966, *30*, 141–150.

Rogers, W. C. A study of like pattern formations in twins. *Journal of Parapsychology*, 1960, *24*, 69. (Abstract)

Rogo, D. S. Psi and psychosis: A review of the experimental evidence. *Journal of Parapsychology*, 1975, *39*, 120–128.

Rogo, D. S. Research in psi-conducive states: Some complicating factors. *Journal of Parapsychology*, 1976, *40*, 34–45.

Rogo, D. S., Smith, M., and Terry, J. The use of short-duration ganzfeld stimulation to facilitate psi-mediated imagery. *European Journal of Parapsychology*, 1976, *1*, (2), 72–77.

Roll, W. G. ESP and memory. *International Journal of Neuropsychiatry*, 1966, *2*, 505–521.

Roll, W. G. Recent research with Lalsingh Harribance: Physical aspects of the target. In W. G. Roll, R. L. Morris, and J. D. Morris (Eds.), *Proceedings of the Parapsychological Association No. 8, 1971.* Durham, North Carolina: Parapsychological Association, 1972. Pp. 67–69.

Roll, W. G., and Klein, J. Further forced-choice ESP experiments with Lalsingh Harribance. *Journal of the American Society for Psychical Research*, 1972, *66*, 103–112.

Roll, W. G., and Solfvin, G. F. Meditation and ESP. In J. D. Morris, W. G. Roll, and R. L. Morris (Eds.), *Research in parapsychology 1975*. Metuchen, New Jersey: Scarecrow Press, 1976. Pp. 92–97.

Roll, W. G., Morris, R. L., Damgaard, J. A., Klein, J., and Roll, M. Free verbal response experiments with Lalsingh Harribance. *Journal of the American Society for Psychical Research*, 1973, *67*, 197–207.

Roll, W. G., Morris, R. L., Harary, S. B., Wells, R., and Hartwell, J. Further OOBE experiments with a cat as detector. In J. D. Morris, W. G. Roll, and R. L. Morris (Eds.), *Research in parapsychology 1974*. Metuchen, New Jersey: Scarecrow Press, 1975. Pp. 55–56.

Rose, L., and Rose, R. Psi experiments with Australian Aborigines. *Journal of Parapsychology*, 1951, *15*, 122–131.

Rose, R. A second report on psi experiments with Australian Aborigines. *Journal of Parapsychology*, 1955, *19*, 92–98.

Ross, A. O., Murphy, G., and Schmeidler, G. R. The spontaneity factor in extrasensory perception. *Journal of the American Society for Psychical Research*, 1952, *46*, 14–16.

Rush, J. H., and Jensen, A. A reciprocal distance GESP test with drawings. *Journal of Parapsychology*, 1949, *13*, 122–134.

Russell, W. Examination of ESP records for displacement effects. *Journal of Parapsychology*, 1943, *7*, 104–117.

Ryzl, M. Training the psi faculty by hypnosis. *Journal of the Society for Psychical Research*, 1962, *41*, 234–252.

Ryzl, M. Precognition scoring and attitude. *Journal of Parapsychology*, 1968, *32*, 183–189. (a)

Ryzl, M. Precognition scoring and attitude toward ESP. *Journal of Parapsychology*, 1968, *32*, 1–8. (b)

Ryzl, M., and Pratt, J. G. A further confirmation of stabilized ESP performance in a selected subject. *Journal of Parapsychology*, 1963, *27*, 73–83.

Sailaja, P. *Confirmatory study of the role of key cards in the language ESP test*. Paper presented at the Eighth Annual Convention of the Parapsychological Association, New York, 1965. (Abstract in *Journal of Parapsychology*, 1965, *27*, 290–291.)

Sailaja, P., and Rao, K. R. *Experimental studies of the differential effect in life setting (Parapsychological Monographs No. 13)*. New York: Parapsychology Foundation, 1973.

Sanders, M. S. A comparison of verbal and written responses in a precognition experiment. *Journal of Parapsychology*, 1962, *26*, 23–34.

Sandford, J. and Keil, H. H. J. The effect of "normal" vs. relaxed states of consciousness on ESP scoring using a GESP feedback testing device. In J. D. Morris, W. G. Roll, and R. L. Morris (Eds.), *Research in parapsychology 1974*. Metuchen, New Jersey: Scarecrow Press, 1975. Pp. 24–27.

Sanjar, M. A study of coincident autonomic activity in closely related persons. *Journal of the American Society for Psychical Research*, 1969, *63*, 88–94.

Schechter, R., Solfvin, G., and McCallum, R. Psi and mental imagery. *Journal of the American Society for Psychical Research*, 1975, *69*, 321–326.

Scherer, W. B. Spontaneity as a factor in ESP. *Journal of Parapsychology*, 1948, *12*, 126–147.

Schmeidler, G. R. Position effects as psychological phenomena. *Journal of Parapsychology*, 1944, *8*, 110–123.

Schmeidler, G. R. Some relations between picture-frustration ratings and ESP scores. *Journal of Personality*, 1950, *18*, 331–343.

Schmeidler, G. R. Picture-frustration ratings and ESP scores for subjects who showed moderate annoyance at the ESP task. *Journal of Parapsychology*, 1954, *18*, 137–152.

Schmeidler, G. R. Agent–percipient relationships. *Journal of the American Society for Psychical Research*, 1958, *42*, 47–69.

Schmeidler, G. R. *ESP in relation to Rorschach test evaluation (Parapsychological Monographs No. 2)*. New York: Parapsychology Foundation, 1960.

Schmeidler, G. R. Evidence for two kinds of telepathy. *International Journal of Parapsychology*, 1961, *3*, 5–43.

Schmeidler, G. R. ESP and tests of perception. *Journal of the American Society for Psychical Research*, 1962, *56*, 48–51. (a)

Schmeidler, G. R. Tests of creative thinking. *Indian Journal of Parapsychology*, 1962, *4*, 51–57. (b)

Schmeidler, G. R. An experiment on precognitive clairvoyance. Part I. The main results. *Journal of Parapsychology*, 1964, *28*, 1–14. (a)

Schmeidler, G. R. An experiment on precognitive clairvoyance. Part II. The reliability of the scores. *Journal of Parapsychology*, 1964, *28*, 15–27. (b)

Schmeidler, G. R. An experiment on precognitive clairvoyance. Part III. Precognition scores related to the subjects' ways of viewing time. *Journal of Parapsychology*, 1964, *28*, 93–101. (c)

Schmeidler, G. R. An experiment on precognitive clairvoyance. Part IV. Precognition scores related to creativity. *Journal of Parapsychology*, 1964, *28*, 102–108. (d)

Schmeidler, G. R. An experiment on precognitive clairvoyance. Part V. Precognition scores related to feelings of success. *Journal of Parapsychology*, 1964, *28*, 109–125. (e)

Schmeidler, G. R. A search for feedback in ESP: Part I. Session salience and stimulus preference. *Journal of the American Society for Psychical Research*, 1968, *62*, 130–141.

Schmeidler, G. R. High ESP scores after a Swami's brief instruction in meditation and breathing. *Journal of the American Society for Psychical Research*, 1970, *64*, 100–103.

Schmeidler, G. R. Mood and attitude on a pretest as predictors of retest ESP performance. *Journal of the American Society for Psychical Research*, 1971, *65*, 324–335.

Schmeidler, G. R., and Allison, L. W. A repetition of Carington's experiments with free drawings. *Journal of the American Society for Psychical Research*, 1948, *42*, 97–107.

Schmeidler, G. R., and Craig, J. G. Moods and ESP scores in group testing. *Journal of the American Society for Psychical Research*, 1972, *66*, 280–287.

Schmeidler, G. R., and LeShan, L. An aspect of body image related to ESP scores. *Journal of the American Society for Psychical Research*, 1970, *64*, 211–218.

Schmeidler, G. R., and Lewis, L. A search for feedback in ESP: Part II. High ESP scores after two successes on triple-aspect targets. *Journal of the American Society for Psychical Research*, 1968, *62*, 255–262.

Schmeidler, G. R., and Lewis, L. A search for feedback in ESP: Part III. The preferential effect and the impatience effect. *Journal of the American Society for Psychical Research*, 1969, *63*, 60–69.

Schmeidler, G. R., and Lindemann, C. ESP calls following an "ESP" test with sensory cues. *Journal of the American Society for Psychical Research*, 1966, *60*, 357–362.

Schmeidler, G. R., and McConnell, R. A. *ESP and personality patterns*. New Haven: Yale University Press, 1958.

Schmeidler, G. R., Friedenberg, W., and Males, P. *Impatience and ESP scores*. Paper presented at the Ninth Annual Convention of the Parapsychological Association, New York, 1966. (Abstract in *Journal of Parapsychology*, 1966, *30*, 275.)

Schmidt, H. Clairvoyance tests with a machine. *Journal of Parapsychology*, 1969, *33*, 300–306. (a)

Schmidt, H. Precognition of a quantum process. *Journal of Parapsychology*, 1969, *33*, 99–108. (b)

Schmidt, H. Toward a mathematical theory of psi. *Journal of the American Society for Psychical Research*, 1975, *69*, 301–319.

Schmidt, H., and Pantas, L. Psi tests with internally different machines. *Journal of Parapsychology*, 1972, *36*, 222–232.

Schouten, S. A. Psi in mice: Positive reinforcement. *Journal of Parapsychology*, 1972, *36*, 261–282.

Schouten, S. A. Effect of reducing response preferences on ESP scores. *European Journal of Parapsychology*, 1975, *1*, (1), 60–66.

Schouten, S. A. Autonomic psychophysiological reactions to sensory and emotive stimuli in a psi experiment. *European Journal of Parapsychology*, 1976, *1*, (2), 57–71. (a)

Schouten, S. A. Psi in mice: Report on several anpsi experiments. *Research Letter of the Parapsychology Laboratory No. 6*. The Netherlands: University of Utrecht, 1976. Pp. 1–58. (b)

Scott, C., and Haskell, P. Fresh light on the Shackleton experiments? *Proceedings of the Society for Psychical Research*, 1974, *56*, 43–72.

Scott, C., and others. The Soal–Goldney experiments with Basil Schackleton: A discussion. *Proceedings of the Society for Psychical Research*, 1974, *56*, 209.

Sharp, V., and Clark, C. C. Group tests for extrasensory perception. *Journal of Parapsychology*, 1937, *1*, 123–142.

Sheehan, P. W. A shortened form of Betts' Questionnaire Upon Mental Imagery. *Journal of Clinical Psychology*, 1967, *23*, 391–398.

Sheehan, P. W., and Neisser, U. Some variables affecting the vividness of imagery in recall. *British Journal of Psychology*, 1969, *60*, 71–80.

Shields, E. Comparison of children's guessing ability (ESP) with personality characteristics. *Journal of Parapsychology*, 1962, *26*, 200–210.

Shields, E. Reading achievement as related to ESP. *Psychics International*, 1964, *1*, 50–54. (Abstract in *Journal of Parapsychology*, 1965, *29*, 66–67.)

Shulman, R. A study of card guessing in psychotic subjects. *Journal of Parapsychology*, 1938, *2*, 95–106.

Sidgwick, E. M. Report on further experiments in thought-transference carried out by Professor Gilbert Murray. *Proceedings of the Society for Psychical Research*, 1924, *34*, 212–274.

Sidgwick, H. President's address. *Proceedings of the Society for Psychical Research*, 1882, *1*, 7–12.

Sinclair, U. *Mental radio* (2nd rev. ed.). Springfield, Illinois: Thomas, 1962.

Skibinsky, M. A comparison of names and symbols in a distance ESP test. *Journal of Parapsychology*, 1950, *14*, 140–156.

Smith, B. M., and Gibson, E. P. Conditions affecting ESP performance. *Journal of Parapsychology*, 1941, *5*, 58–86.

Smith, B. M., and Humphrey, B. M. Some personality characteristics related to ESP performance. *Journal of Parapsychology*, 1946, *10*, 269–289.

Smith, K., and Canon, H. J. A methodological refinement in the study of "ESP" and negative findings. *Science*, 1954, *120*, 148–149.

Smith, M., Tremmel, L., and Honorton, C. A comparison of psi and weak sensory influences on ganzfeld mentation. In J. D. Morris, W. G. Roll, and R. L. Morris (Eds.), *Research in parapsychology 1975*. Metuchen, New Jersey: Scarecrow Press, 1976. Pp. 191–194.

Smith, S. *The mediumship of Mrs. Leonard*. New Hyde Park, New York: University Books, 1964.

Smythies, J., and Beloff, J. The influence of stereotactic surgery on ESP. *Journal of the Society for Psychical Research*, 1965, *43*, 20–24.

Soal, S. G. Reply to Science and the supernatural. *Journal of the Society for Psychical Research*, 1955, *38*, 179–184.

Soal, S. G. A reply to Mr. Hansel. *Proceedings of the Society for Psychical Research*, 1960, *53*, 43–82.

Soal, S. G., and Bateman, F. *Modern experiments in telepathy*. New Haven: Yale University, 1954.

Soal, S. G., and Goldney, K. M. Letter. *Journal of the Society for Psychical Research*, 1960, *40*, 378–381.

Spielberger, C. D. Theory and research in anxiety. In C. D. Spielberger (Ed.), *Anxiety and behavior*. New York: Academic Press, 1966.

Spinelli, E. The effects of chronological age on GESP ability. In J. D. Morris, W. G. Roll, and R. L. Morris (Eds.), *Research in parapsychology 1976*. Metuchen, New Jersey: Scarecrow Press, 1977. Pp. 122–124.

Sprinthall, R. C., and Lubetkin, B. S. ESP: Motivation as a factor in ability. *Journal of Psychology*, 1965, *60*, 313–318.

Stanford, R. G. Attitude and personality variables in ESP scoring. *Journal of Parapsychology*, 1964, *28*, 166–175. (a)

Stanford, R. G. Differential position effects for above-chance scoring sheep and goats. *Journal of Parapsychology*, 1964, *28*, 155–165. (b)

Stanford, R. G. A further study of high- versus low-scoring sheep. *Journal of Parapsychology*, 1965, *29*, 141–158.

Stanford, R. G. The effect of restriction of calling upon run-score variance. *Journal of Parapsychology*, 1966, *30*, 160–171. (a)

Stanford, R. G. A study of the cause of low run-score variance. *Journal of Parapsychology*, 1966, *30*, 236–242. (b)

Stanford, R. G. Response bias and the correctness of ESP test responses. *Journal of Parapsychology*, 1967, *31*, 280–289.

Stanford, R. G. An effect of restricted spontaneity on ESP run scores. In J. B. Rhine and R. Brier (Eds.), *Parapsychology today*. New York: Citadel, 1968.

Stanford, R. G. Extrasensory effects upon "memory." *Journal of the American Society for Psychical Research*, 1970, *64*, 161–186.

Stanford, R. G. EEG alpha activity and ESP performance: A replicative study. *Journal of the American Society for Psychical Research*, 1971, *65*, 144–154.

Stanford, R. G. The differential effect revisited: An interaction of personality and ESP task? In W. G. Roll, R. L. Morris, and J. D. Morris (Eds.), *Proceedings of the Parapsychological Association No. 7, 1970*. Durham, North Carolina: Parapsychological Association, 1972. Pp. 12–13. (a)

Stanford, R. G. Suggestibility and success at augury—divination from "chance" outcomes. *Journal of the American Society for Psychical Research*, 1972, *66*, 42–62. (b)

Stanford, R. G. Extrasensory effects upon associative processes in a directed free-response task. *Journal of the American Society for Psychical Research*, 1973, *67*, 147–190.

Stanford, R. G. An experimentally testable model for spontaneous psi events: I. Extrasensory events. *Journal of the American Society for Psychical Research*, 1974, *68*, 34–57.

Stanford, R. G. Response patterns in extrasensory performance. *Journal of Communication*, 1975, *25*, 153–161.

Stanford, R. G. The application of learning theory to ESP performance: A review of Dr. C. T. Tart's monograph. *Journal of the American Society for Psychical Research*, 1977, *71*, 55–80. (a)

Stanford, R. G. Are parapsychologists paradigmless in psiland? In B. Shapin and L. Coly (Eds.), *The philosophy of parapsychology: Proceedings of an international conference.* New York: Parapsychology Foundation, 1977. (b)

Stanford, R. G. The question is: Good experimentation or not? A reply to Dr. C. T. Tart. *Journal of the American Society for Psychical Research*, 1977, *71*, 191–200. (c)

Stanford, R. G., and Associates. A study of motivational arousal and self-concept in psi-mediated instrumental response. *Journal of the American Society for Psychical Research*, 1976, *70*, 167–178.

Stanford, R. G., and Castello, A. Cognitive mode and extrasensory function in a timing-based PMIR task. In J. D. Morris, W. G. Roll, and R. L. Morris (Eds.), *Research in parapsychology 1976.* Metuchen, New Jersey: Scarecrow Press, 1977. Pp. 142–146.

Stanford, R. G., and Lovin, C. EEG alpha activity and ESP performance. *Journal of the American Society for Psychical Research*, 1970, *64*, 375–384.

Stanford, R. G., and Mayer, B. Relaxation as a psi-conducive state: A replication and exploration of parameters. *Journal of the American Society for Psychical Research*, 1974, *68*, 182–191.

Stanford, R. G., and Neylon, A. Experiential factors related to free-response clairvoyance performance in a sensory uniformity setting (ganzfeld). In J. D. Morris, W. G. Roll, and R. L. Morris (Eds.), *Research in parapsychology 1974.* Metuchen, New Jersey: Scarecrow Press, 1975. Pp. 89–93.

Stanford, R. G., and Palmer, J. Meditation prior to the ESP task: An EEG study with an outstanding ESP subject. In W. G. Roll, R. L. Morris, and J. D. Morris (Eds.), *Research in parapsychology 1972.* Metuchen, New Jersey: Scarecrow Press, 1973. Pp. 34–36.

Stanford, R. G., and Palmer, J. Free-response ESP performance and occipital alpha rhythms. *Journal of the American Society for Psychical Research*, 1975, *69*, 235–243.

Stanford, R. G., and Rust, P. Psi-mediated helping behavior: Experimental paradigm and initial results. In J. D. Morris, W. G. Roll, and R. L. Morris (Eds.), *Research in parapsychology 1976.* Metuchen, New Jersey: Scarecrow Press, 1977. Pp. 109–110.

Stanford, R. G., and Stanford, B. E. Shifts in EEG alpha rhythm as related to calling patterns in ESP run-score variance. *Journal of Parapsychology*, 1969, *33*, 39–47.

Stanford, R. G., and Stevenson, I. EEG correlates of free-response GESP in an individual subject. *Journal of the American Society for Psychical Research*, 1972, *66*, 357–368.

Stanford, R. G., and Stio, A. A study of associative mediation in psi-mediated instrumental response. *Journal of the American Society for Psychical Research*, 1976, *70*, 55–64.

Stanford, R. G., and Thompson, G. Unconscious psi-mediated instrumental response and its relation to conscious ESP performance. In W. G. Roll, R. L. Morris, and J. D. Morris (Eds.), *Research in parapsychology 1973.* Metuchen, New Jersey: Scarecrow Press, 1974. Pp. 99–103.

Steilberg, B. J. Investigation of the paranormal gifts of the Dutch sensitive Lida T. *Journal of Parapsychology*, 1971, *35*, 219–225.

Stephenson, C. J. Cambridge ESP-hypnosis experiments 1958–1964. *Journal of the Society for Psychical Research*, 1965, *43*, 77–91.

Stevenson, I. An antagonist's view of parapsychology. A review of Professor Hansel's *ESP: A scientific evaluation. Journal of the American Society for Psychical Research*, 1967, *61*, 254–267.

Stevenson, I. *Telepathic impressions: A review and report of thirty-five new cases.* Charlottesville: University Press of Virginia, 1970.

Stoyva, J., and Kamiya, J. Electrophysiological studies of dreaming as the prototype of a new strategy in the study of consciousness. *Psychological Review*, 1968, *75*, 192–205.

Stuart, C. E. The effect of rate of movement in card matching tests of extra-sensory perception. *Journal of Parapsychology*, 1938, *2*, 171–183.

Stuart, C. E. An examination of Kennedy's study of the MacFarland data. *Journal of Parapsychology*, 1940, *4*, 135–141.

Stuart, C. E. An analysis to determine a test predictive of extra-chance scoring in card-calling tests. *Journal of Parapsychology*, 1941, *5*, 99–137.

Stuart, C. E. A classroom ESP experiment with the free response method. *Journal of Parapsychology*, 1945, *9*, 92–105.

Stuart, C. E. GESP experiments with the free-response method. *Journal of Parapsychology*, 1946, *10*, 21–35. (a)

Stuart, C. E. An interest inventory relation to ESP scores. *Journal of Parapsychology*, 1946, *10*, 154–161. (b)

Stuart, C. E. A second classroom ESP experiment with the free response method. *Journal of Parapsychology*, 1947, *11*, 14–25.

Stuart, C. E., and Smith, B. M. A second study of the effect of tempo rates of matching. *Journal of Parapsychology*, 1942, *6*, 220–231.

Stuart, C. E., Humphrey, B. M., Smith, B. M., and McMahan, E. Personality measurements and ESP tests with cards and drawings. *Journal of Parapsychology*, 1947, *11*, 118–146.

Stump, J. P., Roll, W. G., and Roll, M. Some exploratory forced-choice ESP experiments with Lalsingh Harribance. *Journal of the American Society for Psychical Research*, 1970, *64*, 421–431.

Szczygielski, D., and Schmeidler, G. ESP and two measures of introversion. In J. D. Morris, W. G. Roll, and R. L. Morris (Eds.), *Research in parapsychology 1974*. Metuchen, New Jersey: Scarecrow Press, 1975. Pp. 15–17.

Taddonio, J. L. Attitudes and expectancies in ESP scoring. *Journal of Parapsychology*, 1975, *39*, 289–296.

Taddonio, J. L. The relationship of experimenter expectancy to performance on ESP tasks. *Journal of Parapsychology*, 1976, *40*, 107–114.

Taddonio, J. L., and O'Brien, D. P. Psi in the classroom: A replication and extension. In J. D. Morris, W. G. Roll, and R. L. Morris (Eds.), *Research in parapsychology 1976*. Metuchen, New Jersey: Scarecrow Press, 1977. Pp. 140–142.

Taetzsch, R. L. *Sheep–goat and decline results of computer-scored audience responses*. Paper presented at the Seventh Annual Convention of the Parapsychological Association, Oxford, England, 1964. (Abstract in *Journal of Parapsychology*, 1964, *28*, 277–278.)

Taetzsch, R. L. *A computer-scored experiment in precognition with company presidents*. Paper presented at the Eighth Annual Convention of the Parapsychological Association, New York, 1965. (Abstract in *Journal of Parapsychology*, 1965, *29*, 288–289.)

Targ, R., and Cole, P. Use of an automatic stimulus generator to teach extrasensory perception. In J. D. Morris, W. G. Roll, and R. L. Morris (Eds.), *Research in parapsychology 1974*. Metuchen, New Jersey: Scarecrow Press, 1975. Pp. 27–29.

Targ, R., and Hurt, D. B. Learning clairvoyance and precognition with an ESP teaching machine. In W. G. Roll, R. L. Morris, and J. D. Morris (Eds.), *Proceedings of the Parapsychological Association No. 8, 1971*. Durham, North Carolina: Parapsychological Association, 1972. Pp. 9–11.

Targ, R., and Puthoff, H. Information transmission under conditions of sensory shielding. *Nature*, 1974, *251*, 602–607.

Targ, R., and Puthoff, H. *Mind-reach*. New York: Delacorte, 1977.

Tart, C. T. Physiological correlates of psi cognition. *International Journal of Parapsychology*, 1963, *5*, 375–386.

Tart, C. T. Card guessing tests: Learning paradigm or extinction paradigm? *Journal of the American Society for Psychical Research*, 1966, *60*, 46–55.

Tart, C. T. A second psychophysiological study of out-of-the-body experiences in a gifted subject. *International Journal of Parapsychology*, 1967, *9*, 251–258.

Tart, C. T. A psychophysiological study of out-of-the-body experiences in a selected subject. *Journal of the American Society for Psychical Research*, 1968, *62*, 3–27.

Tart, C. T. *On being stoned: A psychological study of marijuana intoxication*. Palo Alto: Science and Behavior Books, 1971.

Tart, C. T. *Learning to use extrasensory perception*. Chicago: University of Chicago Press, 1976. (a)

Tart, C. T. Review of *The magic of Uri Geller*, by the Amazing Randi; *The Geller papers: Scientific observations on the paranormal powers of Uri Geller*, by C. Panati (Ed.); and *Uri Geller: My story*, by U. Geller. *Psychology Today*, 1976, *10* (2), 93–94. (b)

Tart, C. T. Improving real time ESP by suppressing the future: Trans-temporal inhibition. In *The state of the art in psychic research*. New York: Institute of Electrical and Electronic Engineers, 1977. (a)

Tart, C. T. Toward humanistic experimentation in parapsychology: A reply to Dr. Stanford's review. *Journal of the American Society for Psychical Research*, 1977, *71*, 81–101. (b)

Taves, E. Some paranormal experiences of hyperthyroid subjects. *Journal of the American Society for Psychical Research*, 1944, *38*, 123–138.

Taves, E., and Dale, L. A. The Midas touch in psychical research. *Journal of the American Society for Psychical Research*, 1943, *37*, 57–83.

Taves, E., Dale, L. A., and Murphy, G. A further report on the Midas touch. *Journal of the American Society for Psychical Research*, 1943, *37*, 111–118.

Tenhaeff, W. H. C. Summary of the results of a psychodiagnostic investigation of forty paragnosts. *Proceedings of the Parapsychological Institute of the State University of Utrecht*, No. 2, 1962.

Terry, J. C. Comparison of stimulus duration in sensory and psi conditions. In J. D. Morris, W. G. Roll, and R. L. Morris (Eds.), *Research in parapsychology 1975*. Metuchen, New Jersey: Scarecrow Press, 1976. Pp. 179–181. (a)

Terry, J. C. Continuation of the rodent precognition experiments. In J. D. Morris, W. G. Roll, and R. L. Morris (Eds.), *Research in parapsychology 1975*. Metuchen, New Jersey: Scarecrow Press, 1976. Pp. 11–14. (b)

Terry, J. C., and Harris, S. A. Precognition in water-deprived rats. In J. D. Morris, W. G. Roll, and R. L. Morris (Eds.), *Research in parapsychology 1974*. Metuchen, New Jersey: Scarecrow Press, 1975. P. 81.

Terry, J. C., and Honorton, C. Psi information retrieval in the ganzfeld: Two confirmatory studies. *Journal of the American Society for Psychical Research*, 1976, *70*, 207–217.

Terry, J. (C.), Tremmel, L., Kelly, M., Harper, S., and Barker, P. L. Psi information rate in guessing and receiver optimization. In J. D. Morris, W. G. Roll, and R. L. Morris (Eds.), *Research in parapsychology 1975*. Metuchen, New Jersey: Scarecrow Press, 1976. Pp. 194–198.

Thouless, R. H. A comparative study of performance in three psi tasks. *Journal of Parapsychology*, 1949, *13*, 263–273.

Thouless, R. H. An examination of the Humphrey–Nicol experiments on the feeling of success in ESP. *Journal of the American Society for Psychical Research*, 1956, *50*, 34–39.

Thouless, R. H. Experiments on psi self-training with Dr. Schmidt's precognitive apparatus. *Journal of the Society for Psychical Research*, 1971, *46*, 15–21.

Thouless, R. H. The effect of the experimenter's attitude on experimental results in parapsychology. *Journal of the Society for Psychical Research*, 1976, *48*, 261–266.

Timm, U. Mixing-up of symbols in ESP card experiments (so-called consistent missing) as a possible cause for psi-missing. *Journal of Parapsychology*, 1969, *33*, 109–124.

Treurniet, W. C., and Craig, J. G. Precognition as a function of environmental enrichment and time of the lunar month. In J. D. Morris, W. G. Roll, and R. L. Morris (Eds.), *Research in parapsychology 1974*. Metuchen, New Jersey: Scarecrow Press, 1975. Pp. 100–102.

Turner, M. E. A space–time experiment. *Psychics International*, 1964, *1*, 71–77. (Abstract in *Journal of Parapsychology*, 1965, *29*, 67.)

Tyrrell, G. N. M. Further research in extrasensory perception. *Proceedings of the Society for Psychical Research*, 1936, *44*, 99–168.

Ullman, M., and Krippner, S. A laboratory approach to the nocturnal dimension of paranormal experience: Report of a confirmatory study using the REM monitoring technique. *Biological Psychiatry*, 1969, *1*, 259–270.

Ullman, M., Krippner, S., and Feldstein, S. Experimentally-induced telepathic dreams: Two studies using EEG-REM monitoring techniques. In G. R. Schmeidler (Ed.), *Extrasensory perception*. New York: Atherton, 1969.

Ullman, M., Krippner, S., and Honorton, C. A review of the Maimonides dream ESP experiments: 1964–1969. *Psychophysiology*, 1970, *7*, 352–353. (Abstract)

Ullman, M., Krippner, S., and Vaughan, A. *Dream telepathy*. New York: Macmillan, 1973.

van Asperen de Boer, S. R., Barkema, P. R., and Kappers, J. Is it possible to induce ESP with psilocybin? An exploratory investigation. *International Journal of Neuropsychiatry*, 1966, *2*, 447–473.

Van Busschbach, J. G. An investigation of extrasensory perception in school children. *Journal of Parapsychology*, 1953, *17*, 210–214.

Van Busschbach, J. G. A further report on an investigation of ESP in school children. *Journal of Parapsychology*, 1955, *19*, 73–81.

Van Busschbach, J. G. An investigation of ESP between teacher and pupils in American schools. *Journal of Parapsychology*, 1956, *20*, 71–80.

Van Busschbach, J. G. An investigation of ESP in the first and second grades of Dutch schools. *Journal of Parapsychology*, 1959, *23*, 227–237.

Van Busschbach, J. G. An investigation of ESP in first and second grades in American schools. *Journal of Parapsychology*, 1961, *25*, 161–174.

Van de Castle, R. L. An exploratory study of some variables relating to individual ESP performance. *Journal of Parapsychology*, 1953, *17*, 61–72.

Van de Castle, R. L. Differential patterns of ESP scoring as a function of differential attitudes toward ESP. *Journal of the American Society for Psychical Research*, 1957, *51*, 43–61.

Van de Castle, R. L. The facilitation of ESP through hypnosis. *American Journal of Clinical Hypnosis*, 1969, *12*, 37–56.

Van de Castle, R. L. An investigation of GESP among the Cuna Indians of Panama. In W. G. Roll, R. L. Morris, and J. D. Morris (Eds.), *Proceedings of the Parapsychological Association No. 6, 1969*. Durham, North Carolina: Parapsychological Association, 1971. Pp. 3–4.

Van de Castle, R. L., and Davis, K. R. *The relationship of suggestibility to ESP scoring level*. Paper presented at the Fifth Annual Convention of the Parapsychological Association, Durham, 1962. (Abstract in *Journal of Parapsychology*, 1962, *26*, 270–271.)

Van de Castle, R. L., and White, R. R. A report on a sentence completion form of sheep–goat attitude scale. *Journal of Parapsychology*, 1955, *19*, 171–179.

Van't Hoff, R., *et al.* [The influence of four variables on telepathic perception, tested by the use of clock-face targets.] *Spiegel der Parapsychologie*, 1972, *2*, 54–66. (Abstract in *Journal of Parapsychology*, 1972, *36*, 252.)

Vasiliev, L. L. *Experiments in mental suggestion.* Hampshire, England: Institute for the Study of Mental Images, 1962.

Vasse, C., and Vasse, P. ESP tests with French first-grade school children. *Journal of Parapsychology*, 1958, *22*, 187–203.

Waldron, S. *Clairvoyance scores of sheep versus goats when subject's attitude toward the experimenter and the purpose of the experiments are manipulated.* Paper presented at the Second Annual Convention of the Parapsychological Association, New York, 1959. (Abstract in *Journal of Parapsychology*, 1959, *23*, 289.)

Wallwork. S. C. ESP experiments with simultaneous electroencephalographic recordings. *Journal of the Society for Psychical Research*, 1952, *36*, 697–701.

Warcollier, R. [A new test with combined targets without emotional value.] *Revue Métapsychique*, 1957, *1*, (6), 29–33 and 1958, *2* (8), 14–20. (Abstract in *Journal of Parapsychology*, 1962, *26*, 70–71.)

West, D. J. ESP performance and the expansion–compression rating. *Journal of the Society for Psychical Research*, 1950, *35*, 295–308.

West, D. J. ESP tests with psychotics. *Journal of the Society for Psychical Research*, 1952, *36*, 619–623.

West, D. J. Home-testing ESP experiments: An examination of displacement effects. *Journal of the Society for Psychical Research*, 1953, *37*, 14–25.

West, D. J. Comment on Dr. Figar's paper. *Journal of the Society for Psychical Research*, 1959, *40*, 172–174.

West, D. J., and Fisk, G. W. A dual ESP experiment with clock cards. *Journal of the Society for Psychical Research*, 1953, *37*, 185–189.

West, L. J. A general theory of hallucinations and dreams. In L. J. West (Ed.), *Hallucinations*. New York: Grune and Stratton, 1962.

White, R. (A.) A comparison of old and new methods of response to targets in ESP experiments. *Journal of the American Society for Psychical Research*, 1964, *58*, 21–56.

White, R. A. The influence of persons other than the experimenter on the subject's scores in psi experiments. *Journal of the American Society for Psychical Research*, 1976, *70*, 133–166. (a)

White, R. A. The limits of experimenter influence on psi test results: Can any be set? *Journal of the American Society for Psychical Research*, 1976, *70*, 333–369. (b)

White, R. (A.), and Angstadt, J. A résumé of research at the A.S.P.R. into teacher–pupil attitudes and clairvoyance test results. *Journal of the American Society for Psychical Research*, 1961, *55*, 142–147.

White, R. (A.), and Angstadt, J. A second classroom GESP experiment with student-agents acting simultaneously. *Journal of the American Society for Psychical Research*, 1963, *57*, 227–232. (a)

White, R. (A.), and Angstadt, J. Student preferences in a two classroom GESP experiment with two student-agents acting simultaneously. *Journal of the American Society for Psychical Research*, 1963, *57*, 32–42. (b)

White, R. A., and Angstadt, J. A review of results and new experiments bearing on teacher-selection methods in the Anderson–White high school experiments. *Journal of the American Society for Psychical Research*, 1965, *59*, 56–84.

Whittlesey, J. R. B. Some curious ESP results in terms of variance. *Journal of Parapsychology*, 1960, *24*, 220–222.

Wiesinger, C. [*Two ESP experiments in the classroom.*] Unpublished doctoral dissertation, Albert-Ludwigs University, Freiburg, Germany, 1971. (Abstract in *Journal of Parapsychology*, 1973, *37*, 76–77.)

Wiklund, N. Aftereffect perception, preconscious perception, and ESP. *Journal of Parapsychology*, 1975, *39*, 106–119.

Wiklund, N. Parapsychological temptations: A discussion on decline-effects, sex-effects, and post-hoc effects. In J. D. Morris, W. G. Roll, and R. L. Morris (Eds.), *Research in parapsychology 1976*. Metuchen, New Jersey: Scarecrow Press, 1977. Pp. 125–128.

Willis, J. Duncan, J., and Udofia, J. ESP in the classroom: Failure to replicate. *Psychological Reports*, 1974, *35*, 582.

Wilson, W. R. Do parapsychologists really believe in ESP? *Journal of Social Psychology*, 1964, *64*, 379–389.

Witkin, H. A., Dyk, R. B., Faterson, H. F., Goodenough, D. R., and Karp, S. A. *Psychological differentiation: Studies of development*. New York: Wiley, 1962.

Wood, G. H., and Cadoret, R. J. Tests of clairvoyance in a man–dog relationship. *Journal of Parapsychology*, 1958, *22*, 29–39.

Woodruff, J. L. ESP tests under various physiological conditions. *Journal of Parapsychology*, 1943, *7*, 264–271.

Woodruff, J. L., and Dale, L. A. Subject and experimenter attitudes in relation to ESP scoring. *Journal of the American Society for Psychical Research*, 1950, *44*, 87–112.

Woodruff, J. L., and Dale, L. A. ESP function and the psychogalvanic response. *Journal of the American Society for Psychical Research*, 1952, *46*, 62–65.

Woodruff, J. L., and George, R. W. Experiments in extrasensory perception. *Journal of Parapsychology*, 1937, *1*, 18–30.

Woodruff, J. L., and Murphy, G. Effect of incentives on ESP and visual perception. *Journal of Parapsychology*, 1943, *7*, 144–157.

York, M. S. The Defense Mechanism Test (DMT) as an indicator of psychic performance as measured by a free-response clairvoyance test using a ganzfeld technique. In J. D. Morris, W. G. Roll, and R. L. Morris (Eds.), *Research in parapsychology 1976*. Metuchen, New Jersey: Scarecrow Press, 1977. Pp. 48–49.

Zenhausern, R., Stanford, R. G., and Esposito, C. The application of signal detection theory to clairvoyance and precognition tasks. In J. D. Morris, W. G. Roll, and R. L. Morris (Eds.), *Research in parapsychology 1976*. Metuchen, New Jersey: Scarecrow Press, 1977. Pp. 170–173.

Zorab, G. ESP experiments with psychotics. *Journal of the Society for Psychical Research*, 1957, *39*, 162–164.

Theories of Psi   3

K. Ramakrishna Rao

1. Introduction

Parapsychological phenomena provide crucial evidence for the falsification of conventionally accepted assumptions concerning human nature. They contradict, as Broad (1953) pointed out, the basic limiting principles that are assumed to govern our cognitions and actions. For example, it is axiomatic, following the prevailing paradigm, that it is impossible for a person to perceive an object without being in a sensory contact with that object. This assumption entails that there can be no such thing as clairvoyance. However, if the existence of psi is independently established, it is tantamount to the falsification of any theory that implies its impossibility. But the acceptance or rejection of evidence is not always as objective and impersonal as one would think. The standards of evidence demanded are likely to vary with the stakes one has invested in terms of one's commitment to the alternate viewpoint.

Behind the resistance to psi and the reluctance to accept what would normally constitute compelling evidence for its existence is the perceived threat of the possible collapse of our secure assumptions concerning our own limitations. In other words, psi constitutes an anomaly in an otherwise relatively orderly universe. Such anomalies in time will precipitate a crisis and may bring about a revolution where the old theories are abandoned in favor of one that could explain the anomalies. Thomas Kuhn

K. Ramakrishna Rao • Institute for Parapsychology, Durham, North Carolina and Department of Psychology, Andhra University, Visakhapatnam, India. A version of this chapter appeared in the *Journal of Parapsychology*, December 1977. Copyright by K. Ramakrishna Rao, 1977.

(1962) in his important book *The Structure of Scientific Revolutions* traced the steps involved in the revolutionary developments of science. He demonstrated that unexplainable anomalies lead to the emergence of new paradigms, which enter into revolutionary struggles with the old ones. Sooner or later, science will have to face the parapsychological facts, for it cannot shut its eyes forever, however compelling the reason for doing so may be. Will this, when it happens, trigger a revolution in science and bring about a paradigmatic change?

There is no lack of theoretical speculation in parapsychology, In fact there are more theories than can be reviewed in this chapter. The primary concern of parapsychological theorizing so far has been directed toward explaining how psi may function relatively unaffected by time–space limitations (Rao, 1966). Some theorists have felt it necessary to postulate new entities, while a few others have expressed hope that an extension of the principles of the physical sciences will suffice to account for psi occurrences. Let us consider briefly some of these theories, (a) to see how successful they are in providing a reasonable explanation of psi phenomena and in suggesting ideas that permit experimental verification, and (b) to determine whether a paradigmatic change is called for or whether psi can be accommodated within the overall framework of the current paradigm by making suitable extensions to it.

2. Physical Theories

For some thinkers such as H. H. Price (1967), psi simply does not fit into a physicalistic world view. Consequently, no extension of "physical" principles would be able to provide a satisfactory explanation of psi. J. B. Rhine, who began in psychical research as a biological mechanist, says that he was eventually led by the cumulative results of psi testing to conclude that no physical correlates of psi have so far been found and confirmed. While Rhine recognizes that the absence of any reliable physical characteristic of psi does not warrant the conclusion that psi is absolutely extraphysical, he is impressed by the evidence that psi is nonphysical and will take such a viewpoint until such time as new research alters this picture. While this view is shared by several psi theorists, an increasing number in recent years seem to think that the nonphysical notion of psi is a reaction more to classical than to contemporary physics. In the "weird wonderland" of subatomic and supergalactic physics, as Koestler (1972) put it, phenomena that appear to be more "occultish" than psi are known to exist. It is therefore argued that no intrinsic incompatibility between physical laws and psi need be assumed and that the manifest anomalies may be resolved by suitably extending or amending physical principles.

Also, it makes sense that we first look into known energetic interactions for an understanding of psi before postulating more esoteric entities or energies. There are a number of early attempts to find physical explanations of psi within the boundaries of electromagnetism and, more recently, by extending quantum physical theories.

2.1. Electromagnetic Theory of Telepathy

The possibility of telepathic communication between minds naturally suggests some form of transmission from one brain to another in a manner analogous to radio. It has long been known that electrical processes take place in the cerebral cortex. In 1929, Berger (1940) showed that rhythmic electrical currents emanate from the brain and that they can be detected at the surface of the scalp by the electroencephalograph, which he invented. This fact suggested the possibility that in a telepathic experiment, the brain of the agent may emit electromagnetic waves corresponding to his or her thought patterns, and that these waves may be afferently received and interpreted by the subject.

One of the objections to an electromagnetic theory of telepathy is that, if there is any transmission of energy between two brains, it must be subject to the inverse square law: that the intensity of an energetic transmission decreases with the square of the distance. But it does not appear that telepathic communication decreases with the square of the distance between the agent and the subject. Successful experiments have been carried out at great distances, and this has been considered sufficient justification for regarding psi as a nonphysical phenomenon. This objective was answered by Hoffman (1940), who argued that while the intensity of an energetic transmission decreases with the square of the distance, its intelligibility (or information) is not greatly affected by distance. Moreover, it is possible to intensify the signals weakened by distance in the same way that "automatic volume controls" are used in radio broadcasts.

The distinguished Soviet physiologist, L. L. Vasiliev (1963/1976), discusses in his book *Experiments in Distant Influence* the attempts of Cazzamalli, Kajinsky, and others to explain telepathy in terms of electromagnetic theory. The Italian neurologist Cazzamalli carried out experiments that indicated to him that the human brain under certain conditions may radiate electromagnetic energy in the form of detectable radio waves of .7 to 100 m. In a case of telepathic transmission, it is assumed that these radio brain waves, emanating from the agent, travel and penetrate into the brain of the subject and excite the cortical center.

The difficulty of finding bioelectric processes that are capable of generating the high-frequency cerebral waves of 10 cm to 1-m wavelength, which would be required for placing any confidence in Cazzamalli's theory, led Kajinsky and others to postulate that the neuron system is vibratory in its nature and that there are closed electric circuits in the nervous system. The basic assumptions of Kajinsky, to quote Vasiliev (1963/1976), are:

1. Both open and closed vibratory currents of the neurons may be interconnected by mutual induction, and the effect in such interaction is marked by the occurrence of combined oscillations as a result of which a detectable electromagnetic wave is generated.
2. The entire nervous system represents one combined system of neuron chains that generate one composite electromagnetic wave.
3. Every thought is accompanied, in the central nervous system, by the generation of electromagnetic waves.
4. The electromagnetic waves of one brain can be afferently received by another brain and excite therein a corresponding psychoneural experience. (p. 27)

Thus, according to Kajinsky, telepathy is caused by the transmission of electromagnetic waves between the agent and the subject by means of a process which he calls "electro-duction."

The results of Vasiliev's own experiments provide evidence against the electromagnetic theory of telepathy. Vasiliev attempted to induce hypnosis in his subjects by telepathy. In a series of experiments, the subject and the hypnotist were placed in metal cabinets, situated in different rooms, which shielded any possible electromagnetic waves within the range of ultrashort, short, and medium wavelengths. The subjects in these experiments were highly successful in responding to the experimenter's telepathic suggestions. The use of the metal cabinets did not produce any diminishing effect on the results. When the experimenter and the subject were separated by as many as 1,700 kilometers, the subject still was successful in responding to telepathic suggestion. Vasiliev's experiments thus rule out the possibility that any short- or ultra-short-wave transmission is associated with telepathy. And it has not been shown that the human brain can emit any long waves that can penetrate metal cabinets. Vasiliev (1963/1976) writes:

Contrary to all expectation, screening by metal did not cause any even faintly perceptible weakening of telepathic transmission. Even under conditions of double screening mental suggestion [telepathy] continued to act with the same degree of effectiveness as without screening. . . . Is it necessary to emphasize that such a conclusion may be of tremendous theoretical importance? According to our conclusion the Cazzamalli "brain wireless waves," if in fact they exist, have no connection whatever with the phenomena of mental suggestion. It follows that the energetic factor in telepathic transmission must be sought in quite a different region of the electromagnetic spectrum: either in the region of radiations with a shorter wave (Röentgen or gamma-rays) which is improbable, or alternatively in the region of kilometre waves, or of static electric fields. However, the possibility of these last two factors playing a part also is hardly feasible. (pp. 126–127)

It should be mentioned, however, that there have been attempts in recent years to postulate electromagnetic waves of the sort that would account for telepathy within the framework of information theory. Another Soviet scientist, I. M. Kogan (1966, 1967, 1968), argues, for example, that "there are reasons for assuming that the existence of telepathy does not contradict the laws of nature, and its carrier could be the electromagnetic field of extra-long waves excited by biocurrents" (1966, p. 81).

2.2. Psychical Energy and Resonance

A variant of electromagnetic theory postulates that cortical changes may be transformed into new forms of energy that escape the limitations of ordinary physical states. For example, Berger (1940), who thought that the changes of electrical brain potential were too small to explain telepathy at great distances, postulated the concept of psychical energy that could travel immense distances and affect brains without itself being affected by the obstructing objects. Berger hypothesized that the physical changes in one's brain might be transformed into *psychical* energies, which, propagating through space in a wavelike manner, could reach another brain and invoke in it mental experiences similar to those of the former. The observations that artificial stimulation of certain cortical parts is known to give rise to subjective experiences and that mental activities seem to involve expending of physical energies suggested to Berger the possibility that psychical energy is but a transformation of the physical activity in the cortex. Berger envisages a reciprocal transformation in which not only do the physical conditions in the brain create consciousness but consciousness also in its turn produces physical changes in other brains. This conversion of physical energy into psychical energy and vice versa explains telepathic transmission, according to Berger. The question as to why telepathic messages from one brain are not received by all living brains is answered by the assumption that the receptivity of one brain to another depends on the sensitivity of the one to the other. This sensitivity may be explained in terms of "resonance," but Berger does not say what the conditions for this "resonance" are. This task was accomplished by Ninian Marshall.

Attempting to explain telepathy in physical terms, Marshall (1960) points out that just as new physical laws are required to account for the behavior of subatomic bodies and those whose speed approaches that of light, new laws may be required to explain the behavior of bodies that attain certain levels of complexity. Marshall postulates that two complex structures with a sufficient degree of similarity, such as two human brains, could act on one another by some kind of direct resonance without being subject to the obstructions of space and time. In the words of Marshall, "any two structures exert an influence on each other which tends to make them become more alike. The strength of this influence increases with the product of their complexities, and decreases with the difference between their patterns" (p. 266). Resonance, then, of a pattern in one brain with another leads to telepathy. The erratic and often distorted as well as unconscious nature of telepathy may be explained, according to Marshall, by the possibility that the brain may resonate with many other structures, resulting in much loss and distortion of the original information. Marshall goes on to suggest that strong resonance from one brain to another may be facilitated by having close relatives act as the subject and the agent or by using emotionally toned material for communication.

The difficulty with Marshall's theory, as with other physical theories, is that in his attempt to find a channel for psi communication, he is led to postulate an interaction that does not require a physical connection between the interacting agencies. Consequently, any energetic interaction involved in such a communication is necessarily acausal. Berger's psychic energy and Marshall's law of resonance, insofar as they transcend time–space obstructions, also transcend causal laws that operate at the level of our communication. Furthermore, what kind of a transmission is possible between an inanimate object like an ESP card and the subject in a clairvoyance test? A card is not complex enough to resonate, nor does it possess consciousness with which to produce psychic energy. All available evidence suggests that telepathy and clairvoyance are not two distinct processes but the same phenomenon manifesting under two different conditions.

2.3. "Physical" Field Theory

Among the field theories of psi, there are some that make use of theoretical constructs in physics, while others postulate nonphysical fields. Wassermann (1956) has no sympathy for the latter. He firmly believes that the vitalist assumptions that postulate a new realm of phenomena different from the physicochemical are unwarranted and that parapsychological phenomena can be explained by the theoretical constructs of physics.

Wassermann postulates a variety of fields to account for various phenomena in biology, psychology, and parapsychology. Among these are the behavior fields or B-fields, psi-fields, and P-fields. The B-fields are associated with neural activity, and they are postulated to explain psychological behavior. Psi-fields, which enable one to have psi experiences, have properties similar to B-fields, but they have "very narrowly spaced energy levels" and occupy "wide regions of space." Psi-fields, according to Wassermann, emit and receive "extremely small quanta of energy"—smaller than the quanta that can be absorbed by matter fields. "Consequently psi-fields could radiate their energy over long distances without it becoming absorbed by matter fields" (1956, p. 66).

Making use of psi-fields, Wassermann explains telepathy this way: When the agent (A) makes a telepathic contact with the subject (S), A's B-field excites a specific psi-field, which in turn excites a corresponding B-field in S. Since telepathic experiences do not always occur, and since time gaps between A's experience and B's experience exist occasionally, Wassermann suggests that the energy transition from one state to another is not always possible and that an excited B-field must wait for suitable circumstances to arise so that it can interact with other fields.

Wassermann postulates P-fields to explain clairvoyance. P-fields are specific energy fields bound to matter fields corresponding to target objects. In clairvoyance, the following chain of processes takes place between the object and the subject. The P-field of an object excites a specific psi-field, which in turn excites a B-field in the subject, causing a clairvoyant experience.

This all sounds very logical, but the question is: Do such fields exist? In spite of Wasserman's rigorous attempts to associate these fields with quantum physics, there can be no doubt that psi-fields have little in common with electromagnetic fields, meson fields, etc. This is not, however, a sufficient reason to reject his hypothesis. What is needed is a deductive development of the hypothesis to arrive at experimentally verifiable predictions.

Wassermann's theory also includes an explanation for precognition. He assumes that the fields (matter fields, electromagnetic fields, psi-fields, B-fields, etc.), which account for all observable events, become duplicated. These "copies," he further suggests, can make faster transitions than their "originals" and thus are potentially capable of giving advance information of field events that will occur only later as far as the originals are concerned. When the copying fields excite psi-fields—and through them the B-fields of a suitable subject—the subject will have a precognitive experience.

Wassermann's hypothesis of precognition, like his explanation of clairvoyance and telepathy, is consistent within itself. Whether such fields do exist and whether they are capable of making the kind of transitions required for them to explain psi phenomena is something that cannot be affirmed or denied without deducing testable implications of the theory. Until then, this theory remains an interesting speculation.

2.4. Quantum Physical Theories

Taking the lead from quantum physics, Dobbs (1965, 1967), among others, argues that there is no intrinsic reason to assume that psi is non-physical. He contests the contention of H. H. Price (1967) that no materialistic explanation of telepathy is feasible because it would assume that some sort of physical radiation is involved in any telepathic communication, and furthermore, that if there are such physical radiations, (a) they should be detectable and (b) the intensity of these supposed radiations should vary with the distance between the agent and the subject. Dobbs (1967) points out:

> According to current quantum theory, whenever a particle or other physical entity is interacting with an electromagnetic or nuclear field of force the interaction takes place through the medium and intervention of the so-called virtual particles, which can have mathematically imaginary mass or momentum . . . . But no one would suggest that these virtual particles . . . could be *directly* detected in any ordinary piece of physical apparatus. Their occurrence has to be *inferred* from the experimental results interpreted in the light of the fundamental physical principles. But this fact about virtual particles does not make them any less *physically* real or *material* than an electron or a neutrino. (p. 247)

Again, "there are physical influences whose intensity is not diminished by the distance over which they have travelled, e.g., the current in a super-conductor . . ." (1967, p. 240). Thus, according to Dobbs, there is no prima facie reason for ruling out a physical explanation of psi. In fact, he goes on to propose one.

2.4.1. Psitrons

Briefly, Dobbs' theory of telepathy is as follows. The cortical excitations in the brain of the agent emit a cloud of particles of imaginary mass which Dobbs calls "psitrons." Insofar as they have only mathematically imaginary mass or energy, psitrons, unlike particles with real mass, are not subject to frictional loss of energy when they travel across physical distances. These psitrons can interact with particles having real mass. In a telepathic situation, the psitrons emitted by the agent's brain impinge on certain neurons that are in a state of unstable equilibrium in the subject's brain and cause a telepathic response. Dobbs here elaborates on the ideas of Eccles concerning the "critically poised neurones" in his theory of "will." Eccles (1953) envisages that a change brought about in a single critically poised neuron in the cortex could cause considerable changes in the activity of the brain and trigger off a chain reaction culminating in an overt response. Dobbs writes: "Now my suggestion is that in certain synaptic contacts between cerebral neurones, at Eccles' critically effective level of excitation, there are particles so delicately poised that they can be caused to trigger off a cascade or chain reaction of neurone discharge, in consequence of capturing particles of imaginary mass" (1965, p. 342).

"The physical basis for ESP would then consist in the interactions between the ordinary particles of mathematically real rest mass (such as the molecular micro-constituents) of a human brain and a gas of particles of mathematically imaginary mass, such interactions triggering the unexpected firing of Eccles' 'critically poised' neurones." (1967, p. 252).

In order to successfully receive a telepathic transmission, the subject, Dobbs (1965) goes on to say, "should be in a properly sensitive state, in which the tiny changes of kinetic energy, produced by capture of particles of imaginary mass by a few particles of real mass (such as orbital electrons of molecules in synaptic junctions), could trigger off a neurone chain reaction, giving rise to an observable modification of some sort in a percipient subject" (p. 343).

Dobbs offers an explanation for precognition as well. Pointing out that a two-dimensional theory of time is "a natural corollary of the admission of imaginary values for energy in physics" (1967, p. 249), he argues that precognition follows the second dimension of time. On this dimension "objective probabilities" play the same role as causal relations in classical physics. Objective probabilities in quantum mechanics mean "*propensities* which influence the outcomes of eventualities in a statistical way . . ." (1967, p. 250). The objective probabilities are contained or "precast" in the second dimension of time. They "predispose the future to occur in certain specific ways" (1967, p. 250). In a precognition situation, these precast dispositional factors are conveyed to the subject through the medium of psitrons. Precognition then is an awareness of "objective probabilities which serve as precasts of future event possibilities" (1967, p. 250). According to this theory, the future therefore is not "predetermined"; it is "predeterminate."

Beloff (1970) criticizes this theory on the ground that physical hypotheses such as Dobbs' do not explain the selection process involved in responding to the right target when there are so many potential targets. As he puts it:

> For the crux of the problem, as I see it, lies, not so much in specifying what kind of energy might surmount spatial and temporal distances or material barriers, but rather in explaining how it comes about that the subject is able to discriminate the target from the infinite number of other objects in his environment. Perhaps my point can best be illustrated with the help of an analogy. Imagine that sound waves were no longer attenuated with distance. It would

follow that every conversation going on for miles around would be equally
audible to you. But by this very fact, every conversation would be equally
unintelligible. Because, of course, every sound would mask every other sound!
By the same token, the closer the physicalists get to explaining the channel
through which the subject receives information of the target, the harder it
becomes to explain how the target is singled out from all the other potential
sources of information. And on this crucial question, none of the physical
theories, however imaginative or ingenious, seems to provide a clue. If telepathy were the only variety of ESP that we need to consider, the situation would
not be so acute, since it would not be quite so difficult to conceive of two
brains acting in resonance with one another; and, not surprisingly, most of the
physicalists do concentrate on telepathy. But when we come to consider clairvoyance, as we must even if Dobbs prefers to ignore it, then the difficulty
becomes so unfathomable that there seems no alternative but to declare that
we are here confronted with a case of information transmission without physical mediation! (p. 138–139)

But it should be pointed out in fairness to Dobbs that the problem of
selection is not peculiar to physical explanations of psi alone. The problem is no less acute with nonphysical theories such as those of Price,
which involve collective unconscious and the like. In fact, Dobbs' explanation here is more satisfactory than several others. He would argue that
the emission of psitrons is of a purely fluctuational character. "From the
standpoint of physics, [fluctuation is] a chance phenomenon for which
one cannot give a fixed rule prescribing its occurrence in advance"
(Dobbs, 1967, p. 254). This theory then implies that psi will ever remain
elusive and unpredictable and "rules out the possibility of harnessing ESP
as a new means of systematic communication analogous to ordinary
radio" (1967, p. 253).

The weakness of the theory, it would appear, is that ESP seems to
occur both unintentionally and sometimes predictably. The unintentional-
ity rules out the exercise of will to emit the necessary psitrons on the
model of Eccles and the discovery of certain relationships between ESP
and such variables as personality mitigates against the contention that
psitron emission is purely fluctuational.

Despite the characteristic quantum approach of Dobbs, his theory in
many respects is similar to that of Berger. The emission of psitrons in
Dobbs' theory parallels the conversion of cortical activity into psychic
energy in Berger's theory. The psychic energy is conceived as having to
have the characteristics that transcend the inhibitory influence of spatial
distance and it may be assumed that it would influence the cortical states
of the recipient subject in telepathy much the same way as psitrons are
supposed to affect the subject. Of course, Berger did not have the advantage of knowing about Eccles's findings.

Dobbs points out interesting test implications of his theory and argues that it can be falsified if "no correlative phase change [in EEG patterns] can be established in the coherent after discharges of [subjects'] frontal lobes in the case of responses scoring 'hits' above chance . . ." (1965, p. 340). This implication makes the dubious assumption that detectable cortical activity is associated with psi-hitting that can be electroencephalographically distinguished from the activity associated with mere guessing, and that this is an essential aspect of this theory as opposed to others. This reasoning needs to be further stretched to account for psi-missing, which is neither hitting nor mere guessing. While some kind of meaningful cortical activity is no doubt implied by Dobbs' theory, it would be hard to be convinced that his theory would be verified if psi-hitting is found to correlate significantly with EEG phase change. Such an observation would easily fit into any nonphysical hypothesis that considers psi as a result of mind–body interaction, because such an interaction would also imply systematic cortical activity during psi manifestations.

The difficulty with these quantum theories of psi is that they assume that the underlying unpredictability at the quantum level may be extended to nonquantum situations. It should be remembered that while quantum theory explains certain anomalies at the subatomic level, as far as the world of our experience is concerned its implications are hardly different from those of classical physics. So any extensions of quantum principles to explain the phenomena at the level of our experience is no less inconsistent with quantum theory than it is with the classical physics.

2.4.2. Hidden Variables

Walker (1970, 1972a,b, 1975) worked out a comprehensive theory of psi that attempts to explain ESP as well as PK. This theory, an extension of Walker's theory of consciousness, is based on the concept of hidden variables in quantum mechanics.

It may be pointed out that classical mechanics assumes that the future state of a physical system can be determined if we have a complete description of the preceding state of the system. In quantum mechanics, however, a given system develops into one of several possible subsequent states and, according to the widely accepted Copenhagen interpretation, the ultimate description or the state vector of the system incorporates all the potential states. However, when a measurement or "observation" is made of the system, the state vector loses this undefined probabilistic quality and gets "reduced" to one real outcome. Unfortunately, the mathematical formalism of quantum mechanics does not specify what exactly constitutes an "observation," and the resulting difficulties lead to the well-known "measurement problem" in quantum mechanics.

One attempt to overcome this problem is to introduce hidden variables that will reconcile the demands of deterministic and stochastic conceptions of the development of the state vector. These hidden variables are conceived to be essentially inaccessible to physical measurement, and to function independently of space–time constraints. In addition, they are so overconstrained in the determination of the collapse of the state vector for a given physical event that separate observers of that event must enter the same resultant state of the system regardless of their spatial separation or lack of direct "physical" interaction.

Walker identifies the hidden variables with consciousness and argues that the specification of these variables by the act of observation renders the physical system deterministic and that prior to such a specification the system is probabilistic. To quote Walker (1975):

> . . . quantum mechanics states that any physical system such as the brain, as a physical object, develops (through the motion and interaction of the constituent particles) with time from any given configuration into a large number of *potential* states. Which of these states actually becomes the observable physical reality is not determined by physical constraints. The development of the system, the brain, is probabilistic. But upon observation (to use the physicists' term), that is, upon the specification of the values of the c_i hidden variables, the consciousness, the state vector is collapsed onto a single component state. The various potential states become the single physical state of the brain. This process continues at such a rapid rate as to present a continuous stream of consciousness. (p. 8)

The hidden variables that bring about the physical changes that cannot be accounted for by any physical variable are equated with the "will," by which Walker means "that part of man's conscious experience postulated to allow him to assert some control over physical events" (1975, p. 9). Walker goes on to argue that "will" can effect changes not only within one's brain but also in the world outside, inasmuch as the brain through its sensory inputs is connected with the external world and therefore forms a part of a larger physical system (described by a collection of state potentialities) which includes both of them and which must be resolved into one single resultant state collectively.

The possibility, then, that observation may bring about a particular state of a physical system out of several possible ones suggests that the observers of the process are not independent and that they are linked with each other insofar as they must agree on the final state of the system. This linking or "coupling" is maintained by the hidden variables via the "will" channel. Since the hidden variables are "nonlocal," not constrained by space–time factors, they are capable of coupling observers separated by distance and time. In telepathy "the will of the subject and the experimenter act together to select the particular state into which the system is collapsed" (1975, p. 10). This means that a successful outcome in a telepathic trial is achieved by the hidden variables. Channeled through the will of the experimenter, the subject, and perhaps the agent, these variables cause a collapse of the state vector which results in an identical call-target state, i.e., a hit. In other words, what is affected is the quantum mechanical process in the brain of the subject. The same process accounts for clairvoyance, because in both clairvoyance and telepathy there is no message transmitted in the usual sense but "a future state is being selected."

Psychokinesis is explained as a process where the will (the hidden variables) of the subject/experimenter determines the collapse of state vector for a physical system at the quantum level with macroscopically diverse potential states. As Walker (1975) puts it, "psychokinesis involves the same basic process as clairvoyance with one change. The system affected is not a quantum mechanical process in the brain determining the call made, but the effect is produced in a physical process that has the character of being *divergent*. The uncertainty in the initial state of the system as imposed by quantum mechanics leads to macroscopically (observably) different potential states" (p. 11).

According to Walker's theory, the magnitude of a psi effect depends on the amount of information transferred through the will channel and the amount needed to collapse the state vector of the given system. The quantum theory of consciousness provides an estimate for the information rate of the will, which is a small part of the total conscious and subconscious mental activity. Since the will data are embedded in total conscious activity, the strength of a psi effect depends on the observers' abilities to utilize the will data. Thus, in principle, quantitative predictions about experimental results can be made based upon a detailed analysis of the psi task and an estimate of the observers' abilities.

Walker's theory is a gallant attempt to explain psi by means of concepts consistent with modern physics. Walker brings together an expertise in theoretical physics and a fair knowledge of parapsychological literature—not a very common combination. Although his theory is the most testable to come out of modern physics, acceptance or rejection may take some time. In applying the theory, the logic is very complicated, the calculations can be quite complex, and many often questionable assumptions and approximations must be made. Also, application of the theory exemplifies the difficulties in testing hypotheses about the psi "channel." As yet, the theory tells essentially nothing about the psychological factors needed for identifying and increasing utilization of the will data, and testing the theory requires very speculative assumptions about the various observers' psi abilities and psychological states. At present, the main difficulty in parapsychological research lies in controlling the psychological characteristics of those involved and this limits the inferences that can be drawn concerning the details of the "channel." Difficulties also arise from the assumptions the theory makes. For example, Walker states "that paranormal phenomena must involve some fundamental 'physical' process and yet clearly become manifest as a part of the will of sentient beings . . ." (1975, p. 34). These assumptions are not as compelling as Walker seems to think.

It is interesting to note that a theory like Walker's, which is said to be an extension of the Copenhagen interpretation of quantum physics, sounds clearly dualistic. The "will" and the "hidden variables" seem to have the same ontological primacy as energy, which accounts for the events in the material world. That the "will" influences only the microlevel quantum systems that rarely manifest in macroscopic physical systems is beside the point. What is important is that even "physical" theories do seem to assume principles or processes that are not a mere extension of what is ordinarily understood as physical, but things that are commonly regarded as mental on a Cartesian model. In an important sense, Walker's theory is a significant reversal of the physicalistic model. One could even characterize it as essentially vitalistic because the central principle that accounts for psi is located in the "will" of the subject. This shift to a response-centered approach from the stimulus-centered physical model is what gives Walker's theory a vitalistic look. Note that Walker is not looking at the process by which the energy patterns emanating from the stimulus objects reach the subject, but rather at the subject and his or her "will" variables. The development of a "dualistic" physics—and this is what this theory attempts to develop—would indeed constitute a paradigmatic change, and its acceptance would have revolutionary consequences for physics.

2.5. Topological Model

Gertrude Schmeidler (1972) suggests a topological rather than a quantum explanation for psi effects. She raises the possibility that psi information is not transmitted across Euclidean space but is a result of direct subject–target contact. She argues that psi produces a sort of "space warp" or bridge across space so that, without disturbing the normal space relationships in a three-dimensional framework, it produces a conjunction between two points normally separated in space (or time, in a four-dimensional framework) when viewed with an extra dimension. "I propose," writes Schmeidler (1972), ". . . that the universe in which ESP or PK is effective has an extra dimension and that this dimension permits topological folding. It thus permits immediate contact between two areas which in an Einsteinian universe would be separated" (p. 124). The failure to find any physical characteristics of targets that limit psi functioning forces us "to conclude that the ESP target is not an object but instead is something like the meaning of an object, or an informational pattern" (p. 125).

Contending that ESP is not an all-or-none process, but that it involves only a partial information transfer "by a fold in the space–time matrix," she speculates on special brain cells or processes that determine ESP receptivity, and proposes that the inhibition of competing brain events is a condition for successful processing of psi information. She argues that "a relational pattern of partial information can come directly to some brain processing center or centers, and that it typically bypasses the periphery. It comes by means of a topological fold in the space–time matrix, so that there is no transmission across space" (p. 130). The area into which it comes determines the form it takes. For example, received in the visual area, it gives visual information. If the sensory projection areas are bypassed, a cognitive change such as an intuitive idea rather than a sensory image would result. Changes in the autonomic nervous system may be caused when it comes into limbic or other noncortical areas.

Once the ESP information reaches some part of the brain, the mechanism or process by which it determines a response may be analogous to the process by which subliminal stimulation elicits a response. In other words, those psychological factors that effect the processing of ambiguous sensory material should also effect the processing of ESP information. This implication is something that can be easily tested.

In another context, Schmeidler (1974) phrased the concept in terms of a "hole in space" instead of a "folding in the space–time matrix," to explain the direct contact between the subject and the target in an ESP situation. Following the suggestion of M. R. Gammon (1973) that the structure of space in Einstein's theory of relativity offers a sensible explanation of psychic sources behind synchronistic events, R. S. McCully (1974) developed hypotheses to account for the Rorschach processes that seem to relate to a "psychically relative space–time continuum." Gammon, inspired by John Wheeler, postulated that the hole-connection (called in physics "wormhole") between two regions of the *same* Euclidean space provides an understanding of the way consciousness is related to the archetypal ground of the psyche. McCully extends this model to draw hypotheses to explain what he considers to be the archetypal connection of certain Rorschach responses, where images seem to "carry threads reaching backward and forward in time" (p. 44). Schmeidler, without agreeing with McCully's synchronistic interpretation, finds the concept of "hole-connection" useful in her topological explanation of psi.

She predicts on the basis of her hypothesis, that people who are friendly, open, and receptive may share the same "psychic space" and therefore share also success in ESP tests. Whether or not research would finally vindicate the speculations of Schmeidler, her creative attempt to integrate physical, physiological, and psychological factors affecting psi in a unified theory is commendable.

3. Nonphysical Theories

H. H. Price, the Oxford philosopher, is convinced that no physical explanation of psi is possible. Characterizing psychical research as "one of the most important branches of investigation which the human mind has ever undertaken" (1967, p. 45), Price argues that the reality of telepathy falsifies the physicalistic world view. "We must conclude," says Price, "that there is no room for telepathy in a Materialistic universe. Telepathy is something which ought not to happen at all, if the Materialistic theory were true. But it does happen. So there must be something seriously wrong with the Materialistic theory, however numerous and imposing the *normal* facts which support it may be" (1967, p. 38). This view, of course, has no universal acceptance. For example, Dobbs (1967) and Cooper (1976), among others, have argued that the assumption that parapsychological findings reject materialism is mistaken.

By and large the nonphysical theories, like the physical theories, seek to find a contact between the subject and the target. This is done by assuming a nonphysical medium in which the subject and the target object are located, or by postulating new entities capable of overcoming space–time constraints. The former assumes that some aspects of our person are at a subliminal level in a continuous contact with others because they are connected by a common unconscious. A variant of this view conceives of a nonphysical field where psi interactions take place. The latter usually takes the form of hypothesizing a mindlike entity that could function independently of the nervous system by projecting itself to reach the target across space–time barriers. So, we find among nonphysical theories (a) subliminal contact theories, (b) field theories, and (c) projection hypotheses.

3.1. Subliminal Contact Theories

3.1.1. Theories of Subliminal Self

Frederic Myers in his monumental *Human Personality*, first published in 1903, argues that the reality of paranormal phenomena such as telepathy, abnormal phenomena like split personality, and even normal phenomena like genius require that we postulate a "subliminal or ultra-marginal consciousness." In addition to our "conscious" or "empirical" self, "there exists a more comprehensive consciousness, a profounder faculty, which for the most part remains potential . . ." (Myers 1903/1915, Vol. 1, p. 12). This Myers calls the subliminal self. "I mean by the subliminal Self," he says, "that part of the Self which is commonly subliminal. . . . And I conceive also that no Self of which we can here have cognizance is in reality more than a fragment of a larger Self-revealed in a fashion at once shifting and limited through an organism not so framed as to afford its full manifestation" (p. 15).

For his time, the ideas of Myers were provocative and seminal. His conception of subliminal mentation in such states as dreams, hypnotic and dissociated states, and genius as subserving our conscious stream of thought was, in a significant sense, the forerunner of modern personality theory.

In his conception of subliminal self, Myers thus postulates an "inward extension of our being," as James put it, "cut off from common consciousness by a screen or diaphragm not absolutely impervious but liable to leakage and to occasional rupture" (Murphy and Ballou, 1960, p. 230). However, Myers was vague as to how the subliminal self makes contact with the "cosmic" environment to bring about paranormal events. Various alternatives suggest themselves: (1) The subliminal selves are but waves in a sea of a supreme self or absolute soul; (2) the subliminal selves themselves are discrete and discontinuous but can interact because they are submerged or situated in a common medium; (3) the subliminal self is inherently capable of interacting with others without being limited by spaciotemporal barriers. The vagueness of Myers' formulation of the psi process had the merit of inspiring a number of subsequent thinkers, from William James to Ehrenwald.

James, for instance, wrote:

> . . . we with our lives are like islands in the sea, or like trees in the forest. The maple and the pine may whisper to each other with their leaves, and Conanicut and Newport hear each other's foghorns. But the trees also commingle their roots in the darkness underground, and the islands also hang together through the ocean's bottom. Just so there is a continuum of cosmic consciousness, against which our individuality builds but accidental fences, and into which our several minds plunge as into a mother-sea or reservoir. Our normal consciousness is circumscribed for adaptation to our external earthly environment, but the fence is weak in spots, and fitful influences from beyond leak in, showing the otherwise unverifiable common connection. Not only psychic research, but metaphysical philosophy, and speculative biology are led in their own ways to look with favor on some such panpsychic view of the universe as this. (Murphy and Ballou, 1960, p. 324)

Kahn (1976) plausibly argued that Myers' hypothesis can be further extended if we assume, like James, that we are linked together in a far more fundamental way than we have hitherto imagined. Psi information may not be conceived of merely as the "subliminal uprush" on rare occasions. It is more pervasive than that, and is, in fact, "an intrinsic component to the human condition" (p. 225). Kahn writes:

> Here the emphasis is on a constantly impinging heteropsychic set of stimuli which occasionally may break through, but which ordinarily press on the stream of thought in such a way as to steadily distort, modify, emphasize, and deflect the ongoing processes of consciousness. Here the occasional breakthrough is less important than the constant interaction between the psi level and the stream of consciousness itself, which now becomes the focus of our attention. (p. 224)

> A search for structural alterations in the ideational organization of both agent and percipient, without regard to traditional "guesses" and "targets," might reveal the presence of psi interaction that, like subatomic particles, are universally present and active, but which remain undetected until they are allowed to act within a matrix so sensitized as to magnify their impact, thus enabling them to cross the threshold of scientific observability. (p. 226)

Thus Kahn, while defending an aspect of Myers' theory, brings it up to date. Even more interesting is the fact that he proposes tests that would verify or falsify some of these assumptions.

Tyrrell (1947b) further developed the concept of the subliminal self to account for extrasensory perception and introduced the concept of mediating vehicles. Telepathy, according to Tyrrell, consists in some sort of cognitive relationship between the subliminal selves of two individuals. "The subliminal or extraconscious region of the self," he says, "contains an enormous range of things, high and low, transcendental and trivial. All are obliged to pass through the bottle-neck at the threshold if they are to reach the normal consciousness, and in doing so, all make use of the principle of mediation by means of constructs" (p. 331).

Now, according to Tyrrell (1947a), the communications and perceptions received at the subliminal level are pushed into consciousness in a symbolic guise or in a distorted form as a mental image or the like. The "tools" by which the unconsciously received psi cognitions are externalized in consciousness are called by Tyrell the "mediating vehicles." These vehicles include dreams, sensory hallucinations, automatic writing, mental images, and strong emotion. Tyrell rightly attaches great significance to this process of mediation. In telepathic dreams, the unconsciously received telepathic contact appears to be exhibited in the same way as the content of normal dreams (Ullman, Krippner, and Vaughan, 1973).

In psi cognitions, according to Tyrell, human personalities are able to overcome the space–time barriers because the subliminal selves, which enter into paranormal cognitive relations, exist not in space and time but "elsewhere," where space and time have no constraining influence. Tyrrell says that he can give no clear description of this "elsewhere." He argues that language is not adequate to deal with these types of phenomena, and he is able to give no lucid description of the nature of subliminal selves. He writes: "Extra-sensory faculty may result from the circumstance that subliminal selves are neither singular nor plural, neither one nor many in their nature, but simply inconceivable" (1948, p. 262).

Tyrrell's views regarding the modus operandi of telepathy may be summarized as follows: In a telepathic cognition, the subliminal selves of the agent and the percipient are in such a relationship that the subliminal self of the percipient has a "propositional awareness" of the agent's subliminal impressions. Telepathic cognition results if the percipient's subliminal awareness regarding the agent is manifested in the consciousness of the percipient by means of a mediating vehicle.

Tyrrell's theory is based on assumptions that need further validation. His exposition of the nature of the subliminal self is ambiguous and vague. Even granting the reality of subliminal selves, we fail to see how these subliminal selves enter into that relationship by virtue of which one *self* can have the propositional awareness of another's subliminal impressions. His conception of the unknown "elsewhere" sounds mystical and does not provide any plausible explanation for the transmission of subliminal impressions from one *self* to another.

Tyrrell's major theoretical contribution lies in his emphasis on the process of mediation. His conception of mediating vehicles and the contention that both telepathic dreams and normal dreams exhibit the same form in externalizing the unconscious contents promise a new and important field of ESP research that might unravel its complexities.

Tyrrell's "elsewhere" takes the form of "collective unconscious" in the theory proposed by H. H. Price (1940, 1948, 1959).

3.1.2. The Collective Unconscious

The telepathic rapport observed by many investigators shows that individual minds have something in common. Price points out that the continuous telepathic rapport between two minds makes it foolish to argue to the plurality of minds. Between one mind and another there are no clear-cut boundaries. The division of minds is not "absolute and unconditional, either." The illusion of the individual mind arises out of the superficial nature of self-consciousness.

Price (1940) thinks that the unconscious portion of one mind may interact with that of another, because they share the "collective uncon-

scious." The collective unconscious that connects all the apparently individual minds is responsible for telepathic cognition. The collective unconscious, according to Price, is not an "entity" or a "thing" but a "field of
interaction." Thus telepathy is possible because minds are not causally
isolated entities. Unconscious events in one mind may produce unconscious events in another mind. Telepathy, according to Price, is not a
form of knowing. Knowing, he says, has an "all or none" character. There
is no intermediary stage between knowing and not knowing; we either
know a thing or do not. But in telepathy the percipient's impression may
be partly true and partly false. Moreover, the percipient's experience
seems to take no notice of the success or failure of his call. If telepathy is
a form of knowing, there ought to be some difference in the experience
when he calls the right card and when he calls the wrong one. Price says
that he has no objection to calling telepathy a form of cognition. But he
contends that telepathy is not knowing others' thoughts; rather a telepathic experience is caused by a similar experience in others. "Telepathy," says Price, "is more like infection than like knowledge" (1940, p.
372).

According to Price, the human mind has developed a repressive
mechanism that suppresses the continual flow of telepathic impact from
one mind to another because there is a biological need for such a
mechanism. Otherwise the thoughts and emotions of all minds would be
constantly received by everyone, and life would very likely become
chaos, and action impossible. Psychoanalysts have indicated that repressive mechanisms are partly in abeyance during states of relaxation
and dreaming. If telepathic influences are suppressed by similar
mechanisms, they should come through more often in these mental states.
Price points out that in fact many spontaneous cases of telepathic nature
do occur during dreams. The existence of a repressive mechanism, he
says, is also suggested by the fact that most mediums enter into a state of
dissociation, which releases the functioning of their abilities.

Price also makes a suggestion regarding the explanation of clairvoyance. He says that the unconscious part of our minds may be capable
of perceiving everything, however remote in space, for the simple reason
that the unconscious may be in contact with all things. But we do not see
all things at once, because the nervous system and the sense organs may
be preventing us from doing so; and this process is, of course, biologically
useful to us. Occasionally, however, when the physiological mechanism
allows it, these unconscious contacts may actualize themselves in the
conscious in the form of psi experiences.

Price's theory leaves the essential intricacies of the modus operandi
of ESP unexplained. His suggestion about the causal interaction of the

unconscious portions of our minds is helpful in explaining telepathy, but Price does not explain in a detailed way the nature and implications of such an interaction. His contention regarding the repressive mechanism is not new, for others, beginning with Bergson (1920), have advocated a similar conception. An important omission is that Price does not seem to suggest any clue to the mysterious riddle of the "selecting process" in ESP, that is, how one is able to select a particular telepathic communication out of the numerous psi impacts that are constantly present in the unconscious. How the repressive mechanism (a screening agent) can also serve as a selecting agent needs to be explained.

3.1.3. Association Theory of Carington

A variant of the idea of the collective unconscious is Carington's (1946b) "association theory of telepathy." This theory is more positivistic than others in this category. The fundamental postulate of his (1949) "radical positivism" is that what is meaningful must be verified by sensation or introspection. He says that an analysis of our perceptions reveals to us that the real or the meaningful in them is only sense data or "cognita." Carington then proceeds to put forward a conception of the mind in terms of cognita and cognitum sequences. He argues that to regard the mind as something other than sense cognita is entirely metaphysical and has no meaning. "The mind," he suggests, could be viewed as "an immense assemblage of discrete particles . . ." (1949, p. 155). Individual minds are the "condensations" formed of cognita. They are not completely "discrete" and "isolate," but are so formed as to possess a common something that may be called the common unconscious or subconscious.

Carington (1949) thinks that this new conception of mind affords a simple and meaningful explanation of the perplexing phenomenon of telepathy. When two or more individuals are faced with similar circumstances they are likely to have similar thoughts or mental images. For example, two persons looking at the sea or thinking about it are likely to imagine boats, waves, or beaches. In a telepathy experiment, the agent concentrates on a target (for example, a picture). The idea of this target is probably associated with various thoughts and ideas about the telepathy experiment. The percipient is likely to have similar thoughts and ideas. Now, granted that the minds of the agent and percipient are related in the common unconscious or subconscious, it is likely, says Carington, that the idea of the target will be brought to the percipient's mind because of its association with the idea of the experiment in the agent's mind. Carington argues that the principle of association of ideas renders this view plausible.

He advances the following line of reasoning in favor of his association theory of telepathy. Soal and his associates reported that subjects in a
telepathy experiment can do well with particular agents alone, which
means that the subject and the agent have something in common that
binds them together. This implies that there are close bonds of association
and similarities between the minds of percipient and agent. This is evident
also in spontaneous telepathy, which usually occurs between near relatives and close friends who have common interests.

Carington introduces the concept of "K-ideas" to render the association theory of telepathy more intelligible. The K-idea is a connecting link,
or an associative bond, between the agent and the percipient. The greater
the number of K-ideas, the greater would be the probability of success in
telepathy experiments. Carington explains the function of K-ideas by the
following analogy. If an individual who is sailing in a boat wishes to send a
heavy object to a person who is in another boat, he would naturally tie a
rope to the object and throw the free end to the other boat. Now, the two
boats are like the mind of the agent and the percipient; the rope is the
connector or the K-idea, and the tying of the rope is the formation of an
associative bond.

The association theory lacks the necessary experimental evidence to
show that the increase in the strength and number of K-ideas necessarily
increases the rate of scoring in ESP experiments. Soal and Bateman (1954)
have experimented with Gloria Stewart, a very successful subject, in
order to test this implication of Carington's theory. They presented
Stewart with a photograph of the agent and later with a detailed sketch of
the objects in the agent's room to increase the strength of K-ideas. The
results of these experiments (the Cambridge–Richmond distance series)
were not statistically significant, and the most that can be said is that they
failed to strengthen Carington's theory. The enormous success recorded
in certain other card-guessing experiments, which did not appear to foster
the formation of associative bonds between the agent and percipient, also
stands against Carington's theory. Finally, Carington's theory gives no
explanation for the clairvoyant mode of ESP, though Carington (1946a)
himself considered that it is inherently impossible to distinguish between
telepathy and clairvoyance.

3.1.4. Psychoanalysis and Psychodynamic Theories of Psi

Less mystical than the concept of the subliminal self is the notion that
psi may function at deeper and more subtle levels of our personality than
recognized so far.

The recognition that psi usually operates at the level of the unconscious raises the possibility that an understanding of the dynamics of the unconscious may give us insights into the way psi manifests in our consciousness. This brings psi and psychoanalysis to share some common ground.

Freud himself (1922/1953, 1925/1953) was quick to see that telepathy, if true, may be governed by the same laws that govern our unconscious mental life. He contended that a telepathic message reaching a sleeper would be treated in a dream like any other external or internal stimulus. Freud argued (1922/1953) that "psychoanalysis may do something to advance the study of telepathy insofar as, by the help of its interpretations, many of the puzzling characteristics of telepathic phenomena may be rendered more intelligible to us; or other, still doubtful phenomena be for the first time definitely ascertained to be of a telepathic nature" (p. 85). Freud suggested also that emotional material may be more successfully transmitted in telepathy. Further, he speculated, "I am inclined to draw the conclusion that thought transference of this kind comes about particularly easily at the moment at which an idea emerges from the unconscious or, in theoretical terms, as it passes over from the 'primary process' to the 'secondary process'" (1925/1953, p. 89). Deutsch (1953), Servadio (1953), Fodor (1951, 1953), Eisenbud (1946, 1952, 1966–67, 1970), and Ehrenwald (1947, 1954, 1968, 1977), among others, paid considerable attention to the telepathic dream and the possibility of telepathic interaction between the patient and the analyst.

His observations led Eisenbud to envisage "two communication systems coexisting, one beneath the other, like the deep tides of the ocean underneath the surface ripples and eddies" (1970, p. 333). A universal psi cognitive field serves "as part of the vegetative nervous system of nature" and helps bring order into the universe. The primary goals served by psi are "not those of the individual at all but of an ascending hierarchy of interrelated systems in which the individual is merely a messenger of sorts" (1970, p. 337). Again, psi "is like other great process-abstractions in nature . . . an integral component in *all* events . . . and as such represented in some measure as a determinant of the final common pathways of these events" (1966–67, p. 161). Eisenbud argued that psi is elusive not so much because it is an unconscious function as because the goals it subserves are not in consciousness. Like the unconscious dynamic factors that go into the determination of our behavior, psi factors also may influence our behavior, whether or not we are able to discern such an influence. Thus, for Eisenbud, psi is a "thorough-going part of the total behavior of the individual." Eisenbud's emphasis on the goal-orientation of psi and his notion of "psi-mediated intercommunication" have been a powerful influence on a number of parapsychologists, not only in their theoretical orientation but also in the interpretation of experimental results (see Stanford, 1974a,b).

Jan Ehrenwald is a psychoanalyst who has written extensively about the theoretical aspects of psi. His theoretical contribution as stated in his most recent book, *The ESP Experience* (1977), may be reviewed as a series of interrelated postulates. First, telepathy is involved in more than an incidental fashion in the early parent–child relationship. It may in fact be the main feature of the mother–child symbiosis. The human infant is more dependent on its parents than is the case among all the other animals. What seems like a communication blackout in the early symbiotic phase is lifted by the telepathic contact between the mother and the child. As Ehrenwald puts it, "owing to the continued fusion of the maternal with the neonatal ego, there is no psychological gap between the two; telepathy follows the patterns of intrapsychic communication within one single, psychologically as yet undifferentiated personality structure" (1977, p. 24). But with the maturation of the child's own nervous system and the delineation of his or her ego boundaries, the telepathic intercommunication becomes unnecessary and even impossible. From the notion of mother–child symbiosis, Ehrenwald goes on to postulate the concept of "symbiotic gradient," which stretches all the way from the early mother–child phase to the doctor–patient, teacher–pupil relationships, to the targets in ESP tests, and in a significant sense, to the universe at large.

The second postulate is that psi is continuous with "our customary sensori-motor behavior." While in normal perceptual processes the effects are limited to the autopsychic sphere, the psi processes extend into the heteropsychic sphere. Just as psychological subject factors such as imagination and emotionally loaded ideas may cause somatic effects like conversion hysteria, "the power of imagination and/or of emotionally charged ideas may extend beyond the boundary lines of the organism into the heteropsychic sphere" (1977, p. 201), resulting in paranormal experiences.

The third postulate assumes a "psychophysical gradient" that closely parallels the "symbiotic gradient" reaching from the ego to the nonego. This postulate leads us to the conception of an "open" personality structure that is not rigidly contained and isolated within an individual. The extension of the sphere of one's personality makes psi interaction possible—an interaction in which experiences are shared and signals exchanged without the benefit of spatially contiguous neural conduction and central processing of neurophysiological events. Ehrenwald points out that there is no special problem involved here because a similar gap between brain events and conscious experience is involved even in the ordinary type of perception.

The fourth postulate is that psi phenomena have their neural bases in the brain stem and the brain cortex. The reticular formation and higher cortical centers function to screen and inhibit psi. The capricious intrusion of psi into our experiential domain or into the results of parapsychological experiments "may be due to the random occurrence of minor flaws in the screening or inhibitory functions of the reticular formation and higher cortical centers" (p. 212). Ehrenwald points out that the distortions and disorganizations of the target picture as drawn by a psi subject are similar to the pictures drawn by some patients suffering from brain damage. He further speculates that in some extreme cases of schizophrenia the "patient's ego may be overwhelmed by psi-pollution" (p. 213).

A number of testable hypotheses can be deduced from the postulates of Ehrenwald. The most important of these is the one that relates to mother–child symbiosis. It should not be very difficult to design tests or make controlled observations of interactions between the infant and the mother that would enable us to verify whether an element of psi is involved that would support Ehrenwald's notion of parent–child symbiosis.

L. E. Rhine (1965), not herself a psychoanalyst, emphasized the unconscious and dynamic aspects of psi as much as any psychoanalyst. Following up on Tyrrell's suggestion, she hypothesized that psi is a two-stage process. While we hardly know anything about Stage I where psi interaction takes place and paranormal information is received, she argued, the process by which the unconscious psi information finds its way into overt behavior may be understood in the same manner as other psychodynamic functions. The four types of psi experiences that her vast collection of spontaneous cases has revealed seem to neatly fit into the hypothesis that they are the "mediating vehicles" that bring the information received at Stage I into Stage II. Also, her analysis of cases that provide incomplete and distorted psi information suggests that these cases are better understood in terms of the two-stage hypothesis. What is important is her observation that the incompleteness, distortions, and imperfections in overt psi responses seem to be traceable to known psychodynamic factors. L. E. Rhine also suggested that psi-missing is due to blocking and repression of Stage I information from reaching Stage II awareness.

3.1.5. LeShan's Clairvoyant Reality

We find a metaphysical culmination of the subliminal contact theories in LeShan's (1969, 1974, 1976) conception of "clairvoyant reality." Reality, he believes, takes on different forms depending on the way we interact with it. The commonsense way of perceiving reality produces the "sensory reality" in which objects and events appear separated by space and time, and information is processed through the senses. Different from this sensory reality is the "clairvoyant reality" where all that ever exists is in the "grand plan and pattern of the universe" and where the known and the knower "are regarded as the same in such a profound fashion that space cannot bar information exchange between them" (LeShan, 1969, p. 103). For LeShan, paranormal communication implies a shift of consciousness from the sensory reality to the clairvoyant reality or access to certain levels of the personality which normally construe reality in this way. He attempted to test this hypothesis by setting up a training program in the paranormal based on learning to alter one's own consciousness toward the clairvoyant reality world view. He reports good success in teaching psychic healing at a distance by this method, but much less success in teaching telepathy or clairvoyance. LeShan's books *The Medium, the Mystic and the Physicist* (1974) and *Alternate Realities* (1976) make fascinating reading as he gropes to find threads to bind the mystical, the paranormal, and the physical worldviews. This may, however, be more a metaphysical theory reminiscent of such Hindu philosophers as Sankara than a scientific explanation of the paranormal.

3.2. Field Theories

The field theories differ from contact theories in their emphasis on interpersonal processes. Among the nonphysical field theories are the idea of a "paranormal matrix" advocated by Murphy and the conception of "psi-fields" by Roll. Gardner Murphy (1945, 1946, 1950, 1952, 1959, 1964), a psychologist of distinction, is a prolific contributor to parapsychological literature. In his varied writings on the subject he has presented several important ideas that deserve careful attention. Since it is not possible to review all of them here, the following discussion will be limited to his field theory.

3.2.1. Murphy's Paranormal Matrix

Psi phenomena, according to Murphy (1945), are not necessarily the result of the processes of isolated individuals but may involve processes that are interpersonal. There is suggestive evidence that psi manifestation depends more on the "relations between persons" than on the ability of the subject alone. The interpersonal relations between the subject and the experimenter, for example, are known to be important for psi functioning. Murphy suggests that the reason for our failure to use psi communication frequently may be found in our "psychological insulation" from one another. Relaxed states and the states in which self-awareness is greatly reduced (which are believed to be states that aid psi functioning) may be the ones that bring us closer to one another at a deeper and more stable level than ordinary awareness does. This may be the level of psi functioning.

If this is so, psi functioning may become understood properly not by analyzing the psi process into distinct activities attributable to distinct things but by applying the concept of field theory and by treating the psi situation, whether experimental or spontaneous, as an indivisible whole of which the subject is only one aspect. "From this point of view," writes Murphy, "a subject and an experimenter in a telepathy experiment represent phases of an organic whole both at the ordinary normal level of interaction and also, more profoundly, at the deeper level at which the paranormal processes occur" (1945, p. 198). Psi phenomena, then, are not produced solely by the individuals who experience them. They are dependent upon interpersonal relations. When individuals act as one "interpersonal entity," Murphy believes, they may possess "extraordinary capacity to make contact with phases of reality which transcend time and space" (1945, p. 192). Thus Murphy seems to anticipate the concept of clairvoyant reality developed later by LeShan.

Now what is the nature of such reality? How are the ordinary psychological processes related to it? The reality constituting the interpersonal psychical field is one in which contacts with remote points in space and time are possible. Every individual exerts influence on the field in varying degrees and is in turn affected by it. Every psychological activity that takes places in a world where time and space are real leaves a "trace" in the world to which psi belongs—a world to which time–space concepts are not applicable. When the present psychological activity makes a contact with that reality directly, we have telepathic or clairvoyant experiences. In order that there be a psi experience, Murphy (1945) points out, "there must be a cosmic system of psychical laws and psychical realities . . . . We may conceive the world of the paranormal as a sort of matrix from which proceed impressions which influence the specific psychological events which happen from day to day, and upon which they in turn make some impression" (p. 203). If these impressions exist over time and if they resemble what we call "mind," then this theory allows the possibility of the survival of the personality after bodily death.

The principal merit of this theory consists in the possibility that certain of its implications are empirically testable. It is, however, a pity that not much was done in the last 30 years since the theory was first published to see whether an enhanced social interaction would result in improved psi performance. It is of interest, however, to note that some special techniques of relaxation have been found useful in eliciting psi (e.g., Braud and Braud, 1973, 1974).

3.2.2. Roll's Psi-Fields

Roll (1961, 1966a,b) has advanced a theory that makes use of the concept of psi-fields. He uses the concept of psi-field as analogous to electromagnetic or gravitational fields and supposes that objects, whether animate or inanimate, possess such fields. Psi-fields interact with known physical fields and with each other. In a case of ESP, a physical or mental event at the target (source) is copied in the target's psi-field; this copy or "psi-trace" is then communicated (over a channel of intermediary psi fields) to the psi-field of the percipient (receiver), where it interacts with his brain to produce an instance of ESP. Roll realizes that a field theory will help to explain psi phenomena only if these in fact obey external objective conditions. He does not deny the importance of psychological conditions such as motivational factors at the source (in the case of telepathy) or receiver (telepathy and clairvoyance), but suggests that the connecting medium is subject to spatiotemporal variables, such as distance in space, "linkage" between the psi fields of objects that have been in physical proximity to each other, frequency and recency of contact.

In addition to transmitting information and energy to other psi-fields and to physical fields, a psi-field also stores information and thus acts somewhat like a memory record. In fact, Roll says that a person's memory record plays a role both in the transmission of information (in telepathy) and in the reception of information (ESP in general), and he suggests that the memory record may be part of the psi-field of an organism. This leads Roll to the suggestion that another set of hypotheses, namely, the so-called laws of learning (recency, frequency, and vividness) govern the reception and transmission of ESP. There have been some experimental attempts to test a few of the implications of this theory (Kanthamani and Rao, 1974, 1975; Stanford, 1973). The results are somewhat equivocal. Blackmore (1977), for example, argues that some of the implications that are tested by Kanthamani and Rao do not follow logically from Roll's memory–ESP hypothesis.

Roll extends his theory to explain precognition. He states that mental and physical events are copied in the psi-fields of animate and inanimate physical objects as psi-traces. The latter possess a certain energy that can be communicated to other psi-fields and to the physical systems these psi-fields are connected with. Consequently, if a person has a desire for a certain event or if an image referring to some occurrence is created in his mind, this image or desire increases the probability that the occurrence will happen. Roll does not say that the person who has the precognitive dream *causes* the later events to happen by PK, but rather that the dream (as a psi-trace) possesses a PK "charge" and thus the precognized event is likely to become "materialized" no matter what the desires of the dreamer may be when this happens. The dream may have been due to ESP from some other psi-field in the universe. In that case, the precognitive experience and the verifying events are both effects of the same cause. The energy involved in bringing about the verifying events is no greater than laboratory PK effects and is supposed to effect only the physically indeterminate links in the normal course of events. He explains experimental cases of precognition involving dice throws and mathematical calculations in the same way, suggesting that the brain processes that enable us to perform the highly complex calculations underlying ordinary perceptual activities are also brought to bear in these experiments so as to make "targets" conform to "precognitions." Roll emphasizes that his theory is subject to empirical verification and would be disproved if the spatiotemporal conditions supposedly governing psi-fields are found to have no effect. He points out that the theory is in agreement with those cases of precognition where the events foreseen were prevented from happening on the basis of the precognitive experience itself.

Following the publication of Roll's theory in 1961, there was a lively discussion by some of the eminent thinkers in the field. For a criticism of this theory, one could do no better than refer to these comments (Broad, 1962b; Chari, 1962; Ducasse, 1962).

3.3. Projection Hypotheses

The theories considered thus far assume either that the individual is in touch at some level with all that exists or that the objects of psi experience (targets) somehow make a contact with the subject through a nonphysical medium. In either case, the individual subject's problem is to select the desired information out of the multitude with which he or she is potentially in contact. The projection hypotheses seek to overcome this problem by according to the individual the ability to make paranormal contact with the target. In other words, the subject is not a passive receptor of psi information but an active agent who reaches out to the object of his or her psi cognition.

3.3.1. J. B. Rhine's Relativism

It is difficult to write in any convincing way about J. B. Rhine's theory. First and foremost he is an experimental scientist who abhorred theorizing, which he felt would shackle the research worker. McDougall (1934/1973) observed: "When he [J. B. Rhine] comes into my room and finds me reading a book on metaphysics or religion, he scratches his head and . . . wonders whether, after all, I, in my later years, am becoming a renegade" (p. xv). Rhine has said repeatedly that a theory is a closed gateway. What we need in parapsychology, he argued, are hypotheses that are questions that open up pathways. He disclaims having any theory of his own, apart from the working hypotheses he employed as an inquiring scientist.

Yet Rhine did write on theoretical issues and even gave a name to his theoretical position. He stated hypotheses broader than his experimental manipulations would have permitted him to test. Whether or not he recognized the theoretical relevance of some of his ideas, there is an unmistakable *weltanschauung* whose influence on the thinking of subsequent parapsychologists is not inconsiderable. To this we now turn, recognizing that he may not approve of our pigeonholing him in any of our theoretical categories.

In an editorial in 1945, Rhine sketched a point of view which he termed *relativism*. According to the relativistic hypothesis, the mind and the body, the psychical and physical processes, are both real and relatively distinct. But they are "rooted in a common system of energetic determinants which as yet is not known to science" (p. 228). Inasmuch as all knowable events presuppose a psychophysical interaction, we must infer a "fundament for the interaction of body and mind" (p. 228). In a footnote (p. 228). Rhine quoted from the presidential address of C. D. Broad to the Society for Psychical Research in 1935, in which Broad postulated an "extended pervasive medium, capable of receiving and retaining modifications of local structure or internal motion," and commented that Broad's hypothetical medium is probably identifiable with the fundament that he saw as necessary for all psychophysical interaction.

In *New World of the Mind*, Rhine (1953) considers the possibility of a mental energy operative in psi phenomena, an energy not subject to the familiar conditions of space, time, and mass. This energy, like the more familiar energies, is convertible to other forms, and in this way its operations can be detected by its secondary effects. The cognitive (ESP) effects of psi result from converting parapsychical energy to the physiological energy of the brain system; the psychokinetic effects of psi result from conversion of parapsychical energy to mechanical energy so that it acts on a material system such as rolling dice. The question is left as to whether psi may not operate in an energetic order that in itself has no space–time. Rhine emphasizes the unifying interaction of the mind with the physical world, even while calling attention to the valid distinctions parapsychology has established.

To explain how we acquire paranormal information, Rhine suggested an interesting hypothesis in his very first book (1934/1973), which may be called the projection hypothesis. This little-known hypothesis rests on two assumptions: (1) that some agency of the mind that can function to some extent independently of the physical world is operative in ESP, and (2) that this agency has the capacity to "go out" to meet the object that is outside the organism it occupies.

According to Rhine, psi phenomena suggest the existence of mind that under certain circumstances and to some degree can function independently of the physical limitations of the material body. Relation to space has been considered an invariable characteristic of physical operations. All our perceptual experiences, insofar as they relate to the material world, are organized into the framework of space. But with regard to ESP, space apparently has no influence, and effects of distance such as the inverse square law are inapplicable to it. No reliable relation has been found between the distance of the subject from the target or the agent and the degree of success of one's calls in ESP tests. In view of this fact and of the evidence of precognition, Rhine goes on to suggest that, unknown to the physical world, there might well be some other energy, one peculiar to mind, which is radically different from material energies. He considers that the source of these distinctive results must be sought in the nature of the mind capable of such effects.

Further, success in ESP experiments is relatively independent of the nature of the item to be cognized. It does not make any difference whether the target of the subject's guess is something material like an ESP test card, or a thought, as in the case of pure telepathy. Several outstanding subjects in ESP experiments have averaged about the same in telepathy and clairvoyance tests, and successful results are obtained with a diversity of stimulation, ranging from a material object to a mental image and even to an object that will exist only at a future time. In sensory experience, to the contrary, we find different stimuli giving rise to different types of experience. Hence, argues Rhine, the only way to render these facts intelligible is to recognize the need of a mental function capable of action independent of the limitations that define physical reality.

Rhine goes on to make an important suggestion. He writes:

> The diversity of the "stimulus objects" here is so great as to suggest that the agency responsible is the percipient's mind—that his mind, in effect, "goes out to" the object. Such different objects could not be expected to give such similar stimulation. It is much more reasonable to suppose that the percipient's mind can perceive in E.S.P. fashion a wide enough range of "objects" to include thoughts and cards. It is this "going out" to perceive that points in our present picture of mind–body limitations to a relative independence of the material laws, as known. A "going out" to great distances in defiance of "inverse square" laws that all known matter-bound energies obey, as well as a "going

out" to a solid pack of cards and the selection of the right ones in the right order; and, again, a "going out" first to the right mind in a heavily populated region 250 miles away and selecting its thoughts, while evading doubtlessly similar thoughts originating nearer the percipient (circle, star, plus, etc.), selecting from the chosen agent's mind not the thoughts arising from her reading the book before her, but the very images intended for the very moment when the call is made; and, finally, a "going out" of mind that selects one card on a table 250 yards away, when there are hundreds of similar cards in adjoining rooms that are nearer the percipient, many others in his own room and in the observer's room—such facts and conditions come close to persuasion of the necessity for the active and selective agency of the percipient's own mind, in escaping the limitations of its material nerves and sense organs, penetrating stone walls and evading distance, and accurately apprehending the desired "object" on a level or scale or condition that is non-material and non-spatial. (1934/1973, pp. 192–193)

This view is indeed radical in that it implies reverse causation. Unlike sensory perception, where external objects radiate energy patterns that are efferently received by the receiver, in extrasensory perception the cognizing mind itself makes the contact with the external object or an agency of it by actually "going out" to the object.

3.3.2. Broad's Compound Theory

What we described as Rhine's hypothesis was anticipated by the British philosopher C. D. Broad in his "compound theory" (1925/1951, 1962a). Broad uses the concept "paranormal" to include such psi phenomena as clairvoyance, telepathy, precognition, and psychokinesis. According to Broad, there are certain synthetic principles that help to integrate various aspects of human experience. These he calls the "basic limiting principles"; an event is paranormal if it seems prima facie to conflict with any of these principles. For instance, a clairvoyant event is paranormal because it contradicts the basic limiting principle that "it is impossible for a person to perceive a physical event or a material thing except by means of sensations which that event or thing produces in the mind" (1953, p. 10).

Broad's definition of the paranormal is one of the most analytic definitions in the field of parapsychology, but one wonders if it is not simply a negative description of what the paranormal is not, rather than a positive assertion of what it is. However, this criticism should not belittle the importance of Broad's analysis since what we know of psi is indeed limited.

As early as 1925, Broad (1951) put forward a hypothesis to explain the mind–body relation. Convinced as he was of the reality of psi as revealed in spontaneous case material and the phenomena of trance mediumship, he directed his hypothesis beyond the mind–body relation to accommodate the paranormal and the possibility of survival. According to this hypothesis, which he calls the "compound theory," the mind is not a single substance. It is a compound of two substances, and neither of them by itself has the characteristics of mind. These two substances are the "psychic factor" or "psychogenic factor" or "psi component" as he later called it, and the "bodily factor."

Such acts as perception, reasoning, and remembering are not the functions of either of the factors by itself. Just as a chemical compound possesses characteristics that do not belong individually to either of the constituents, so the functions of the mind are not to be found solely in one or the other of its constituent elements.

Broad goes on to say that the psychic factor could persist even after the cessation of the body after death. When a psychic factor is united with a body, it functions as a mind and certain traces are formed. When a person dies, this factor separates; thus a discarnate psychic factor will not have a mind or consciousness. If it so happens that a psychic factor after its dissolution from the body with which it has so long been associated comes into contact with the body of a living organism, as would be the case of an entranced medium, the newly formed "mind" may, in virtue of the impressions this psychic factor had in the form of traces, recall the experiences of the deceased person with whose body the psychic factor had been united.

If we extend the compound theory to cover ESP and PK phenomena, we then have to assume that the psychic factor goes out to reach for the object or thought in psi cognitive operations or that it is in constant touch with all things and thoughts at all times. If we admit the latter, that is, universal and omniscient ESP, there would be no need for any traces in the psychic factor in order to recall the experiences, since it is actually in touch with all that is. Thus Broad's compound theory logically entails the "going out" hypothesis that Rhine later made explicit in his monograph.

3.3.3. The "Shin" Theory of Thouless and Wiesner

Another projection hypothesis is the Shin theory jointly formulated by Thouless and Wiesner (1948). This hypothesis observes the similarity between normal and paranormal processes and suggests that these two processes are not radically different. In either case, no unusual entity is operative nor is there an actual representation of the cognized object. In all the spontaneous manifestations of ESP, the symbolic or distorted representation of psi cognitions is evident. In normal sense perception also, the image of the object that is cognized is not perceived directly. It is true, of course, that the content of a cognition resembles the object in most cases, but the immediate causal antecedent of our sense perception is not the object but the nervous system and the brain. Hence, both psi cognition and sense perception are but the results of processes in the brain and the nervous system.

"*In normal thinking and perceiving*," Thouless and Wiesner write, "*I am in the same sort of relation to what is going on in the sensory part of my brain and nervous system as that of the successful clairvoyant to some external event, and that this relation is established by the same means*" (p. 196). In an act of perception, according to this view, we are not aware of the immediate cause of our perceptions, the cause being the changes in the brain and nervous system. So also, a successful clairvoyant is not aware of the object of his or her cognition, which is the immediate "causal ancestor" of one's cognition. Then normal perception differs from clairvoyance in that the former is mediated by the brain and nervous system while in the case of clairvoyant perception a direct contact between the subject and the object is established.

Thouless and Wiesner (along with some of the 19th-century thinkers, notably Braid) assume that there is some entity that is involved in our processes of volition and perception, which they call "Shin." Shin is almost like the soul, but they prefer to avoid the usage of the concept "soul," as it carries a certain connotation that is partly outside the field of parapsychology. Shin is always operative in sensory as well as extrasensory cognitions. It is constantly being informed of our sensory perceptions. Its cognitions are received from the perceptual side and its volitions are activated on the motor side. In normal perceptions, Shin is mediated by the brain and nervous system, and in psi cognitions, such as clairvoyance, it is directly connected with the object.

Stimuli from the object act on the sensory part of the nervous system. Shin is informed by the processes in the nervous system, and, in turn, Shin controls the motor part of the nervous system. On the other hand, in the processes of clairvoyance, direct connections are established between Shin and the object, without the intervention of the brain and the nervous system. Thus psi cognitions are not supernormal but, as Thouless and Wiesner (1948) put it, are "exosomatic forms of processes which are normally endo-somatic" (p. 199).

Thouless and Wiesner (1948) define telepathy as a "process of Shin acting on, or being acted on by, a nervous system other than its own" (p. 206). In every normal act of perception, Shin is informed of the processes in its own nervous system. Thouless and Wiesner suggest that it might happen sometimes that Shin develops contacts with some nervous system other than its own and is thus aware of processes of that other nervous system. Telepathy, then, would be like any other process of perception except that it would involve cognitive relations with a nervous system that is outside the body in which Shin is residing.

Thouless and Wiesner point out that a volitional effort in ESP often tends to inhibit success. They seek to interpret this in support of their hypothesis. Thus they argue that the volitional efforts put forth are likely to direct Shin activity to the habitual sensory modes of perception and, consequently, prevent Shin's direct contact with the object. This is, however, a questionable argument. Many successful clairvoyants, particularly mediums, claim to exercise considerable volitional effort to achieve success. Miss Johnson, who showed ESP to a remarkable degree, did this "successfully, but not without great nervous strain" (Tyrrell, 1938). Rhine's brilliant subject Pearce correctly guessed all 25 cards when Rhine (1934/1973) goaded him by betting on the outcome. Thouless and Wiesner suspect that the action of the nervous system may inhibit psi-functioning. But volitional effort need not put the nervous system into action; on the other hand, it may control its activity. As pointed out by Craig Sinclair, concentration and relaxation may be equally necessary for success. Sinclair perhaps means the same when she observes, "A part of concentration is complete relaxation" (in U. Sinclair, 1930, p. 179).

There is a considerable similarity between Rhine's hypothesis and the Shin theory. According to Thouless and Wiesner, the direct contact of Shin with an object, without the mediation of the brain and the nervous system, is the necessary condition of clairvoyant cognition, and the direct contact of Shin with a brain and a nervous system other than its own is telepathy. Now it may be asked, "How is the percipient's Shin able to reach the object that is outside the body it occupies?" The laws of causation do not permit us to assume that Shin sits inside and yet is capable of perceiving distant objects without any causal connections in between.

Broad's analysis (1937) of causal objection to precognition applies mutatis mutandis to the Shin activity. Therefore, it is evidently impossible for Shin to perceive objects unless the radiating patterns of energy emanating from the object are reflected without sensory aid on Shin, or Shin is assumed to be capable of forcing itself on the objects external to the organism and extending in space, without itself being subjected to the laws of space. The known laws of nature render the first alternative impossible. Hence, we need to assume that Shin, a part of it, or an agent of it "goes out" to the object to perceive extrasensorially.

This is essentially what Rhine (1934/1973) seems to mean when he writes that the mind or an agent of it "goes out" to perceive extrasensorially, or, alternately, when he later adds that the mind may function through an energy form not conditioned to time–space–mass relations

(1953). The difference between Rhine and Thouless consists in the use of different terms, *mind* and *Shin*. Perhaps Thouless and Wiesner are justified in giving currency to the new term *Shin* since it is not vitiated by any previous metaphysical connotation, as is the case with the term *mind*.

3.3.4. Stanford's PMIR

Stanford (1974a,b, 1977a,b) has proposed a model for understanding psi which appears to incorporate and elaborate on the idea of mind projection implicit in Rhine's theory. Stanford postulates that the organism uses psi to scan its environment, as it does with its available sensory resources. This scanning, according to him, is need-based. "*In the presence of a particular need*," writes Stanford (1974a), "*the organism uses psi (ESP), as well as sensory means, to scan its environment for objects and events relevant to that need and for information crucially related to such objects and events* (p. 43)." When extrasensory information is obtained to subserve a need, the organism tends to behave in ways to satisfy the need, resulting in what Stanford calls the psi-mediated instrumental response or PMIR. In other words, when an organism receives psi information, it tends "to act in ways which are instrumental in satisfying its needs in relation to the need-relevant object or event" (1974a, p. 44). Stanford goes on to state several other propositions that develop this basic idea of PMIR, to explain some of the experimental results in terms of PMIR concepts, and also to suggest further areas of research.

Stanford (1974b) extends his model to explain psychokinesis. PK is regarded as "a response mode for PMIR." PMIR may be any kind of goal-relevant response made possible through extrasensory means by PK. Stanford distinguishes two kinds of telepathy: the "percipient-active" and the "agent-active" forms. Telepathy, where the percipient actively scans the internal states of the agent, is the first kind. The second form of telepathy is one in which the agent actively influences the internal states of the percipient by means of PK. In other words, the agent-active telepathy is really a form of PK. An important aspect of Stanford's theory is that PMIR is conceived as disposition-subserving rather than intrinsically perceptual or cognitive in character and that psi tends to influence behavior in appropriate ways, not necessarily striving for perceptual–cognitive expression.

The central idea in this model is that all psi responses are mediated, are instrumental, and subserve the "entire range of needs." The emphasis on the nonintentional character of psi scanning reiterates the assumptions that psi is somewhat similar to our autonomic activity, in that it functions without our conscious intent and that the extrasensory information received at the level of the unconscious requires a mediating instrument if it is to be manifest in consciousness. It is not clear, however, whether Stanford rules out completely the possibility of having direct awareness of extrasensory information and holds that ESP can only be inferred from the responses it is believed to mediate. Also, it is not clear whether, according to this model, psi is an entity, a structure, or a process. If it is an entity, what are its characteristics? What is its ontological status? Also, what is its relation to our body and sensorimotor system? Again, the model suggests very little about the underlying structure or process of psi. How is psi able to scan in such a way as to be independent of time–space constraints, as far as we know?

Stanford brings together a number of psi findings with commendable ingenuity and candor. His stress on the nonintentional character of psi makes sense. Yet the basic model is hardly an advance over the projection hypothesis. While Stanford may be correct in his thinking about the goal-directedness of PMIR, one will find it hard to believe that the strength and importance of the need is as relevant to psi as Stanford's model implies. Many subjects who are successful on trivial psi tasks have reported no psi experiences on matters that must have been tremendously important to them in life. In defense of Stanford's theory, it may be pointed out that the theory makes several assumptions concerning the conditions that block psi functioning, which presumably explain why we do not always experience psi in response to our need demands.

Subsequent to his publication of the PMIR theory, Stanford has developed his theory to include assumptions explaining the underlying character of psi phenomena. These new ideas make it clear that the "scanning" mentioned in the PMIR model is not literal—that psi often occurs so that it looks *as if* scanning has occurred, but that scanning is not what actually activates psi response (Stanford, 1977a,b).

In a paper presented at the Parapsychology Foundation conference, Stanford (1977a) attempted to make explicit the assumptions implied in the traditional model which he calls the "*psychobiological* paradigm," and argues that his revised version of the PMIR model is an alternative. Crediting this paradigm with a strong and constraining influence on the course of parapsychological research in the past, he identifies the following preconceptions it is believed to imply: (1) that ESP is an information-receiving capacity and that "in some sense either a specialized receptor or the brain and nervous system must have the capacity to receive and process such information" (p. 2), and (2) that "extrasensory information is used, albeit unconsciously, to guide and thus to control the outcome" (p. 2). Stanford refers to J. B. Rhine's view that assumes ESP and PK to be the nonphysical analogues of sensory perception and motor action, as an example of the psychobiological paradigm that, he says, has been rarely questioned by parapsychological researchers.

While Stanford is correct in assuming that Rhine's characterization of psi as an extrasensorimotor function has guided most of psi research, the two "preconceptions" referred to above are not necessarily implied by the psychobiological paradigm. In fact, the second part of the first preconception, that "a specialized receptor or the brain and nervous system has the capacity to receive and process" psi information, is patently alien to Rhine's thinking on this matter. Again, it is true that Rhine advocates the idea of implicit extrasensory monitoring of the target system for guiding PK, but this is an ad hoc hypothesis and not a logical deduction from the so-called psychobiological model.

Stanford emphasizes that we should depart from the notion that ESP is a kind of information-processing factor and think of it as a disposition-subserving function. This seems to be a misplaced emphasis because there is no logical incompatibility between the two points of view. The "dirigibility" idea that Rhine repeatedly stressed is the purposive aspect of psi. The concept of goal-directedness hardly seems alien to Rhine, whose psychological roots are in McDougall's hormic psychology. Stanford also seems to miss the significance of the term *target* as traditionally used by parapsychologists. If *target* were identical with *stimulus*, there would have been no need to use the former expression. *Target* has a teleological dimension insofar as it is goal-orienting to the subject.

Extending and revising his PMIR model, Stanford has proposed in a preliminary form a theory of "conformance behavior," which attempts to explain ESP in the following way. The nervous system or the brain is a complex and sophisticated random event generator (REG). The ESP subject (or the experimenter), insofar as he or she has a need, wish, or want to succeed in the test, is a disposed system. A disposed system is contingently linked to an REG under circumstances that are favorable in such a manner that the outputs of the latter fulfill the dispositions of the former. When such conformance behavior manifests, we have ESP. In plain language, what Stanford is saying here is this: If the subject has a wish or need to succeed in an ESP test, under favorable circumstances his or her brain or nervous system will be biased to make correct calls. This is possible because a "contingent linkage" exists between a successful subject's disposition and brain, or between a successful experimenter and his or her subjects in the case of experimenter effect, or between the agent and the percipient in some forms of telepathy. But the concept of contingent linkage makes some of the same assumptions as the variety of hypotheses based on the so-called psychobiological model. Stanford's theory resembles that of Walker (1975) without the latter's explanatory and predictive value.

4. Acausal Theories

The physical as well as nonphysical theories of psi find it necessary to postulate an agency that is endowed with the ability to make a direct contact with the target, transcending the inhibitory effects of space and time, or a medium that provides the necessary link of contact between the subject and the target. In either case some kind of causal interaction is assumed. There are, however, a few who question the basic assumptions underlying these theories and suggested acausal models. For example, Dommeyer (1977) suggests that the anomalies of psi that arouse the antagonism of scientists could be resolved by an acausal theory of ESP and PK. He proposes that there is in nature acausal uniformity in addition to the well-known causal uniformity.

Dommeyer distinguishes among three types of acausality. The first type is implied in the kind of uniformity that exists between two clocks showing the same time, even though one is not the cause of the other. The second type of acausal relationship is one where two causally independent events have a common causal antecendent(s), as in two apple trees blooming about the same time. The third type of acausality involves "intermittent acausal uniformity." "In this sort," says Dommeyer, "the uniform occurrence of the kinds of events that A and B are is not constant. It can be sufficiently present, however, to be statistically significant" (p. 90). Dommeyer argues that the fact that no intelligible causal relationship is found between a psychic event such as a premonition and the verifying referent indicates that there may be no such causal relation. This would call for a change in our interpretational framework from a causal model to an acausal one.

Another critic of vitalistic theories in parapsychology is Flew (1951, 1953–54), who has characterized the "mind talk" of Rhine and others as "philosophical sensationalism" born out of inappropriate explanatory models and a misunderstanding of the "logic of terms."

The concept of extrasensory perception, Flew argues, suggests an explanatory model of perception, but ESP is very different from perception in essential respects. He goes on to say that such paradoxes as serial concepts of time are patently due to taking seriously the perceptive models of ESP. If we cannot explain ESP on the model of perception, how else can we explain it? Flew thinks that it is more fruitful to consider ESP a "species of guess work." But one fails to see, even granting an explainable connection between the subject's guesses and some other psychological factors associated with it, what purpose this new model would serve for ESP. As Mundle (1952) succinctly points out, Flew's "guesswork" model could neither *describe* nor *explain* the facts of ESP any more appropriately than the perception model of the parapsychologists.

4.1. Synchronicity

The best known acausal explanation of psi is Jung's synchronicity hypothesis. According to Jung (Jung and Pauli, 1955), any causal explanation of paranormal phenomena such as ESP is "unthinkable," because a causal interaction is always on "energetic" phenomenon bound by space–time limitations. Parapsychological phenomena are known to be at least partially independent of space and time; therefore, they should belong to another order of the universe. In contradistinction to the familiar causal order, Jung postulates a noncausal order that is composed of synchronistic phenomena. By synchronicity Jung means a noncausal relationship that links two events together in a meaningful way. It is a sort of meaningful coincidence, a coincidence that makes sense. Synchronicity, says Jung, applies to those cases of simultaneous occurrence of a certain psychological condition with one or more objective phenomena in which the meaning of the first is similar to the others that follow.

Synchronistic coincidences include not only the significant results in psi experiments and spontaneous psi occurrences but also the omens, successful astrological predictions, *I Ching* readings, and all kinds of physical effects that have no normal explanation. The following is one of the several personal experiences of synchronicity Jung (1963) reports, one that occurred in 1909 when Jung and Freud were discussing paranormal phenomena:

> While Freud was going on this way, I had a curious sensation. It was as if my diaphragm were made of iron and becoming red-hot—a glowing vault. And at that moment there was such a loud report in the bookcase, which stood right next to us, that we both started up in alarm, fearing the thing was going to topple over on us. I said to Freud: "There, that is an example of a so-called catalytic exteriorization phenomenon."
> "Oh come," he exclaimed. "That is sheer bosh."
> "It is not," I replied. "You are mistaken, Herr Professor. And to prove my point I now predict that in a moment there will be another such loud report!" Sure enough, no sooner had I said the words than the same detonation went off in the bookcase. (p. 155)

Even though synchronous events literally mean those events that are simultaneous occurrences, Jung uses the concept of synchronicity to include even precognitive events. In the experience cited above, for example, the second explosion occurred after Jung's prediction of it. Spontaneous precognitive events do sometimes occur considerably later in time than their predictions. Jung did not seem to be concerned about the extent of duration between the event and its foreknowledge as a precondition for synchronistic precognition.

Flew (1953–54) criticized this concept on the ground that "meaningful coincidence" is a tautology, He argued that concidences are concidences because they are meaningful. But by *meaningful* Jung seems to imply more than what Flew grants him, even though some examples of synchronicity given by Jung himself, devoid of their symbolism, appear to be no more than mere coincidences. In the experience of Jung narrated above, the meaningfulness of the coincidence is derived by three factors: (1) The explosions occurred when the two men were discussing paranormal phenomena; (2) Jung predicted the occurrence of the second explosion with no ordinary means of knowing that such an explosion would occur again; and (3) no causal relationship is discernable between the discussion of paranormal phenomena by Jung and Freud and the first explosion or between Jung's awareness of the impending explosion and the subsequent detonation in the bookcase.

While Jung is unequivocal in his denial of any causal relationship between the synchronistic events, he does not deny that each of the synchronistically related events may have its own causal ancestors. For example, it is possible that the explosions may have had natural explanations; but what is of interest is that they happened when they did.

Even granting Jung's assumption that it is futile to look for causal connections between synchronistic events, we are still left with the problem of distinguishing true synchronistic events from chance coincidences; i.e., the coincidences that are "meaningful" from those that are not. The concept would make sense if we could explain how the synchronistic events, as opposed to nonsynchronistic coincidences, come to pass. This is the most crucial aspect of synchronistic theory and unfortunately the most difficult one from the point of view of knowing what precisely were Jung's views. It is no easy task to reconcile Jung's own writings on this subject or the interpretations given by his followers. One reason for this state of affairs is that, for Jung, synchronicity is a metaphysical principle and is intended to explain more than what we now regard as parapsychological phenomena.

A parapsychological situation, whether it is causal or synchronistic, has two elements that need to be related: a series of mental events within the subject and one or more events outside of the subject. The subjective psychic events have their own causation. According to Jung, in a synchronistic situation the psychic events are mediated by the archetypes, which are dispositions of the collective unconscious. The archetypes are not themselves in consciousness but are represented in it by archetypal images and symbols. As mediators or vehicles, the archetypes themselves are insufficient to account for the content of the synchronistic psychic event. The true source is located at the deeper levels of our psyche—the psychoid level. At this level, the psyche, a microcosm, "reflects" the universe, the macrocosm. While discussing Swedenborg's vision of the Stockholm fire Jung (1969) says, "The fire in Stockholm was, in a sense, burning in him too" (p. 481). As Progoff has pointed out, Jung seems to be providing the psychological phenomenology of Leibniz's concept of the monad "mirroring" the universe. To quote Progoff (1973): "Once the functioning of a significant part of the psyche has dropped to the psychoid depth, the individual, as microcosm, is in a condition at which a part of his psyche is able to "catch" the "reflections" of the surrounding macrocosm to describe them and make them articulate" (p. 115).

The basic assumption, then, is that there is a latent capacity in the unconscious of foreknowledge that can operate without such intermediaries as the senses. In extrasensory perception, we draw on this latent capacity by the process of *abaissement*, a "lowering of the mental level." Since the psyche functions by means of a "dynamic balancing process," a lowering of consciousness on one side leads to a corresponding intensification of consciousness on the other. Such a "lowering," then, makes the psyche open to the full impact of the archetypal factors at the psychoid level and activates the latent capacity for extended awareness that results in parapsychological experiences. The extended awareness without the usual intermediaries is possible because the psyche at its deepest level is a microcosm that "reflects" the universe in macrocosm.

Thus, in his attempts to avoid any explanation of the paranormal based on "magical causality," Jung is led to assume that our unconscious in a significant sense is capable of "absolute knowledge," which on occasions becomes available to conscious experience through archetypal images and symbols. The emergence of these images into consciousness may be simultaneous with, prior to, or after the occurrence of the related external event. So we have contemporaneous, precognitive, or retrocognitive psi experiences. The "meaningfulness" of the coincidence is then a function of the "mirroring" effect, i.e., the reflection of the macroscopic event in the microcosm of our unconscious. In nonsynchronistic coincidences, there are presumably no such reflections.

Now, let us take the detonation in Freud's bookcase as an example of a paranormal event and attempt to interpret it in synchronistic acausal terms. The knowledge of the detonations is potentially available to the unconscious of Jung as well as Freud. But this knowledge was mediated into Jung's awareness alone after the first detonation and shortly before the second. Therefore, the coincidences became meaningful to Jung and not to Freud, who apparently did not experience a similar "reflection" of his unconscious.* The alternative explanations to this are (1) that the impending detonation somehow caused awareness in Jung, or (2) that Jung himself in some paranormal way caused the explosion in the bookcase. The first of these two is ruled out because it is impossible for a nonexistent external event to cause awareness. The second involves some sort of a PK effect, which would imply again a cause–effect relationship. If a natural sequence of events is shown to have caused the detonation in the bookcase, then, of course PK is ruled out. But whether PK occurred in this instance or not, in the light of substantial evidence for PK, Jung's hypothesis that in synchronistic situations external events are experienced as reflections in the unconscious through the mediation of the archetypes needs extension.

As Aniela Jaffe (quoted by Bender, 1977) points out, synchronicity is scarcely an explanation of PK:

> Jung's hint at the psychical relativity of time and space, "then the moving body must possess, or be subject to, corresponding relativity," does not lead us much further. He did not mention the question of psychokinesis with much more than this short remark. But in his work as well as in his letters he does hint at a possibility that the psyche can influence non-psychical things in some way and that, therefore, there may exist some so-to-speak causal relation. (p. 75)

In order to explain PK, Jung would have to assume that the archetypes, which are assumed to be capable of mediating the unconscious "knowledge" into consciousness, may also be able to exert their influence on and create events extending beyond the experiencing subject. This idea is implied in the concept of archetype as "psychoid." Being at the limits of our observational ability, it eludes our categorization into physical or psychical. When an archetype is activated, it may influence the external events as well as the images in the mind of the person involved in the synchronistic situation.

The omniscience of the unconscious and its capacity to effect changes in the environment are no new assumptions in parapsychology. What seems to be important in Jung's theory is the suggestion that the archetypes are involved as mediating agents and that the process of

---

*Gertrude Schmeidler suggests in a personal communication that Freud did not *consciously* experience it because, as Jung's symbolic father, the aggression was too threatening to him.

abaissement is important for archetypal activation that would result in paranormal experiences. These ideas are capable of empirical testing and provide the basis for interaction between Jungians and parapsychologists.

Gatlin (1977) makes use of Jung's synchronicity concept for a genetic interpretation of psi. She argues that the failure to identify a physical carrier of psi information suggests that there is no such carrier and that no transmission of information takes place in ESP. Instead, information is created via the mechanism of synchronicity. Gatlin questions the commonly made assumption that there is some kind of an interaction between the target and the subject. The possibility of success in a precognitive situation rules this out because meaningful information cannot be transmitted backward in time.

Psi situations may be regarded as hierarchically structured situations of ascending levels of complexity where a unit can be seen either as a part of a larger whole or as the whole of some parts. The hit is ordinarily considered to be the elementary unit of psi, and the parapsychologists had hoped to find an explanation in an interaction that would bring about the target–response match. Gatlin argues that this is a wrong way of looking at the psi situation. The subject's response is not caused by the target; at the same time the response is not causeless. Again, the target sequence is not so random as we often tend to believe. The concept of a "random finite sequence is an unattainable ideal" (p. 8). Thus, once we realize what the hierarchies involved are, we could see that the individual hits are acausal inasmuch as the target response matchings may now be seen as the matching of bias in target and response sources. Gatlin points out:

> It does seem intuitively reasonable that two biased sources chosen at random from nature would not match to the extent we sometimes observe, but have been "tuned" to synchronize by some kind of interaction. However, and this is the heart of the matter, this tuning process does not have to occur (a) during the course of the experiment per se (ESP, PK, etc.). It does not even have to occur (b) in the pre-experiment subject–experimenter–environment interaction. It could possibly have occurred (c) even further back in time by slow evolutionary processes which have sorted biological sources into a finite number of discrete informational categories such that the probability is high that two of them will match by coincidence without significant interaction in the present. (p. 14)

Gatlin recognizes that the matching of target and response biases may itself be acausal and that such a matching, in its turn, may be traced to "higher level synchronistic mechanisms which operate on a cosmic scale" (p. 15).

While Gatlin's conjecture may seem prima facie plausible to explain spontaneous ESP, particularly of the telepathic kind where one could assume synchronization between the built-in biases of the two biological sources (the percipient and the agent), it is difficult to conceive that in an experimental psi situation the subjective and genetic bias of the subject somehow mysteriously synchronizes with the assumed bias of the target sequence. Gatlin has not shown convincingly how and at what level of the hierarchical organization the acausal relation between the subject source and the target source becomes causally related. One implication of Gatlin's theory, however, has some merit. It makes sense to assume that in some cases the subject may not respond in a target-by-target fashion. In fact, psi may simply instigate a bias in the subject's response pattern, a bias that would synchronize with the inherent bias of the target sequence so that more of his responses would match with the targets than otherwise. Some research on this question is clearly called for.

Koestler (1972) found it painful to see Jung entangle himself in the verbiage of causality when he seemed to assign a causative role to archetypes in producing psi effects. He argued that synchronicity is an ultimate and irreducible principle and is complementary to mechanical causation. Parapsychological phenomena are the highest manifestation of nature's integrative tendency to create order out of disorder. Recent developments in physics and biology as well as parapsychology seem to point this out. "Everything," writes Koestler, "hangs together; no atom is an island; microcosm reflects macrocosm, and is reflected by it" (Hardy, Harvie, and Koestler, 1973, p. 261). Elsewhere he writes about some sort of "psychomagnetic field" that is credited with producing synchronistic or confluential events that are not subject to the laws of classical physics. Its modus operandi at this time is unknown, but it may be "related to that striving towards higher forms of order and unity-in-variety which we observe in the evolution of the universe . . ." (Koestler, 1972, p. 128).

5. Summary

Writing about theories and models of psi, Chari (1977) observes that the "field is strewn with dead and dying hypotheses and desperate expedients" (p. 806). Many of the theories we have surveyed are tentative and exploratory hypotheses, often no more than descriptions. While none is entirely satisfactory in explaining psi, each of them seems to contain some fruitful ideas. Together they may indicate broad categories of theorizing in parapsychology and perhaps even imply the directions future theories and even research may take. The growing emphasis on testable hypotheses and falsifiable models augurs well for the advancement of psi research. The factor that distinguishes parapsychology from the occult is the former's commitment to scientific method. A theory that permits no de-

ductive development and makes no verifiable predictions seldom contributes to the growth of a science. The critical need is for theory and research to go hand in hand. The indications are that they will do so, and
that state of affairs is beneficial for parapsychology.

Investigation of the "physical" hypotheses, directed toward finding a
new medium of psi communication, will likely reveal the limiting conditions of psi. Today, no one really knows what the outer boundaries of psi
are. To assume a priori that ESP can reach any object however remote it
may be in space or time, that it can make possible such feats as speaking
in unknown languages and exhibiting unlearned skills, or that PK can
influence any target without regard to its size and kind, indicates a naive
optimism, which, unchecked, could lead us to overlook some basic facts
about psi. It is just as important to learn what psi cannot accomplish as it
is to discover what it can accomplish.

The "nonphysical" hypotheses are likely to be the ones that will give
us insights into the psychological processes involved in psi cognitions.
The theories that postulate the common or collective unconscious offer
explanatory models that provide clues for the discovery of the dynamics
that govern psi manifestation. However, they are confronted with the
problem of explaining the selection process involved in receiving psi messages. Projection hypotheses attempt to overcome this problem by postulating such entities as mind and Shin. The testing of the projection
hypotheses, which place the principle of psi operation and its energetic
source in the individual rather than in the target object, will likely give us
important information about subject variables.

Most of the nonphysical hypotheses, like the physical ones, are derived from what may be called the *interactionist model*—a model that
assumes the independence of the subject and the target in a psi situation
and regards the subject–target interaction as essential for psi manifestation. Acausal theories plead for abandoning the interactionist model in
favor of the *intuitionalist model*.

Acausal hypotheses have the merit of questioning some of the classical assumptions concerning subject–target relationships. They, more
than any others, show the basic inappropriateness of the stimulus–
response model of psi. In a significant sense there is a prima facie absur-
dity in any attempt to connect the subject and the target in a psi situation.
Take for example the question of precognition. The target by definition is
nonexistent at the moment of the subject's cognition of it. The vain attempts to connect the subject with a nonexisting event lead us to such
paradoxical notions of other dimensions of time and different orders of
reality (Flew, 1976). Acausal models assume a subject–target identification. Thus there is no distance to travel or no time to scan between the

subject and the target. Every subject is a microcosm, potentially capable of reflecting the whole cosmos. This potential is not realized because we are habitually and constitutionally given to respond to and interact with our environment rather than to probe within to discover hidden knowledge. Psi events do seem to indicate, however, that this is not an irreversible process and that on occasion knowledge can be had by tapping our inner resources. Thus we are led to postulate an ominscience inherent in our very being.

Whether we opt for the intuitionalist model or the interactionist model to explain psi, it would seem to portend a paradigmatic shift in our view concerning human beings and their place in nature.

6. References

Beloff, J. Parapsychology and its neighbors. *Journal of Parapsychology*, 1970, *34*, 129–142.

Bender, H. Meaningful coincidences in the light of Jung–Pauli's theory of synchronicity. In B. Shapin and L. Coly (Eds.), *The philosophy of parapsychology: Proceedings of an international conference*. New York: Parapsychology Foundation, 1977.

Berger, H. *Psyche*. Jena: Verlag Gustav Fischer, 1940.

Bergson, H. *Mind energy*. New York: Henry Holt, 1920.

Blackmore, S. *Memory as an alternative to perception for modelling E.S.P.* Paper presented at the conference of the Society for Psychical Research, London, April 1977.

Braud, L. W., and Braud, W. G. Further studies of relaxation as a psi-conducive state. *Journal of the American Society for Psychical Research*, 1974, *68*, 229–245.

Braud, W. G., and Braud, L. W. Preliminary explorations of psi-conducive states: Progressive muscular relaxation. *Journal of the American Society for Psychical Research*, 1973, *67*, 26–46.

Broad, C. D. *Mind and its place in nature*. New York: Humanities Press, 1951. (Originally published, 1925.)

Broad, C. D. The philosophical implications of foreknowledge. *Proceedings of the Aristotelian Society, 1937, 16* (Suppl.), 177–209.

Broad, C. D. Book review of "Symposium: Is psychical research relevant to philosophy?" by M. Kneale, R. Robinson, and C. W. K. Mundle. In *Aristotelian Society's Supplementary Vol. 24: Psychical research, ethics, and logic. Journal of Parapsychology*, 1951, *15*, 216–223.

Broad, C. D. *Religion, philosophy and psychical research*. New York: Harcourt Brace, 1953.

Broad, C. D. *Lectures on psychical research*. New York: Humanities Press, 1962. (a)

Broad, C. D. The problem of precognition: Notes on Mr. Roll's paper and comments evoked. *Journal of the Society for Psychical Research*, 1962, *41*, 225–234. (b)

Carington, W. W. Comments on Doctor Rhine's "Telepathy and clairvoyance reconsidered." *Proceedings of the Society for Psychical Research*, 1946, *48*, 8–27. (a)

Carington, W. W. *Thought transference: An outline of facts, theory and implications of telepathy*. New York: Creative Age Press, 1946. (b)

Carington, W. W. *Matter, mind and meaning*. New Haven: Yale University Press, 1949.

Chari, C. T. K. W. G. Roll's PK and precognition hypotheses, an Indian philosopher's reactions. *Journal of the Society for Psychical Research*, 1962, *41*, 417–422.

Chari, C. T. K. Some generalized theories and models of psi: A critical evaluation. In B. Wolman (Ed.), *Handbook of parapsychology*, New York: Van Nostrand Reinhold, 1977.

Cooper, D. E. ESP and the materialist theory of mind. In S. Thakur (Ed.), *Philosophy and psychical research*. New York: Humanities Press, 1976.

Dobbs, H. A. C. Time and extrasensory perception. *Proceedings of the Society for Psychical Research*, 1965, *54*, 249–361.

Dobbs, H. A. C. The feasibility of a physical theory of ESP. In J. R. Smythies (Ed.), *Science and ESP*. New York: Humanities Press, 1967.

Dommeyer, F. C. An acausal theory of extrasensory perception and psychokinesis. In B. Shapin and L. Coly (Eds.), *The philosophy of parapsychology: Proceedings of an international conference*. New York: Parapsychology Foundation, 1977.

Deutsch, H. Occult processes occurring during psychoanalysis. In G. Devereaux (Ed.), *Psychoanalysis and the occult*. New York: International Universities Press, 1953.

Ducasse, C. J. What would constitute conclusive evidence of survival? *Journal of the Society for Psychical Research*, 1962, *41*, 401–406.

Eccles, J. *The neurophysiological basis of mind*. Oxford: Clarendon Press, 1953.

Ehrenwald, J. *Telepathy and medical psychology*. London: George Allen & Unwin, 1947.

Ehrenwald, J. *New dimensions of deep analysis*. London: George Allen & Unwin, 1954.

Ehrenwald, J. Human personality and the nature of psi phenomena. *Journal of the American Society for Psychical Research*, 1968, *62*, 366–380.

Ehrenwald, J. *The ESP experience: A psychiatric validation*. New York: Basic Books, 1977.

Eisenbud, J. Telepathy and problems of psychoanalysis. *Psychoanalytic Quarterly*, 1946, *15*, 32–87.

Eisenbud, J. The use of the telepathy hypothesis in psychotherapy. In G. Bychowski and L. Despert (Eds.), *Specialized techniques in psychotherapy*. New York: Basic Books, 1952.

Eisenbud, J. Why psi? *Psychoanalytic Review*, 1966–67, *54* (Winter), 147–163.

Eisenbud, J. *Psi and psychoanalysis*. New York: Grune and Stratton, 1970.

Flew, A. G. N. Minds and mystifications. *The Listener*, September 27, 1951.

Flew, A. G. N. Coincidence and synchronicity. *Journal of the Society for Psychical Research*, 1953–54, *38*, 198–201.

Flew, A. G. N. The sources of serialism. In S. Thakur (Ed.), *Philosophy and psychical research*. New York: Humanities Press, 1976.

Fodor, N. *New approaches to dream interpretation*. New York: Citadel, 1951.

Fodor, N. Telepathy in analysis. In G. Devereaux (Ed.), *Psychoanalysis and the occult*. New York: International Universities Press, 1953.

Freud, S. Dreams and telepathy. In G. Devereaux (Ed.), *Psychoanalysis and the occult*. New York: International Universities Press, 1953. (Originally published, 1922.)

Freud, S. The occult significance of dreams. In G. Devereaux (Ed.), *Psychoanalysis and the occult*. New York: International Universities Press, 1953. (Originally published, 1925.)

Gammon, M. R. Windows into eternity: Archetype and relativity. *Journal of Analytical Psychology*, 1973, *18*, 11–24.

Gatlin, L. L. Meaningful information creation: An alternative interpretation of the psi phenomenon. *Journal of the American Society for Psychical Research*, 1977, *71*, 1–18.

Hardy, A., Harvie, R., and Koestler, A. *The challenge of chance*. New York: Random House, 1973.

Hoffman, B. ESP and the inverse square law. *Journal of Parapsychology*, 1940, *4*, 149–152.

Jung, C. G. *Memories, dreams, reflections* (Recorded and edited by A. Jaffé). New York: Pantheon, 1963.

Jung, C. G. *The structure and dynamics of the psyche* (*Collected works*, Vol. 8). Princeton: Princeton University Press, 1969.

Jung, C. G., and Pauli, W. *The interpretation of nature and the psyche: Synchronicity and the influence of archetypal ideas on the scientific theories of Kepler*. New York: Pantheon, 1955.

Kahn, S. D. "Myers' problem" revisited. In G. R. Schmeidler (Ed.), *Parapsychology: Its relationship to physics, biology, psychology, and psychiatry*. Metuchen, New Jersey: Scarecrow Press, 1976.

Kanthamani, H. (B. K.), and Rao, H. H. A study of memory–ESP relationships using linguistic forms. *Journal of Parapsychology*, 1974, *38*, 286–300.

Kanthamani, H. (B. K.), and Rao, H. H. The role of association strength in memory– ESP interaction. *Journal of Parapsychology*, 1975, *39*, 1–11.

Koestler, A. *The roots of coincidence*. New York: Random House, 1972.

Kogan, I. M. Is telepathy possible? *Telecommunication and Radio Engineering*, 1966, *21* (1, Pt. 2), 75–81.

Kogan, I. M. Telepathy—hypotheses and observations. *Telecommunication and Radio Engineering*, 1967, *22* (1, Pt. 2), 141–144.

Kogan, I. M. Information theory analysis of telepathic communication experiments. *Telecommunication and Radio Engineering*, 1968, *23* (3, Pt. 2), 122–125.

Kuhn, T. S. *The structure of scientific revolutions*. Chicago: University of Chicago Press, Phoenix Books, 1962.

LeShan, L. *Toward a general theory of the paranormal (Parapsychological monographs No. 9.)* New York: Parapsychology Foundation, 1969.

LeShan, L. *The medium, the mystic and the physicist*. New York: Viking Press, 1974.

LeShan, L. *Alternate realities*. New York: M. Evans, 1976.

Marshall, N. ESP and memory: A physical theory. *British Journal for the Philosophy of Science*, 1960, *10*, 265–286.

McCully, R. S. The Rorschach, synchronicity, and relativity. In R. W. Davis (Ed.), *Special monograph: Toward a discovery of the person*. Burbank: Society for Personality Assessment, 1974.

McDougall, W. In J. B. Rhine, *Extra-sensory perception*. Boston: Branden Press, 1973. (Originally published, 1934.)

Mundle, C. W. K. Some philosophical perspectives for parapsychology. *Journal of Parapsychology*, 1952, *16*, 257–272.

Murphy, G. Field theory and survival. *Journal of the American Society for Psychical Research*, 1945, *39*, 181–209.

Murphy, G. Psychical research and the mind–body relation. *Journal of the American Society for Psychical Research*, 1946, *40*, 189–207.

Murphy, G. Psychical research and personality. *Journal of the American Society for Psychical Research*, 1950, *44*, 3–20.

Murphy, G. The natural, the mystical and the paranormal. *Journal of the American Society for Psychical Research*, 1952, *46*, 125–142.

Murphy, G. A comparison of India and the West in viewpoints regarding psychical phenomena. *Journal of the American Society for Psychical Research*, 1959, *53*, 43–49.

Murphy, G. Lawfulness versus caprice: Is there a "law of psychic phenomena"? *Journal of the American Society for Psychical Research*, 1964, *58*, 238–249.

Murphy, G., and Ballou, R. O. (Eds.). *William James on psychical research*. New York: Viking Press, 1960.

Myers, F. W. H. *Human personality* (2 vols.). New York: Longmans, Green, 1915. (Originally published, 1903.)

Price, H. H. Some philosophical questions about telepathy and clairvoyance. *Philosophy*, 1940, *15*, 363–374.

Price, H. H. Psychical research and human personality. *Hibbert Journal*, 1948, *47*, 105–113.

Price, H. H. Psychical research and human nature. *Journal of Parapsychology*, 1959, *23*, 178–185.

Price, H. H. Psychical research and human personality. In J. R. Smythies (Ed.), *Science and ESP*. New York: Humanities Press, 1967.

Progoff, I. *Jung, synchronicity and human destiny*. New York: Julian Press, 1973.

Rao, K. R. *Experimental parapsychology*. Springfield, Illinois: Charles C. Thomas, 1966.

Rhine, J. B. *Extra-sensory perception*. Boston: Branden Press, 1973. (Originally published, 1934.)

Rhine, J. B. Editorial: Parapsychology and dualism. *Journal of Parapsychology*, 1945, *9*, 225–228.

Rhine, J. B. *New world of the mind*. New York: Wm. Sloane, 1953.

Rhine, L. E. Toward understanding psi-missing. *Journal of Parapsychology*, 1965, *29*, 259–274.

Roll, W. G. The problem of precognition. *Journal of the Society for Psychical Research*, 1961, *41*, 115–128.

Roll, W. G. The psi field. *Proceedings of the Parapsychological Association No. 1, 1957–1964*. Durham, North Carolina: Parapsychological Association, 1966, Pp. 32–65. (a)

Roll, W. G. ESP and memory. *International Journal of Parapsychology*, 1966, *2*, 505–521. (b)

Schmeidler, G. R. Respice, adspice, prospice, In W. G. Roll, R. L. Morris, and J. D. Morris (Eds.), *Proceedings of the Parapsychological Association No. 8, 1971*. Durham, North Carolina: Parapsychological Association, 1972. Pp. 117–145.

Schmeidler, G. R. Psychological lawfulness and physical theory. In R. W. Davis (Ed.), *Special monograph: Toward a discovery of the person*. Burbank: Society for Personality Assessment, 1974.

Servadio, E. Psychoanalysis and telepathy. In G. Devereaux (Ed.), *Psychoanalysis and the occult*. New York: International Universities Press, 1953.

Sinclair, U. *Mental radio*. Monrovia, California: Upton Sinclair, 1930.

Soal, S. G., and Bateman, F. *Modern experiments in telepathy*. New Haven: Yale University Press, 1954.

Stanford, R. G. Extrasensory effects upon associative processes in a directed free-response task. *Journal of the American Society for Psychical Research*, 1973, *67*, 147–190.

Stanford, R. G. An experimentally testable model for spontaneous psi events. I. Extrasensory events. *Journal of the American Society for Psychical Research*, 1974, *68*, 34–57. (a)

Stanford, R. G. An experimentally testable model for spontaneous psi events. II. Psychokinetic events. *Journal of the American Society for Psychical Research*, 1974, *68*, 321–356. (b)

Stanford, R. G. Are parapsychologists paradigmless in psiland? In B. Shapin and L. Coly (Eds.), *The philosophy of parapsychology: Proceedings of an international conference*. New York: Parapsychology Foundation, 1977. (a)

Stanford, R. G. Conceptual frameworks of contemporary psi research. In B. Wolman (Ed.), *Handbook of parapsychology*, New York: Van Nostrand Reinhold, 1977. (b)

Thouless, R. H., and Wiesner, B. P. The psi processes in normal and paranormal psychology. *Journal of Parapsychology*, 1948, *12*, 192–212.

Tyrrell, G. N. M. *Science and psychical phenomena*. London: Methuen, 1938.

Tyrrell, G. N. M. The *modus operandi* of paranormal cognition. *Proceedings of the Society for Psychical Research*, 1947, *48*, 65–120. (a)

Tyrrell, G. N. M. Reason, inspiration and telepathy. *Hibbert Journal*, 1947, *45*, 327–333. (b)

Tyrrell, G. N. M. *The personality of man*. West Drayton: Penguin Books. 1948.

Ullman, M., Krippner, S., and Vaughan, A. *Dream telepathy*. New York: Macmillan, 1973.

Vasiliev, L. L. *Experiments in distant influence*. New York: E. P. Dutton, 1976. (Originally published as *Experiments in mental suggestion*, 1963.)

Walker, E. H. The nature of consciousness. *Mathematical Biosciences*, 1970, *7*, 131–178.

Walker, E. H. Consciousness in the quantum theory of measurement. Part I. *Journal for the Study of Consciousness*, 1972, *5*, 46–63. (a)

Walker, E. H. Consciousness in the quantum theory of measurement. Part II. *Journal for the Study of Consciousness*, 1972, *5*, 257–277. (b)

Walker, E. H. Foundations of paraphysical and parapsychological phenomena. In L. Oteri (Ed.), *Quantum physics and parapsychology*. New York: Parapsychology Foundation, 1975.

Wassermann, G. D. An outline of a field theory of organismic form and behaviour. In G. E. Wolstenholme and E. C. P. Millar (Eds.), *Ciba Foundation symposium on extrasensory perception*. Boston: Little, Brown, 1956.

Name Index

Adams, J. Q., 105
Adcock, C. J., 97, 154
Alkokar, V. V., 156, 159
Altom, K., 97, 114
Altrocchi, J., 62
Anderson, M., 74, 79, 81, 101, 104–105, 136–137, 138, 147, 148, 169, 181
Angstadt, J., 101, 145, 147
Aström, J., 132

Ballard, J. A., 131, 164, 191–192
Banham, K. M., 155, 163, 180, 186
Barber, T. X., 209
Barkema, P. R., 122
Barrington, M. R., 155
Barron, F., 49, 149
Barry, J., 194
Bate, D., 103, 159, 195
Bateman, F., 266
Bates, K. E., 103, 142
Becker, R. O., 1
Beer, D., 101
Behrendt, T., 149, 196
Beloff, J., 80, 97, 101, 103, 111, 112, 130, 143, 154, 159, 184, 195, 253–254
Belvedere, E., 121

Bender, H., 287
Berger, H., 247, 249–250, 254
Bergson, H., 265
Bertini, M., 115
Bessent, M., 79, 120, 127
Bestall, C. M., 39
Bevan, J. M., 92, 97, 154, 165–166
Bhadra, B. H., 154–155, 159
Bierman, D. J., 98, 145, 147
Birge, W. R., 96–97
Bisaha, J. P., 63, 80
Blackmore, S., 272
Bleksley, A. E. H., 26, 74
Blom, J. G., 62
Bogart, D. N., 93
Bokert, E., 117
Bond, E. M., 136, 173
Boss, M., 3
Braid, J., 278
Braud, L. W., 41, 114, 115, 119, 128, 131, 132, 159, 163, 271
Braud, W. G., 28, 41, 113–114, 115, 119, 121, 128, 159, 163, 185–186, 190
Brier, R., 107

Brinkman, W., 102
Broad, C. D., 245, 273, 274, 276–277, 279
Brodbeck, T. J., 130, 132, 148
Broughton, R. S., 95, 108, 128–129, 152, 175
Brugmans, H. J. F. W., 60, 180
Burdick, D. S., 54
Buzby, D. E., 80, 134, 141, 149, 156–157, 207

"C. J.," 61, 199
Cabibbo, C., 103
Cadoret, R. J., 40, 91, 92, 121–122, 125, 153, 169, 200
Camstra, B., 98, 147
Carbone, M., 124–125, 181
Carington, W. W., 74, 75, 77–78, 265–266
Carlson, M. L., 23
Carpenter, J. C., 23, 25, 130, 131, 134, 135, 154, 155, 158, 161, 162–163, 165, 169, 170, 182, 191–192, 193
Casler, L., 93, 97, 102, 109, 110
Casper, G. W., 97, 101,

297

Casper, G. W. *(cont.)*
   132, 135, 155, 159, 166,
   182
Castello, A., 128, 129
Cattell, R. B., 130
Cavanna, R., 123
Cazzamali, F., 247, 248
Chari, C. T. K., 273, 289
Charlesworth, E. A., 42,
   114, 118, 133, 149
Chauvin, R., 82
Child, I. L., 26, 37, 62, 99,
   169, 174, 202–203, 209
Clark, C. C., 102
Cohen, D., 91, 92
Cooper, D. E., 260
Coover, J. E., 60, 99
Cowles, M., 195
Craig, J. G., 49, 108, 152
Crookall, R., 117
Crumbaugh, J. C., 130, 155

Dagel, L. T., 184–185
Dale, L. A., 106, 129, 181,
   184, 195
Dalton, G. F., 194
Damgaard, J. A., 30, 62
Davis, K. R., 111
Dean, E. D., 31, 49, 80,
   103, 146, 155, 169,
   181–182, 194–195, 196
Deguisne, A., 104
Delmore, W., 62, 87–88,
   177, 181, 186, 200
Deutsch, H., 267
Dimond, S., 128
Dingwall, E. J., 109
Dobbs, H. A. C., 252–255,
   260
Dommeyer, F. C., 283
Drake, R. M., 136, 143,
   180
Drucker, S. A., 42, 93,
   116, 184, 187
Duane, D. T., 48, 149, 196
Ducasse, C. J., 273
Dukhan, H., 62, 117
Dunne, B. J., 115
Durkin, M. G., 111, 169

Duval, P., 27, 40, 150–151,
   175

Eason, M. J. C., 136
Eastman, M., 148
Eccles, J., 252–253, 254
Edmunds, S., 111
Ehrenwald, J., 4, 261, 267,
   268–269
Eilbert, L., 93, 133, 155,
   159
Einstein, A., 259
Eisenbud, J., 105, 108, 120,
   154, 159, 267–268
Elkisch, P., 166
Erwin, W., 120
Esser, A. H., 149, 194
Estabrooks, G. H., 60, 170
Extra, J. F. M. W., 100,
   151
Eysenck, H. J., 40, 130,
   133, 151

Fahler, J., 37, 76, 109–110,
   177–178
Feather, S. R., 107, 137,
   157, 159, 176
Feola, J., 125
Figar, S., 193–194
Fishbein, M., 160
Fisk, G. W., 23, 74,
   106–107, 108, 161,
   198–199, 200, 201,
   202–203
Flew, A. G. N., 283–284,
   285, 290
Fodor, N., 267
Foster, A., 25
Foster, E. B., 25, 27, 39,
   87, 199
Foulkes, D., 75, 121
Fox, W., 111
France, G. A., 149
Freeman, J. A., 26, 27, 80,
   83, 84, 85, 130, 136,
   145–146, 162,
   176–177, 180, 181
Freud, S., 267, 284–287
Friedman, R. M., 146, 154,

Friedman, R. M. *(cont.)*
   157, 159, 164

Gambale, J., 175, 176
Gammon, M. R., 259
Garrett, E. J., 16, 97
Gatlin, L. L., 209, 288–289
Gauld, A., 59
Gelade, G., 139, 159, 179
Geller, U., 63–64
George, R. W., 83, 94
Gerber, R., 122
Gerstein, P., 155
Gibson, E. P., 74, 75, 76,
   93, 169
Glick, B. S., 111
Glidden, S. H., 174
Globus, G., 121
Goldberg, J., 134
Goldstone, G., 105
Greely, A. M., 70
Green, C. E., 74, 130, 131,
   132, 147, 148
Greenwood, J. A., 54, 172
Grela, J. J., 111
Gurney, E., 59, 70

Habel, M. M., 115, 145
Haight, M. J., 142
Hall, C., 29, 120, 121
Hall, J. A., 105
Hallett, S. J., 83, 88
Hammid, H., 79–80
Hanlon, J., 63
Hansel, C. E. M., 65–67
Haraldsson, E., 70, 79,
   132, 140, 155, 184, 186,
   194
Harary, S. B., 155, 159,
   176
Hardy, A., 289
Harper, S., 42, 115
Harribance, L., 16, 30, 46,
   62, 98, 125, 169, 172,
   173, 181, 202
Harris, S. A., 151, 175
Harvie, R., 139
Haskell, P., 67
Hebda, H. C., 87, 89

Hermon, H., 42, 116
Hess, W. R., 3
Heyman, S., 90, 134
Hodgson, R., 60
Hoffman, B., 247
Hogan, R. A., 149
Honorton, C., 28, 29, 41,
    42, 45, 79, 92, 103,
    109, 110–111, 112,
    113, 114–115, 116,
    119, 121, 124–125,
    126, 127, 130, 134, 135,
    138, 139, 140, 154, 179,
    180, 181, 185, 206, 209
Huby, P. M., 122
Hudesman, J., 141–142,
    164
Hume, D., 64
Humphrey, B. M., 131,
    132, 135, 136,
    142–143, 165, 166,
    168, 169, 170, 178, 179,
    181, 207
Hurt, D. B., 184
Hutchinson, L., 81
Hyman, R., 47

Ivnisky, D., 178, 185

Jackson, M., 139, 155, 179,
    185
Jacobson, E., 113
Jaffe, A., 287
James, W., 261–262
Jampolsky, G. G., 142,
    143, 184
Janet, P., 109
Jensen, A., 75
Joesting, R., 169
Johnson, M., 131, 140,
    189–190, 192, 193
Johnson, (Miss), 279
Jolliffe, D., 111
Jones, J. N., 157, 159
Jones, S. M., 93
Jung, C. G., 2, 284–288,
    289

Kahn, S. D., 74, 131, 154,

Kahn, S. D. *(cont.)*
    155, 159, 160, 166,
    181–182, 262
Kajinsky, B. B., 247–248
Kamiya, J., 127
Kanthamani, H. (B.K.),
    62, 79, 85, 88, 130,
    131, 132, 133, 135, 136,
    137, 166, 174, 175–176,
    177, 186, 200, 272
Kappers, J., 122
Keeling, K. R., 111, 181
Keil, H. H. J., 170
Kelly, E. F., 48, 54, 62, 79,
    125, 197, 200, 202
Kennedy, J. E., 108, 209
Kennedy, J. L., 98
Kimura, S., 111
Klein, J. L., 30, 62, 98
Koestler, A., 209, 246, 289
Kogan, I. M., 249
Kogen, J., 111
Kramer, J. K., 130
Kreiman, N., 175, 178,
    179, 185
Kreitler, H., 21, 38, 98–99,
    145
Kreitler, S., 38, 98–99
Krippner, S., 49, 75, 79,
    83, 111, 112, 118–119,
    120–121, 145
Kubis, J. F., 148
Kuhn, T. S., 245–246

Lancaster, J. B., 88
Layton, B. D., 146, 156,
    157, 160
Leonard, G., 60
"Leonie," 109
LeShan, L., 269–270, 271
Levin, J., 40, 49, 151
Levine, F., 138
Levy, W. J., 68, 151
Lewis, H., 115
Lewis, L., 88, 124
Lieberman, R., 134, 176
Lloyd, D. H., 49, 197
Louwerens, N. G., 101,
    144–145

Lubetkin, B. S., 94
Lubke, C., 98
Lucas, D., 84, 202

McBain, W. N., 111, 134,
    145, 157
McCallam, E., 37, 139,
    179, 180, 185
McConnell, R. A., 156,
    158
McCully, R. S., 259
McDougall, W., 273–274,
    282
McElroy, W. A., 131, 132,
    184
MacFarland, J. D., 83, 98,
    103, 170
McGuire, K., 134–135,
    138, 155, 164
McMahan, E. A., 22–23,
    74, 80, 93, 96–97, 99,
    166, 169, 177, 180, 182
Maher, M., 129
Mangan, G. L., 74, 79, 88,
    180, 198
Manning, R., 99
Marchesi, C., 74, 93, 169,
    177
Marks, D. F., 140
Marsh, M. C., 132
Marshall, N., 249–250
Martin, D. R., 61, 169,
    170, 172, 180, 199
Mayer, B., 114, 163
Medhurst, G., 67
Medhurst, R. G., 66
Michie, D., 74, 106, 159
Mihalasky, J., 134, 146
Millar, B., 49, 53, 197
Miller, A., 94, 158, 159
Miller, S. W., 114, 131
Mitchell, A. M. J., 180
Mitchell, E. D., 75, 170
Monroe, R. A., 117
Montredon, E., 150, 175
Mordkoff, A. M., 149
Morris, R. L., 1, 2, 20, 30,
    36, 46, 49, 51, 52, 53,
    62, 91, 92, 98, 108,

Morris, R. L. *(cont.)*
  118, 124, 125, 150, 151,
  152, 153, 172, 209
Moss, T., 101, 112,
  138–139, 155, 159
Mundle, C. W. K., 284
Murphy, G., 3, 90, 94, 95,
  261, 270–271
Mussig, G. F., 163
Musso, J. R., 63, 108, 147,
  159
Myers, F. W. H., 59, 96,
  260–262

Nakanishi, M., 111
Nash, C. B., 83, 84, 89,
  105, 111, 130, 131, 132,
  134, 136, 141, 149, 154,
  155, 156, 157, 159, 163,
  165, 169, 178, 194, 196,
  208
Nash, C. S., 80, 83, 84, 89,
  141, 157, 178, 194, 208
Newton, M., 142
Neylon, A., 116
Nicol, J. F., 130, 131, 132,
  133, 136, 178
Nielsen, W., 74, 79, 130,
  131, 132, 158, 161–162,
  177, 207
Nordbeck, B., 192
Nowlis, D. P., 124

O'Brien, D. P., 175
Osis, K., 23, 27, 39, 74,
  76–77, 79, 80, 81, 89,
  92, 103, 107, 116–117,
  130, 132, 133, 134, 150,
  155, 156, 159, 164, 169,
  174, 181
Otani, S., 129

Palmer, J., 1, 2, 70, 93, 94,
  97, 100, 115–116, 118,
  131, 133, 134, 139, 140,
  154, 155, 157–158,
  159–160, 163, 166,
  182, 201, 205
Parker, A., 39, 103–104,
  107, 108, 111, 115,

Parker, A. *(cont.)*
  137–138, 152, 159,
  163, 175, 176, 181, 182
Patanjali, 109
Pearce, H., 60–61, 65–67,
  75, 172–173, 199, 279
Pegram, M. H., 169
Pehek, J. O., 49
Percy, E., 134
Peterson, C. J., 155
Pettijohn, C., 105
Pfungst, O., 40, 152
Pienaar, D. C., 89
Piper, L., 60
Placer, J., 53
Pleshette, G., 125, 139, 163
Pratt, J. G., 21, 23, 25, 40,
  52, 54, 60–61, 65–67,
  68, 74, 75, 76, 82, 91,
  93, 103, 112, 130, 142,
  169, 172, 180, 181, 198,
  199, 200, 201, 202
Price, A. D., 107, 108, 130,
  139–140, 193
Price, G. R., 64–65, 67
Price, H. H., 246, 252, 254,
  260, 263–265
Price, M. M., 103, 108,
  142, 143
Progoff, I., 286
Puryear, H. B., 184
Puthoff, H. E., 27, 31, 47,
  63, 75, 79–80, 196

Raburn, L., 99, 115
Ramsey, M., 103
Randall, J. L., 100, 130,
  131, 132, 140, 142
Randi, J., 16, 63
Ransom, C., 68, 69
Rao, H. H., 137, 174, 175,
  176, 272
Rao, K. R., 1, 2, 22, 25, 84,
  85, 86, 100, 111, 117,
  125–126, 130, 131,
  137, 145, 146, 164, 176,
  179, 182, 203, 208, 209,
  246
Redington, D., 97
Reed, B., 93

Rhine, J. B., 21, 26, 36, 37,
  52, 54, 60–61, 67, 68,
  74, 75, 76, 77, 78–79,
  80, 94–95, 96, 99, 109,
  120, 121, 147, 149, 151,
  152, 167–169, 170,
  171, 172, 180, 183, 198,
  206, 207, 246,
  273–276, 277,
  279–280, 281–282, 283
Rhine, L. E., 10–11, 82,
  120, 155, 269
Rice, G. E., 31, 49, 101
Richet, C., 24
Riess, B. F., 143–144, 180
Rilling, M. E., 105
Rivers, O. B., 97, 131, 136
Rogers, D. P., 156, 161,
  162–163, 165, 169,
  171, 182, 192, 209
Rogers, W. C., 149
Rogo, D. S., 115, 119, 120,
  143
Rohr, W., 98
Roll, M., 30
Roll, W. G., 30, 46–47, 62,
  98, 116–117, 130, 131,
  134, 139, 150, 155, 159,
  169, 174, 176, 181, 202,
  270, 272–273
Rose, L., 170, 181, 199
Rose, R., 170, 180, 181
Ross, A. O., 90
Rouke, F. L., 148
Rush, J. H., 75
Russell, W., 198, 199
Rust, P., 189
Ryzl, M., 35, 61, 112, 154,
  155, 159, 160, 172

Sailaja, P., 85, 108, 130,
  131, 164, 182, 190–191
Sanders, M. S., 86
Sandford, J., 114
Sanjar, M., 49, 194, 195
Sankara, 270
Schechter, R., 92, 139, 179
Scherer, W. B., 90–91, 92
Schmeidler, G. R., 22, 74,
  75, 86–87, 88, 90, 93,

Schmeidler, G. R. *(cont.)*
  95, 99 –100, 117, 122,
  129, 130, 131, 133, 134,
  135, 136, 137, 138,
  141 –142, 143, 146,
  148, 153 –158, 159,
  160, 163 –164, 169,
  170, 178 –179, 182,
  258 –260, 287
Schmidt, H., 27, 37, 52–53,
  71, 79, 95, 184, 186
Schouten, S. A., 39, 91, 92,
  100, 151–152, 175,
  195, 196
Scott, C., 67–68
Servadio, E., 123, 267
Shackleton, B., 61, 67, 97,
  198
Sharp, V., 102, 169
Sheehan, P. W., 139, 140
Shields, E., 132, 136, 147
Shulman, R., 142
Sidgwick, E. M., 62
Sidgwick, H., 64
Sinclair, M. C. (Mrs. U.),
  62, 279
Sinclair, U., 28, 62, 279
Singer, J. D., 26
Skibinsky, M., 74, 84
Smith, B. M., 54, 93, 130,
  166
Smith, K., 155
Smith, M., 115, 139
Smith, S., 60
Smythies, J., 143
Soal, S. G., 61, 67–68, 87,
  96, 97, 172, 180, 198,
  199, 266
Solfvin, G. F., 117, 131,
  134
Spielberger, C. D., 160
Spinelli, E., 147
Sprinthall, R. C., 94
Stanford, B. E., 125
• Stanford, R. G., 22, 23, 26,
  27, 38, 91, 92,
  105–106, 114,
  115–116, 124, 125,
  126, 127, 128, 129, 133,
  134, 135, 157, 159, 163,

Stanford, R. G. *(cont.)*
  170, 171, 172,
  173–174, 175, 176,
  187, 188–189, 190,
  191, 201, 208, 209, 268,
  272, 280–283
Steilberg, B. J., 169, 170
Stent, G. S., 3
Stepanek, P., 35, 61–62,
  112, 172, 181, 201–202
Stephenson, C.J., 111,
  112
Stevenson, I., 10, 11, 14,
  66, 70
Stewart, G., 61, 67, 97,
  172, 199, 200, 266
Stio, A., 38, 189
Stowell, J., 138
Stoyva, J., 127
Stribic, F. P., 169, 170,
  180, 199
Stuart, C. E., 54, 89–90,
  93, 98, 101, 130, 131,
  135, 165, 166, 182
Stump, J. P., 62, 169
Swann, I., 16
Swedenborg, E., 286
Szczygielski, D., 132

Taddonio, J. L., 104, 156,
  182
Taetzsch, R. L., 134, 155,
  169, 182
Tanous, A., 16
Targ, R., 21, 29–30, 31, 47,
  48, 53, 63, 79–80, 184,
  196–197
Tart, C. T., 19, 28, 31, 37,
  48, 53, 63, 89, 93, 97,
  100, 117, 122, 126, 129,
  141, 183, 186–187,
  195, 196, 199, 200, 209
Taves, E., 143, 181, 182,
  184
Tenhaeff, W. H. C., 130
Terry, J. C., 39, 40, 115,
  151–152, 175
Thompson, G., 190
Thouless, R. H., 80, 108,
  179, 184, 277–280

Timm, U., 200
Tirado, J., 111
Treurniet, W. C., 152
Turnbull, B., 156, 157
Turner, M. E., 76, 77, 81,
  181
Tyrell, G. N. M., 78,
  262–263, 269, 279

Ullman, M., 28, 42, 120,
  121, 262

van Asperen de Boer,
  S. R., 122
Van Busschbach, J. G.,
  83, 101, 144, 145, 147,
  182
Van De Castle, R. L., 29,
  84, 89, 111, 112, 120,
  145, 146, 155, 156
Van't Hoff, R., 102
Vasiliev, L. L., 109,
  247–248
Vasse, C., 136
Velissaris, C. N., 87
Velissaris, C. R., 87

Waldron, S., 156
Walker, E. H., 2, 255–258,
  283
Wallwork, S. C., 124, 125,
  197
Warcollier, R., 88
Wasserman, G. D., 250,
  251
Weiner, D., 209
Weiskopf, V. F., 3
West, D. J., 23, 97,
  106–107, 142, 161,
  165, 166, 194, 198, 201,
  202
West, L. J., 115
Wheeler, J., 259
White, R. A., 101,
  104–105, 108, 113,
  124, 136, 145,
  147–148, 154
Whittlesey, J. R. B.,
  122–123
Wiesinger, C., 101

Wiesner, B. P., 277–280
Wiklund, N., 146, 192
Willis, J., 190
Wilson, C. W. M., 122
Wilson, R., 51
Wilson, W. R., 154

Witkin, H. A., 115, 140
Wood, G. H., 40, 153
Wood, R., 185
Woodruff, J. L., 25, 66–67,
   68, 82, 93, 94, 95, 106,
   129, 155, 159, 163, 195

York, M., 114, 115, 131

Zener, K., 26
Zenhausern, R., 80–81,
   146
Zorab, G., 142

Subject Index

Acausal theories of psi, 2–3, 250, 283–291
Age and ESP performance, 18, 78, 94, 105, 123, 144, 146–149, 207
Agents, 4, 21–23, 28–31, 38, 42, 51, 73, 96–103, 108, 110–112, 120, 144–150, 153, 166, 194–197, 206–207, 247, 251–252, 257, 265–266, 280, 282, 289. *See also* General ESP; Telepathy
Aggressiveness and ESP performance, 133, 135
Alpha. *See* Electroencephalograph
Altered states of consciousness and ESP, 4, 42, 73, 109–123, 126–127, 129, 165, 205–206, 261
Animals, ESP in
  "clever," 40, 152–153
  as experimental subjects, 19, 21, 27, 39–40, 49, 100, 144, 149–153, 174–176, 184
  cats, 19, 27, 32, 92, 117–118, 150, 174
  dogs, 8, 19, 40, 152–153
  gerbils, 152, 175
  goldfish, 152
  horses, 19, 40, 152
  mice, 32, 100, 151
  pigs, 40
  rats, 100, 151–152, 175
  psi-trailing, 149
Archetypes, 259, 286–287, 289
Artists as ESP subjects, 138–139

Association theory of psi, 265–266
Attitude toward ESP, 38, 101, 123, 156, 160

Belief systems and psi, 4, 104. *See also* Sheep-goat effect
Below-chance scoring. *See* Psi-missing
Birth order and ESP performance, 144, 148
Blindness and ESP performance, 18, 143
Brain injury and ESP performance, 143–144

Card-guessing
  basic technique (BT), 24, 32–34, 60–61, 89, 94, 97–99, 121–122, 129, 167–168, 171, 177, 191
  blind matching (BM), 25, 35, 117, 191–192
  closed deck, 34, 52, 91
  down through technique (DT), 24, 33, 61, 78, 80, 91–93, 98, 103, 106, 110–111, 122–123, 139, 149, 167–171, 177, 199
  open deck, 34–35
  open matching, 25, 35, 91
  screened touch matching (STM), 25, 35, 66, 82, 84–85, 89, 142
  unspecified techniques, 26, 32–37, 52, 60–62, 74–80, 86, 89, 93, 96–99, 109–111, 122, 124–125, 132,

Card guessing *(cont.)*
  unspecified techniques *(cont.)*
      134–135, 137, 139–146, 148–149,
      153, 166, 171–172, 178, 180–182,
      185–186, 198, 201–203, 250, 266
    See also Targets, restricted-choice
Channel for psi, 250, 257–258
Clairvoyance
  definition, 7–8
  in experiments, 21–24, 28, 40, 63, 65, 79,
      82–83, 85–86, 88, 91–92, 104, 114,
      117, 134, 141, 145–146, 149,
      165–167, 184
  and other forms of psi, 22, 34, 36, 80–82,
      96–100, 102
  theories of, 250–251, 254, 257, 264, 266,
      270, 272, 275–276, 278
Clairvoyant reality theory of psi, 269–270
Collective unconscious, 254, 260,
      263–265, 290
Compound theory of psi, 276–277
Confidence
  of success in an ESP experiment, 15–17,
      76, 97, 110–113, 119, 154, 159–160,
      206
  of success on an ESP trial, 27, 37,
      177–180, 185, 206
Covert ESP testing, 17, 21–23, 37–39, 98,
      105–107, 145, 173, 188–193
Creativity and ESP performance, 3–4, 10,
      138–139, 207
Criticism. *See* Parapsychology, criticisms of
"Crucial experiment," 68–69

Death, survival of, 59–60, 277
Decline effects, 81–83, 85, 99, 101,
      157–158, 167–170, 180–184,
      186–187
Diametric (direct) ESP, 25, 39
Differential effect. *See* Preferential effect
Disguised ESP testing. *See* Covert ESP
      testing
Displacement effects, 76–77, 86–87, 90,
      97, 141, 148, 166, 198–201
Distance and psi, 50, 73–77, 143, 207,
      247–248, 250–251, 253–254, 275,
      290
Dreams. *See* Hypnotic dreams;
      Nocturnal dreams
Drugs and ESP performance, 121–123

ESP. *See* Extrasensory perception
Electroencephalograph (EEG), 42, 48–49,
      123–128, 139, 149, 196–197, 207,
      247, 255
Electromagnetic theory of psi, 247–249,
      251
Environmental conditions and ESP
      performance, 92–93, 147, 206
Experimenter effects, 17–18, 20, 23,
      39–40, 52–53, 69, 100, 102–108,
      142, 150, 153, 182, 196, 206, 209,
      257, 270, 282
Extrasensory perception
  anecdotal evidence, 7–10, 31, 70, 109,
      149, 208
  case studies, 10–12, 59, 109, 120, 269,
      276
  definition, 7
  experimental findings, 1–2, 60–207
    ego processes, avoidance of, 187–197
    physical variables, 73–83, 207
    psi-prone trials, selection of, 167–187
    response modes, 86–87, 89–92, 193
    social-psychological variables,
        96–108, 206
    subject variables, 92, 96, 123–167,
        205–207
    target variables, 82–88, 207
  field investigations, 12–14, 16, 59–60,
      109
  research methods, 1, 7–54
  theories of. *See* Psi, theories of
  types of. *See* Clairvoyance;
      Precognition
Extraversion and ESP performance, 19,
      132–133, 142, 161–162, 206

Feedback of ESP results, 28, 51–52,
      94–96, 183–187, 206
Field dependence and ESP performance,
      140–141, 207
Field theories of psi
  physical, 250–251
  psychological, 4, 260, 267, 270–273
Focussing effect, 62, 201–202
Forced-choice ESP tests. *See* Targets,
      restricted-choice
Fraud in ESP research
  cases of, 59, 68, 151
  charges of, 63–68, 87, 172

Fraud in ESP research *(cont.)*
  precautions against, 10–14, 16, 20, 26,
    32, 35, 49 –51, 53, 60, 63, 66, 68,
    101
Free-response ESP tests. *See* Targets,
  free-response

Galvanic skin response (GSR), 49, 129,
  195–196
Ganzfeld, 42, 93, 99, 115–116, 119, 185,
  201
General ESP (GESP)
  definition, 21
  in experiments, 21–24, 39, 63, 83–84,
    89, 92, 96–104, 108, 111, 119–120,
    125, 134, 139, 143, 145–150,
    165–167, 170–171, 173, 199–200
Gifted subjects
  in experiments, 15–17, 28, 60–67, 74,
    76, 79, 82, 87–88, 93, 97–99,
    112–113, 120, 125, 127, 143–144,
    169–170, 172–173, 177, 180–183,
    186, 199–202, 266
  field studies, 12–14, 16, 59–60
Graphic expansiveness and ESP
  performance, 165–167, 206–207
Guesswork theory of psi, 283–284

Hemispheric specialization, 112, 128–129
Hidden variable theory of psi, 2, 255–258
History of psi research. *See*
  Parapsychology, history and
  development of
Holistic ESP effects, 88, 202–203
"Hume Game," 64–68
Hypnagogic-like states and ESP, 43,
  113–121, 128, 205
Hypnosis and ESP, 41, 73, 83, 102,
  109–113, 118–119, 133–135, 160,
  177–178
Hypnotic dreams and ESP, 111–112,
  118–119

Imagery
  ability, as variable, 43, 92, 139–140, 207
  enhancement of, 41–43, 113–115,
    127–128
  as ESP response, 32, 35, 37, 42, 91–92,
    118, 262
  reporting of, 43–44

Incentives. *See* Reward in ESP
  experiments
Intelligence and ESP performance,
  136–138, 184–187, 206
Interactionist model of psi, 290–291
Interpersonal relationships and psi, 3–4,
  12–14, 16–18, 32, 96–108, 110,
  132–133, 139, 147, 166, 206–207,
  259–260, 266–268, 270–271
Intuitionist theories of psi, 290–291

Judging of free-response material, 28–29,
  41, 44–48, 50–51, 79–80, 101

K-ideas. *See* Association theory of psi
Kirlian photography, 49
Knowledge of results. *See* Feedback of
  ESP results

Maimonides Medical Center Dream
  Laboratory, 29, 42, 120–121, 145
Maze targets, 26–27, 37, 39, 174
Meditation and ESP, 41, 109, 116–117, 126
Mediumship, 59–60, 97, 109, 276
Memory and ESP, 111, 137–138, 140, 173,
  175–176, 272
Mental illness and ESP performance,
  141–144, 269
Mood and ESP performance, 23, 103, 107,
  123, 143, 156, 160–165, 207
Motivation and ESP performance, 18, 26,
  93, 97, 103, 182–183, 187, 272

Neuroticism and ESP performance,
  130–133, 158, 161–162, 206
Nocturnal dreams and ESP, 9, 11, 42–43,
  63, 75, 79, 118–121, 140, 261–262,
  264, 267

Out-of-body experiences, 116–118, 150,
  159–160

PK. *See* Psychokinesis
Paranormal matrix, 270–271
Parapsychology
  criticisms of, 60, 63–71, 194
  history and development of, 1–4, 59–61,
    70–72, 109, 203–204, 289–290
Perceptual deprivation, 41, 114–116. *See
  also* Ganzfeld; Witch's cradle

Personality and ESP performance. *See* Psychological tests and ESP performance; Subjects in ESP research

Philosophy and psi. *See* Psi, theories of

Physicality of psi, question of, 3, 246–247, 252–255, 258, 269, 274, 290

Physiological ESP responses, 48–49, 115, 123–130, 193–196, 199, 208

Plethysmograph, 49, 149, 193–196

Position effects, 67–68, 85, 167, 171, 197, 206

Precognition
definition, 7–9
in experiments, 27, 30, 39–40, 77–82, 94, 97, 102, 140–141, 145–146, 162–163, 166, 168, 184, 197, 207
and other forms of psi, 22–23, 34, 36–37, 39, 52, 78–82, 102
theories of, 251, 253, 272–273, 275–276, 283, 285, 290

Preferential effect, 85–87, 100, 179, 208

Projection theories of psi, 260, 273–283, 290

Progressive relaxation technique, 41–42, 113–114, 118, 271

Psi fields. *See* Field theories of psi

Psi-mediated instrumental response (PMIR), 188–191, 193, 280–283

Psi-missing, 54, 74–75, 79–81, 83–84, 86, 91–94, 100, 102–105, 110–111, 115, 117, 119, 122, 129, 138, 142, 145–146, 148, 153–154, 159, 166, 168–171, 175, 178–182, 185–186, 197, 199–201, 205, 208, 255, 269

Psi phenomena
definition, 7
existence of, 9, 59–73, 245
evolution of, 4, 289
limitations of, 290
and science, 1–4, 64, 68, 70, 81, 108, 203, 209, 245–246, 250, 258
theories of, 1–4, 207–209, 245–291

Psitrons, theory of, 252–255

Psychic experiences and ESP performance, 157, 159–160

Psychic readings, 30, 46–47, 62, 127, 130

Psychic shuffle, 36–37, 52, 78, 88, 177, 200

Psychical energy, theory of, 249–250

Psychoanalytic theories of psi, 4, 266–269

Psychokinesis
definition, 7
and ESP, 21, 34, 36–37, 39–40, 47, 52–53, 78–79, 81, 108, 133–134
theory of, 255, 257, 270, 272–274, 277, 280–281, 283, 287, 290

Psychological tests and ESP performance
Allport's Ascendence–Submission Scale, 135
Allport–Vernon Scale of Values, 134
Barber Suggestibility Scale, 133–134
Barron's Independence of Judgment Scale, 138
Bernreuter Personality Inventory, 131–132, 161–162
Betts Questionnaire upon Mental Imagery, 92, 139–140
Blacky Pictures Test, 131
California F Scale, 134
California Psychological Inventory, 134
Cason's Test of Annoyance, 133
Cattell's 16PF, 130–132
Cattell's HSPQ, 130–133
Draw-A-Person Test, 141
Edwards Personal Preference Schedule, 135
Embedded Figures Test, 140–141
Eysenck Personality Inventory, 130, 132, 161–162
Gordon Test of Visual Imagery, 139–140
Guilford's Personality Scales, 130, 132
Heston Personal Adjustment Inventory, 131
Junior Eysenck Personality Inventory, 131
Kragh's Defense Mechanisms Test, 131, 192
Maslow's Security-Insecurity Questionnaire, 130
Maudsley Personality Inventory, 130
Mental Health Analysis, 131
Minnesota Multiphasic Personality Inventory, 130, 132
Mosher Sex Guilt Scale, 131, 192
Muller-Lyon Illusion, 98
Nowlis's Mood Adjective Checklist, 162–164

Rokeach's Dogmatism Scale, 135
Rorschach Test, 100, 131, 158, 259
Rosenzweig Picture Frustration Study,
    133
Rotter's Internal-External Control of
    Reinforcement Scale, 135
Semantic Differential, 134
Spielberger's State-Trait Anxiety
    Inventory, 130–131, 164, 191–192
Stanford Hypnotic Susceptibility Scale,
    134
Stuart Interest Inventory, 135–136
Taylor Manifest Anxiety Scale, 131,
    164, 191
Thematic Apperception Test, 99
Time Competence Scale, Personal
    Orientation Inventory, 134
Time Metaphor Test, 134
Torrance's Social Motivation
    Inventory, 138
Welsh Figure Preference Test, 138
Psychotherapy and ESP, 4, 120, 141–142,
    267–269
Punishment in ESP experiments, 20, 38,
    40, 100, 129, 150–153, 188

Quantum physics and psi theory, 2,
    246–247, 249, 252–258

Rand Corporation, 52
Random number generator, 27–28, 40,
    52–53, 79, 95, 103, 184–187
Randomization. See Targets, random
    selection of
Rate of response, 24, 33–34, 43, 89–90
Recording of ESP responses, 24–27,
    32–33, 35–37, 41, 43–44, 48–50
Relativism theory of psi, 273–274
Relaxation and ESP performance, 97,
    112–114, 122–123, 127, 129, 264,
    270–271, 279
Remote viewing technique, 29–30, 47, 63,
    79–80
Repeatability in psi research, 1, 4, 17,
    69–71, 105, 108, 167, 203–204
Resonance theory of psi, 249–250
Response bias, 26, 34–35, 45, 51, 91–92,
    108, 119, 125, 150–151, 171–177,
    205–206, 288–289

Response mode, 32–50, 86–87, 89–92, 193
Retrocognition, 9
Reward in ESP experiments, 20, 38–39,
    73, 93–96, 100, 150–153, 158,
    174–175, 188

Salience effects. See Position effects
Sampling problems, 11–12, 18, 46, 62, 69,
    72–73, 154, 180, 203–204
Schmidt's machine. See Random number
    generator
Selected subjects. See Gifted subjects
Selection process in psi reception,
    253–254, 264–265
Self concept and psi performance,
    134–135, 189
Sensory and inferential cues, precautions
    against, 14–15, 20, 24, 26, 42, 47,
    49–51, 60, 81, 87, 98–99, 117, 143,
    150, 179, 202
Sex differences and ESP performance, 81,
    85, 105–106, 120, 123, 144–146,
    148, 157–158, 189, 191–192
Sheep-goat effect
    belief in psi, 18, 103, 134–136, 153–158,
        160, 170, 192, 206
    questions related to belief, 158–160
Shin theory of psi, 277–280, 290
Skinner box ESP tests, 39, 152, 175
Society for Psychical Research, 59
Spontaneity and ESP performance, 15,
    90–92, 103, 172, 174, 176, 187,
    205–207
Statistics in ESP research
    direction of difference from chance
        expectation, 73, 110, 116, 119, 132,
        142–143, 149, 154, 164, 179,
        204–207
    general, 29, 45, 47, 51, 53–54, 69, 73, 84,
        204
    magnitude of difference from chance
        expectation, 15, 73, 91, 116, 119,
        132, 142–143, 204–207
    variance, 91–92, 148, 156–159, 162–163,
        169–171, 182–183, 197, 205,
        209
    See also Sampling problems
Subatomic physics. See Quantum physics
    and psi theory

Subjects in ESP research
    characteristics and ESP performance.
        18, 90, 96, 123–167, 199, 268, 290
    experimenters as, 20, 194
    recruitment of, 17–19
    screening of, 17, 19, 76, 186–187, 199
    special subject populations, 17–18
    See also Gifted subjects
Symbiosis and psi, 268–269
Synchronicity, 2, 208–209, 259, 284–289.
        See also Acausal theories of psi

Targets
    characteristics of, 21–23, 26–28, 73,
        83–87, 136, 146, 206
        complexity, 22, 25, 28–29, 39, 41, 83
        meaningfulness, 13, 15, 23, 28–29, 31,
            83–85, 191, 194–196, 267
        multiple-aspect, 86–88
        physical dimensions, 82–83, 207, 259
    definition, 13, 15
    emotional events as, 31, 48–49, 149, 267
    free-response, 28–31, 41–48, 50, 62–63,
        74–75, 79–80, 86, 93, 99, 100,
        111–113, 115–122, 125–128, 132,
        134, 138–139, 149, 154, 159,
        165–166, 179, 182, 201, 205
    random selection of, 22, 45, 50–53, 63,
        78–79, 81–82, 147, 288–289
    restricted-choice, 23–28, 32–40, 48–49,
        51–53, 60–63, 66–67, 74–77, 82–99,
        104–107, 109–112, 114, 117,

Targets *(cont.)*
    restricted-choice *(cont.)*
        121–125, 128, 134–147, 150–164,
        166–193, 198–203. *See also*
        Card-guessing; Random number
        generator
    See also Preferential effect
Teacher-pupil ESP, 101–102, 104–105,
    144–146
Telepathy
    and clairvoyance, 21–23, 96–102
    definition, 7–8
    in experiments, 20–23, 96–97, 99, 102,
        149
    theories of, 247, 249–254, 256, 262–268,
        270, 272, 275–276, 278–280, 282,
        288–289
Thyroid conditions and ESP performance,
    143–144
Time perception and ESP performance,
    90, 134
Topological theory of psi, 258–260
Twins as ESP subjects, 118, 132, 148–149,
    196

Unintended psi effects, 20, 23, 45, 47,
    102–108, 197–203, 254, 280–281.
        See also Experimenter effects

Witch's cradle, 42, 116

Zener cards. *See* Card-guessing